Rethinking Choice of Law in Cross-Border Sales

Rethinking Choice of Law in Cross-Border Sales

Gustavo Moser

eleven
international publishing

Published, sold and distributed by Eleven International Publishing
P.O. Box 85576
2508 CG The Hague
The Netherlands
Tel.: +31 70 33 070 33
Fax: +31 70 33 070 30
e-mail: sales@elevenpub.nl
www.elevenpub.com

Sold and distributed in USA and Canada
International Specialized Book Services
920 NE 58th Avenue, Suite 300
Portland, OR 97213-3786, USA
Tel.: 1-800-944-6190 (toll-free)
Fax: +1 503 280-8832
orders@isbs.com
www.isbs.com

Eleven International Publishing is an imprint of Boom uitgevers Den Haag.

ISBN 978-94-6236-846-0
ISBN 978-94-6274-852-1 (E-book)

Preface

Whatever the nature of the transaction, in international business there is one prime question fundamental to the validity, interpretation, effectiveness and enforceability of the contract: what law governs?

Businesses frequently see the transaction in practical terms: to provide needed services or equipment, investments and expansion, control and management, or ensuring rights and obligations *inter partes*. It is for this reason that contracting parties will inevitably spend enormous time, energy and even money in negotiating and agreeing the specifics of a contract. Often, the law will be secondary or not even considered.

In very many contracts, advised by professional law organisations, there is a strong recommendation that contracts expressly provide for the law to apply. The issue in many circumstances is whether the law controls the specific terms agreed or if the applicable law is there to supplement and support the parties' agreement. In very significant part, most national laws are permissive and allow parties to agree their own arrangements. National laws will give effect to the terms agreed, provided they do not breach any mandatory laws or fundamental international public policy of the jurisdiction before which the issue is brought. On the other hand, contracts are inevitably incomplete with issues unforeseen or not provided for. In such circumstances, where necessary the applicable law may be required to play a key role in implying terms or filling the gaps to give the contract meaning and effect.

In some cases parties may not agree on a choice of national or other law. There are many reasons. The 'deal' is agreed, perhaps after hard bargaining. The parties (or their lawyers) cannot agree on the law of the other party, and no neutral law is acceptable. In the circumstances, the parties do not wish to scupper their agreement because of a pure choice of law which, in turn, would appear to have only limited relevance at least at the time of contracting and until a dispute arises. Most terms recording obligations, undertakings, promises, warranties, prices, penalties, remedies, etc. are self-explanatory. They are agreed and – at least at the outset – are clear and of mutual benefit and they have built-in protections that are seen as sufficient for the parties.

Even where there is an agreed choice of applicable law, there will always be other legal influences, such as national law specific to an aspect of the contract, the capacity of a party to the transaction, the existence of a corporation, effect of a shareholders' agreement, contract interpretation, enforceability of provisions in given jurisdictions and, of course, dispute resolution agreements.

Developed through business transactions, international and national institutional efforts, industry practices and the decisions of international arbitration tribunals, general principles of law which can be applied to specific transactions and situations have emerged. What rules should be applied and in what circumstances is not always clear but it does allow arbitrators and even national court judges to interpret and enforce the contract terms through these international practices and rules.

Much has been written about *lex mercatoria*, including what it is and whether it has sufficient status to be applied to international business transactions. This issue is well discussed in this book by Dr Gustavo Moser. Whilst this issue is controversial – to the extent of which a majority of scholars approach it with scepticism and often challenge the very existence of *lex mercatoria* as an 'autonomous legal system' – the role of transnational rules in international contracts is notable and relevant.

Various organisations have undertaken initiatives to recognise the commercial relevance of these general and often transnational principles. These principles include *pacta sunt servanda*, the obligation to compensate for breach to place the victim financially in the place it would have been, but for the breach and the duty to mitigate the effects of the breach. Model contracts providing for optional choice-of-law clauses referring to 'principles of law generally recognized in international trade' in conjunction with other rules are often used. There are widely accepted neutral legal standards, such as the Unidroit Principles and the principles in the United Nations Convention on Contracts for the International Sale of Goods (CISG). Another example are the Hague Principles on the Choice of Law in International Contracts, which established a set of general principles to guide the interpretation of the choice of law in international agreements.

The *lex mercatoria* will not replace national law. However, it can have an influence on the way national law is applied in given circumstances of international transactions. It may also be applied directly to the meaning of the contract terms as part of general principles of law or to the specific contract itself. It may further be used as an integrated choice (in conjunction with Unidroit Principles, for example CISG, or specific trade usages), and provide a neutral or transnational playing field for contracting parties.

This book, *Rethinking Choice of Law in Cross-Border Sales*, provides an in-depth analysis of the sources of these general principles and standards and how they are and can be applied. Dr Moser has brought together many of the sources and opinions on these issues and has provided an analysis which will be useful both prospectively, when choosing the law to apply, and retrospectively, when seeking to understand what the contract means, how it could or should be applied, and how international arbitrators and judges can use them to give commercial effect to an agreed transaction.

The book will assist parties and lawyers to limit difficulties which can occur with the selection of a national law which may not properly support the contract. It discusses alternatives to overcome or control the effects of uncertain intentions and mistaken choices that are made by parties and their lawyers when selecting the governing law for their transactions. Here, Dr Moser explains factors which may assist lawyers and decision-makers to make rational and efficient choices of the laws and rules to apply.

Rethinking Choice of Law in Cross-Border Sales will be a useful tool to all those involved in choosing, determining and applying law and rules to international transactions. Dr Moser is to be commended for a timely book which fills a gap in the readily available materials on the subject.

London, April 2018
Professor Julian D M Lew QC

Table of Contents

Acknowledgments

The history behind this book reflects how fascinating, plural and international the topic of choice of law is.

This work is the product of a research carried out for many years, which has led me to appreciate to an even greater level the intricacies of choice of law in various contexts. It was built upon my own legal experiences in common and civil law jurisdictions worldwide.

There is also a peculiarity in this book in that it was written in the four corners of the world; more precisely, four continents and in many cities and libraries, for which I am most grateful. I hope that the discussions within this book will inspire readers to continue the research in the various aspects of choice of law.

This book would not have been accomplished without the generosity and support of many legal professionals around the world who dedicated their time and knowledge to contribute to this project. I will forever be indebted to you all. My special thanks go to a pre-eminent mind in this field and my mentor Professor Dr Ingeborg Schwenzer for inspiring and guiding me, and for the enlightening conversations around this challenging topic. I would also like thank the author of my preface, a luminaire in the international arbitration community, the one and only Professor Dr Julian D M Lew QC, for his belief and contribution to this work.

Last but not least, my thanks also to my family and friends, for their ongoing patience and encouragement.

Introduction

The choice of governing contract law has historically been conceived as a paramount decision in cross-border negotiation of contracts, inasmuch as it governs a contract's life from beginning to end. As a matter of fact, the governing contract law dictates and regulates a party's behaviour by attaching legal and economic consequences to each step taken in the course of the contractual relationship. Whilst this choice may often result in anticipating the allocation of stakes (monetary value) between the parties, the economic analysis of law assists us in understanding law as incentives for changing behaviour (implicit prices) and as instruments for policy objectives (efficiency and distribution).[1] Consequently, parties will cooperate or not depending on the incentives in play which, as readers will appreciate, may vary greatly.

In a cross-border sale, where parties may come from vastly different jurisdictions, both in terms of cultural and legal traditions, one may wonder which law should regulate the deal. Would domestic law better fit that purpose? Perhaps third-party law? Or a neutral legal framework? How can parties find the right balance? Is there a right balance, after all? More importantly, do they want to find it at all?

Despite its acknowledged theoretical importance, it is often suggested that negotiators might dedicate less attention than they should to the particulars of the choice of law clause. Instead, negotiators tend to opt for law that may be convenient for business, or be the result of previous experiences, including, for example, following in a partner's footsteps, or a successful deal in the past, without further deliberation.

In light of this apparent discrepancy between theory and practice, we decided to investigate further how traders actually choose the law for their deals. We also wanted to find out the reasons for these decisions and the foundations on which these decisions are based. This is how the Global Empirical Survey on Choice of Law, which will be discussed in detail in this book, was conceived in 2014. The survey was essentially designed to investigate parties' concerns regarding choice of law and to assess whether neutral legal frameworks were welcome in addressing these concerns.

It is undisputed that negotiators have traditionally tried to impose their own law in deciding which system of law is to govern a contract. This tendency can pose hindrances, as parties might not make the best decision they could. This is precisely our first point of concern: we aim to reveal how and what factors determine the way contracting parties choose the law to govern their agreements. We shall also elaborate on whether parties are

1 See R. Cooter & T. Ulen, *Law and Economics*, Addison-Wesley, Boston, 2007, p. 9.

actually aware of biases and heuristics,[2] cognitive blinders that might simply cloud or blur a decision. Alternatives to 'home turf' and 'arm-wrestling' tactics, which are often seen in practice, will also be discussed.

Readers will subsequently be invited to consider the major market distortions and failures to which contracting parties are routinely exposed. We shall demonstrate that, with the increase of market activities and complexity of deals worldwide, parties need to be equipped with the most efficient tools to maximize gains from cross-border contracts, thereby avoiding risks and costly mistakes. With this purpose in mind, we shall analyze choice of law studies undertaken and offer alternatives to be used in practice, which seek to overcome recurrent complaints, uncertainties and fears when it comes to choosing governing contract law. We shall also attempt to verify the effectiveness of these solutions in light of the evidence presented.

It is the aim of this book to examine the position of the choice of law in the decision-making processes in cross-border sales. The first part of the book sets out evidence on the choice of law: the available data will be explored in fine detail, including a focus on how negotiators typically approach the subject and what are the main drives and triggers of this decision. We shall further investigate whether contracting parties are aware of the vast legal market options available and whether they actually enjoy their benefits. In the second and third chapters, we shall map out some of the market distortions and imperfections to which negotiators are (consciously or not) routinely exposed. We shall also reveal the common psychological triggers that influence decision-making processes and how to identify and better control them to a party's best advantage. We shall further shed light on the idiosyncratic contract design and the mechanisms to manage this properly in an international context, all in an attempt to identify and use the appropriate tools to make better decisions and obtain more efficient outcomes.

The final part of the book (Chapters 4 and 5) will concentrate on alternatives to escape 'arm-wrestling', 'home turf', deadlock situations and other tactical scenarios in cross-border sales. We shall present and compare alternatives which can be used in international contract settings and then test the effectiveness of the solutions they can provide, taking into account both the legal and economic aspects and contracting parties' real-life concerns and preferences collected in the earlier chapters. Readers are invited to find out the answers to the following questions: what really matters to contracting parties when drafting choice-of-law clauses? Are there key provisions, 'backbones', legal standards or frameworks that are indeed indispensable? Do contracting parties consider legal and economic choices at all? With this in mind, we aim to offer to legal practitioners tools that enable them to excel and effectively optimize, at a rather even level between parties, the exchange of goods worldwide.

---

2 Cognitive biases are mental shortcuts commonly used in making daily decisions. Because a decision can (and usually does) take time and effort, the mind uses routes (heuristics) to facilitate the process of reaching a conclusion or making a decision. The topic will be further discussed in Chapter 2.

1 Choice of Law in Practice – Empirical Studies

1.1 Efforts to Reveal Parties' Preferences

Hermetic and mostly confusing formulas have been exhaustively discussed worldwide in an attempt to explain choice of law theories and methods that lead to the governing contract law, or, in some scenarios, to multiple laws. However, despite the myriad theories of the vagaries of private international law, few legal sources have been able to identify and reveal in empirical terms the parties' choices and preferences in cross-border contracts.[1] The factors and underlying motives that influence certain decisions are often unavailable to market players and laymen in general.[2] Likewise, the identification and control of decision-making triggers, as well as methods of influencing and possibly improving decisions, are typically not explored or discussed.

A few practical questions are routinely left unanswered: how do contracting parties make decisions in real-world environments? What determines key contractual choices such as the governing contract law in a cross-border sale? What are the economic consequences of this choice? Is it possible to anticipate and manage external factors? How can contracting parties influence and thereby improve their decisions?

In this chapter we shall unveil, assess and compare the available data on parties' choice of law decisions in the context of cross-border contracts. We aim to disclose and discuss the main driving forces and motives for this choice, as well as investigate possible interplay with choice of forum decisions. The above will hopefully extract elements that shed light on what can influence and possibly improve contracting parties' decisions. Before doing so, one caveat is in order, as discussed below.

Unfortunately, information on choice of law decisions is not readily available and even more difficult to collect than overall use of dispute resolution mechanisms worldwide. Such data often remain inaccessible to the general public for various reasons. In the first instance, contracts are typically confidential, especially if they contain arbitration clauses. This is particularly so in most cross-border sales. In addition, court statistics do not usually list choice of law information but rather, *inter alia,* the subject matter of contracts, the nationality of the parties, and the amount in dispute. Empirical studies such as those discussed in this chapter present different ways researchers have attempted to obtain data on cross-border contracts.

1 Previous empirical research efforts will be further discussed *infra* p. 7 *et seq.*

2 For reference of previous studies, see I. Schwenzer & C. Kee, 'International Sales Law: The Actual Practice', *Pennsylvania State International Law Review*, Vol. 29, Issue 3, 2011, pp. 425-447.

In the first part of the following discussion, several studies are presented in chronological order, accompanied by general comment on the findings. We shall focus on the highlights of the data obtained from these studies and then draw a conclusion, based upon the various empirical studies undertaken thus far, as to how parties generally choose the law that governs their transactions. We shall also examine whether parties appreciate the extent of their freedom of contract, whether they are aware of available options and whether this choice is constrained by rational factors or bound by other considerations. The selected works – selective and non-exhaustive – are primarily based on the following criteria: innovation, chronology, scope and reach. Hence, the earlier studies that were chosen were limited to pioneering works and surveys where either a representative economic region was surveyed, or a large number of countries were involved. These earlier studies serve predominantly as a parameter for comparison with the efforts undertaken in the Global Empirical Survey on Choice of Law (hereinafter the Survey[3]).

In the second part we shall discuss the evidence obtained as part of a recent, interdisciplinary and pioneering Survey. This Survey is a study of the specifics behind the contracting parties' mindset in choosing governing contract law in cross-border sales. The Survey findings, however, will be explored to a greater extent in the subsequent chapters of this book.

In the final part of Chapter 1, we shall undertake a brief and non-exhaustive comparative analysis of all of the empirical studies discussed in this chapter. This final section will highlight the similarities of the results obtained in all of these studies, identify the differences and note the behavioural patterns, main preferences and concerns of the respondents of the Survey. The chapter further aims to determine the impact of these studies in a quest to understand the decisions made by contracting parties in cross-border sales.

1.1.1 Previous Studies on Choice of Law Decision-Making Processes

The discussion on previous studies on choice of law decisions will be divided into two parts. The first part of this subchapter will present the pre-2008 studies, *i.e.* the studies that were positioned at the forefront of the empirical efforts concerning choice of law decisions. We shall present some of the pioneering initiatives, which were instrumental in revealing both the preferred laws and contracting parties' general concerns and preferences on this topic. The second part, named 'post-2008: innovative works', will introduce a set of studies that were innovative in their use of different tools and approaches. These included efforts to recycle earlier ideas and using them in different contexts and targeting specific industry-sector contracts and respondents. Overall, it can be concluded that the 'post-2008' studies were wider in scope.

---

3 The Survey results were first published in L. G. Meira Moser, 'Parties' Preferences in International Sales Contracts: An Empirical Analysis of the Choice of Law', *Uniform Law Review*, Vol. 20, Issue 1, 2015, pp. 19-55.

1.1.1.1 Pre-2008 Studies: Pioneering Initiatives

1.1.1.1.1 Studies on Choice of Law

In 1995 a private practitioner from San Francisco, Barton S. Selden,[4] made an enquiry among 23 practitioners from ten countries[5] on the use of the *lex mercatoria*. The study was conducted informally and most recipients replied that they would strongly advise against a choice of the *lex mercatoria* in an international contract and would prefer a 'definitive' and 'provable' law.[6] Barton S. Selden further remarks that "by 'definitive' it is meant that the chosen law consists of a comprehensive set of decision-making rules which can be applied to resolve a dispute. 'Provable' refers to those rules embodied in a fixed form which can be presented to dispute resolution forum".[7] Hence, Barton S. Selden concluded that despite discussions of *lex mercatoria* in academic writings, the popularity of the *lex mercatoria* as a choice of law was not found on any empirical data.[8]

In 1999 the CENTRAL[9] Research Project on Transnational Commercial law started its project entitled "The Role of Merchants, their Lawyers and their Arbitral Tribunals in the Evolution and Development of Transnational Commercial Law". The goal of the project was to clarify whether the conduct of international businessmen was in fact determined by transnational law. This involved the question whether transnational law was being used and accepted by international legal practice in contract negotiation, contract drafting and in dispute resolution through international commercial arbitration. It also involved more specific questions regarding concrete rules or principles of transnational commercial law.[10] In order to do so the questionnaire, which formed the basis for a worldwide empirical study on the *Use of Transnational Law in International Contract Law and Arbitration*, was sent to in-house counsel, attorneys, arbitrators and experts in international business law. The CENTRAL Enquiry covered a broad range of transactions: sales contracts, joint ventures, construction, distribution, licensing contracts and contracts for the exploitation of natural resources and M&A contracts. The questionnaire received 808 answers, from 51 countries, although there was no even regional distribution among those who responded to the enquiry. As to the outcome, the CENTRAL team advised that one of the most important results was the inter-

4 B. S. Selden, 'Lex Mercatoria in European and US Trade Practice: Time to Take a Closer Look', *Annual Survey of International & Comparative Law*, 1995, pp. 111-129.

5 The authors states that the attorneys, 'active in international commercial matters', were from the following countries: Belgium; France; Germany; Italy; Japan; Korea; the Netherlands; Panama; Philippines; and the United Kingdom. See B. S. Selden, *supra* note 4, p. 129 (note 43).

6 B. S. Selden, *supra* note 4, pp. 118-119. See also, K. P. Berger *et al.*, 'The CENTRAL Enquiry on the Use of Transnational Law in International Contract Law and Arbitration – Background, Procedure and Selected Results', p. 3, available at [https://www.trans-lex.org/3/_/background-procedure-and-selected-results/].

7 B. S. Selden, *supra* note 4, p. 119.

8 *Id.*, p. 113.

9 Trans-lex-.org is a free research and knowledge platform on transnational law and is available at [https://www.trans-lex.org/].

10 K. P. Berger *et al.*, *supra* note 6, p. 5.

national practitioners' awareness of the use of transnational law in international practice: about one-third of the respondents indicated that they were aware of the use of transnational commercial law in international contract negotiation and choice of law clauses, and the result was even higher in the context of international commercial arbitration (42%).[11] The CENTRAL Enquiry team showed surprise at such a high percentage of respondents indicating their awareness of the use of transnational law in legal practice and concluded that this could mean that there was a high number of arbitration experts among the respondents.[12] 68.86% of the respondents revealed a positive or neutral attitude to the new *lex mercatoria*, while only 19.56% rejected this concept altogether.[13] The CENTRAL Enquiry further concluded that the alleged incompleteness of the *lex mercatoria* and enforcement concerns do not play a major role in legal practice, even though the results also revealed that practitioners attach substantial weight to the issue of enforceability. It was also reported by the CENTRAL Enquiry team that answers citing the vagueness and uncertainty of transnational commercial law were 'by far outweighed by those replies that refer to the lack of practical experience and the fact that no information has been available on the subject of transnational commercial law'.[14] Lastly, the CENTRAL Enquiry team reported two tentative conclusions: one, that transnational commercial law was being used in international legal practice (and was more popular among civil law practitioners) and secondly, that there was a substantial gap between the assumptions of lawyers who discuss the theory of transnational commercial law and the assumptions and viewpoints of international legal practice.[15]

Despite the generality of its inferences and a lack of clear breakdown of the evidentiary source in terms of contract surveyed and respondent profile, the study was one of the first of its kind to discuss this topical matter. The CENTRAL project has been instrumental in its mandate to provide awareness to businessmen and practitioners of the use of transnational law and this is confirmed by the website [trans-lex.org],[16] which compiles a comprehensive list of principles drawn up from the market, a truly up-to-date working tool in the field of transnational commercial law and a user-friendly database of that matter.

One of the first studies of choice of law was conducted by Eva-Maria Kieninger, published in 2002.[17] The study was limited to Europe and the author analyzed the available legal manuals on the practice of international contracts. With respect to the German manuals analyzed, the results revealed that 'the suitability and the superiority of German law is simply assumed

11 *Id.*, p. 14.
12 *Id.*
13 K. P. Berger *et al.*, *supra* note 6, p. 22.
14 *Id.*, p. 20.
15 *Id.*, p. 21.
16 For further information, please consult [https://www.trans-lex.org/].
17 E.-M. Kieninger, *Wettbewerb der Privatrechtsordnungen im Europäischen Binnenmarkt*, Tübingen: Mohr Siebeck, 2002. Additional information regarding this study can be found in S. Vogenauer, 'Regulatory Competition through Choice of Contract Law and Choice of Forum in Europe: Theory and Evidence', *European Review of Private Law*, Vol. 1, 2013, pp. 13-78, p. 37.

and is never questioned'.[18] Ms Kieninger also found that there were occasional suggestions by the respondents to choose law that had a certain degree of similarity to German law, such as Swiss or Austrian law, in cases where no German law was applicable. The results indicated that German contracting parties would predominantly choose their own law as the governing contract law – if this was not available, a similar law was selected instead.

Legal manuals from other European jurisdictions were also surveyed and revealed the same pattern: the respondents' preference for their own laws.[19] The study also revealed that, in cross-border trade of derivatives, for instance, parties would prefer English or New York law, in line with the standard practice in this industry.

The study results allow us to conclude that familiarity of domestic law was ranked as a priority and a deal-breaker by the respondents. Moreover, when 'home law' was not available, parties would likely look for similarities in other law in order to make and justify their choice. This indicates that similarity serves as a cue for decision-making, and contracting parties will tend, by the device of representativeness,[20] to identify features similar to their own law and tend to choose that law. In addition, in some instances, instead of choosing their 'home law', respondents would simply opt to follow trade practice (*e.g.*, derivative contracts), a choice that may also be justified as an attempt to reduce the level of asymmetry of information[21] often seen between traders and financial institutions. In other words, as financial institutions might not be willing to share all information they possess, choosing a law that is a trade practice could reduce the level of uncertainty[22] of a dispute outcome.

This study is of great importance as it signals some general preferences of respondents in a decision-making context and inaugurates a series of empirical efforts regarding cross-border transactions. However, the study was limited in scope: analysis of legal manuals available for the practice of international contracts in Europe.

---

18 *Id.*

19 S. Vogenauer, *supra* note 17, p. 37.

20 A thorough analysis of judgment devices can be found in Section 2.2.1.

21 Asymmetry of information is generally acknowledged in scenarios where one party possesses information unavailable (or more detailed than) (that of) to the counterparty. Examples of asymmetry of information in contractual negotiations are discussed in Section 3.2.

22 V. Gessner explains the differences in levels of uncertainty through the lenses of sociology. Citing Geet Hofsted, Gessner remarks "uncertainty avoidance is a cultural dimension and some societies socialize their members into accepting the uncertainty of the future and not becoming upset by it. People of such countries will take risks rather easily. Hofsted calls such societies 'weak uncertainty avoidance' societies. Other societies socialize their people into trying to beat the future. Because the future remains essentially unpredictable, in those societies there will be a higher level of anxiety in people, which becomes manifest in greater nervousness, emotionality, and aggressiveness. Such societies, called 'strong uncertainty avoidance' societies, also have institutions that try to create security and avoid risk, among others legal institutions, public law and private contracts. Hofstede gives as examples Germany as a 'strong uncertainty avoidance' society, and India as a 'weak uncertainty avoidance' society", 'Global Legal Interaction and Legal Cultures', *Ratio Juris*, Vol. 7, Issue 2, 1994, p. 142. See also V. Gessner & A. Schade, 'Conflicts of Culture in Cross-Border Legal Relations: The Conception of a Research Topic in the Sociology of Law', *Theory, Culture & Society*, Vol. 7, No. 2, Issue 6, 1990, pp. 253-277.

Also in 2002, Cam Quyen Corinne Truong[23] analyzed 141 arbitral awards in cases involving international distribution agreements submitted to the International Chamber of Commerce (ICC[24]) between 1984 and 2000. The author confirmed that, in cases where the parties had chosen national law, 75% had opted for civil law jurisdiction and 25% for common law jurisdiction. In addition, the top three preferred systems of laws were: French (27%), American (15%), and Swiss (12%).

The author went further to investigate the nationality of the parties and found that 108 contracts out of the 141 analyzed involved parties based in different countries. From this new data she found that in 80% of the 108 contracts, the 'home law' of one of the parties was chosen in the following order: law of the supplier (52%) and law of the distributor (28%). In only 13% of the 108 contracts did parties choose 'neutral law', and in 50% of the 108 contracts they agreed on Swiss law.

Truong's findings demonstrate that the law of the supplier in a given contract is the preferred choice of law decision. For the first time, a sequence of preferred laws was disclosed. Moreover, it appears that 'arm-wrestling', or so-called bargaining power,[25] had been exercised to a full extent in the 108 contracts.

Although this study is arguably of great statistical value, it was based on a rather limited sample of respondents, therefore unrepresentative, *i.e.*, one single arbitration court (ICC), and was restricted to a specific contract (distribution agreements). As such, the study not fully have disclosed the reasons for the respondent's choices on a worldwide scale and may not be applicable to all types of contractual agreement.

In 2005 the Oxford Institute of European and Comparative Law, in partnership with Clifford Chance, conducted a survey[26] of 157 European companies based in eight European Union Member States: France, Germany, Hungary, Italy, the Netherlands, Portugal, Spain and the United Kingdom. The Survey aimed to reveal some aspects of the practices in undertaking cross-border transactions.

The results indicated that 83% of the respondents believed that the ability to choose a governing regime of law was 'important'. When asked about their preferences in making such choice, 66% said that they preferred their 'home law'. Only 21% expressed a preference for law other than their own (domestic). Interestingly, 41% had occasionally

23 C. C. Q. Truong & P. Fouchard, *Les différends liés à la rupture des contrats internationaux de distribution dans les sentences arbitrales CCI*, Litec, Paris, 2002. For a summary of the findings, see C. C. Q. Truong & P. Fouchard, 'The Law Applicable to the Merits in International Distribution Contracts: An Analysis of ICC Arbitral Awards', *ICC International Court of Arbitration Bulletin*, Vol. 12, 2001, p. 37; pp. 38-39.

24 International Chamber of Commerce (ICC), available at [www.iccwbo.org/].

25 Bargaining is usually defined as the power to negotiate and conclude deals. By bargaining, people frequently agree on the terms for interaction and cooperation. The authors Cooter and Ulen explain that the process of bargaining can be divided into three steps: (i) establishing the threat values; (ii) determining the cooperative surplus; and (iii) agreeing on terms for distributing the surplus from cooperation. See more in R. Cooter & T. Ulen, *supra* note 1 in Introduction, p. 48.

26 S. Vogenauer, *supra* note 17, pp. 39-41.

chosen foreign contract law because their home law had not been suitable to their aims. Among the preferred foreign regimes, American law was cited by 1%.

Respondents were also asked to indicate which law, in their view, was most used in cross-border transactions. The result showed that 26% cited English law; 11% French, and 10% German.

The reasons given by the respondents for avoidance of certain regimes were the judiciary's being 'too arbitrary' or a law 'too protectionist'. In addition, the law's being 'different' from their home law was indicated by some respondents as a preponderant reason for its avoidance.[27]

This survey endorsed earlier findings where familiarity played a key role in a party's choice of governing law. The study also showed that parties gave due consideration to the choice of law process and would likely impose their own law by the use of bargaining power. The respondents signalled concern at the adequacy and convenience of the forum for potential dispute (*e.g.* 'judiciary's being too arbitrary') and would likely elect the law of the forum chosen.

Despite the number of companies surveyed, this study was limited to eight countries only, which may have led to certain cognitive biases, *e.g.* availability and anchoring-and-adjustment[28] – that do not allow us to generalize the findings, in particular due to the lack of representativeness of the sample.

As we shall see in the next chapter, cognitive biases are mental shortcuts commonly used in making daily decisions. They could also be named as 'hidden forces' that routinely influence our decisions without our further reflection.

Because a decision can (and usually does) take time and effort, the mind uses routes to facilitate the process of reaching a conclusion or making a decision. However, the power of cognitive biases is such that they routinely produce imperfections in the end result, for example by providing wrong estimates or departing from imprecise starting points.

As typical examples of cognitive bias in contract negotiation we could list the halo effect, the 'status quo' bias and the framing effect. The halo effect is a common cognitive bias easily identified in contract negotiation: once a good or bad impression is formed, it is often extended more generally and exaggerated.[29] For example, in the 2005 Survey the percentage of English law as the most used law in cross-border transactions (26%). Indicating a 'preference', in its own view and not necessarily by experience, could of itself be a product of cognitive biases.

According to the 'status quo' bias', individuals will tend to prefer an option consistent with the current state of affairs.[30] For example, the preference that respondents demon-

---

27 *Id.*

28 The topic 'heuristics and cognitive biases' is explored in fine detail in Section 2.2.1.

29 J. A. Maule & G. P. Hodgkinson, 'Heuristics, Biases and Strategic Decision Making', *The Psychologist*, Vol. 15, Issue 2, 2002, pp. 68-71.

30 R. Korobkin & C. Guthrie, 'Heuristics and Biases at the Bargaining Table', *Marquette Law Review*, Vol. 87, 2003, p. 805.

strated for their home law (66%) endorsed this bias. With respect to the framing effect, differences in the way a question is posed may generate very different answers. We use the term 'decision frame' to refer to the decision-maker's conception of the acts, outcomes and contingencies associated with a particular choice. The frame that a decision-maker adopts is controlled partly by the formulation of the problem and partly by the norms, habits and personal characteristics of the decision-maker.[31]

Another example of cognitive bias that appears to be prevalent in the results of this study can be revealed through the question 'Which law in their view was most used in cross-border transactions'. Respondents ranked only European systems as, in their view, the top three most used laws in cross-border transactions worldwide. *A contrario sensu*, respondents could arguably have thought that this question was limited to European boundaries and therefore, influenced by the framing effects, by anchoring-and-adjustment and availability heuristics,[32] named only European laws.

1.1.1.1.2 Studies on CISG Opt-Outs

Empirical Studies have also been undertaken with a particular emphasis on international sales law,[33] focusing primarily on the United Nations Convention on Contracts for the International Sale of Goods (CISG) and its interactions with the market, with the aim of assessing the CISG's popularity in certain jurisdictions.[34]

As early as 1997 a study conducted by Michael Wallace Gordon in Florida, United States, revealed the unfamiliarity of the respondents with the CISG.[35] Mr. Gordon surveyed 100 selected members of the Florida Bar's Section on International Law and the 24 members of that section's Executive Committee. Although professed as specialists in international law, the survey concluded that about 30% of the respondents indicated having 'reasonable knowledge' of the CISG and only two indicated 'strong knowledge'.[36]

---

31 A. Tversky & D. Kahneman, 'The Framing of Decisions and the Psychology of Choice', *Science,* Vol. 221, 1981, p. 453.

32 According to the anchoring-and-adjustment heuristic, we evaluate a problem by starting from an initial reference point – often one suggested to us – but we then make insufficient adjustments from it. Anchoring-and-adjustment refers to a tendency for judgments to be biased towards an initial value arrived at from partial or no computation. In its turn, according to availability heuristic, a decision-making is often based on what is most easily remembered at a given moment. It refers to the way in which probability or frequency judgments are influenced by the ease with which past examples are recalled. See more in A. Tversky & D. Kahneman, 'Judgment Under Uncertainty: Heuristics and Biases', *Science,* Vol. 185, 1974, pp. 1124-1131.

33 The list of studies discussed in this chapter is non-exhaustive. The surveys were selected on the criteria of relevance and importance to the topic of this book.

34 A complete study on how the CISG has influenced national law is available in F. Ferrari (Ed.), *The CISG and Its Impact on National Legal Systems,* Sellier, Munich, 2008.

35 M. W. Gordon, 'Some Thoughts on the Receptiveness of Contract Rules in the CISG and UNIDROIT Principles as Reflected in One State's (Florida) Experience of (1) Law School Faculty, (2) Members of the Bar with an International Practice, and (3) Judges', *American Journal of Comparative Law,* Vol. 46 (Suppl.), 1998, pp. 361-374.

36 W. S. Dodge, 'Teaching the CISG in Contracts', *Journal of Legal Education,* Vol. 50, 2000, pp. 72-94, available at [https://www.cisg.law.pace.edu/cisg/biblio/dodge.html].

90% of the respondents were of the opinion that the national sales law of Florida had prior applicability.[37] Mr Gordon also surveyed the faculties of Florida law schools[38] and found little attention to the CISG, noting in particular the absence of the CISG from casebooks.[39]

Mr Gordon's study attested to ignorance of the CISG among lawyers in the 1990s.[40] The study further hinted at the possibility that it was not dogmatic concerns but rather lack of information which might have contributed to the reluctance of practitioners to accept and apply the CISG.[41] However, it is necessary, once again, to put these figures into context: a survey conducted in 1997, among members of a state bar, who were already practitioners (presumably of a few years' standing) and not yet familiar with the CISG for reasons that are understandable, *inter alia*, the lack of representativeness of the sample (members of a single bar) and the number of CISG contracting States at that time (less than 50 states[42]). However, what probably most if not all practitioners could not predict was how costly this ignorance would be.[43] In the same direction, Seven Regula undertook a survey which found that only 10% of German purchasing and sales personnel had any knowledge of the CISG.[44]

Many years later, in 2004, Justus Meyer undertook a survey among 479 German lawyers specialized in international sales contracts.[45] The author reported that CISG opt-outs were 'normal practice' for 45% of the respondents. In 2007 the survey was replicated in

37 M. Koehler, 'Survey Regarding the Relevance of the United Nations Convention for the International Sale of Goods (CISG) in Legal Practice and the Exclusion of Its Application', *CISG Database*, 2006, available at [http://cisgw3.law.pace.edu/cisg/biblio/koehler.html].

38 The (costly) lack of awareness of the CISG is discussed in W. S. Dodge, *supra* note 36.

39 *Id.*

40 Despite this state of ignorance, the CISG was gradually starting to get noticed, thanks to the work of notable scholars like A. H. Kritzer, who remarked "The CISG is a collegial undertaking adopted to help remove barriers to world trade. Collegial sharing of data on the CISG can help the world trade community achieve this goal. The CISG W3 database is a platform for such collaboration designed to make information on this uniform sales law more readily available. All who practice, rule upon, or study international commercial law are invited to link to and draw on this database, and to help expand and improve its contents", 'The Convention on Contracts for the International Sale of Goods: Scope, Interpretation and Resources', *Cornell Review of the Convention on Contracts for the International Sale of Goods*, 1995, p. 187.

41 K. P. Berger *et al.*, *supra* note 6, p. 4.

42 Full list of contracting States available at [www.uncitral.org/uncitral/en/uncitral_texts/sale_goods/1980CISG_status_chronological.html].

43 See, J. E. Murray Jr, 'The Neglect of CISG: A Workable Solution', *Journal of Law & Commerce*, Vol. 17, 1998, pp. 365-379; P. Windship, 'Domesticating International Commercial Law: Revising UCC Article 2 in Light of the UN Sales Convention', *Loyola Law Review*, Vol. 37, 1991, pp. 43-68; H. D. Gabriel, 'The Inapplicability of the United Nations Convention on the International Sale of Goods as a Model for the Revision of Article Two of the Uniform Commercial Code', *Tulane Law Review*, Vol. 72, 1998, pp. 1995-2014; D. A. Thompson, 'Commentary, Buyer Beware: German Interpretation of the CISG Has Led to Results Unfavourable to Buyers', *Journal of Law & Commerce*, Vol. 19, 2000, pp. 245-263.

44 S. Regula & B. Kannowski, 'Nochmals: UN Kaufrecht oder BGB? Erwägungen zur Rechtswahl aufgrund einer vergleichenden Betrachtung', *Internationales Handelsrecht*, 2004/2, pp. 45-54.

45 J. Meyer, 'UN-Kaufrecht in der deutschen Anwaltspraxis', *Rabels Zeitschrift für ausländisches und internationales Privatrecht*, Vol. 69, 2005, pp. 457-486.

Austria (319) and Switzerland (396).[46] The author reported that 41% of the Swiss lawyers and 55% of the Austrian opted out of the CISG.[47]

At the same time Martin Koehler conducted a survey from October 2004 to September 2005 of the relevance of the CISG in legal practice and the exclusion of its application. The investigation took place in Germany and the United States and, whilst more than 3,000 practitioners were invited to participate, only 81 questionnaires were returned: 48 from the United States and 33 from Germany. Of these 49 were returned by law firms, 22 by company lawyers and 2 by the legal departments of public institutions; and 8 respondents supplied no information regarding their status.[48] Martin Koehler's findings show that only 4% of the respondents indicated never having had any contact with the CISG; 69.7% of the German respondents had contact with the CISG in their day-to-day work; whereas in the United States the figure was 29.2%. 58.2% of the United States practitioners knew of the CISG only from studies or the literature, as compared with 27.3% in Germany. Martin Koehler's findings indicate that only 9.9% of the respondents answered that they never excluded the application of the CISG, whereas 71.6% excluded the CISG (70.8% in the United States and 72.7% in Germany).[49]

When asked to spell out the reasons for such exclusion, the respondents' most frequent answer was 'because the CISG is generally not very widely known' (53.1%). The runner-up reason was 'there was no need for application' (38.3%) and in third place, 'advantage was seen in the application of the uniform law' (35.8%). Other reasons included that their business partners or those of their respective clients could not be dissuaded from application of national law (32.1%), because they or their companies had insufficient experience of the application of the CISG (28.4%), or because their company or the client, due to a leading position in the market, had the power to retain the application of its national law (25.9%).[50]

A finding that, albeit relevant, comes as a no surprise is that 33.3% of the American respondents indicated that they excluded the CISG because of insufficient case law, as compared with 6.1% of German respondents.

In his analysis of results, Martin Koehler concludes that the

> central – although hardly the most surprising – finding of the empirical survey shows that the overriding reasons for an exclusion of the Convention are practical and the lack of familiarity of the convention provides by far the most important reason for exclusion.

46 J. Meyer, 'UN-Kaufrecht in der schweizerischen Anwaltspraxis', *Schweizerische Juristen-Zeitung/Revue suisse de jurisprudence*, Vol. 104, 2008, pp. 421-428.

47 J. Meyer, 'UN-Kaufrecht in der österreichischen Anwaltspraxis', *Österreichische Juristen-Zeitung*, Vol. 63, 2008, pp. 792-798.

48 M. Koehler, *supra* note 37.

49 *Id.*

50 *Id.*

The study also investigated whether respondents, in cases where they understand that the CISG applies and is not entirely excluded, undertake any modification of the CISG; exclude, replace or vary any individual provision or parts thereof. The majority of the respondents (58%) denied undertaking any modification. Those who did were mostly concerned with extending or limiting liability provisions.[51]

Lastly, Martin Koehler rightly raised a crucial element of concern regarding familiarity, conveying the message that this is a 'self-generating circulus vitiosus', inasmuch as familiarity with and acceptance of a given legal framework arise by use and positive experience.

It is important to contextualize Martin Koehler's study, in particular given the increasing exchange of goods in global markets since 2005 and, in consequence, the impact and development of new legal standards and legal frameworks worldwide. The findings, however, confirm that familiarity is and continues to be a key element in the decision-making processes. The study is also helpful in signalling some features of the CISG that could be modified or improved.

A subsequent survey was conducted by Martin Koehler and Guo Yujun in 2007 in China,[52] in which a total of 27 questionnaires were completed by 18 attorneys in private practice and 9 in-house counsel. The authors reported that the Chinese responses were very much similar to those of the United States respondents: 30% had contact with the CISG in their day-to-day work; a further 60% had contact with the CISG in other ways: 13.3% knew of the CISG from hearsay, 26.7% from their studies; 16.6% from the literature; and 3.4% from colleagues.

With respect to the reasons for exclusion of the CISG in China, the first was that 'there is no reason to make use of the unified law as long as our business partners or the business partners of our client continue to apply national law' (51.9%); 'because it is not possible to dissuade our business partners or the business partners of our clients from the application of their national law' (37%); and 'insufficient case law to date related to the CISG' (29.6%). As to the modifications of the provisions of the CISG, 44.4% of the Chinese respondents indicated not having made any.

Lastly, the authors concluded that there was a trend towards citing irrelevance of the legal aspects, on the one hand, and the familiarity, or lack thereof, as the paramount reason for exclusion, on the other hand. The authors further noted that the respondents had not yet taken the trouble to compare the legal aspects of the two regimes of law in detail.[53] The authors further stated that the CISG's goal of unifying the law and the

51 *Id.*

52 M. Koehler & G. Yujun, 'The Acceptance of the Unified Sales Law (CISG) in Different Legal Systems: An International Comparison of Three Surveys on the Exclusion of the CISG's Application Conducted in the United States, Germany and China', available at [www.cisg.law.pace.edu/cisg/biblio/koehler-yujun.html].

53 M. Koehler & G. Yujun, *supra* note 52.

literature's much-vaunted advantages of a unified law are 'victims of certain indolence in practice'.[54]

More or less simultaneously with Martin Koehler's study, Gilles Cuniberti conducted a study of 181 cases in the United States, Germany and France, where the CISG was applied, in order to assess the effect of the CISG on contractual practice and whether it had been beneficial.[55] The study encompassed both court decisions and arbitral awards.

Cuniberti found that the revealing message was that parties to international sale are generally not concerned with the legal regime governing their contract. This is supported by the fact that in 63% of the cases decided by American courts the parties were not sufficiently concerned with the applicable law to include a provision in respect of the choice of law or to ensure that it would be enforceable.[56] As regards arbitral awards, in 60% of the cases the parties had not provided for the applicable law. Cuniberti concludes that most parties who failed to provide, had probably neglected the issue of the legal regime governing their contract for a simpler reason: 'the parties are just unaware of the importance of the applicable law and of the issue generally'.[57]

Cuniberti further submitted that the cases reviewed demonstrated that the buyers and sellers were unsophisticated, not concerned with the legal regime governing their contracts, and that the CISG had not brought them any *ex ante* benefit.[58] In addition, Cuniberti argued that the data provided allow us to identify two scenarios in which the CISG could benefit players: firstly, unsophisticated parties, as they are not concerned *ex ante* with the legal regime, if an issue arises, may wonder what the law is and seek legal advice. In such a scenario the CISG would thus bring benefits as it would facilitate the resolution of a dispute regarding the law applicable. Secondly, the CISG could also benefit some sophisticated parties who would not retain a lawyer for domestic transactions but would do so for international transactions. Therefore, a harmonized set of rules would avoid bargains and learning costs, thereby reducing transaction costs.[59]

Cuniberti's study is also of value as it reveals a striking lack of attention paid to the choice of law matters. While the topic of choice of law is routinely regarded as arid and often presented as complex, it is surprising that parties would understand that this topic is not a contractual issue *ex ante, i.e.*, an issue which parties should discuss and negotiate rather than defer it to an *ex post* scenario. The parties seemed to have neglected that the applicable rules, if not rationally thought through, may intervene and prevent international sales from taking effect.

---

54 *Id.*

55 G. Cuniberti, 'Is the CISG Benefiting Anybody?', *Vanderbilt Journal of Transnational Law*, Vol. 39, 2006, pp. 1511-1550.

56 G. Cuniberti, *supra* note 55, pp. 1534-1535.

57 *Id.*

58 G. Cuniberti, *supra* note 55, pp. 1544-1545.

59 *Id.*

In 2006 and 2007 Peter Fitzgerald[60] conducted a survey of 47 respondents who effectively addressed the substance of this question: 55% (US lawyers) typically opted out of the CISG.

Likewise in 2007 George Philippopoulos[61] reported, from a sample of 46 commercial litigation lawyers, that an 'overwhelming majority' preferred to opt out of the CISG, albeit no percentage was reported.

1.1.2 *Post-2008 Studies: Innovative Works*

1.1.2.1 Studies on Choice of Law

The studies from 2008 onwards inaugurate what we consider a new phase in terms of evidence found in choice of law decisions. Some of the studies were pioneering in the contract surveyed or subjects interviewed; others used previous ideas but put them in different contexts and others updated earlier studies by extending considerably the pool of respondents surveyed.

In 2008 Stefan Voigt published a study on choices of law,[62] based on the ICC Statistical Report for the year 2003, where 580 cases were filed and involved parties from 123 countries. It revealed that 82% of the contracts surveyed contained a choice of law clause. English law was chosen in 24% of the contracts that contained a choice of law clause, Swiss law in 20%, French in 19% and US – Canadian in 10%.

The study validated previous conclusions that parties will attempt, if context allows, to impose their home law on their transactions. If this option were unsuitable or unavailable, it appeared that the above systems would be preferred. The study also offered a list of preferred systems, and it is noted that English and Swiss law feature once more as 'key players'. However, the study is not entirely clear on the type of contract involved and the nationalities of the parties profiled and surveyed. In addition, this study was based on data provided by only one arbitral institution (the ICC). Hence it would be difficult for readers to generalize on parties' preferences in all types of contractual agreement.

In 2008 the Oxford Civil Justice Survey,[63] jointly conducted by the Oxford Institute of European and Comparative Law and the Oxford Center for Socio-Legal Studies, aimed to

60 P. L. Fitzgerald, 'The International Contracting Practices Survey Project: An Empirical Study of the Value and Utility of the United Nations Convention on the International Sale of Goods (CISG) and the UNIDROIT Principles of International Commercial Contracts to Practitioners, Jurists, and Legal Academics in the United States', *Journal of Law & Commerce*, Vol. 27, 2008, pp. 1-34.

61 G. Philippopoulos, 'Awareness of the CISG Among American Attorneys', *UCC Law Journal*, Vol. 40, Issue 3, 2008, pp. 357-569.

62 S. Voigt, 'Are International Merchants Stupid? Their Choice of Law Sheds Doubt on the Legal Origin Theory', *Journal of Empirical Legal Studies*, Vol. 5, Issue 1, 2008, pp. 1-20.

63 S. Vogenauer, 'Perceptions of Civil Justice Systems in Europe and Their Implications for Choice of Forum and Choice of Contract Law: An Empirical Analysis', *in* S. Vogenauer & C. Hodges (Eds.), *Civil Justice Systems in Europe: Implications for Choice of Forum and Choice of Contract Law*, Hart Publishing, Oxford,

assess companies' perceptions of national contract law and the civil justice systems in Europe.

The survey mapped out the preferences of 100 European companies. The results showed that 85% of the companies surveyed occasionally chose foreign law to govern their transactions. The survey indicated that the following regimes were preferred: English law (21%); German (16%); French and Swiss law (14%); and Dutch (9%). Respondents were further asked to indicate the factors that triggered this choice: they answered that the most important factor was the quality of the contract law.

The survey went further and concluded that in reality the preferences were related predominantly to the surveyed companies' 'home law'. When home choices were unavailable, Swiss law (28%) and English law (23%) led the preferences. With respect to the forum, 'home turf' also appeared to be the choice of the respondent companies.

This survey had broader scope than those of earlier studies and included choice of forum considerations in addition to choice of law. It also encompassed a larger sample of respondents, although the focus remained on Europe. While these limitations arguably prevented broader conclusions from being drawn, especially in relation to non-European parties, some previous conclusions were again confirmed, such as the 'familiarity' ideal sought in any transaction.

Interestingly, 'quality of the law' was indicated as the most important consideration in choosing governing law. What does this represent in real-world practice? How can one assess such quality? While 'quality of the law' might be seen as imprecise and vague, this does prompt the idea that further analysis of these features should be explored in future surveys or studies.

In 2009 Theodore Eisenberg and Geoffrey Miller published a study[64] based on 2,882 contracts publicly available due to a reporting requirement of the United States Securities and Exchange Commission. The contracts were reported in 2002 and covered a wide range of topics: commercial transactions, asset sales, purchases through to licensing, mergers and trust agreements. The contracting parties were in the United States. The study showed that 46% of the contracts were subject to the law of New York; 15% to that of Delaware; and 8% to the law of California. 39% included a choice of forum clause, in the following order of preference: 41% New York; 11% Delaware and 7% California as the preferred forum for potential disputes.

The authors concluded that the preference for New York law endorsed the inferences that choices of law will tend to cluster around one or a few states (in the United States)

2017, p. 1 *et seq*. The Survey results are also available at www.fondation-droitcontinental.org/fr/wp-content/uploads/2013/12/oxford_civil_justice_survey_-_summary_of_results_final.pdf.

64 T. Eisenberg & G. P. Miller, 'The Flight to New York: An Empirical Study of Choice of Law and Choice of Forum Clauses in Publicly-Held Companies' Contracts', *Cardozo Law Review*, Vol. 30, 2009, pp. 1475-1512.

because of the increased development of the law in those states.[65] Moreover, a substantial degree of overlap was identified between choice of forum and choice of law: if a particular state's law is chosen as the governing contract law, then that state's forum is likely to be selected to hear potential disputes.[66] The study was of local or regional scope and, although it did not specify the reasons for this, it did reveal a sort of interplay between choice of law and choice of forum.

Following the trend of empirical studies, Thomas Dietz examined the enforcement of cross-border contracts in the software industry.[67] The results were published in 2010 and were based on 31 qualitative interviews, of which 27 were with business managers in the software industry and four with representatives of trade associations in 2005 and 2006.

Dietz found that the contracts were governed by the law and, unless an arbitration clause was inserted, the forum of the purchaser. All these choices were driven by negative perceptions of the quality of the civil justice systems in the software developers' jurisdictions. Included in this equation were untrustworthy judges, delayed proceedings, unpredictable costs, and problems in enforcing judgment. It appeared that choice of law simply echoed choice of forum – the interviewees did not seem to draw a clear distinction.[68]

As further explained by Stefan Vogenauer while analyzing Dietz's findings, the parties to these transactions worked on the assumption that the contracts would never be enforced in the state courts – and in fact they never were: purchasers did not even try to obtain judgment in their favour in their home courts because they feared delay and difficulties in enforcing these judgments in the developers' jurisdictions. Nor did developers sue in the purchasers' home courts because they regarded the costs of litigating in a Western European jurisdiction as prohibitive and felt they were not sufficiently familiar with the law of these jurisdictions. The parties to these transactions therefore tended to rely on so-called 'private order contract enforcement institutions' in order to protect their cross-border transactions against fraud and opportunism.[69]

This study identified a clear interplay between choice of law and choice of forum, yet the scope and spread of the study is limited – it focused on a particular single contract and had only regional reach. Once again, these data are of direct relevance, although they leave open the question of what the driving forces and major concerns of parties in choice of law and choice of forum decisions are, thereby warranting further studies in the future on this point.

Since 2006 Queen Mary, University of London has been conducting studies focused on international arbitration preferences and contracting parties' main concerns. Previous

---

65 T. Eisenberg & G. P. Miller, *supra* note 64, p. 1490.

66 *Id.*, p. 1511.

67 T. Dietz, *Institutionen und Globalisierung: eine empirische Untersuchung am Beispiel grenzüberschreitender Softwareentwicklungsverträge*, Mohr Siebeck, Heidelberg, 2010. For a summary in English of Dietz's findings, see S. Vogenauer, *supra* note 17, pp. 45-46.

68 S. Vogenauer, *supra* note 17, pp. 45-46.

69 *Id.*

editions have been helpful in demonstrating that arbitration has become the preferred dispute-resolution method for cross-border disputes.[70]

For methodological purposes this chapter will refer to the 2010 edition only and some of the other editions will be discussed in other chapters of this book.[71] We have taken this approach because the main drive behind the current chapter is to present studies of choice of law decisions in cross-border transactions. It would be counterproductive to engage readers in discussion of choice of forum at this stage, noting in particular that there will a subsequent chapter dedicated to dispute resolution concerns and their interaction with choice of law decisions.[72] Consequently, the following discussion will present the Queen Mary University of London Survey (2010 edition), in which elements of choice of law were added to the traditional choice of forum-driven questionnaire.

As mentioned above, the 2010 edition[73] was innovative in including choice of law questions. The study was based on 136 responses to an online questionnaire and 63 face-to-face and telephone interviews.

The results showed that 44% of the respondents selected their domestic law, if they had this choice, followed by English law (25%), Swiss law (9%), and New York law (6%).[74] The law most frequently chosen by the counterparties was that of their own jurisdiction (53%), English law (21%) and New York law (10%).[75] It is interesting that 40% of the respondents, unsurprisingly, believed that the most frequently used law was English law, followed by New York law (17%), and Swiss law (8%).[76]

The respondents' choice was mostly influenced by the perceived neutrality and impartiality of the chosen legal system with regard to the parties and their contract (66%), the appropriateness of the law to the type of contract (60%), and the parties' familiarity with and experience of the particular law (58%).[77]

As to the reasons for selecting the preferred law, most respondents cited familiarity and legal certainty (or 'predictability', 'foreseeability'). They also mentioned being influenced by a 'well developed jurisprudence' and 'international acceptance'.[78] Some respondents also referred to the substantive qualities of the law chosen, such as its appropriateness to particular types of contract or general principles, *e.g.* respect for freedom of contract. Some respondents indicated that 'strategy also has an impact': they would at-

---

70 Previous editions of the Queen Mary University of London surveys will be the subject of deeper analysis in *infra* Section 4.1.1.

71 In this connection, please refer to *infra* Section 4.1.1.

72 *Id.*

73 2010 International Arbitration Survey: Choices in International Arbitration, full data available at [www.arbitration.qmul.ac.uk/docs/123290.pdf].

74 *Id.*, p. 13, Chart 9.

75 *Id.*, p. 13, Chart 10.

76 *Id.*, p. 14, Chart 11.

77 *Id.*, p. 12, Chart 8.

78 *Id.*, p. 13.

tempt to anticipate which national laws might provide them with an advantage in case of dispute.

The study did reveal data on the relationship between choice of law and arbitration clauses. An indication of the respondents' position with regard to this relationship might be found in their attitude to choice of the seat of arbitration (which determines the procedural law applicable to proceedings to the extent that the parties have not stipulated otherwise[79]): 51% of the respondents decided on the governing law before they selected arbitration. Conversely, the latter choice did not appear to have influenced the respondents' choice of law.[80]

All in all, the 2010 Queen Mary Survey shows that familiarity and neutrality of the chosen law are the most desirable aspects, whereas the respondents briefly mentioned substantive qualities, *e.g.* appropriateness to type of contract, and respect for freedom of contract.[81] The results appear to indicate that choice of law and choice of forum are interconnected to a degree, and that choice of law might determine choice of forum.

In 2010 the Law Society of England and Wales conducted telephone interviews with senior representatives of 602 law firms across England and Wales.[82] Among those interviewed 91 had advised on deals with a party from another jurisdiction in the previous year. In 78% of these the parties had chosen English law 'to govern the whole deal (all contracts)'; in 8% of these the parties had chosen English law 'to govern a part of the deal'. In only 2% had the parties chosen 'the law(s) of other jurisdiction(s) to govern the whole deal'.[83]

Among the 91 firms the most important factors for the choice of governing law were 'legal certainty' (73%) and 'familiarity with the legal system of the contracting parties' (67%), rather than concerns pertaining to the inherent qualities of contract law, measured in terms of the 'attractiveness of the legal principles' of a particular legal system (47%) and 'the ease of use of the legal system' (53%).

This study has the same limitations as those discussed above: a regional approach and limited scope. Nevertheless, it has the virtue of endorsing previous conclusions and disclosing new findings. For example, it noted that some respondents rated the 'attractiveness of the legal principles' and the 'ease of use of the legal system' as important factors. However, unfortunately, the study did not clarify what the terms 'attractiveness' and 'ease of use' represent in real-life practice, which would be desirable in order better to understand contracting parties' minds in this instance.

79 S.Vogenauer, *supra* note 17, pp. 48-49.
80 2010 International Arbitration Survey: Choices in International Arbitration, p. 9, Chart 5.
81 *Id.*, pp. 12-13.
82 S. Vogenauer, *supra* note 17, pp. 49-50.
83 *Id.*

During the academic year 2010-2011 the *Fondation pour le droit continental* in France conducted a study on choice of law.[84] The project focused on three types of international transaction: sales contracts and contracts for works and services; mergers and acquisitions, and financial transactions. The study was based on questionnaire-led qualitative interview with Paris-based legal practitioners involved in making choices of law in international transactions.[85]

For the first two types of contract, 25 practitioners were interviewed, with a more or less equal distribution between in-house counsel and external legal advisors. With regard to financial transactions, there were roughly 40 interviewees. Half of them were banking lawyers and the remainder was made up of in-house counsel and external advisors.[86] The study found that choice of law was mostly made by in-house counsel or, in the case of financial transactions, by the banks' lawyers. In short the results appeared to indicate that relatively little attention was given to choice of law during the negotiations.

The study revealed that the issue of choice of law is typically not a deal-breaker.[87] The findings demonstrate that choice of law is given less attention than it probably deserves at the negotiation table. The limitations mentioned above also apply to the findings in the study conducted by the *Fondation pour le droit continental*: a limited sample and narrow scope. The focus was placed on 'who' makes the choice of law decision and how this choice is ranked in terms of importance.

Whilst it is certainly relevant to understand who are the actors involved and the extent of their power in the decision-making processes, the underlying reasons for their decisions were never among the study goals. Unfortunately, the findings do not allow us to extract perceptions and draw guidelines on choice of law processes. For instance, generalizations regarding respondents' views on whether more or less attention is given if you are a supplier or a buyer, or whether this decision is influenced by other variables, *inter alia*, the type of agreement and potential amount at stake, the nationality of the parties, the jurisdiction(s) where obligations are likely to be enforced.

Let us take as an example the hypothesis 'choice of law is not a deal-breaker'. Does the study's findings confirm this assumption? Alternatively, under what conditions or circumstances would the choice of law decision be seen as a deal-breaker? Further, would this perception be modified if the choice of law decision is, say, combined with a dispute resolution clause over which parties have/will bargain(ed)? Or would that change if you negotiate this clause as a supplier or a purchaser?

---

84 The *Fondation pour le droit continental* undertakes, *inter alia*, studies on the economic consequences of the law chosen by the parties to international contract. The studies aimed to better understand parties' motives in negotiating applicable law clauses. See *e.g.*, the 'Index of Legal Certainty', basis of an evaluation of legal certainty in a context of international comparison, available at [www.fondation-droitcontinental.org/en/wp-content/uploads/2015/06/NS_Rapport-complet-5-juin-2015_EN.pdf]

85 S. Vogenauer, *supra* note 17, p. 50.

86 *Id.*

87 *Id.*

The findings in this study indicated that in-house counsel mostly make the choice of law decision in international sales contracts. Do the findings confirm this inference worldwide? If the study reveals tendencies, could we focus on this point and analyze why this is the case from the available data? Could we conclude that in-house counsel might be more risk-averse[88] (or have fewer incentives to change policy) than external counsel and this is one of the reasons why some laws are preferred to others? Are there rational elements involved in this choice or are there primarily intuitive-based factors?

As we can see, although the findings are relevant to understand who are the actors involved in the process of choosing governing contract law, and even indicate behavioural patterns and tendencies, there are certainly open questions that deserve further study. Due to its limited scope the study failed to allow generalization, as stated above.

In 2013 Gilles Cuniberti published his study[89] based on an analysis of more than 4,400 international contracts submitted to ICC arbitration in the period 2007 to 2012.[90] Cuniberti's findings revealed five jurisdictions that have laws considered more attractive in the international market for contracts. They follow this order of preference: English, Swiss, US State laws, French and German.[91]

While analyzing the results, Cuniberti further discussed the underlying reasons for different levels of attractiveness of certain systems. As extrinsic factors, he lists seat of arbitration, language, neutrality, model contracts, law firms and colonial empires.[92] As intrinsic qualities of contract law, he lists marketing materials, general features of legal systems, and some peculiarities of English and Swiss Contract Law.[93]

Among Cuniberti's explored reasons, 'colonial empires' calls for particular attention. The author asserts

> [I]n the international success of certain contract laws could be that a number of jurisdictions are former colonies of two European countries.

Cuniberti further asserts that the law of these European countries would often closely follow the law of the country that once occupied them. And he concludes that

88 R. Cooter & T. Ulen remark that "a person is said to be risk-averse if she considers the utility of a certain prospect of money income to be higher than the expected utility of an uncertain prospect of equal expected monetary value", *supra* note 1 in Introduction, p. 46.

89 G. Cuniberti, 'International Market for Contracts: The Most Attractive Contract Laws', *Northwestern Journal of International Law & Business*, Vol. 34, Issue 3, 2013, pp. 455-517. See also Cuniberti's proposal that the attractiveness of a given contract law can be assessed by determining the number of cases in which it was chosen as the third-state law.

90 A search for the terms 'CISG' and 'CVIM' (French acronym for CISG) in the 'awards tab' of the ICC Digital Library returned 99 results. A further investigation revealed that the CISG was cited in 50 ICC awards out of 762 awards published on the database. Further information is available at [http://library.iccwbo.org/].

91 G. Cuniberti, *supra* note 89, p. 517.

92 *Id.*, p. 490.

93 *Id.*, pp. 475-501.

> The law of the former colonial power will thus be at least familiar to any actor originating from one of these colonies. So it could be predicted that those parties would view the law of the former colonial power as not truly foreign, and would thus be happy to provide for its application.

Cuniberti's study has undeniable value because it maps out the preferred law in the context of international contracts. It offers an update of Truong's findings but is broader in scope. Cuniberti also discusses a theoretical perspective with new elements, such as extrinsic factors and intrinsic qualities of contract law, in an attempt to explain why certain law stands out among others. However, it is arguable that this is another study heavily focused on statistics and thus not helpful to understand the mechanics of this choice, and less on a respondents' substantive concerns regarding governing contract law or the driving forces that guide this choice.

In 2017 Linn Bergman published a study[94] on how arbitrators determine and deal with governing contract law in cross-borders disputes. Ms Bergman analyzed 101 previously unpublished Stockholm Chamber of Commerce (SCC[95]) awards and decisions from 1993 to 2017. While it is not entirely clear how this selection was made by the author, the underlying purpose was to allow academics and practitioners to understand when choice of law issues may arise and how they can be addressed, thereby increasing foreseeability in choice of law decisions.[96] The study organized the decisions by choice of law themes[97] and provided to each of them a succinct factual background accompanied by the legal reasoning. For example, the study recorded five[98] referrals to the UNIDROIT Principles[99] and one referral[100] to *lex mercatoria.*[101]

For purposes of this book we are mostly concerned with decisions where the CISG was applied by the arbitrators as the governing contract law. We noted that Bergman's study listed 41 referrals[102] to the CISG by the arbitral tribunals. This is a very significant number and one that confirms earlier inferences that the CISG may indeed be popular in

---

94 L. Bergman, *A Casebook on Choice of Law in Arbitration*, Landa, Stockholm, 2017.

95 Further information about the Arbitration Institute of the Stockholm Chamber of Commerce is available at [www.sccinstitute.com].

96 L. Bergman, *supra* note 94, p. 5.

97 The themes were divided into three groups 'Contract', 'Decision' and 'Method', L. Bergman, *supra* note 94, pp. 15-18.

98 In only one of these five cases had the parties agreed that the contract was governed by 'international commercial law', which the arbitrators understood to refer to CISG with the exclusion of national reservations and the UNIDROIT Principles. See L. Bergman, *supra* note 94, pp. 213-214.

99 Further information about the The International Institute for the Unification of Private Law (UNIDROIT) is available at [www.unidroit.org].

100 The reference was made in the context of the arbitrators' remarking that the applicable arbitration rules allow them, in the absence of an agreed choice of law or rules of law, to apply the law or rules of law which they consider to be most appropriate, including *lex mercatoria.* See L. Bergman, *supra* note 94, pp. 208-210.

101 Please see discussion on *lex mercatoria* in *infra* Section 5.1.2.2, note 72 in Chapter 5.

102 See L. Bergman, *supra* note 94, p. 9.

international arbitration,[103] despite the difficulties of measuring this worldwide given the confidentiality inherent to these proceedings.

Given our interest in the topic, we have independently examined these 41 arbitration cases. Out of these 41, in 2 of them the CISG was referred *in obiter* and not applied.[104] Hence, we took into account the 39 arbitration cases where the CISG was applied and thus classified them in four groups: (i) application of the CISG by the arbitral tribunal's own initiative; (ii) direct application by recourse to domestic conflict of law rules, Article 1(1)(a) of the CISG; (iii) application by virtue of domestic conflict of laws rules, Article 1 (1)(b) of the CISG; and (iv) choice of the CISG by parties' agreement.

Group (i) comprises cases where the arbitrators autonomously applied the CISG without recourse to conflict of law rules but rather as an expression of the proper law of the contract or a neutral legal standard to govern the cross-border dispute. In this group there was no choice of governing contract law in the parties' agreements and the application of the CISG was made by the arbitral tribunal without regard to Article 1[105] of the CISG.[106]

Group (ii) consists of cases where the arbitrators applied the CISG via Article 1(1)(a), *i.e.* where both parties were located in contracting States. As above, the cases in group (ii) had no choice of governing contract law and domestic law had been applied in some cases to supplement the matters uncovered by the CISG via Article 7(2).[107]

---

103 See *infra* note 119.

104 Of these 41 cases, in 1 (SCC Arbitration, Code 246 (2002): R (France) vs. H and N (China)), the parties had subsequently agreed that Chinese law should govern the contract and the CISG was mentioned by the arbitrators *in obiter*: "[...] In the absence of an agreement between the parties, CISG and – to the extent required for supplementing CISG – French law could arguably be the proper law of the Contract, at least as far as the sale of goods is concerned...". However, the controversy revolved around agency and legal competence, matters not governed by the CISG. See L. Bergman, *supra* note 94, pp. 159-162. In the other case (SCC Arbitration, Code 239 (2002) O (Italy) vs. N (China)), the arbitral tribunal did not apply any legal rule when interpreting the contract but did mention the CISG *in obiter* "[...] We note that Italy and China have both ratified the UN Convention of 1980 on International Sales of Goods". See L. Bergman, *supra* note 94, pp. 155-156. Therefore, these cases have been excluded from the independent analysis undertaken by this author.

105 Article 1(1) This Convention applies to contracts of sale of goods between parties whose places of business are in different States:
a. when the States are contracting States; or
b. when the rules of private international law lead to the application of the law of a contracting State.

106 See commentary of Article 1 of the CISG by I. Schwenzer & P. Hachem, *in* I. Schwenzer (Ed.), *Schlechtriem & Schwenzer, Commentary on the United Nations Convention on the International Sale of Goods (CISG)*, 4th ed., Oxford University Press, Oxford, 2016, pp. 27-46.

107 Article 7(2) Questions concerning matters governed by this Convention which are not expressly settled in it are to be settled in conformity with the general principles on which it is based or, in the absence of such principles, in conformity with the law applicable by virtue of the rules of private international law.

Group (iii) consists of cases where the arbitrators had recourse to domestic conflict of law rules to elect the CISG (Article 1(1)(b)). As above, the cases in group (iii) had no choice of governing contract law. In this group domestic law had also been applied in some cases to supplement the matters uncovered by the CISG via Article 7(2).

Lastly, group (iv) comprises cases where the parties have elected the CISG expressly in their agreements.

The results obtained, detailed in the below graph, show a prevalence of application of the CISG by virtue of Article 1(1)(a) (20 cases), followed by parties' agreement (8 cases), application of the CISG by virtue of domestic conflict of laws rules (7 cases) and autonomous application by the arbitral tribunal (4 cases[108]).

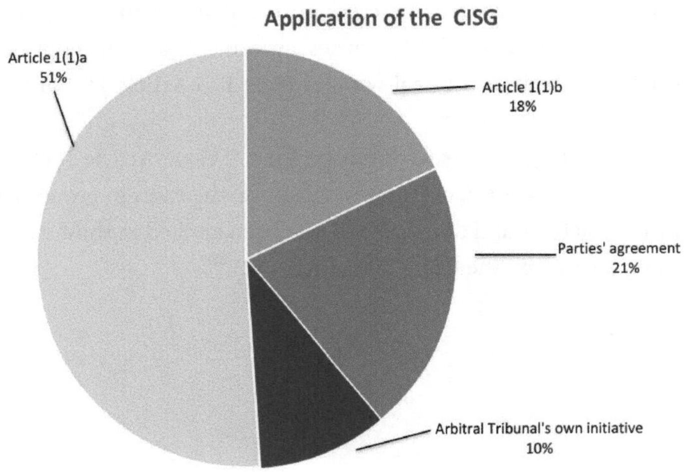

We have also examined whether these contracts have choice of law clauses and if so, whether they expressly elected CISG or domestic law as governing contract law. A choice of law clause was present in 10 or 25% of these contracts in the following proportion: domestic laws (5), CISG (4[109]) and 'International Commercial Law' (1[110]).

108 The first case dates back to 1999 and the last one to 2008.

109 These cases dated from 2005 to 2011.

110 SCC Arbitration, Code 428 (2008): B (China) vs. E (Germany). In this case, the arbitration clause read as follows 'On this contract shall apply International Commercial Law'. See L. Bergman, *supra* note 94, pp. 213-214.

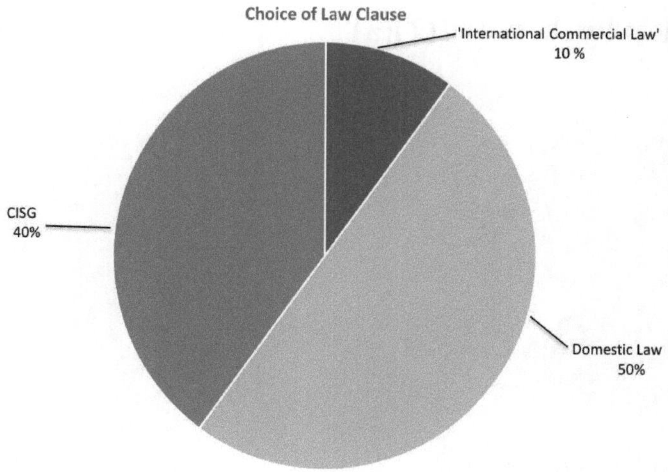

The percentage of cases with absence of a choice of law clause is, in this author's view, the most surprising finding obtained above (75%[111]). This is particularly striking in the context of international arbitration, where players are, or at the very least professed to be, sophisticated and aware of the effects and consequences flowing from their contractual arrangements. However, this may also point to two possible scenarios: (i) the involvement of unsophisticated parties in some of these cases,[112] who may have entered into these agreements without knowing the exact legal consequences of their choices (it is unclear from the cases surveyed what is the size and nature of the disputes[113]); and (ii) a 'laid-back'[114] approach adopted by these parties who would – perhaps too optimistically – defer this matter to the arbitrator, whom they rely on to determine the governing contract law.[115]

Given that Berman's study encompassed decisions from 1994 to 2017, we have also decided to generate graphs[116] disclosing the relevant period of time in which the decisions were made.

111 The latest case dates back to 2014.

112 In his study, although conducted in the context of court proceedings, Cuniberti submitted that the cases reviewed demonstrated that the buyers and sellers are unsophisticated parties who are not concerned with the legal regime governing their contracts and that the CISG has not brought them any *ex ante* benefit. See G. Cuniberti, *supra* note 55, pp. 1540-1541.

113 The factual background summaries provide limited information as to the case particulars and this is arguably due to the confidentiality of the arbitral awards. In this regard the author advises that the disputed matter 'has been generalised', L. Bergman, *supra* note 94, p. 5.

114 See more of this discussion in *infra* Chapter 4.

115 *Id.*

116 In light of the low number obtained in group 2, there will be no graph generated by time. However, the decisions were rendered in 1999 (1), 2003 (1), 2006 (1), and 2008 (1).

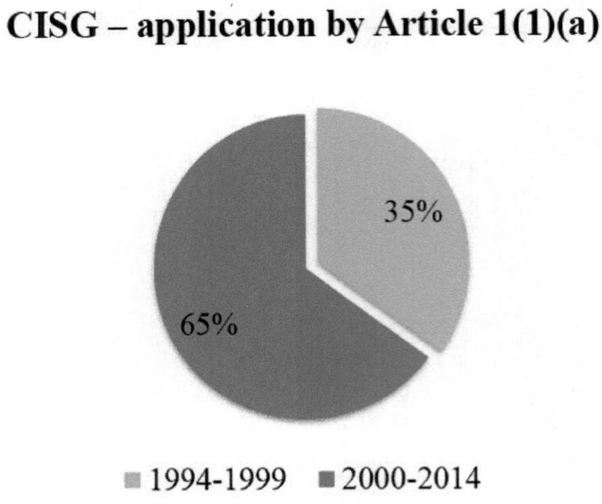
CISG – application by Article 1(1)(a)
35%
65%
1994-1999
2000-2014

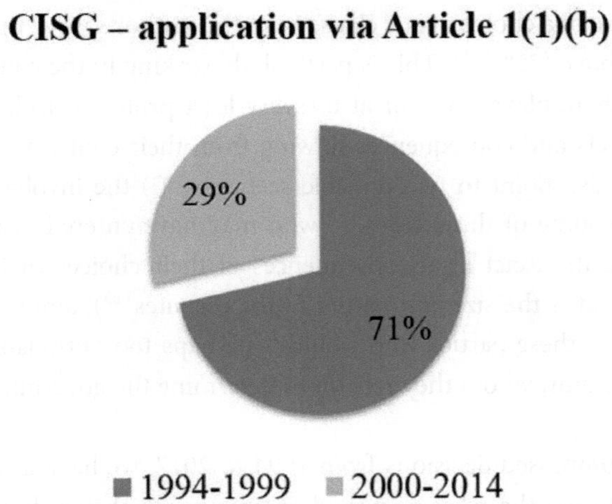
CISG – application via Article 1(1)(b)
29%
71%
1994-1999
2000-2014

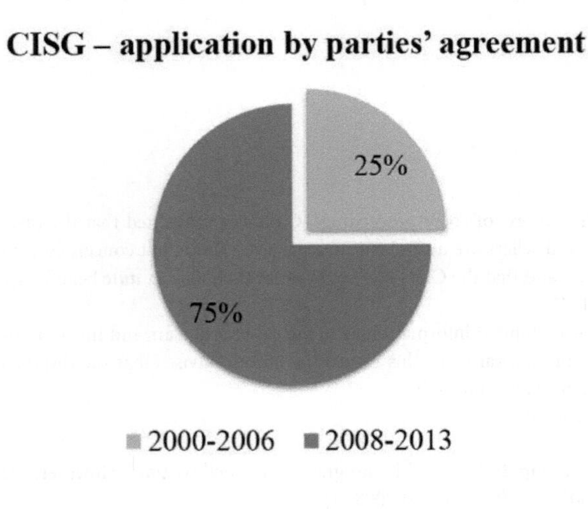
CISG – application by parties' agreement
25%
75%
2000-2006
2008-2013

CISG – application by Arbitral Tribunal's own initiative

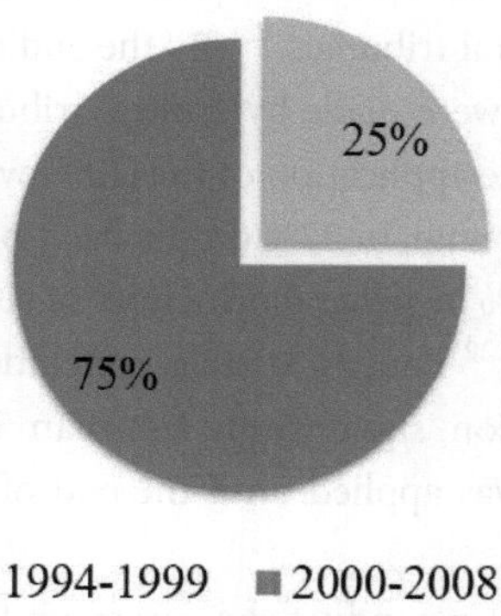

The above timeframes confirm the gradual increase in the level of awareness of the parties and arbitrators of the CISG in SCC international arbitration cases. The figure of 75% attests to the fact that rather recently parties have decided more often to use this legal framework to govern their cross-border deals. The identical figure of 75% also attests to the popularity of the CISG among arbitrators in SCC international arbitration cases. The decrease of application of the CISG via Article 1(1)(b) from 2000 may be a consequence of the increase in the number of contracting States in the same period of time, which is also shown in the higher number of application via Article 1(1)(a).

All in all, despite a lack of clarity with respect to the sample of cases surveyed, the results obtained in Bergman's study are certainly encouraging: a steady use of the CISG as the governing contract law in SCC international arbitration cases from 1994 to 2014.[117]

1.1.2.2 Studies on CISG Opt-Outs

Inaugurating a new phase of study, Widmer & Hachem reported a survey conducted in early 2008 of 153 Swiss lawyers of whom 62% 'regularly' opt out of the CISG. The authors found that Swiss lawyers are 5 times more likely to accept a counterparty's proposal to opt out rather than to opt in.[118]

117 The latest CISG -applied case reported in Bergman's study dates back to 2014 but the study included 1 case from 2017. See, in this regard, L. Bergman, *supra* note 94, pp. 297-299.

118 The latest CISG -applied case reported in Bergman's study dates back to 2014 but the study included 1 case from 2017. See, in this regard, L. Bergman, *supra* note 94, pp. 297-299. 170 lawyers responded, 17 were not involved in international sales. See L. Spagnolo, *CISG Exclusion and Legal Efficiency*, Wolters Kluwer, Alphen aan den Rijn, 2014, p. 151.

In 2008 Loukas Mistelis,[119] while not properly delving into CISG opt-outs, undertook a study on the CISG Database of the Pace Law University[120] to map out the application of the CISG by judicial courts and arbitral tribunals.[121] By the end of 2008 he observed that over a quarter of the 2000 decisions were made by arbitral tribunals. According to Mistelis' study, in these 2000 decisions the application of the CISG was determined in 57% of the cases by choice of the arbitral tribunal, in 22% on the basis of conflict of law rules, in 11% by choice of the parties and in 2% by general principles of law. No reason was clearly determined as to the remaining 8%.[122] Loukas Mistelis concluded that, given the confidentiality policy applying to arbitration, significantly less than 5% of arbitration awards are published; therefore, the CISG was applied until the end of 2008, in 4,250 to 5,000 arbitration cases.[123]

In 2009 and 2010 Lisa Spagnolo also conducted a survey on the available evidence on contractual opt-outs from the CISG.[124] Ms Spagnolo categorized the US as occupying one end of the spectrum, that of prevalently 'blind' or 'automatic' opt-outs from the CISG in practice, and China at the other end, being a 'pro-CISG' jurisdiction. The author further categorized Canada and Australia as aligned with the American position and Switzerland, Germany and Austria, in that order, appearing to fall between the two poles. Ms Spagnolo analyzed fundamental economic and psychological causes of the prevalence of opt-outs in some jurisdictions and markets.[125] The author found that 'lack of familiarity' was a main driver of such choices. Ms Spagnolo's study is certainly relevant in connection with CISG's opt-outs as her analysis endorsed earlier findings regarding familiarity but was 'boosted' with an economic analysis focus, with elements such as 'costs to become proficient' and 'bargaining power' being discussed.

119 See L. Mistelis, 'CISG and Arbitration', *in* A. Janssen & O. Meyer (Eds.), *CISG Methodology*, Sellier European Law Publishers, Munich, 2009, pp. 375-395.

120 CISG Database available at [http://iicl.law.pace.edu/cisg/cisg].

121 See recent study conducted by L. Bergman, *supra* note 94, pp. 36-39.

122 L. Mistelis, *supra* note 119, p. 386 *et seq.*

123 *Id.* See also, A. Janssen & M. Spilker, 'The Relationship Between the CISG and International Arbitration: A Love with Obstacles?', *Contratto e impresa / Europa*, Vol. 1, 2015, pp. 44-74.

124 L. Spagnolo, 'A Glimpse through the Kaleidoscope: Choices of Law and the CISG (Kaleidoscope Part I)', *Vindobona Journal of International Commercial Law and Arbitration*, Vol. 13, 2009, p. 135; L. Spagnolo, 'Rats in Kaleidoscope: Rationality, Irrationality, and the Economics and Psychology of Opting In and Out of the CISG', *Vindobona Journal of International Commercial Law and Arbitration*, Vol. 13, 2009, p. 163; L. Spagnolo, 'Green Eggs and Ham: The CISG, Path Dependence, and the Behavioural Economics of Lawyers' Choices of Law in International Sales Contracts', *Journal of Private International Law*, Vol. 6, 2009, p. 438; L. Spagnolo, 'The Last Outpost: Automatic CISG Opt Outs, Misapplications and the Costs of Ignoring the Vienna Sales Convention for Australian Lawyers', *Melbourne Journal of International Law*, Vol. 10, 2009, pp. 141-216. Further information is also available in L. Spagnolo, *supra* note 118, pp. 150-181.

125 L. Spagnolo, 'Green Eggs and Ham', *supra* note 124, p. 438.

Ingeborg Schwenzer and Christopher Kee[126] published a comprehensive report of a survey on CISG opt-outs, which collected 640 answers from 66 countries and the respondents' profile included practising attorneys (347 answers), arbitrators (98 answers), entrepreneurs (60 answers), and academics (135 answers). According to this survey only 13% and 32% of the practising lawyers always exclude the CISG or do so sometimes, while the remaining 55% rarely or never opt out of the CISG.[127] The survey also asked whether businesses included a choice-of-law clause in their standard terms and conditions and to identify which law parties chose in their contracts. The results revealed that 47% included a choice-of-law clause and references to English and Swiss law have consistently recurred, with participants, especially from South America, referring to the law of the place of performance of the contract as the most popular.[128] The study also revealed that arbitrators indicated that between 20% and 36% of cases involving the sale of goods applied non-national law such as PICC[129] and *lex mercatoria*.[130]

I. Schwenzer & C. Kee remark that, whilst familiarity with the CISG has reached good levels, evidence suggests that it still remains in practice what they termed 'the domestic orientation of lawyers' and they also raised an issue with the standard of legal education.[131] In effect, the cost of becoming accustomed to the CISG is certainly one of the concerns affecting 'lack of familiarity' that should be explored in further detail in future studies. In addition, the bargaining power of contracting parties may have played a significant role.

Further studies have been carried out in the United States in order to analyze decisions and how US courts generally approach the CISG. Ann Morales-Olazábal, Robert W. Emerson, Karen D. Turner & René Sacasas[132] researched court decisions from 2004 to 2012 and found that popularity of the CISG is still low, concluding that "much research remains to be done in this area to inform US courts and practitioners involved in deciding or advising in the context of international sales".[133]

A more recent US study published in 2016 was conducted by John Coyle.[134] Coyle collected a dataset of more than 5,000 contracts (between 2009 and 2014) to determine

---

126 I. Schwenzer & C. Kee, 'Global Sales Law – Theory and Practice', *in* I. Schwenzer & L. Spagnolo (Eds.), *Towards Uniformity: The 2nd Annual MAA Schlechtriem CISG Conference*, Eleven International Publishing, The Hague, 2011, pp. 155-164.

127 I. Schwenzer & C. Kee, *supra* note 2, p. 436.

128 *Id.*

129 'PICC' stands for 'Principles for International Commercial Contracts' and the content of which is available at [www.unidroit.org].

130 I. Schwenzer & C. Kee, *supra* note 2, p. 436.

131 *Id.*, p. 438.

132 A. Morales-Olazábal *et al.*, 'Global Sales Law: An Analysis of Recent CISG Precedents in US Courts 2004-2012', *Business Lawyer*, Vol. 67, No. 4, 2012, pp. 1351-1381, available at: [www.americanbar.org/publications/the_business_lawyer/volume_67/number_4.html].

133 *Id.*

134 J. F. Coyle, 'The Role of the CISG in US Contract Practice: An Empirical Study', *University of Pennsylvania Journal of International Law*, Vol. 38, Issue 1, 2016, pp. 195-240.

the extent to which private parties select or exclude the CISG,[135] and followed up with interviews to better understand the role that the CISG plays in US contract practice. In order to do so, Coyle examined contracts registered with the Securities and Exchange Commission ('SEC'[136]) by searching through the EDGAR database[137] the term 'international sales of goods'. The author advised that this group of 5,000 contracts "includes a wide range of contract types and is not comprised exclusively of international sales agreements; any contract that referenced the CISG was included".[138] The author then examined the contracts to ascertain whether there was an exclusion of the CISG or a choice of it as a source of governing contract law.

While investigating the available data, Coyle noted that there were hundreds of dataset contracts in which the parties opted out of the CISG even though the contract in question did not involve the sale of goods.[139] Coyle advised that approximately 69% of the US dataset contracts filed with the SEC opted-out of the CISG did so 'needlessly'.[140] The author thus concluded that "the fact that just over two-thirds of these contracts opted out of the CISG when there was no need to do so suggests that the default position is to exclude the treaty from any and all contracts. This pattern of practice indicates that many US companies reflexively exclude the CISG with inquiring as to whether it would apply of its own force".[141]

As regards opt-in of the CISG, the author advised that in only 1% of the contracts surveyed the parties refer to the CISG to state that they want it to govern the agreement.[142] Of this number, the majority of the companies belonged to manufacturing (semiconductor companies), IT and pharmaceutical sectors. As to products most popular, electronic equipments and computer softwares, followed by medical equipment, industrial equipment and pharmaceuticals.[143] Sellers were mostly located in California and buyers in Europe, North America, China or Japan.[144] Coyle further reported a number of responses regarding the CISG collected in the telephone interviews, among which are 'inconsistency', 'CISG generally disfavours sellers', 'everyone is spooked by the CISG'.[145]

Coyle also undertook a secondary contract dataset between 2011 and 2015 to identify international supply agreements. He found 248 and then undertook a review to determine: (i) whether it excluded the CISG; (ii) whether the foreign counterparty had its

135 J. F. Coyle, *supra* note 134, p. 199.

136 Further information about the US Securities and Exchange Commission (SEC) is available at [https://www.sec.gov/].

137 The SEC maintains a public repository that contains private contracts. This database is called EDGAR (The Electronic Data Gathering, Analysis, and Retrieval system).

138 J. F. Coyle, *supra* note 134, p. 211.

139 *Id.*, p. 218.

140 *Id.*, p. 219.

141 *Id.* p. 220.

142 *Id.*

143 J. F. Coyle, *supra* note 134, p. 224.

144 *Id.*, p. 225.

145 *Id.*, p. 226.

principal place of business in a country that had not ratified the CISG; (iii) whether the agreement was an amendment to a prior agreement; (iv) whether the agreement in question selected foreign law; and (v) whether it was a repeat of another contract in the secondary dataset. After this review, Coyle found 44 international supply agreements, each of which contained a choice of law clause selecting the law of a US state and none of which excluded the CISG.[146]

Coyle therefore concluded that the dataset supports a number of observations: (i) US companies routinely exclude the CISG from contracts to which it would not otherwise apply; (ii) the number of US companies that select the CISG to govern their contracts is small and declining; (iii) the CISG lacks broad support within any industry or geographic region within the United States; and (iv) some companies that had selected the CISG in the past now have a policy of excluding it from their contracts.[147]

Despite Coyle's sceptical analysis of the datasets, there are a number of considerations to be discussed in terms of the method adopted in the study and the conclusions drawn up by the author. The results also serve to alert readers to the rather (and surprising) limited information of parties in relation to their legal options.

To start with, the author admitted that it is common for US companies to exclude the CISG from wholly domestic contracts.[148] Hence, the study failed to offer clear data as to the proportion of domestic and international contracts out of the 5,000 surveyed. Also, it is not obvious from the findings how EDGAR database indexes the contracts subject to Coyle's study.

In addition, Coyle also mentioned that there were a number of dataset contracts, where the CISG is excluded from a contract involving a foreign counterparty whose home country has not ratified the CISG.[149] While we were not given precise numbers, this behaviour signals a lack of familiarity in relation to the CISG, and also a fear of unpredictable outcome from the courts that may end up hearing a potential dispute.[150] These exclusions could thus have been the product of a bargain between the parties.

Finally, it is worth remembering that there were hundreds of dataset contracts in which the parties opted out of the CISG even though the contract in question did not even involve the sale of goods. This demonstrates that the sample surveyed may have failed to provide accurate data on what Coyle had sought to find at the outset of his study, *i.e.* 'to better understand the role that the CISG plays in US contract practice.'

P. Perales Viscasillas studied CISG cases in Spanish courts and concluded that "it is somehow frustrating to see that the Spanish courts do not seem to be aware of the existence of legal literature or cases on the CISG, not even of the Spanish doctrine and case

146 *Id.*, p. 235.
147 *Id.*, p. 216.
148 *Id.*, p. 217.
149 *Id.*
150 Familiarity with the law is first discussed *infra* pp. 31.

law".[151] Pilar Viscasillas further remarks "[...] Sometimes, and this is not the fault of the courts but that of the lawyers, it can be seen that the courts are not at all aware of the existence of the CISG".[152]

Yehuda Adar[153] surveyed the status of CISG in Israel and reported that practising attorneys frequently opt out of the CISG. The author further reported a rather ambivalent policy: "on one hand, most of the Israeli cases reflect a sympathetic approach towards the idea of a uniform sales law. At other times the courts have ignored the CISG without a sufficient clear reason".[154] Similarly, Petra Butler[155] undertook a study in New Zealand and concluded that companies rarely choose the CISG as the governing law of their international sales.

Edoardo Ferrante[156] conducted a study which concluded that the exclusion of the CISG as governing law of an international sale is common practice in Italy. Jorge Oviedo-Albán has also attested to a similar policy in Colombia.[157]

Further study has been conducted on CISG case law in the Balkan peninsula, [158] reporting that the practice of excluding the CISG is common, but also for reasons of unfamiliarity.[159]

As the main reasons for CISG exclusion in Switzerland,[160] Corinne Widmer-Lüchinger[161] states that there are still many attorneys who opt out of the CISG due to lack of certainty, and that its scope is limited. Contracting parties are likely to prefer one set of legal rules to govern their deals.

---

151 P. Perales Viscasillas, 'CISG Case Law in Spain', *in* C. B. Andersen & U. Schroeter (Eds.), *Sharing International Commercial Law across National Boundaries: Festschrift for Albert H. Krtizer on the Occasion of his Eightieth Birthday*, Wildy, Simmonds & Hill Publishing, London, 2008, p. 379.

152 *Id.*

153 Y. Adar, 'The CISG in Israel', *in* L. A. DiMatteo (Ed.), *International Sales Law: A Global Challenge*, Cambridge University Press, New York, 2014, pp. 518-538.

154 Y. Adar, *supra* note 153, p. 538.

155 P. Butler, 'New Zealand', *in* L. A. DiMatteo (Ed.), *International Sales Law: A Global Challenge*, Cambridge University Press, New York, 2014, pp. 539-547.

156 E. Ferrante, 'Italy', *in* L. A. DiMatteo (Ed.), *International Sales Law: A Global Challenge*, Cambridge University Press, New York, 2014, p. 403.

157 J. Oviedo-Albán, 'La Convención sobre Compraventa Internacional de Mercaderías: antecedentes y desarrollos alternativos', *Foro de Derecho Mercantil*, Vol. 29, 2010, pp. 37-89; see also J. A. Gaviria-Gil, 'The Puzzle of the Lack of Colombian Case Law on the CISG', *International Law: Revista Colombiana de Derecho Internacional*, 2015, pp. 289-328.

158 The analysis of CISG case law in the Balkan peninsula comprised, for the purpose of the study: Bosnia and Herzegovina, Bulgaria, Croatia, Greece, FYR Macedonia, Montenegro, Romania, Serbia and Slovenia. V. Pavić & M. Djordjevic, 'The Scope and Sphere of Application of the CISG in the Balkans', *in* J. Stamm (Ed.), *Festscrift für Helmut Rüßmann*, Juris, Saarbrücken, 2013, p. 888.

159 V. Pavić & M. Djordjevic, *supra* note 158, p. 893.

160 A summary of the Swiss case law on the CISG from 2008 to 2013, by P. Landolt, can be found at [www.landoltandkoch.com/medias/landolt_jusletter_cisg.pdf].

161 C. Widmer-Lüchinger, 'Switzerland', *in* L. A. DiMatteo (Ed.), *International Sales Law: A Global Challenge*, Cambridge University Press, New York, 2014, pp. 466-485.

Davies and Snyder[162] also reported data collected among practising attorneys in the United States, Germany, and China. The rates of CISG opt-outs were as follows: 70.8% in the United States, 72.7% in Germany, and 44.4% in China.

A further study has claimed that, according to a survey made in 2004, only 8% of German practising attorneys preferred the CISG as the governing law of the contracts that they negotiated for their clients, while 42% expressly exclude this legal instrument.[163]

As Ulrich Schroeter rightfully notes, the existing evidence on the CISG as a law in practice comes in two forms: (1) the number of court decisions and arbitral awards applying the CISG; and (2) surveys among lawyers.[164] Although we believe that there is a great deal of value in these efforts, we concur with Ulrich Schroeter's reasoning that a number of these existing surveys lacked statistical power.[165] The reasons for this are the small sample size and the limited geographical focus.

These studies were instrumental in mapping out and measuring the popularity of the CISG in local markets and in certain jurisdictions. They were also of great value in spelling out for the first time common criticisms of the CISG, such as its 'lack of certainty' and 'incompleteness' of its legal framework.

Whilst the rate of CISG opt-out cannot be overlooked and should be further discussed and investigated, a commonality to note among all these studies is that such rate appears to be linked to 'lack of familiarity'[166] with the CISG and perhaps a 'fear of the unknown'.[167] However, the claim that the CISG is 'widely excluded' is not supported by empirical evidence. Some general trends, of an inextricable relationship with the 'home turf', have been identified in these surveys.

With respect to this particular topic of familiarity with the law, Martin Khoeler was most apt in describing 'lack of familiarity'[168] as a 'self-generating circulus vitiosus',[169] and we would add that this indicates that further studies should be carried out to reveal the underlying reasons and motives for the high rate of CISG opt-out.

---

162 M. Davies & D. V. Snyder, *International Transactions in Goods: Global Sales in Comparative Context*, Oxford University Press, New York, 2014, pp. 40-42.

163 S. Kiene, 'German Country Analysis: Part II', *in* L. A. DiMatteo (Ed.), *International Sales Law: A Global Challenge*, Cambridge University Press, New York, 2014, p. 377.

164 U. Schroeter, 'Empirical Evidence of Courts' and Counsels' Approach to the CISG (with Some Remarks on Professional Liability)', *in* L. A. DiMatteo (Ed.), *International Sales Law: A Global Challenge*, Cambridge University Press, New York, 2014, p. 650.

165 U. Schroeter, *supra* note 164, p. 651.

166 The costs to become familiar with the CISG has long been argued as one of the reasons for the CISG exclusion. See, *e.g.* J. S. Ziegel, 'The Future of the International Sales Convention from a Common Law Perspective', *New Zealand Business Law Quarterly*, Vol. 6, 2000, pp. 336-346.

167 This 'fear of unknown' is further explored in *infra* Section 1.2.4.4.

168 H. Flechtner contends that the investment in familiarization is amortized over long periods, 'Changing the Opt-Out Tradition in the United States', *University of Pittsburgh Legal Studies Research Paper Series* No. 2010-10, available at [https://papers.ssrn.com/abstract=1571281]. See also a discussion on learning (information) costs, or costs to become proficient, in L. Spagnolo, *supra* note 118, p. 155.

169 M. Koehler, *supra* note 37.

On this matter Ulrich Schroeter further raises a topical question of 'professional liability', including malpractice in lawyers that exclude the CISG in their own interest, in order to escape the need to deal with its unfamiliar rules[170] and concludes that "an attorney's ignorance of the CISG exposes him or her to the risks of professional liability, given the deep and easily accessible body of case law and scholarship on the CISG".[171] Would this perhaps be one of the driving forces behind the CISG opt-outs? Would 'unfamiliarity' be the 'mask' that hides other reasons such as malpractice? This is a serious matter that deserves to be further investigated.[172]

The above studies failed to provide a rather and comprehensive list of the main criticisms of the CISG and the preferred features or attributes of a most desirable legal framework to govern cross-border sales. From the results collected above, several questions remain unanswered: to what extent is the CISG incomplete, unable to provide legal solutions to cross-border sales disputes? Is redress to domestic law a weakness of the CISG? Are parties fully aware of CISG provisions regarding the steps prior to this redress? As we can see, 'incompleteness' and 'lack of legal certainty' in this context are vague, undetermined concepts that needed to be further clarified and explored.

1.1.3 *Screening the Results or What Have We Learned from These Studies?*

1.1.3.1 Overlaps and General Trends

As we have seen thus far, studies undertaken have undoubtedly been useful in identifying, evaluating and improving dispute-resolution methods in cross-border disputes. They have also accurately identified most of the markets' and industries' internal and external concerns and choices in dispute-resolution mechanisms, *e.g.* a fear of a judiciary 'too arbitrary' or 'too protectionist',[173] and overall negative perceptions of the quality of civil justice systems.[174] Likewise, they have provided a guide to benefits, risks and missteps of choice of forum, allowing contracting parties to take precautions in order to find the most appropriate dispute-resolution method.[175] Additionally, some studies have been able to identify preferred laws and general principles that play a role in this choice.[176]

The more recent studies on CISG perceptions and practices were also important to identifying data on rates of opt-out and general preference. They were seemingly instrumental in prompting and fostering further studies in this area, in particular to exploring

170 U. Schroeter, *supra* note 164, p. 663.

171 M. Koehler, *supra* note 37.

172 A future research is also aimed to address professional liability's concerns regarding the topic of CISG opt-outs. See, in this sense, *infra* Section 5.2.

173 See *supra* note 26.

174 *Id.*

175 See *supra* note 70.

176 See, in this sense, *supra* Section 1.1.2.

the causes of CISG opt-outs and the reasons why certain laws are preferred to others, and whether certain legal features or attributes might be the cause of attraction or rejection.

However, surveys worldwide have found little convincing data to shed light on the intricate concerns and questions faced by contracting parties regarding choice of law matters. Questions such as what triggers and drives this decision and why certain laws are preferred to others are often unanswered. Likewise, the legal standards and features of most and least desirable governing contract law remain unavailable. Equally, the mechanisms to improve and optimize decisions of choice of law are routinely unexplored.

The data collected in the above studies lightly touch upon general preferences for certain law but do not fully address the particulars of this choice. Most studies and surveys analyzed above were arbitration-based, *i.e.* the surveyed contracts were subject to arbitration, which may assist in revealing a particular set of preferences but not necessarily the interplay between choice of law and of forum. More importantly, the above studies do not reveal the relevant triggers of choice of law decisions on a more global scale.

1.1.3.2 The Foundations for a Global Study

It is noteworthy that the choice of governing contract law is of utmost importance in any bargain; this choice will regulate the deal, define how contracting parties will behave and allow them to set their strategies in the course of the contract, in addition to governing the life of the contract from beginning to end.

Despite its unquestionable importance, scarce information is available on how this decision is taken, and the main factors informing choice of governing contract law. The alternatives available to improving and optimizing this choice are likewise unexplored.

Additionally, the connection and role of law, economics and psychology in decision-making processes is often underexplored and possibly underestimated. Unfortunately, in a dynamic, globalized and complex world of contracts, interdisciplinary approaches are rarely studied. Therefore, there does not seem to be any answer to these practical questions:

- Are contracting parties maximizers of their welfare?
- Are they, generally speaking, self-interested players who seek to reach efficient results?
- Does it depend on the context and external stimuli?
- Do emotions play any role in the choice?
- Can these emotions cloud or enlighten the judgment of these choices? If so, to what extent?
- How can we avoid, control or minimize the effects of these emotional factors?
- How can parties seek to influence and improve choice of governing contract law?

To address these questions as well as note possible correlations between them, we hoped another survey would assist in offering more elements to identify clearer what the process of choice of law does entail and how can we improve this process. Therefore, recognizing a gap in the existing research, a Global Survey on Choice of Law ('Survey on Choice of Law') was designed.

1.2 A Global Empirical Survey

The Survey took on a rather diverse and interdisciplinary approach. In order to provide a multi-faceted analysis of the choice of law, the Survey combined questions mixed with elements of law, economics and psychology. The objectives were to unveil, provide understanding of, and also tackle, control or improve imperfections and incongruities in the decision-making process. In doing so, parties would be provided with assistance in making rational decisions and obtaining efficient results from their transactions. Hence, we aimed to delve into the unexplored world of contracting parties' minds.

Readers should not be surprised at the questionnaire's design in the Survey: some of the questions had deliberately mixed legal and economic perspectives, as well as choice of law and choice of forum considerations.

Indeed, the Survey sought to reveal the prevalent interests and preferences of parties when faced with a full list of choices. This method would, it is hoped, deliver data on the underlying motives that trigger these choices. The Survey is also intended to investigate whether there were (and if so, why and to what extent) any interplay or interaction between choice of forum and choice of law considerations. The idea behind the questionnaire design was to investigate fully how decisions are taken and what factors play a part in parties' real-life negotiations.

In an attempt to achieve the aims of the Survey, ready-made answers were deliberately blended with legal and economic considerations in the same question. The goal was to assess the level of rationality of the respondent in the decision-making process, and to better identify the drives behind these choices.

Both questions and answers were carefully chosen to include fine-tuned responses, allowing respondents to indicate non-listed options, which could be either a comment or further note or even a link to one of the other questions. For methodological purposes – to test as to what extent the respondents would or would not use cognitive biases –, provided answers appeared to be repeated in the different questions.

The questionnaire was designed to include all potential areas of concern or sensitivities found in a contract negotiation context. This would assist respondents in identifying the main triggers of these concerns or sensitivities and their order of prevalence and importance. The wording of the answers, as well as their order displayed in each question, varied. This was all in an attempt to avoid – or at the very least minimize – a respondent's use of mental shortcuts, such as availability, which would cloud the accuracy of the results. According to the availability heuristic, decision-making is often based on what is most easily remembered at a given moment. Judgments are influenced by the ease with which past examples are recalled.[177]

Upon a quick review of the Survey questions and answers one might think that the provided answers followed a coherent structure that might have aided respondents in making rational choices. However, this was not the intention, for the following reasons:

Firstly, the answers to the questions contained both rational and intuitive elements that could be encountered in any decision-making context.

Secondly, respondents were free to choose suitable answers and even indicate non-listed ones.

Finally, the Survey contained ready-made answers to assist respondents to reveal data that they otherwise would likely not be able to reveal in their choices.

The Survey provided respondents with seven initial questions where a list of options was provided, and one question positioned at the end of the questionnaire. The final question was designed to help respondents to recall remote memories and provide a better understanding of the opt-out scene. The tailored questionnaire represents one of its outstanding features of the Survey in comparison to the studies already undertaken.

To sum up, the Survey was an invitation to explore the exciting and yet unexplored world of the contracting parties' minds; idiosyncratic and seemingly driven by multiple stimuli. In the following discussion, we open and attempt to understand the black box of the decision-making processes in cross-border transactions.

1.2.1 Survey Goals

In contract negotiations parties may frequently choose the governing contract law in light of positive and negative experience related to the trading partner and/or the transaction. Parties may attribute a 'tag' to this experience and evaluate it according to the outcomes achieved in these previous experiences. However, these evaluations may not always be accurate and can be clouded by emotion. Is there (ir)rationality involved? How can we ascertain these elements?

The governing law sets out the standards, defines the effects of acts and omissions of the contracting parties, and dictates and guides the parties' conduct in the course of a contract's life.[178] For example, such decisions may include whether to perform or act in breach of the contract, to remain silent with respect to an offer, to claim damages or

177 A. Tversky & D. Kahneman, *supra* note 32, pp. 1124-1131.

178 See A. W. Katz, 'Contract Formation and Interpretation', *in* Peter Newman (Ed.), *The New Palgrave Dictionary of Economics and the Law,* Macmillan, London, 1998, p. 2, available at [http://ssrn.com/abstract=69534].

mitigate loss, to gather evidence, to exchange and communicate information, to manage, transfer or allocate risks, to behave opportunistically, to adopt recalcitrant tactics, and to spend resources in resolving dispute.

The above factors are those that parties should evaluate and take into consideration while assessing the pros and cons of any governing contract law at the choice-of-law decision stage.

From a purely rational perspective, individuals make decisions using a compensatory strategy. They identify and evaluate all available options, assess and weigh all relevant aspects of each option, and then select that which they believe most favourable.[179] This requires actors to infer facts by applying principles of deductive logic to all known and relevant information. While choosing governing contract law, parties would process all available information, make choices and execute behaviour in a way calculated to maximize their expected utility, *i.e.* maximize the differential between expected benefits and costs.[180] And the difficulties lie with the attempt to specify as precisely as possible the valued attributes involved in the exchange process.[181]

On the other hand, under a heuristic-based approach,[182] or an intuitive process, the choice of law decision may be based on previous experience (good or bad), meaning that individuals use mental shortcuts to make decisions due to limited available information. In these scenarios a certain decision would be chosen according to its success or failure in real-world environments and not according to logical and mathematical rules.[183] Heur-

179 C. Guthrie, 'Law, Information, and Choice: Capitalizing on Heuristic Habits of Thought', *in* G. Gigerenzer & C. Engel (Eds.), *Heuristics and the Law*, MIT Press, Cambridge MA, 2006, p. 427.

180 R. B. Korobkin, '*The Problems with Heuristics for Law (February 1, 2004)*', *UCLA School of Law, Law & Econ Research Paper No. 4-1*, p. 2, available at [http://papers.ssrn.com/sol3/papers.cfm?abstract_id=496462].

181 Douglass C. North uses a rather trivial example to explain the intricacies of our daily contractual choices: "[...] take something as simple as the purchase of oranges for orange juice. What I would really like to purchase is a quantity of juice with a tart flavor and a certain amount of vitamin C; but the amount of juice, the flavor and vitamin C are all valued attributes that are costly to measure separately. Instead, we buy oranges by number or by weight; and these are poor surrogates for what we really are looking for. To the degree that any valued attribute is too costly to be able to measure perfectly then, we have some dissipation of income as a result of a failure to be able to measure it". And the author remarks that 'as long as some of these valued attributes are imperfectly measured', the costs will continue to rise, 'The New Institutional Economics: A Symposium', *Zeitschrift für die gesamte Staatswissenschaft / Journal of Institutional and Theoretical Economics* Bd. 140, H. 1, 1984, p. 9.

182 R. B. Korobkin, *supra* note 180. In this connection, see also M. I. Fraidin, 'Decision-Making in Dependency Court: Heuristics, Cognitive Biases, and Accountability', *Cleveland State Law Review*, Vol. 60, 2013, pp. 913-974, noting that "[...] heuristics devices include 'availability' and 'representativeness', among other 'mental shortcuts' ...The availability heuristic allows a decision-maker to reach a decision by immediate, reflexive reference to a different situation that comes readily to mind... The 'representativeness' heuristic similarly reflects a decision-maker's substitution of one item for another. A decision-maker who relies on the representativeness heuristic assesses a probability 'by the degree to which A is representative of B, that is, by the degree to which A resembles B'... 'Affect' or the good or bad feelings generated by a person or event, is another heuristic that sometimes drives decision-making" (pp. 919-920).

183 For further information on heuristics and choice of law processes, see L. Spagnolo, 'Green Eggs and Ham', *supra* note 124, p. 438; L. Spagnolo, *supra* note 118, pp. 189-194.

istic-based decision-making is rather a simplified cognitive process of making decisions when parties are faced with uncertainties.

While the choice of law process may seldom be regarded as a rational choice, there are many factors, including legal, economic and even psychological, which may influence and guide this choice.

This is precisely what the Survey envisioned to achieve: a critical discussion of parties' preferences in international contract negotiation. This includes the parties' strategies and choices while they assess and decide on the governing contract law of international sales, including the advanced precautions taken, and the legal and economic considerations and concerns arising out of such negotiation. In addition to unveiling the factors prompting the choice of law, another aim of the Survey was to find out the features that make certain governing contract law more appealing than others, in an effort to measure contracting parties' degree of rationality in their choices.

Finally, the Survey brings to readers, including parties to an agreement, party advisors, decision-makers, legal practitioners and other interested individuals, empirical knowledge of parties' preferences in international sales negotiations. The Survey also intended to shed light on the commercial tactics adopted by parties in international negotiation. It also includes an assessment of the main concerns associated with the substantive law, an analysis of advantages and disadvantages of choosing, determining and applying domestic law and uniform laws to govern international sales contracts and the exclusions and opt-out mechanisms available to contracting parties.

1.2.2 *Respondent Profile*

The respondents were profiled for professional experience, legal background and geographical location. Counsel and party advisors with significant experience in international sales contracts were invited to participate in the Survey. In order to identify a respondent's most suitable profile, strict regard was given to expertise, years of standing and location of residence.

The sample of respondents included in-house lawyers and legal practitioners whose primary role was to negotiate international sales contracts and/or provide advice on cross-border sales dispute. However, as the aim was to capture and understand how governing contract law is chosen in various areas, respondents who combined experience in both cross-border sales and other areas of law were also approached.[184] The minimum requirement was 10 years' standing and a geographical balance was sought.

184 Although some respondents were also experienced in other areas of law, such as construction, energy and intellectual property, the respondents' main role was to participate in the negotiation of international sales contracts and/or to provide advice on cross-border sales dispute. Therefore, all the respondents were familiar with choice-of-law matters in cross-border sales.

The respondents were leading counsel[185] in the subject matter in their respective countries. All of the professionals invited to participate in the Survey were carefully selected through a series of searches on the above criteria.

Finally, counsel who combined international sales law experience with expertise in other areas of law or practice areas were also approached, as the Survey aimed to offer an interdisciplinary view of the choice-of-law process, and a clear view of this practice worldwide. However, the Survey was not intended to investigate results by industry sector or different areas of law in addition to international sales law, the reason why there are no data by industry sector or area of law.

The questionnaire was sent to seasoned specialists who were known or professed to have regular dealings in international sales law.

1.2.3 Method

The Survey consisted of an online questionnaire accessible by invitation only. The content of the Survey was available via a click-through link that guided the respondent to eight multiple-choice questions. The respondents were invited to participate in the Survey from July to September 2014.

In the online invitation the respondent was made aware of the 2014 Survey goals, as well as of its structure, the estimated time required to respond, and the web link.

After being directed to the Survey webpage, the respondent was firstly informed of the Survey goals. Following this, as a preliminary request, the respondent was invited to indicate his or her country of residence.

In completing the questionnaire the respondent was allowed to specify other choices, preferences and/or concerns not listed in the provided answers and/or to make comments that he or she might wish to include regarding the choice-of-law decision-making process.

The questionnaire offered a non-exhaustive list of preferences that was, to a great extent, focused on legal and economic aspects, with some variations of terms for adequacy and methodological purposes. Nonetheless, in all questions, the respondent was offered a blank box in which to identify or specify other choices, preferences and/or concerns, which could also be used to link a non-listed choice to precedent questions and for additional thoughts and comments. A respondent should have taken around 10 minutes to respond to the questionnaire. The eight questions displayed choices in random order each time a new respondent accessed the questionnaire.

Questions 1 and 4 allowed the respondent to select only three answers or preferences – the reason for this was to better assess the main legal and economic considerations. The respondent could specify in a blank box his or her choice(s), preference(s) and/or con-

185 Counsel used here as both private practice and in-house lawyer.

cern(s) not listed. Questions 2, 3, 5, 6 and 7 allowed the respondent to select an unlimited number of options, preferences and/or concerns – the Survey was intended to give the respondent more alternatives that would help draw inferences regarding parties' preferences in these questions. Finally, Question 8 could be skipped or, if selected by the respondent, the reason for the exclusion or opting-out option could be disclosed or omitted. Questions 1 to 8 are reproduced later in this chapter.

1.2.4 Survey Results

228 respondents[186] from 93 jurisdictions[187] completed the Survey. They are located in Europe, Asia, the Americas and Caribbean, Africa and Oceania. They represented 40 of the world's largest national economies and some of their jurisdictions are listed in the top 100, in accordance with the World Bank's figures that measure economic growth by gross domestic product.[188]

The chart below shows the percentage of jurisdictions per geographical region.[189]

---

186 The IP addresses of the respondents were verified to confirm the exact number. While there is a certain margin of error as some may have been using a proxy server, the author considers this to be unlikely and, if it did happen, with exceptional incidence.

187 Out of the 93 jurisdictions, 35 of them, or 37%, were not contracting States at the time of the Survey. The list of these jurisdictions (in no particular order) reads as follows: Cameroon; Mozambique; Namibia; Nigeria; Zimbabwe; Barbados; Bermuda; Bolivia (Plurinational State of); Guatemala; Jamaica; Nicaragua; Panama; Venezuela (Bolivarian Republic of); South Africa; Tanzania (Republic of); Cambodia; Indonesia; India; Iran (Islamic Republic of); Azerbaijan*; Kuwait; *Bahrain; Macao; Malaysia; Myanmar; Nepal; Philippines; Saudi Arabia; Sri Lanka; Thailand; United Arab Emirates; *Viet Nam; Portugal; Malta; and Ireland. Out of these 35, in three (*) jurisdictions the CISG came into force subsequently to the Survey's launch: Bahrain (October 2014); Azerbaijan (2017); and Viet Nam (2017). For statistical purposes, it is also worth noting that out of these 37%, the distribution by legal families is as follows: 30% (civil law); 25% (common law); and 45% (mixed legal systems: civil and customary/religious). List of legal systems extracted from the World Factbook of the Central Intelligence Agency Library, available at [www.cia.gov/library/publications/the-world-factbook/fields/2100.html].

188 Further information and data available at [http://data.worldbank.org/indicator].

189 The full list of jurisdictions in alphabetical order: Albania, Argentina, Armenia, Australia, Austria, Azerbaijan, Bahrain, Bangladesh, Barbados, Belarus, Belgium, Bermuda, Bolivia (Plurinational State of), Brazil, Bulgaria, Cambodia, Cameroon, Canada, Chile, China, Colombia, Costa Rica, Croatia, Cyprus, Czech Republic, Denmark, Ecuador, Egypt, El Salvador, Finland, France, Germany, Greece, Guatemala, Hong Kong (China), Hungary, Iceland, India, Indonesia, Iran (Islamic Republic of), Ireland, Israel, Italy, Jamaica, Japan, Kuwait, Latvia, Luxembourg, Macao (China), Malaysia, Malta, Mexico, Mozambique, Myanmar, Namibia, Nepal, Netherlands, New Zealand, Nicaragua, Nigeria, Norway, Panama, Paraguay, Peru, Philippines, Poland, Portugal, Republic of Korea, Romania, Russian Federation, Saudi Arabia, Serbia, Singapore, Slovakia, Slovenia, South Africa, Spain, Sri Lanka, Sweden, Switzerland, Taiwan (Province of China), Tanzania (United Republic of), Thailand, Turkey, Ukraine, United Arab Emirates, United Kingdom of Great Britain and Northern Ireland, United States of America, Uruguay, Venezuela (Bolivarian Republic of), Viet Nam, Zambia and Zimbabwe. With the except of Taiwan, please note that the author classified the jurisdictions according to geographical regions according to the United Nations Statistics Division. Further information available at [http://unstats.un.org/unsd/methods/m49/m49regin.htm].

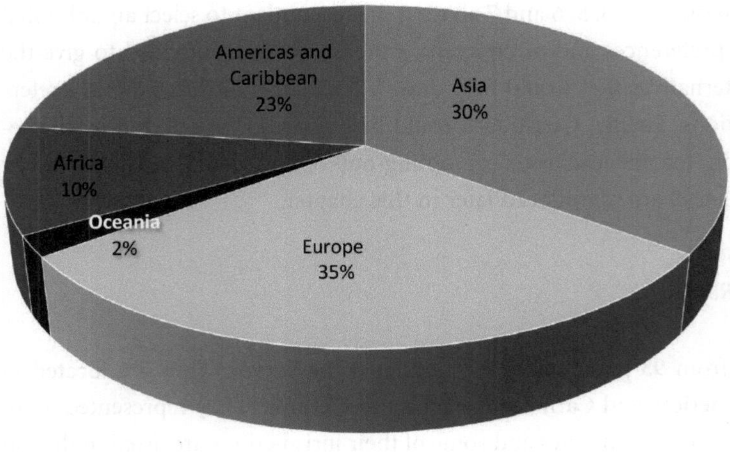

Africa
Cameroon, Egypt, Mozambique, Namibia, Nigeria, South Africa, Tanzania (United Republic of), Zambia, Zimbabwe.
Americas and Caribbean
Argentina, Barbados, Bermuda, Bolivia (Plurinational State of), Brazil, Canada, Colombia, Costa Rica, Chile, Ecuador, El Salvador, Guatemala, Jamaica, Mexico, Nicaragua, Panama, Paraguay, Peru, United States of America, Uruguay, Venezuela (Bolivarian Republic of).
Asia
Armenia, Azerbaijan, Bahrain, Bangladesh, Cambodia, China, Cyprus, Hong Kong (China), Indonesia, India, Iran (Islamic Republic of), Israel, Japan, Kuwait, Macao (China), Malaysia, Myanmar, Nepal, Philippines, Republic of Korea, Saudi Arabia, Singapore, Sri Lanka, Taiwan (Province of China), Thailand, Turkey, United Arab Emirates, Viet Nam.
Europe
Albania, Austria, Belarus, Belgium, Bulgaria, Croatia, Czech Republic, Denmark, Finland, France, Germany, Greece, Hungary, Iceland, Ireland, Italy, Latvia, Luxembourg, Malta, Netherlands, Norway, Poland, Portugal, Romania, Russian Federation, Serbia, Slovakia, Slovenia, Spain, Sweden, Switzerland, United Kingdom of Great Britain and Northern Ireland, Ukraine.
Oceania
Australia, New Zealand.

The following charts serve as an indicator of the global scope of the Survey:

Survey Results - Global

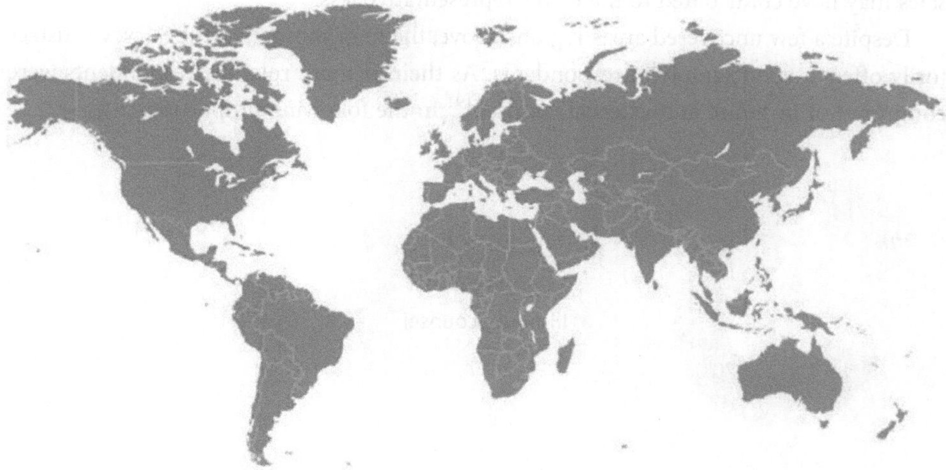

The chart below, in its darker portions, indicates the number of jurisdictions covered by the Survey:

Survey Results - Reach

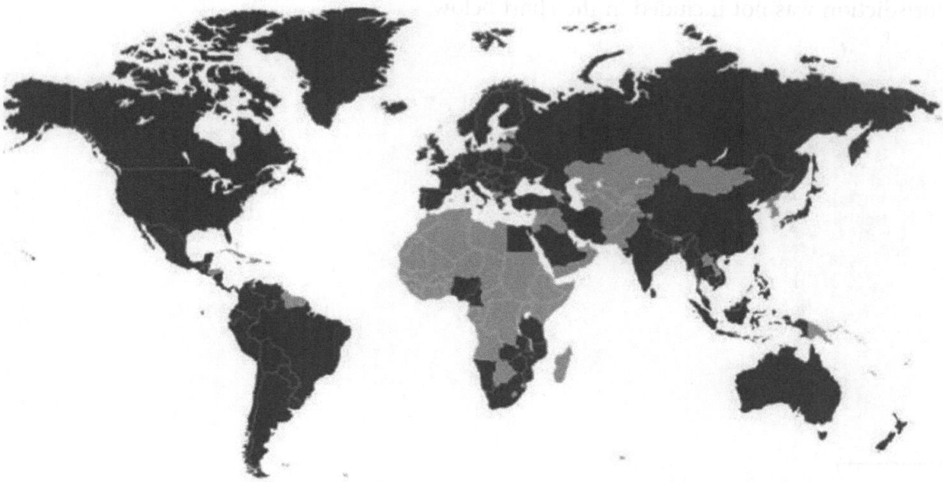

As we can see, the respondents represented 40 of the largest national economies in the world and some of the jurisdictions are listed in the top 100.[190] Naturally, there are a few areas/regions shaded grey, predominantly in Africa and parts of Asia. This can be explained by the overall limitations imposed by online surveys, where databases and e-mail blocking systems may have hindered a larger reach on these continents. Likewise, in some countries, the lack of information regarding professionals well versed in cross-border sales may have contributed to their non-representativeness.

Despite a few uncovered areas/regions above, the map shows that the Survey satisfactorily offers a good sample of respondents. As their primary role, the respondents were comprised of in-house and external counsel,[191] in the following proportion:

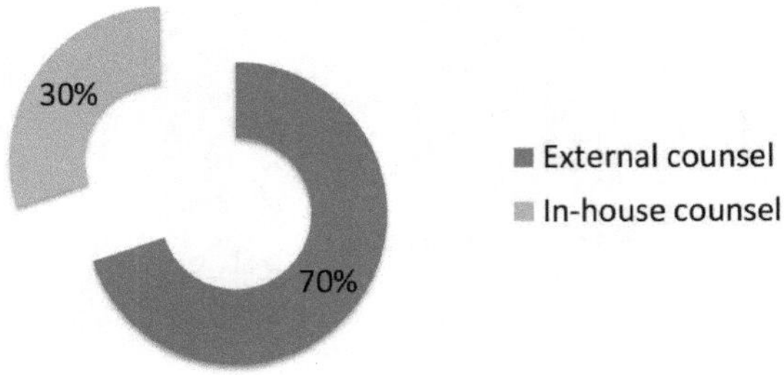

Finally, the following chart offers a breakdown of respondents' jurisdiction by legal systems.[192] For methodological reasons – in particular given the majority of jurisdictions belonging to these families – we have listed only the two most prevalent legal systems, civil law and common law.

Jurisdictions with mixed legal systems were classified according to the prevalent influence, either civil or common law. In the absence of a clear predominant influence, the jurisdiction was not included in the chart below.

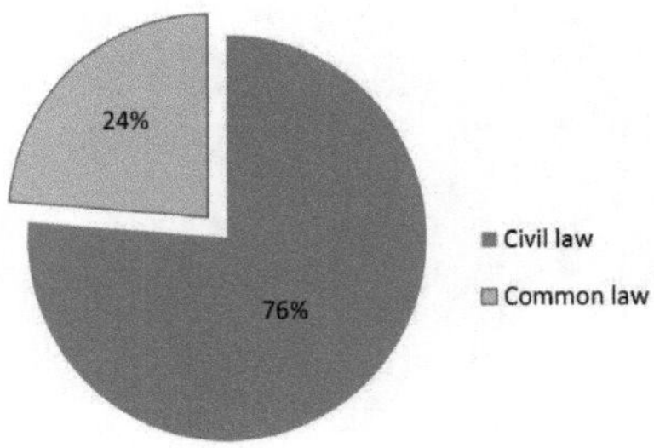

190 Due to overall limitations imposed by online surveys, some large economies were not surveyed, such as Pakistan, Bangladesh, Qatar, Kazakhstan, Morocco, Angola, among others.

191 External counsel understood here as private practice lawyer.

192 List of legal systems per country extracted from the World Factbook of the Central Intelligence Agency Library, available at [https://www.cia.gov/library/publications/the-world-factbook/fields/2100.html].

Readers should not be surprised at the prevalence of civil law jurisdictions in the Survey results. As a matter of fact, the number of civil law jurisdictions worldwide is substantially higher than common law, which may *per se* justify the discrepancy of numbers.[193]

The Survey did not target a specific legal family but rather focused on the practice of negotiating governing contract law worldwide. That the majority of respondents resided in civil-law jurisdictions does not undermine the global scope of the Survey. Appropriate comparison between civil and common law families will be drawn below to also reveal commonalities and differences between these two legal families and disclose the way the choice of governing contract law is approached.

We shall now move to the results obtained in the 8 questions, answers and additional comments (hereinafter Survey Questions). As mentioned before, the Survey Questions will also be accompanied by a comparison of civil law and common law families per question.

1.2.4.1 Legal Considerations

Question 1: When choosing a substantive law to govern an international sales contract, what are your three (3) main legal considerations?

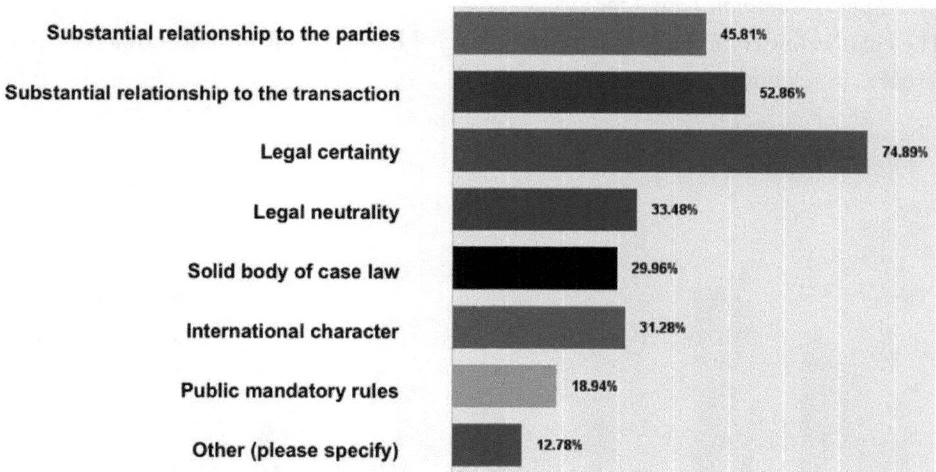

With respect to the main legal considerations in a choice-of-law decision-making process, the respondents elected legal certainty (74.89%), substantial relationship to the transaction (52.86%) and substantial relationship to the parties (45.81%).

The respondents indicated the following additional main legal considerations:

- level of development of the proposed governing law;

193 See, in this sense, World Factbook of the Central Intelligence Agency Library, available at [https://www.cia.gov/library/publications/the-world-factbook/fields/2100.html].

- degree of familiarity with the law;
- cost and time;
- clients' interests;
- for a sale on credit basis, law of the buyer's jurisdiction;
- flexibility;
- accessibility to the law;
- legal rules easy to ascertain;
- 'home turf' advantage where possible;
- enforceability;
- positive effects on the party who seeks advise;
- forum for dispute resolution;
- independent and corruption-free judiciary;
- habit – use of standard contracts;
- counsel and client's favourable experiences with and knowledge of the law;
- arbitration know-how available;
- enforceability of resulting judgment or award; and
- familiarity to lawyers acting.

Civil Law vs Common Law Approaches

The chart below compares common law and civil law respondents and shows their preferences in relation to Question 1.

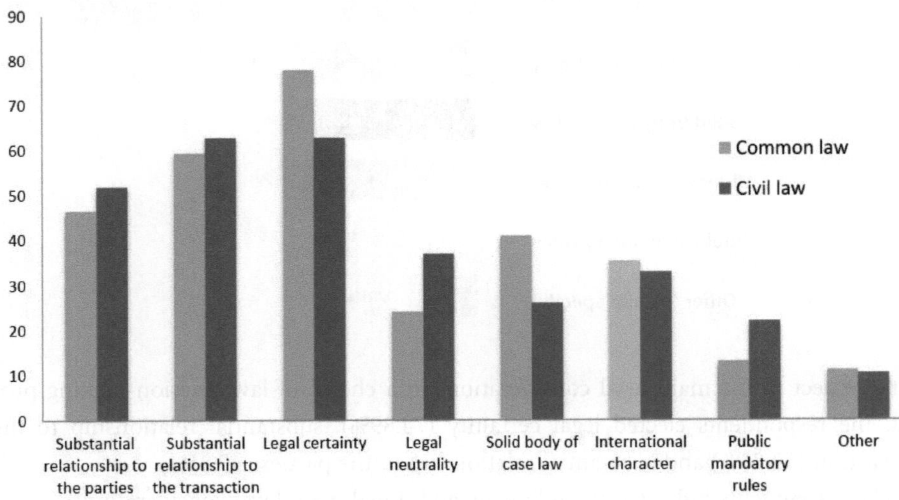

There was a parity of preferences between common law and civil law respondents in relation to some options, such as 'international character', 'substantial relationship to the parties' and 'substantial relationship to the transaction'. The reasons for these commonalities may be that these options would generally be more counter-intuitive than others in any cross-border sales negotiation. Contracting parties are likely to appreciate the international aspect of the contract coupled with substantial relationship to the parties and the parties. In other terms, the use of 'home turf' is likely to be exercised where possible and a good dose of strategy when it comes to deciding where contractual obligations will need to be performed.

Apparent disparity has been noted in the level of importance of 'legal certainty' and 'solid body of case law' between common law and civil law. Responses here are 'legal certainty' and 'solid body of case law', both options being most preferred by common law respondents. This discrepancy confirms assumptions that common law parties will tend to look for 'legal certainty' (or at the very least its appearance), in conjunction with a body of case law perhaps influenced by their doctrine of binding precedent. It is interesting to tease out the relationship between these independent variables. There might be a correlation between 'legal certainty' and a 'solid body of case law', which is also confirmed throughout the Survey.[194]

Lastly, it is worth noting, perhaps surprisingly, that civil law respondents prefer 'legal neutrality' to common law respondents. Whilst *neutrality* may have various facets,[195] which we shall investigate in the next chapters,[196] this answer taken solely certainly shows that civil law respondents are inclined to make use of third jurisdiction laws or neutral legal frameworks, to govern their cross-border sales. These inferences and their plural underlying reasons will be explored in the next chapter.

Question 2: Under a legal perspective approach, while analyzing the provisions of a substantive law, please indicate the features that may call particular attention and contribute to a decision in favour of the substantive law under analysis:

194 See, for example, Survey results in Question 7, where 'solid body of case law' was cited as one of the most important features of a governing contract law, *infra* Section 1.2.4.3.

195 See C. Fountoulakis, 'The Parties' Choice of 'Neutral Law' in International Sales Contracts', *European Journal of Law Reform*, Vol. VII, Issue 3/4, 2005, pp. 303-329; see also I. Schwenzer, 'Who Needs a Uniform Contract Law, And Why?', *Villanova Law Review*, Vol. 58, Issue 4, 2013, pp. 723-732.

196 In this connection, please refer to *infra* Chapter 5.

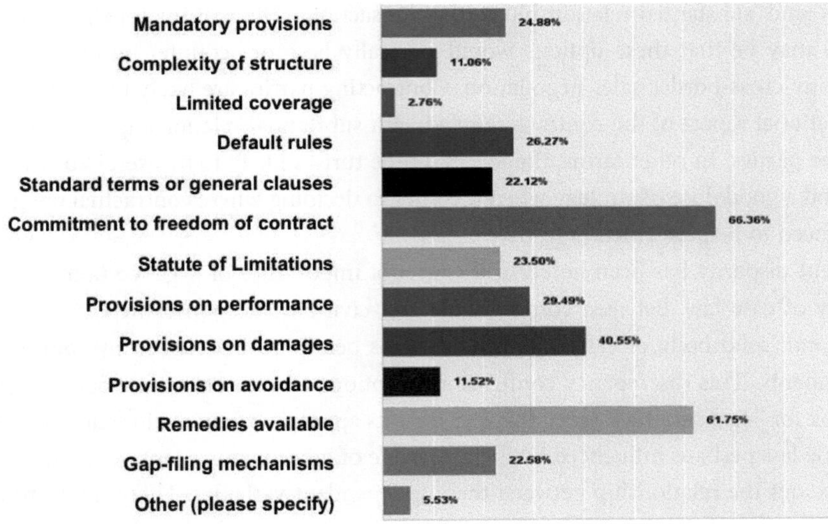

With respect to the positive legal features of governing contract law, the respondents favoured commitment to freedom of contract (66.36%), remedies available (61.75%) and provisions on damages (40.55%).

The respondents indicated the following additional positive legal features of governing contract law:

- predictability;
- enforcement rules and procedure;
- familiarity with the law of the jurisdiction by the parties;
- cost/convenience of resolving disputes;
- language considerations;
- depends on whether one is representing seller or buyer. For example: buyer's duties to verify; goods and related time limits; extent of seller's warranty;
- whether the jurisdiction has ratified the UN Convention on Contracts for the International Sale of Goods (CISG);
- quality of available arbitrators;
- provisions on discovery;
- contract law rules; and
- provisions on limitation of liability.

Civil Law vs Common Law Approaches

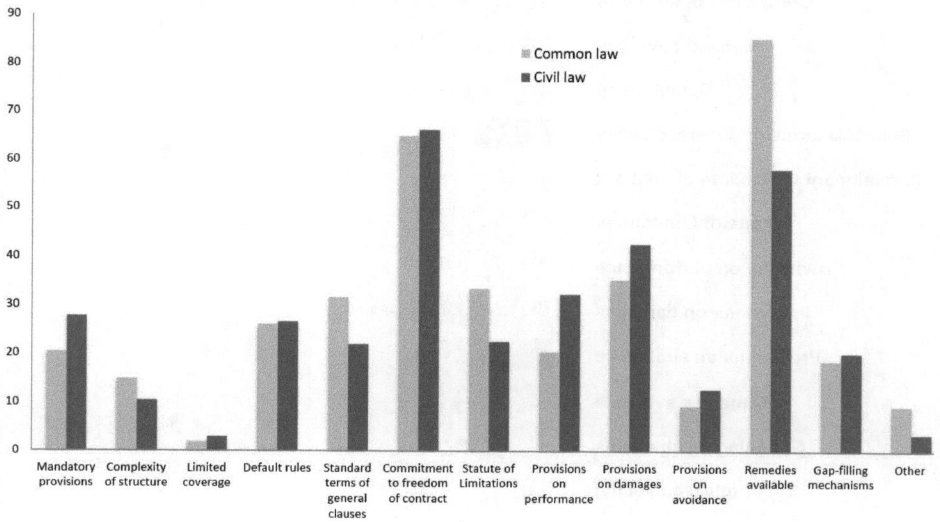

Unsurprisingly, 'freedom of contract', 'default rules', 'limited coverage' and 'gap-filling mechanisms' were common choices by the respondents. As explained in question 1 above, these options seem also to be more counter-intuitive and part of a respondent's general 'checklist', even if in some cases these options are not easily accessible and therefore not thoroughly examined. For example, 'freedom of contract' found in a certain governing contract law which is subject to restrictions not easily ascertainable by the respondent.

The most notable disparity in question 2 relates to 'remedies available', which a significant majority of common law respondents regard as an attribute more appealing in a governing contract law than civil law respondents. The reason may perhaps be that parties from common law background would be more akin to the 'full picture' of the governing contract law, thereby anticipating scenarios where remedies will be instrumental[197] and perhaps be determinative of the fate of the contract, whether to limit options to remedy default scenarios or to offer a broad array of tools to maintain the contract alive.

Question 3: Under a legal perspective approach, while analyzing the provisions of a substantive law, please indicate the features that may call particular attention and contribute to a decision against the substantive law under analysis:

197 The importance of legal remedies is discussed in detail in *infra* Section 5.1.9.

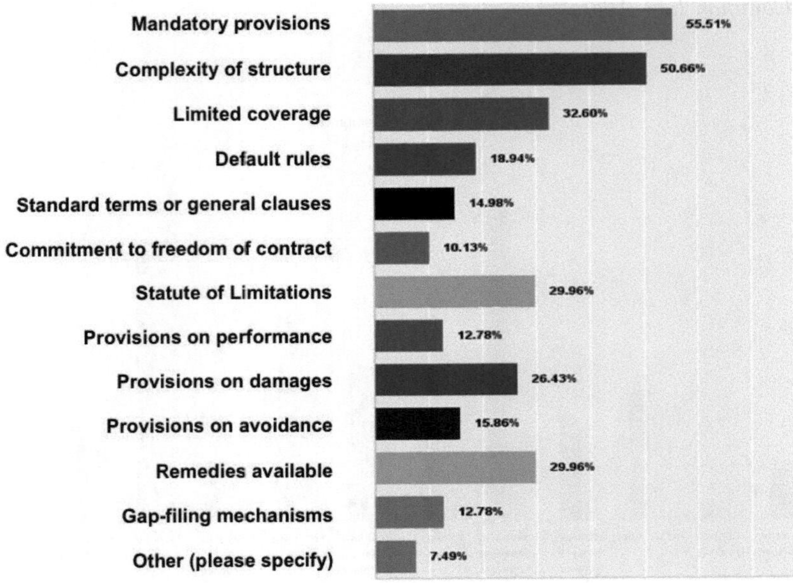

With respect to the negative legal features of governing contract law, the respondents elected mandatory provisions (55.51%), complexity of structure (50.66%) and limited coverage (32.60%).

The respondents indicated the following additional negative legal features of governing contract law:

- restriction of parties' rights under a commercial transaction;
- unfamiliarity with the law of the particular jurisdiction;
- state of administration of justice in applicable jurisdiction;
- cost/convenience of resolving disputes;
- language considerations;
- lack of qualified and impartial arbitrators in the relevant jurisdiction;
- independence and impartiality (or lack thereof) of judiciary;
- depends on whether one is representing seller or buyer;
- mandatory provisions curtailing the freedom of contract;
- lack of case law and doctrine;
- law different from that of the place of performance;
- potential enforcement issues; and
- unpredictability.

Civil Law vs Common Law Approaches

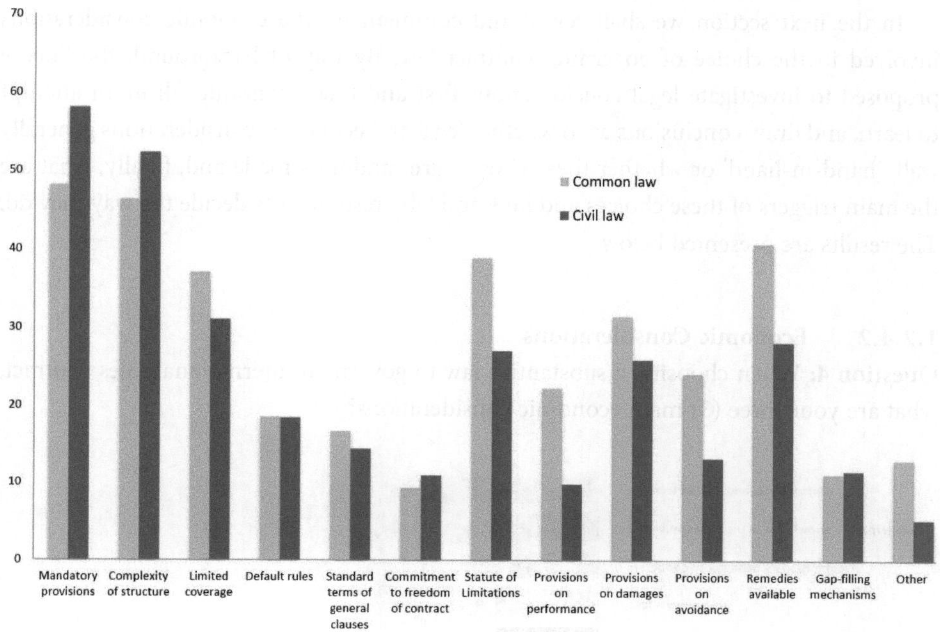

Concerning the negative attributes of governing contract law, similar results were obtained in most of the available options, with the exceptions of 'statute of limitations', 'provisions on performance', 'provisions on avoidance' and 'remedies available'.

In all the above-cited options, common law respondents accorded these attributes as greater importance than did civil law respondents. Once again this proves that these common law respondents have undertaken a legal strategy analysis in responding to this question. As we shall see in the next chapters,[198] these features of governing contract law will dictate how a contract is executed and the consequences attached to it, including in circumstances of breach and where contractual claims need to be filed with courts or otherwise (*i.e.* concerns of a statute of limitations).

From a civil law perspective, it is worth noting an expressive rejection of 'complexity structure' and 'mandatory provisions', which also accompanies the answers obtained earlier. Civil law respondents would also be willing to find law which would not curtail rights and complicate matters when it comes to managing the legal tools available.

This completes the respondents' legal considerations in electing their governing contract law in international sales contracts. We have seen thus far that overall the respondents show clear rationality in their answers, common law respondents showing a more strategic approach to the question than civil law respondents, albeit that the latter de-

198 See *infra* Chapters 3 and 5.

monstrate an increasing awareness of 'legal neutrality', 'uncomplex structure' and 'freedom of contract'.

In the next section we shall reveal and comment on the economic considerations involved in the choice of governing contract law. By way of background, the Survey proposed to investigate legal considerations first and then economic, all in an attempt to learn, and draw conclusions as to whether legal and economic considerations generally walk 'hand-in-hand' or whether these choices are randomly made and, finally, what are the main triggers of these choices and how and why respondents decide the way they do. The results are presented below.

1.2.4.2 Economic Considerations

Question 4: When choosing a substantive law to govern an international sales contract, what are your three (3) main economic considerations?

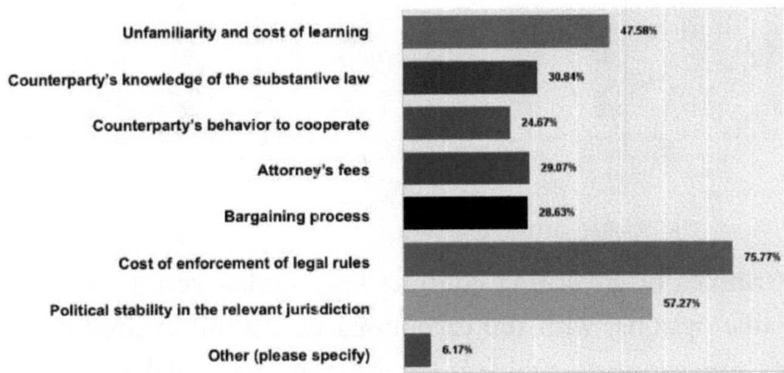

The respondents indicated cost of enforcement of legal rules (75.77%), political stability in the relevant jurisdiction (57.27%) and unfamiliarity and cost of learning (47.58%) as their chief concerns.

The respondents indicated the following additional main economic considerations:

- predictability of outcome coupled with law's recognition of freedom of parties to a contract;
- level of education of the judges;
- own knowledge of the substantive law;
- what courts will decide on potential disputes;
- if arbitration is chosen, then this consideration is of minor importance;
- depends on whether one is representing seller or buyer;
- how to financially secure the transaction;
- enforceability;
- breadth of available discovery;
- relationship to parties transaction; and
- similarity of chosen law to law of the client.

Civil Law vs Common Law Approaches

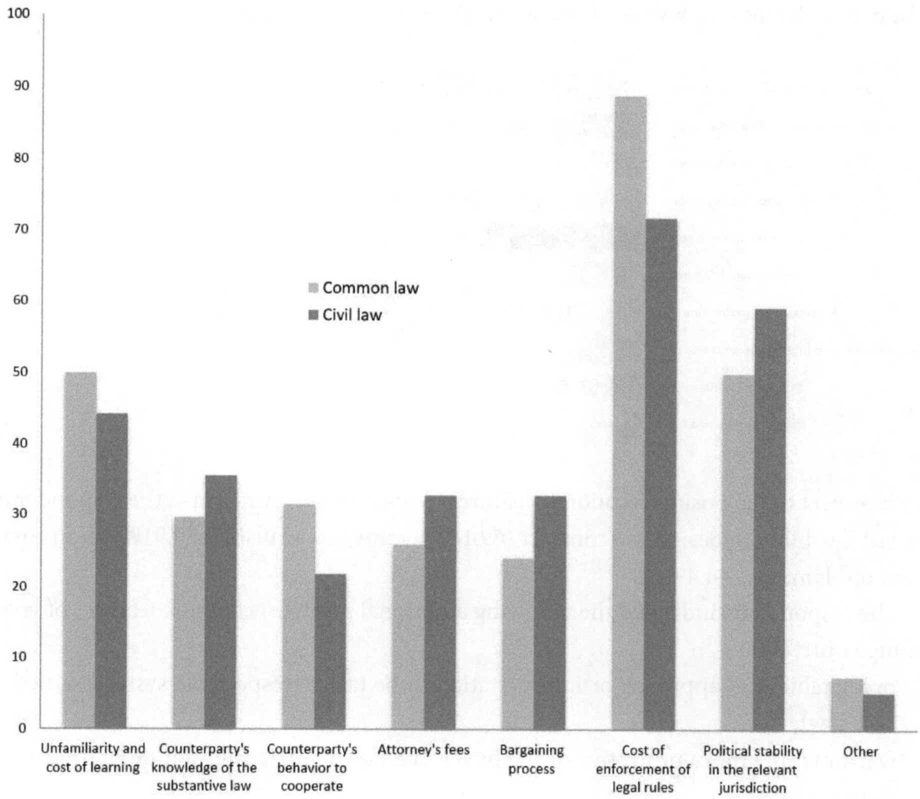

Asked about economic considerations, common law and civil law respondents differed most notably in the weight they attached to 'cost of enforcement of legal rules', 'political stability in the relevant jurisdiction' and 'bargaining process'.

'Cost of enforcement of legal rules' was more important to common law than civil law respondents, a finding which corresponds to earlier inferences that these respondents seem to have undertaken a more rational approach, and is also consistent with the set of answers to questions 1 to 3 above.

'Political stability in the relevant jurisdiction' and 'bargaining process' were more important to civil law than common law respondents. 'Political stability in the relevant jurisdiction' may somehow be associated with 'cost of enforcement', reason why the former has also been selected by a significant number of common law respondents. It might be that the civil law respondents assessed this as a 'game changer' and so of considerable importance. We should also not overlook the possibility that preferences may routinely be influenced by the position of a party – buyer or supplier – and where there is greater likelihood of breach.

Question 5: Under an economic perspective approach, while analyzing the provisions of a substantive law, please indicate the features that may call particular attention and contribute to a decision in favour of the substantive law under analysis:

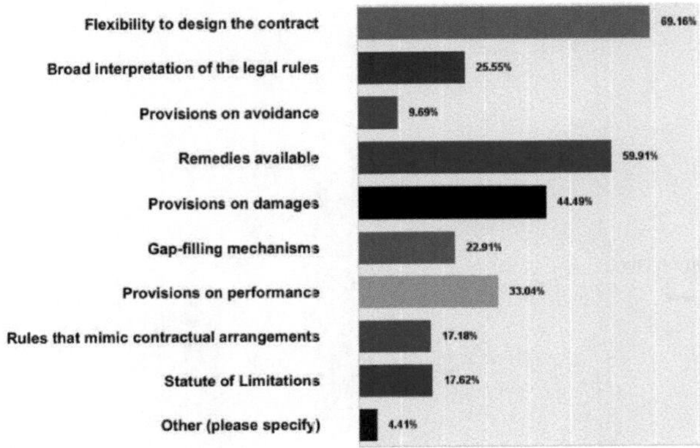

With respect to the positive economic features of governing contract law, the respondents elected flexibility to design the contract (69.16%), remedies available (59.91%) and provisions on damages (44.49%).

The respondents indicated the following additional positive economic features of governing contract law:

- predictability of approach or interpretation to be taken (respectable system, settled case law);
- warranty: the more protective of the buyer, the better (including statute of limitations);
- familiarity/unfamiliarity of a party with the law – if a party always needs to retain foreign legal advice whenever a legal issue arises under a contract this increases cost and incentivizes early moving or settlement;
- independent and corruption-free judiciary; and
- breadth of discovery, strict construction of contractual terms.

Civil Law vs Common Law Approaches

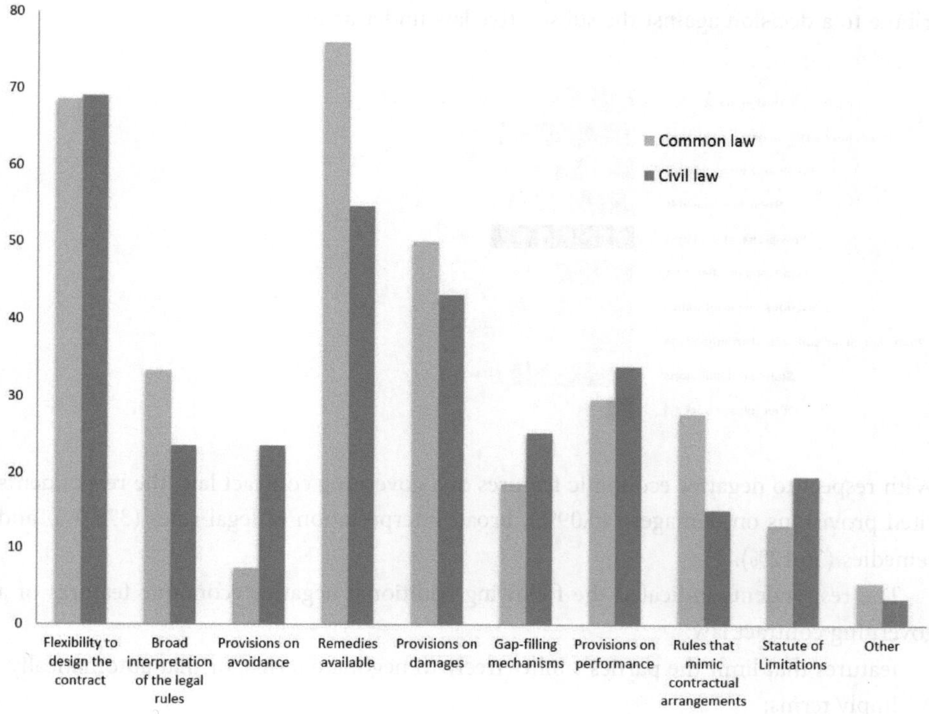

It comes as a no surprise that 'remedies available' were ranked higher by common law respondents, following the answers above.

There is a clear discrepancy between common law and civil law respondents in relation to 'provisions of avoidance', with a substantially higher rate for civil law respondents. This does not seem entirely consistent with responses to question 3 above, where common law respondents indicated 'provisions of avoidance' as a higher negative legal feature of governing contract law than did civil law respondents. This may be explained by the fact that civil law respondents, moving to the section on 'economic considerations' started effectively to undertake a more economic analysis of the choice of law provisions. This inference may be confirmed, for example, by the higher rate of responses to 'statute of limitations' and 'provisions on performance'.

Lastly, it is worth noting common law respondents' preference for 'broad interpretation of the legal rules' and 'rules that mimic contractual arrangements', reinforcing inferences that common law respondents will be looking for rules easy to ascertain and whose content provides business-look responses.

Question 6: Under an economic perspective approach, while analyzing the provisions of a substantive law, please indicate the features that may call particular attention and contribute to a decision against the substantive law under analysis:

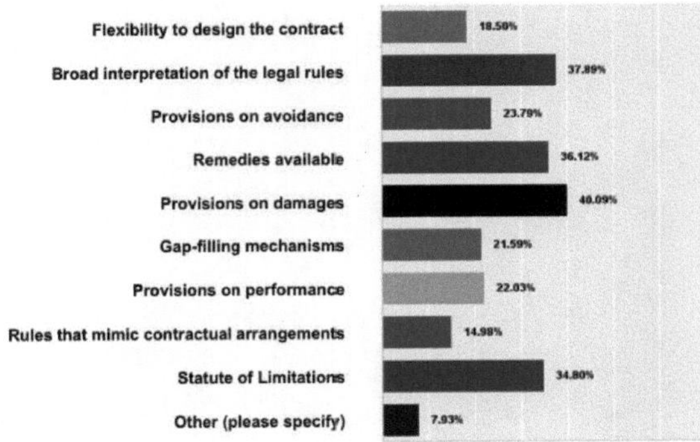

With respect to negative economic features of a governing contract law, the respondents cited provisions on damages (40.09%), broad interpretation of legal rules (37.89%) and remedies (36.12%).

The respondents indicated the following additional negative economic features of a governing contract law:

- features that limit the parties' ability freely to negotiate terms, or that automatically imply terms;
- unpredictable approach/interpretation;
- costly to access;
- mandatory indemnities;
- unclear gap-filling schemes; no freedom to adapt legal solutions;
- mandatory law provision;
- too favourable to the counterparty;
- from seller's perspective: the more protective of the buyer, the more reason against;
- average speed of legal enforcement processes;
- difficult enforcement in the jurisdiction;
- corrupt judiciary; and
- legal uncertainty.

Civil Law vs Common Law Approaches

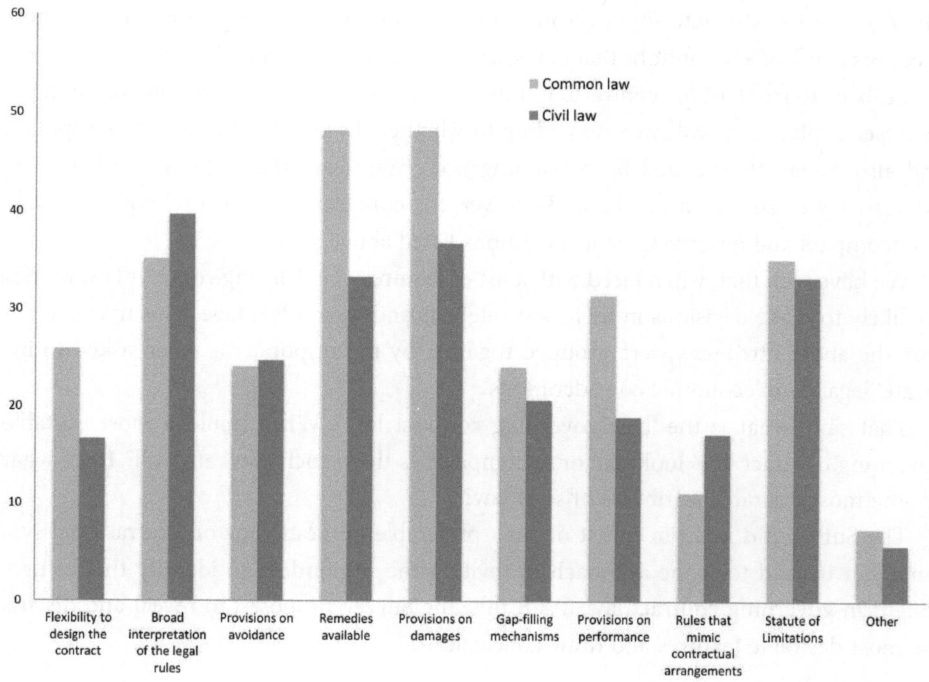

Concerning negative economic attributes of a governing contract law, perhaps the most notable discrepancy between civil law and common law respondents is 'remedies available' and 'provisions on damages', attributes that common law respondents seem to value more highly than do civil law respondents. The results also show that 'rules that mimic contractual arrangements' are not popular among civil law respondents, *i.e.* rules lacking an element of indeterminacy.

The Survey results further demonstrated that answers to the first six questions, although not in the same order of importance or priority, indicated a coincidence of legal and economic choices in the process of negotiating and deciding governing contract law.[199] The overlapping aspects comprise the following considerations:

- statute of limitations;
- provisions on performance;
- provisions on avoidance;
- provisions on damages;
- gap-filling mechanisms;
- remedies available; and

199 L. G. Meira Moser, *supra* note 3, p. 43.

- flexibility to design the contract/commitment to freedom of contract.

The overlapping attributes of governing contract law from both legal or economic perspectives confirm assumptions that parties, at least in theory, will look at the 'full picture', or the 'back to front' of the contract, and then design it as they see fit, bearing in mind the interests at play. This will vary according to whether the client is the buyer or supplier, and also be largely dictated by bargaining power, among other factors which will be exhaustively discussed in this book. However, the core elements, or 'backbone', is likely to encompass and observe the considerations listed above.

We have seen that, when faced with a list of features of governing contract law, parties are likely to make decisions in their best interests and their advantage. This may explain why the above attributes were grouped together by the respondents when asked to indicate 'legal' and 'economic considerations'.

That said, what is the 'best governing contract law'? What would a most 'suitable governing contract law' look like or encompass? Is there such 'law' after all? If so, what are the most desirable attributes of such law?

The Survey did not aim to list or rank preferable domestic law or neutral legal systems, but instead took the approach of inviting the respondent to identify the features sought in governing contract law. With this, the Survey proposed to reveal and discuss the most desirable features and draw conclusions.

1.2.4.3 Most Desirable Substantive Law: Features

Question 7: Please indicate the features of a most desirable substantive law:

The respondents were required to indicate the features they most desired in governing contract law. As mentioned earlier, the intention was to determine and understand the vital attributes sought by the respondents in making such decision.

The results were as follows: legal rules easy to ascertain (68.72%), a body of case law that facilitates interpretation of legal rules (53.74%), limited restriction on party autonomy (46.70%), neutrality (42.29%) and international character (42.29%).

The respondents also indicated the following additional features as most desirable:

- gap-filling mechanisms easy to ascertain;
- applicable jurisdiction member of the CISG;
- whether or not mandatory rules (are in) favour of one of the parties;
- language; and
- ability to enforce.

Civil Law vs Common Law Approaches

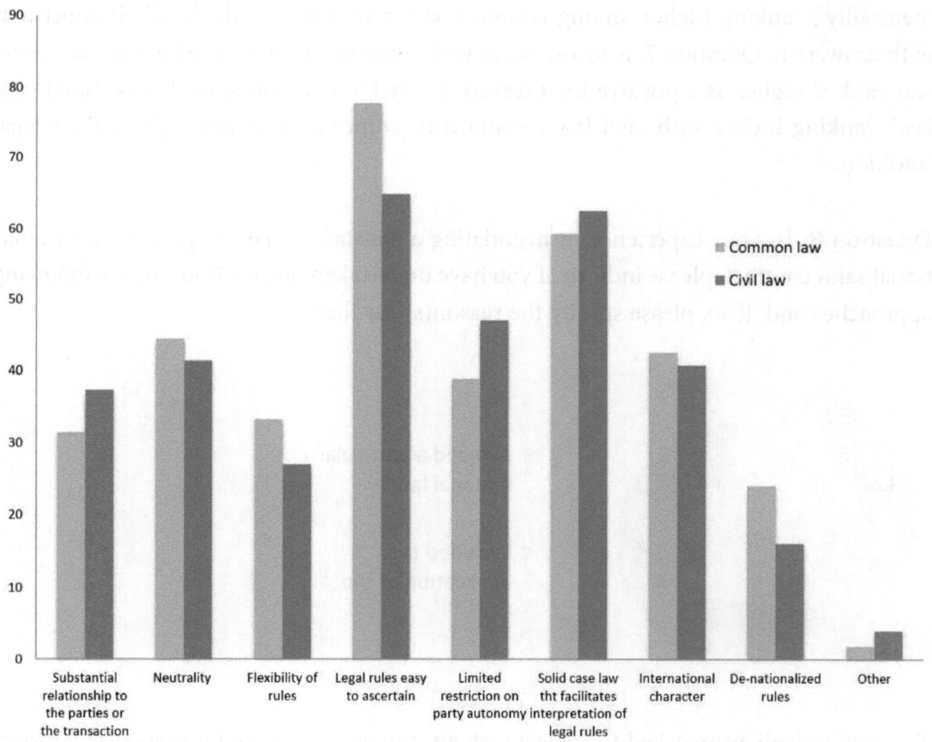

What may call for particular attention is the civil law respondents' desire for 'solid case law', who accorded this slightly greater importance than their common law colleagues did. This is particularly surprising, given the tradition of non-binding precedent in civil law jurisdictions.[200]

200 See, *e.g.* T. M. Cooper, 'The Common and the Civil Law. A Scot's View', *Harvard Law Review*, Vol. 63, Isssue 3, 1950, pp. 468-475.

Common law respondents expressed a higher preference for 'Denationalized rules' and 'legal rules easy to ascertain'. This is a rather interesting development. One would have thought, noting a preference for 'Denationalized rules', that the rate of opt-outs of the CISG would be significantly lower among common law respondents, which does not seem to have been confirmed by the responses to Question 8 (discussed below). This inconsistency will be explored in the chapters to follow.

There appears to be a correlation between some of the independent variables, for example between 'legal certainty' (Question 1), which in Question 7 is framed as 'legal rules easy to ascertain', and 'a solid body of case law'. These variables seem to walk hand-in-hand and may justify why in Question 7, 'a solid body of case law' has been cited as one of the most attractive features of governing contract law.[201]

With respect to the commonalities, none has struck as a major surprise, save for 'neutrality', ranking higher among common law respondents, which, albeit consistent with answers to Question 7, is inconsistent with those to Question 1, where this attribute was ranked higher as a positive legal feature by civil law respondents. Lastly, 'solid case law', ranking higher with civil law respondents, comes as a surprise, given their legal tradition.

Question 8: In your experience in negotiating a substantive law to govern an international sales contract, please indicate if you have undertaken one (or both) of the following approaches and, if so, please specify the reason(s) for that:

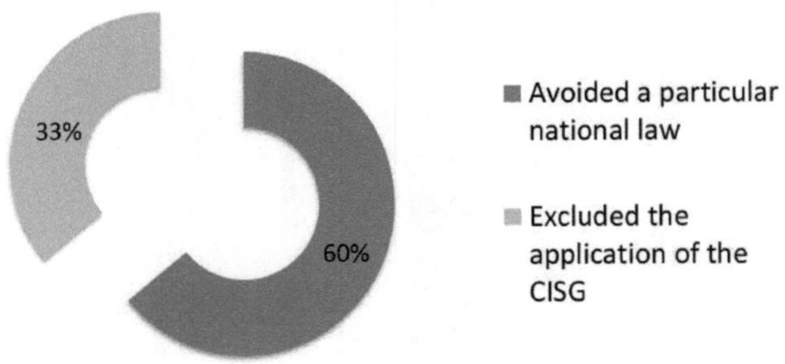

The respondents were asked to indicate whether they had avoided a particular national law or opted out of the CISG in their past practice. Question 8 (hereinafter Q8) thus included two options: 'CISG' or 'particular national law'. Whilst readers are aware that the CISG, once the administrative requirements are met in the ratifying jurisdiction, becomes 'national law', the purpose of Q8 was to investigate the underlying rational and non-rational factors and elements that dictate the parties' behaviour of avoiding a particular national law and opting out of the CISG. Q8 was meant to elicit the parties'

201 See *supra* Section 1.2.4.3 regarding this correlation.

attitude to 'opt-out', including scenarios where a particular national law was avoided in order (i) to prevent a less credible domestic sales law's application, and securing parties' benefit from a more acceptable legal framework; (ii) to avoid a particular national law so as to escape the CISG's application (for various reasons, including lack of trust of some of these respondents in the CISG's application by state court judges[202]); and (iii) to ensure that a given legal framework within which the parties have bargained would fully apply.

That said, the author submits that some respondents may indeed have avoided particular national law in order (indirectly) to opt in or out of the CISG. The respondents' comments, which will be discussed below, attest to this inference: 'doubts on the correct application of the law by the courts' and 'international sales of goods are international in essence, so a particular national law might bring obligations not conceived for international trade'. For these respondents, particular national law may have been avoided so as to allow for the CISG to apply to these deals.

The Survey has not sought to map out the respondents' experience in a given period (5 or 10 years, for example), nor was it intended to be restricted to state court or arbitration cases in isolation. The author thus acknowledges that the absence both of timeframes or timescales and dispute resolution options could have influenced the overall rates of Q8. For example, a respondent who had avoided or opted-out of a particular national law 10 years ago could change his or her mind today by virtue of a new and modern domestic sale law or act, or even by the fact that the jurisdiction has now ratified the CISG or had ratified with some reservations which are no longer in force.

The Survey was not intended to show similarities and differences between the choices 'in arbitration' and 'state court'. Nevertheless, we should understand that this may also have affected the results, given that some of these respondents, although seasoned practitioners in international sales law, may have had more experience with court cases than arbitration cases or vice-versa, and that they could have adopted a practice in the past which would not be repeated some few years later, perhaps given their positive or negative experience with dispute resolution method A or B.

That caveats stated, the numbers show that 33% of these respondents opted-out of the CISG and 60% avoided a particular national law.

In light of the non-negligible numbers obtained in the above chart, we decided to investigate this data in further detail. The results are discussed below.

202 See reasons of CISG opt-outs *infra* Section 1.2.4.5.

Civil Law vs Common Law Approaches

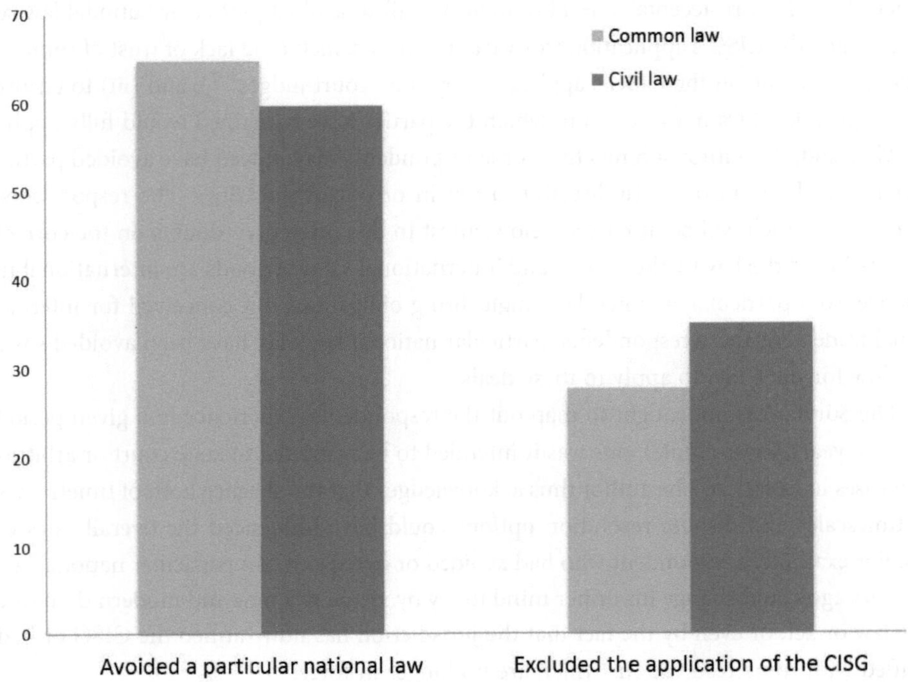

The above graph compares civil and common law responses to Q8. In terms of avoidance of particular national law, the results are fairly even as between the two legal families, with a slight higher rate of avoidance among common law respondents.

We understand that the overall high rate of 'avoidance of a particular national law' is in line with the respondents' expressed preferences in answer to the previous 7 questions, in which they undertook an analysis and advanced attributes of a governing contract law that would fit their interests. There is thus nothing abnormal in obtaining this high rate of 'avoidance of a particular national law'. However, this author was keen to learn from these respondents why they avoided these laws. Were the reasons for this avoidance disclosed or informed?

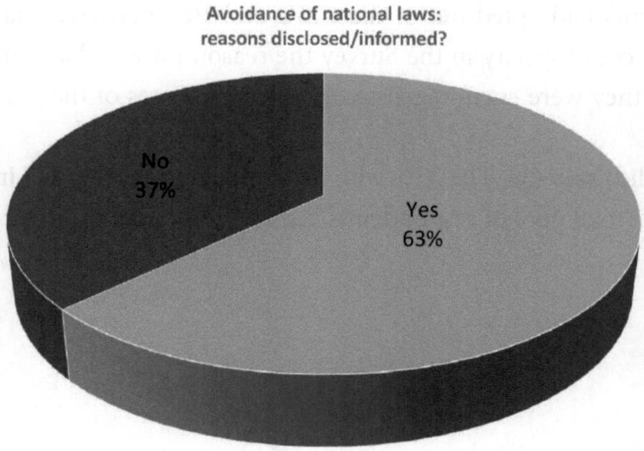

Of the 60% of the respondents who avoided a particular national law, 37% did not or disclose their reasons. There are a number of reasons non-disclosure which, unfortunately, fail to serve further analysis and study but it might be that avoidance was due to non-legal or economic considerations and simply based on other factors, which we shall explore later in this book.[203]

These respondents (37%) belong to the legal families identified in the chart below:

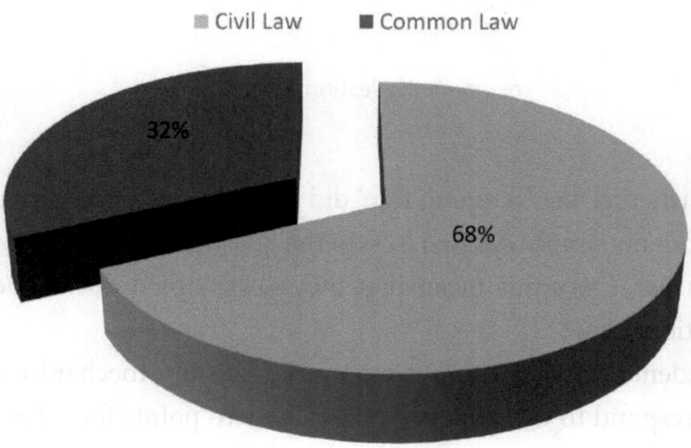

There is a prevalence of civil law respondents among those who, for undisclosed reasons, avoid particular national law. Whilst the parallel between the two legal families may signal certain trends, it is unfortunate that such a high rate of avoidance (37%) cannot be further analyzed. However, we are here principally concerned, for purposes of this book, with the CISG opt-outs rates.

203 The other factors that may influence respondents to opt-out of the CISG will be further discussed in *infra* Chapter 2.

In total, 33% of the respondents had opted out of the CISG and 60% particular national law. As we have seen, they could specify in the Survey the reason for avoidance or exclusion of the CISG, although they were encouraged to do so for purposes of the Survey.

The respondents could (and did) skip Q8. The 33% who had opted out of the CISG in fact were 33% of the 76.5% of the 'total pool of respondents', *i.e.* 228 respondents. Therefore 23.5% skipped Q8.

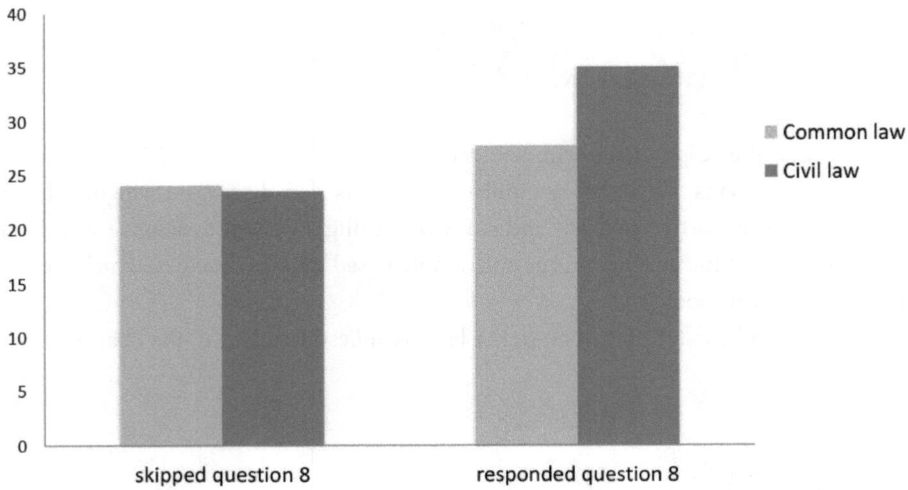

Of course, it remains to be seen whether the 'skipping rate' did in fact reflect an absence of opt-outs or whether the respondents simply decided to skip the question for the sake of completing the questionnaire earlier. Does this mean that they never opted out of the CISG or avoided a particular national law?

We could assume that respondents familiar with opt-outs and exclusions mechanisms were probably more inclined to respond to Q8. However, there are two points for reflection here: 1) the pool of experienced respondents might have guessed they could opt out; and (perhaps, more intriguingly) 2) the respondents were not informed that they could skip Q8, *i.e.* the 'skip option' was not part of the questionnaire instructions. This leads us to infer that some of the respondents who skipped Q8 (maybe most?) had in fact probably never opted out of the CISG. This could be the case, but some readers may think that only an additional option such as 'I did neither of these' in the questionnaire could allow this conclusion, and to read the minds of those who skipped Q8.

In light of the above considerations we decided to investigate further the exclusion of the CISG. To this end, the chart below provides a breakdown of the CISG opt-out rates among respondents who answered Q8:

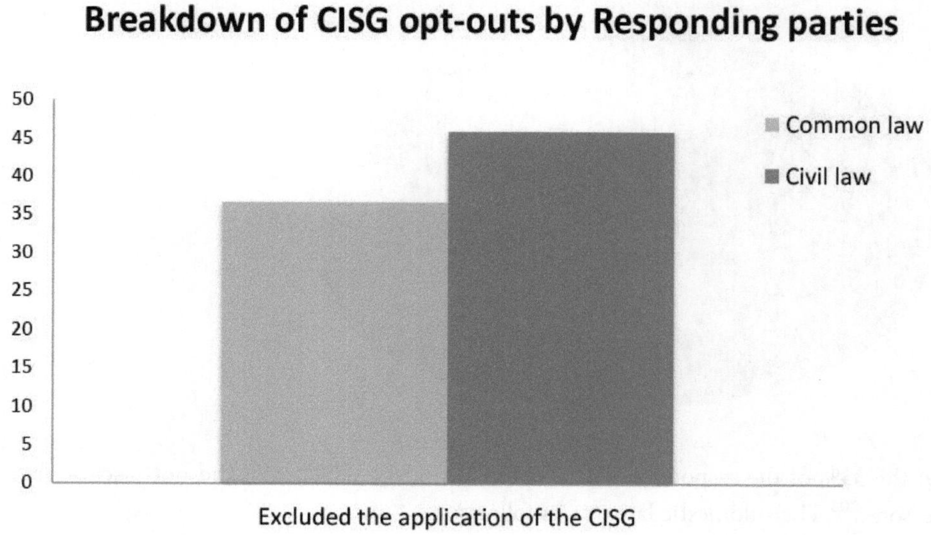

As we can see, when we examine the responses from those who did not skip Q8, a higher rate of opt-out is obtained, with civil law respondents taking the lead by a not very significant margin. This may also indicate a relatively higher rate of common law exclusions of the CISG, given its smaller pool of participants.[204]

As mentioned above,[205] Q8 could be skipped or, if selected by the respondent, the reason for the exclusion or opting-out choice could be disclosed or omitted. Although commendable, it was not requested that respondents spell out the reason(s) for exclusion. The chart below provides a clearer picture of these data.

The below chart elucidates the percentage of reasons informed or disclosed by the Survey respondents who indicated to have opted-out of the CISG:

204 The Survey participants from common law jurisdictions accounted for 24%.
205 Please see Survey instructions *supra* Section 1.2.3.

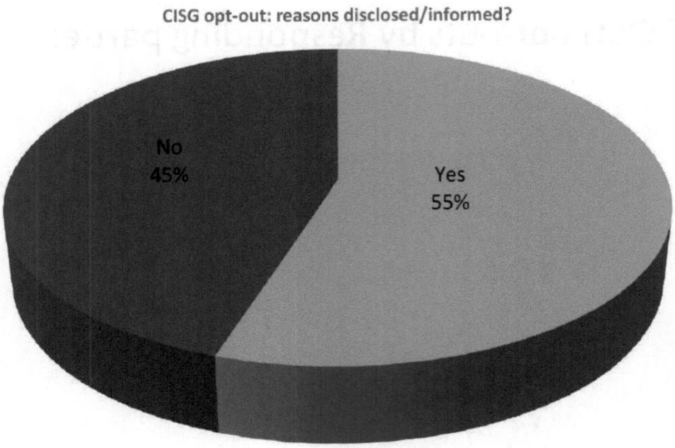

Of the 33% of the respondents who opted out of the CISG, 45% did not disclose their reasons.[206] Their domestic law was as follows:

CISG Opt-out by Legal Families

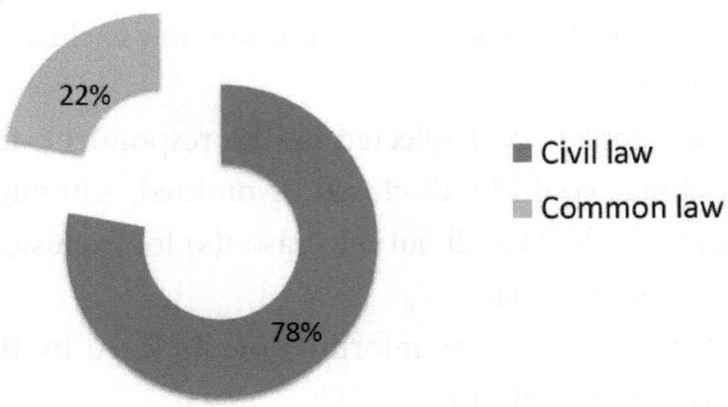

The percentage of undisclosed reasons is highly significant but, unfortunately, fails to contribute to what could be a more thorough understanding of the underlying reasons for CISG exclusion. This high rate of omission prevents and holds off potential legal improvements and solutions, not to mention the lack of economic analysis of these decisions, which may not have been thought through. However, in the following chapters, we shall attempt to understand this rate by making use of multi-disciplinary tools, in addition to offering to those who chose not to disclose some further reflection which we hope will serve better to equip them in future choice of law decisions.

206 See reasons of opt-out of the CISG *infra* Section 1.2.4.5.

1.2.4.4 National Law

Below are the reasons[207] cited by the respondents for avoidance of certain national law.[208] For ease of reference, we divided them in two: (i) substantive considerations and (ii) non-substantive. Such categorization is a mere device to facilitate discussion and further understanding of the matter and is not intended to limit inferences developed below.

1.2.4.4.1 Substantive Considerations

- since the national law requires multiple signatures or other arcane contract formation elements;
- for contracts involving intellectual property national laws were chosen because of stronger copyright protection for software and less confusion about moral rights;
- international sales of goods are international in essence, so a particular national law might bring obligations not conceived for international trade;
- it contained a prohibited penalty clause;
- it is not adequate to the parties' juridical culture;
- difficulty of enforcement;
- uncertainty and difficulty in interpretation of that country's law;
- in matters of first demand guarantee, a national law was recommended to be avoided as it meant less difficulty in obtaining an order to prevent payment to the beneficiary;
- it did not apply to the place of execution of the agreement;
- more flexible approach regarding the limitation of liability;
- national law was not favourable for specific transactions;
- in order to avoid punitive damages and not to be stuck in very costly litigation;
- certainty and predictability;
- preference for freedom to contract and avoidance of jurisdictions with less developed judicial systems;
- limited freedom of contract; no reliable gap-filling mechanisms;
- certain jurisdictions restrict party autonomy and have introduced mandatory statutory provisions, which is highly undesirable;
- unfair terms or higher learning costs of gaining understanding of the law;
- the substantive law has unfavourable provisions on time limitation, limitations of liability or other provision which can be unfavourable for our client;
- parties needed more flexibility to design their particular contracts;
- for reasons of its contents and the remedies available;
- to avoid the application of specific mandatory provisions;
- generally preferred common law and therefore avoided civil law as being less flexible;

207 The respondents who indicated avoidance of particular national law without specifying the reason constitute 37%. Therefore this list compiles the reasons of 63% of the respondents.

208 Duplicated entries or slightly different wording were eliminated from the sample.

- does not meet the positive satisfactory requirements;
- lack of available legal framework;
- complex and dogmatic interpretation of parties' intention and broad interpretation of mandatory rules which significantly limits contractual freedom;
- due to potential invalidity of standard terms;
- risk of damages in case of breach of contract;
- whenever provisions regarding filling in the gaps are absent from the text or adversely affected by other provisions; and
- national law not flexible enough and restricts party autonomy.

1.2.4.4.2 Non-Substantive Considerations

- client's request;
- particular national law most of the time meant a benefit to only one party, usually the party familiar with such law;
- it is considered a 'weak law';
- it avoids the law of the counterparty's domicile because choosing that law might encourage the counterparty to breach the contract relying on legal advice available in its own country, instead of trying to cooperate in the full performance of the contract;
- it demonstrates a lack of knowledge of that national law in order to determine whether that was the best option;
- opposing party's law;
- the limitations of the substantive law of many under-developed countries;
- international organization is involved;
- law not developed in the energy sector;
- to avoid uncertainty or inconvenience/cost issues;
- substantive law not sufficiently developed to govern the main aspects of contractual matters;
- extremely costly to use;
- 'exotic' laws that we always advise against applying;
- uncertainty;
- cost of enforcement;
- doubt concerning the correct application of the law by the courts;
- best practice to avoid choosing substantive law from any jurisdiction where the legal system is not stable, neutral and fair, to the extent possible, given the wishes of the parties and the particular circumstances of the transaction;
- political and social instability;
- uncertain rule of law, protection of national parties by court;
- neutral law instead of the law of the counterparty's country;
- 'neutrality of law' concern;

- unpredictable jurisprudence; and
- civil law jurisdiction.

The percentages of main reasons can be summarized as follows (see figure 1 on page 85): 'Substantive design' (36%), 'lawyer's strategy' (19%) and 'unfamiliarity' (14%) are the three main reasons disclosed by the respondents for avoidance of certain national law.

For purposes of completeness we shall briefly refer to the 3 main reasons individually.

The most popular reason for avoiding a particular national is 'substantive design' (36%). This incorporates answers relating to inefficient or undesirable legal framework, or unwelcome provisions encountered in the national law.

While the details of these deals have not been disclosed, it could well be that these respondents took a rational approach in evaluating the efficiency and (non-)attractiveness of certain provisions in a given national law before deciding to choose one over the other. The respondents' comments confirm this hypothesis: 'the substantive law has unfavourable provisions on time limitation, limitations of liability or other provisions which can be unfavourable for our client'; 'in order to avoid punitive damages and not to be stuck in a very costly litigation; more flexible approach regarding the limitation of liability'. It is possible to infer that these respondents undertook the laborious work of testing provisions and assessing their legal and economic adequacy to a given deal.

Avoidance of national laws: substantive design

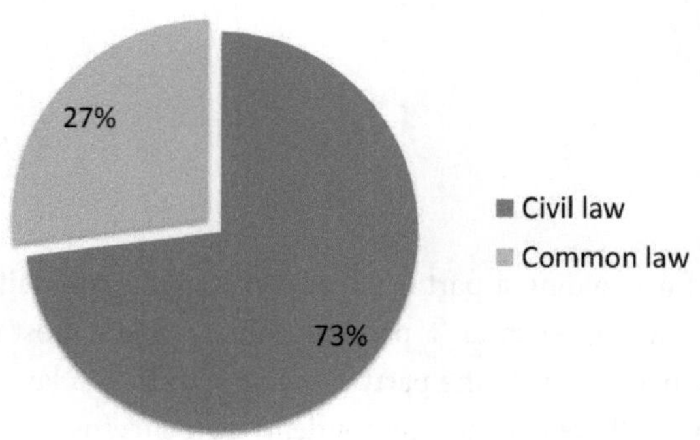

The runner-up reason for avoiding a particular national law is 'lawyer's strategy' (22%) and includes answers where respondents deliberately and tactically avoided a particular national law, either because it was the opposing party's law, or a law whose attributes did not correspond to, or match the interests at stake, or even as leeway to seek easier enforcement of certain matters in dispute. For example, 'it did not apply to the place of execution of the agreement', 'political and social instability'; 'cost of enforcement'; 'opposing party's law'.

Some of these respondents may have avoided a particular national law because it lacked a credible sales law, thereby allowing a more acceptable or receptive legal framework to apply. Nor should we overlook the possibility that some respondents might have avoided a particular law in order to ensure or prevent the application of the CISG.[209] This could encompass strategies such as bargaining over the place of performance or of conclusion of the contract so as to avoid certain conflict of law rules, ensuring that a given regime be the governing contract law.

This lawyer's strategy has been acknowledged throughout the Survey and is also evidenced in the consideration 'whether the jurisdiction has ratified the UN Convention on Contracts for the International Sale of Goods (CISG)'.[210] While this can be taken as justification of the proposition that ratification of the CISG by a given jurisdiction is a factor militating in favour of a choice of law of that jurisdiction, the answer may also imply that ratification of the CISG is a reason for not choosing the law of that jurisdiction.

In this category, comment also included adequacy of the juridical culture, accessibility, international character, costs, enforcement concerns, and political and social instability.

Avoidance of national laws: lawyer's strategy

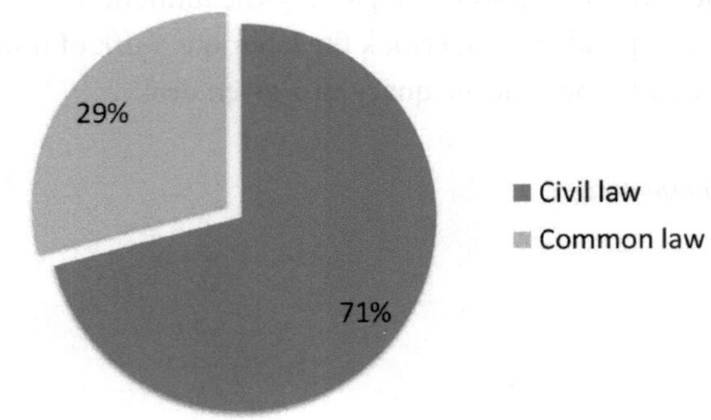

The third most popular reason for avoiding a particular national law is 'unfamiliarity' (14%). This category includes comments such as 'a particular national law most of the time meant a benefit to only one party, usually the party familiar with such a law'.

It may be that 'unfamiliarity' is linked by the respondents to concerns about the application of a particular national law by state court judges. In other words the 'familiarity' aspect could be connected to the decision-maker. The possibility is suggested by this comment: 'doubts on the correct application of the law by the courts', that is, unfamiliarity of state judges approaching the nuances of a given law. The overall positive attitude of Survey respondents to arbitration endorses this view.[211]

209 See, in this sense, Article 1 of the CISG.

210 Responses to Question 2 *supra* Section 1.2.4.1.

211 See, *e.g.*, additional comments in relation to Question 1 (Section 1.2.4.1) and Question 4 (Section 1.2.4.2).

Avoidance of national laws: unfamiliarity

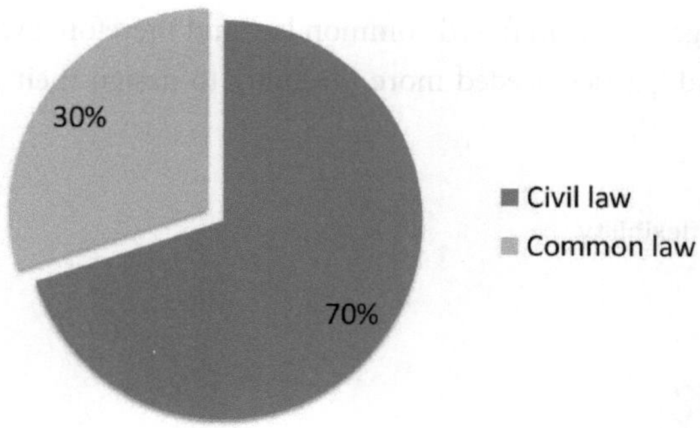

'Predictability/legal certainty' (11%) is the fourth most common reason for avoiding national law. Survey comments which fall within this category include: 'unpredictable jurisprudence'; 'uncertain rule of law, protection of national parties by court'; 'to avoid uncertainty or inconvenience/cost issues'; 'lack of available legal framework'; 'certainty and predictability'; and 'uncertainty and difficulty in interpretation of that country's law'.

In this category some respondents expressed their fear that the courts would not be in a position to apply the law. This could be a law over which the parties have bargained, considered, or avoided because of concerns regarding possible unwanted outcomes. Once again, this could also be interpreted as a 'fear of the unknown'[212] but also as 'unfamiliarity' of the decision-maker with the legal framework.

Avoidance of national laws: predictability/legal certainty

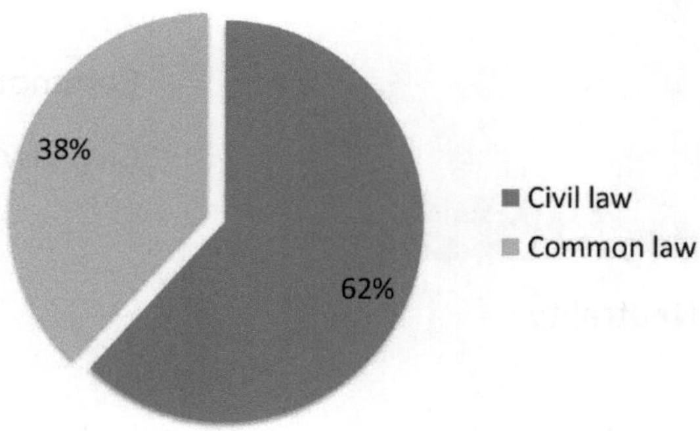

The above chart shows that, among lawyers from civil law jurisdictions, 'predictability/legal certainty' was more frequently cited than was the case with their common law counterparts.

212 See *supra* note 168.

The reason for avoiding a national law, 'Flexibility' (9%) was the fifth most frequently cited concern and includes comments such as 'national law not flexible enough and restricts the party autonomy'; 'generally preferred common law and therefore avoided civil law as being less flexible'; and 'parties needed more flexibility to design their particular contracts'.

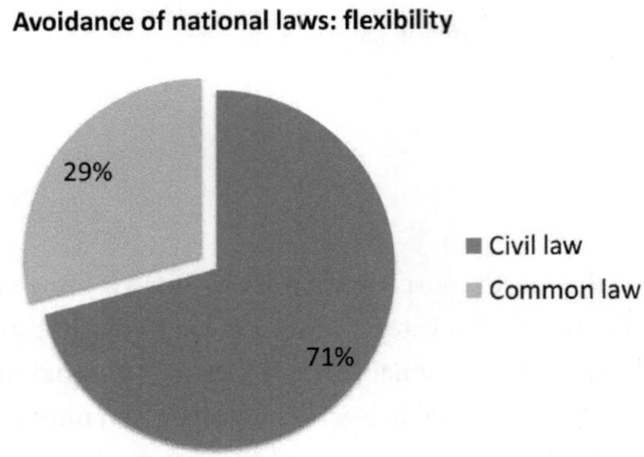

For purposes of our discussion below of CISG opt-outs, it is also worth mentioning 'Neutrality', which was indicated as a main reason cited by 5.7% of the respondents who answered Q8, in the following proportion of common law and civil law participants:

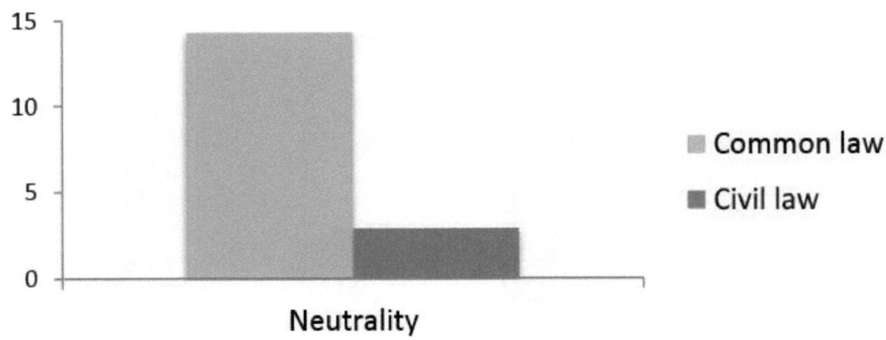

There is a considerable difference between the proportions of common law and civil law respondents who excluded national law for reasons of 'neutrality' (14% against 2.8% respectively). Arguably, these respondents, in deciding on the governing contract law of their deals, opted for a 'neutral legal framework'. It is not entirely clear what circumstances led these respondents to take such approach, nor whether this was part of bargaining process which had resulted in a 'middle-ground solution' or whether this was decided because of positive or negative experience with such neutral law.

Another aspect to note is the underlying idea of a 'neutral law', *i.e.* whether it is a third country's law or a neutral legal framework such as the CISG.[213] The respondents' comments may endorse the view that certain domestic law has been avoided in order to allow neutral legal regimes to operate fully or to their fullest capacity. These include 'international sale of goods are international in essence, so a particular national law might bring interpretations of obligations not conceived for international sale'; 'the parties agreed to have a neutral governing law'; and 'better to have even a neutral law that the law of the counterparty's country'.

These data on 'neutrality' conflict somewhat with the results obtained in response to Question 1, where civil law participants indicated a higher preference for 'legal neutrality'[214] than did common law. It might well be that the concept and extent to which 'neutrality' plays a role in this decision have not been fully considered by some respondents. However, the results of Question 8 followed the trend in Question 7, where more common law respondents regarded 'neutrality' as one of the most desirable attributes in governing contract law.

The reasons for avoidance of national law are not surprising; in particular, 'substantive design' (36%) and 'lawyer's strategy' (19%). Let us not forget that these respondents, as experienced practitioners, would have compared certain key attributes in state law by recourse to rational exercise. This is confirmed, *inter alia*, by comments: 'more flexible approach regarding the limitation of liability'; 'in order to avoid punitive damages and not to be stuck in a very costly litigation'; and 'the substantive law has unfavourable provisions on time limitation, limitations of liability or other provisions which can be unfavourable for our client'.

The results also show that not only rational elements have driven these choices. This is confirmed by comments, *inter alia*, 'weak law', 'exotic law'.[215]

Have these decisions been thought through carefully after all? Would the outcome of these decisions be different had respondents been aware of the non-rational elements that routinely affect our decisions? These are questions the author will attempt to address and answer in the following lines.

213 See C. Fountoulakis, *supra* note 195, pp. 305-307; see also L. Spagnolo, *supra* note 118, pp. 115-116.
214 Survey Question 1 *supra* Section 1.2.4.1.
215 These quotes will be further discussed in *supra* Chapter 2.

1.2.4.5 CISG

Below are the reasons[216] cited by the respondents for the exclusion of the CISG.[217] For ease of reference, we divided them into two categories: (i) substantive considerations and (ii) non-substantive considerations. Such categorization is a mere device to facilitate understanding and not intended to limit analysis which is developed below.

1.2.4.5.1 Substantive Considerations

- the CISG was excluded because of the contracts involve service and intellectual property as well as goods, and the CISG is not well suited to those aspects of the transaction and may produce unwanted results;
- unconvinced that CISG struck the right balance;
- it is a question of balance. If I want balance, I go for the CISG. If I want to enforce obligations strictly, I go for specific national state law;
- lack of knowledge of particular body of law and its consequences for contract performance and avoidance;
- national law more favourable than CISG;
- national law more advantageous to the seller;
- the desire is to have the entire agreement between the parties reflected within the four corners of the contract, without importing – perhaps unintentionally – CISG provisions;
- less legal certainty; CISG does not cover all issues usually relevant in a contract law dispute;
- especially in software-related contracts, counterparties expect the CISG to be excluded;
- to make sure specified states apply the law without exception;
- uncertain outcome of application in particular by state courts;
- the national rules available are more flexible than the CISG;
- the CISG can sometimes add to perceived complexity, which may not be favourable to parties, notably also for negotiation of the contract;
- if national courts have jurisdiction, application of domestic civil code is more predictable;
- lack of safety rules;
- lack of a body of case law;
- it all depends on who you represent – buyer or seller. Buyer-friendly law is a reason for seller's representatives to avoid this law;
- undesirable solutions;

216 The respondents who indicated the exclusion of the CISG without specifying a reason amount to 45%. Therefore this list compiles the reasons of 55% of the respondents.

217 Duplicated entries or slightly different wording were eliminated from the sample.

- the CISG is excluded whenever we assist a seller. If we assist a buyer, the seller's national law is avoided if the differences between buyer's and seller's national law are considered to be too great;
- provisions were more favourable to the counterparty;
- because of the doubts on the application of the said rules since there are no established precedents;
- risk of different interpretation of the same rules in different jurisdictions;
- excluded the application of the CISG because it may interfere with the contract in an unpractical manner;
- principle of good faith;
- certain CISG provisions, *e.g.* that on consequential damages – are not necessarily more advantageous than the available national alternatives.

1.2.4.5.2 Non-Substantive Considerations

- lack of familiarity and lower degree of legal certainty;
- client's request;
- the CISG was considered weighted in favour of buyers;
- use of precedent contract that excluded CISG;
- the other side refused to have the CISG applied;
- The CISG is one-sided;
- have only excluded CISG where other party insisted or there was a particular reason;
- depending on client's position and interests;
- international conventions, especially UN, embody political compromises between a large number of states, representing different interests. Therefore these compromise solutions do not always fit the interests of parties to international sale contracts;
- excluded the CISG only in cases where the client prefers arbitration in common law jurisdictions as lawyers and arbitrators in these are familiar with common law;
- to avoid uncertainty or inconvenience/cost issues;
- no experience;
- clients do not like the CISG because it is often excluded ; and
- the cost of advising under CISG is greater than under national law.

The percentage of main reasons can be summarized as follows (see figure 2 on page 85): 'Lawyer's strategy' (23%), 'substantive design' (20%), and 'predictability /legal certainty' (15%) are the three main reasons for the respondents' opting out of the CISG.

For purposes of completeness we shall break down the statistics on all the reasons for CISG's exclusion by legal traditions.

Before doing so we should keep in mind the distribution of the respondents' legal tradition:

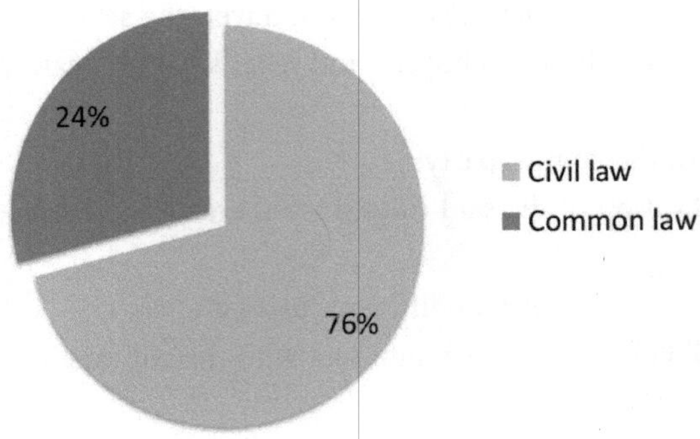

'Lawyer's strategy' (22%) encompasses a broad range of answers connected, *inter alia*, to the type of agreement; the contract design, the place(s) of potential enforcement, the nature of likely dispute and the resolution method agreed.

We should remember that there is a level of indeterminacy associated with 'lawyer's strategy' and it could well be that this reason was used to mask other reasons such as 'unfamiliarity', 'fear or the unknown' and even others that could constitute grounds for professional negligence claims.[218]

CISG opt-out: lawyer's strategy

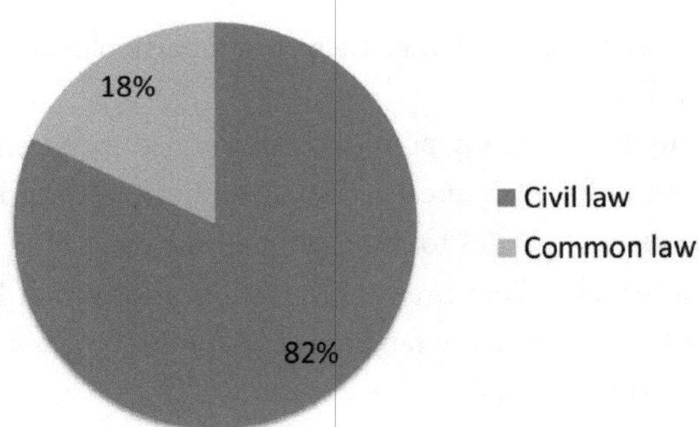

'Substantive design' (20%) encompasses a large array of answers, which include, for example: national law's being more advantageous; the CISG's being 'one-sided'; certain provisions unfavourable to these respondents or their clients, and overall substantive design concerns.

No reference was made in the Survey to the 'seller-friendliness' of the CISG,[219] which has nevertheless been discussed by academics as an allegation by representatives of devel-

218 See, in this sense, U. Schroeter, *supra* note 164, pp. 650-651; and L. Spagnolo, *supra* note 118, p. 128.

219 M. Koehler refers to the CISG's 'seller-friendliness', which the author argues has been 'very much emphasized by academics', *supra* note 37.

oping countries.[220] However, Survey respondents have regarded the CISG as 'buyer-friendly'.[221] This could indicate that the CISG may strike the right balance between buyer and seller, as it is suggested that the CISG 'actually achieves fair and reasonable results for both parties'.[222] Despite this, it is important to assess the level of rationality behind these 'buyer-friendly' opinions and investigate whether these may also have been the product of bad experience rather than criticism of the substantive provisions of the CISG.

On this matter, the author believes that it is difficult to see how a set of rules can be regarded by users as 'buyer' or 'seller' friendly if not all of its provisions have been tested in various contractual scenarios. While there may be provisions that exempt one or the other from performing certain obligations, thereby restricting or expanding their duties as the case may be, the author contends that non-rational factors may have blurred the analysis by these respondents.

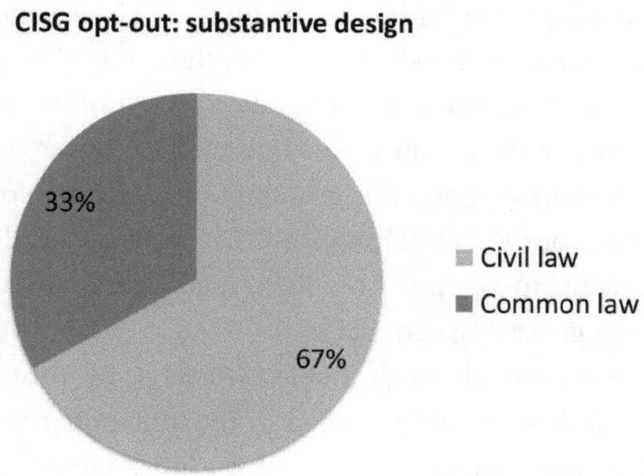

The reason 'Predictability/legal certainty' (15%), while it may misleadingly be seen as self-explanatory, carries a great deal of indeterminacy and will be further discussed in this book. How predictable should certain governing contract law be? What would this entail

220 I. Schwenzer & P. Hachem, 'The CISG: Successes and Pitfalls', *American Journal of Comparative Law*, Vol. 57, 2009, pp. 475, advising that 'representatives of developing countries have argued that the CISG is too seller friendly. This allegation focuses mainly on the obligation of the buyer to examine the goods and give notice of any non-conformity.'

221 Survey Question 8 and reasons to CISG opt-outs *supra* Section 1.2.4.3.

222 I. Schwenzer & P. Hachem, *supra* note 220, p. 476.

and what would be the main underlying reasons[223]? Is 'legal certainty'[224] a concept separate from other legal concerns and self-sufficient? Do parties challenge the CISG's intended degree of legal certainty sought?

The comments associated with these reasons are, in the author's view, unconvincing. The following endorse this view: 'lack of safety rules' and 'to avoid uncertainty or inconvenience/cost issues'. While there might be doubt and hesitation about the CISG ('costs' issues may also be linked to learning costs[225]), there is a significant element of subjectivism in these comments and it is rather unclear what are the underlying reasons for which these respondents are inclined to opt out of the CISG.

The 'uncertainty issues' referred to may be linked to the respondents' fears of state courts' interpretation of CISG provisions, rather than CISG provisions themselves. In other words, 'uncertainty' here might be associated concerning how a state court judge would approach a topic and whether he or she would be sufficiently skilled to appreciate the CISG's nuances and deliver a satisfactory result. This could be limited to jurisdictions where the CISG has recently come into force, or jurisdictions where there might be political instability or social unrest, or even those where there is a low record of international transaction and thus where there could possibly be some level of uncertainty among stakeholders. The following comment supports this presumption: 'uncertain outcome of application in particular by state courts'. Let us not forget that 'political stability' has been acknowledged by the respondents to be one of the three main economic considerations in approaching and selecting governing contract law.[226]

'Uncertainty issues' could also be explained, although to a lesser extent, by virtue of the idea of 'unfamiliarity issues'. Would these issues be linked to the 'unfamiliarity' of decision-makers with the CISG and its applicable provisions? If so, 'uncertainty' here would be connected to the 'uncertain' result of a state court decision's applying the CISG rather than the 'uncertain' meaning or functionality of any of the CISG provisions.

'Predictability/legal certainty' may also be connected to 'unfamiliarity' and 'lack of case law'. These three reasons are intertwined and could be part of the large umbrella 'fear of the unknown', *i.e.* a 'mask' of ignorance worn by some respondents in dealing

223 For a sociological approach of the topic, see V. Gessner, *supra* note 22, p. 142; see also N. Luhmann, *A Sociological Theory of Law*, translated by E. King and M. Albrow, Rutledge and Kegan Paul, London, 2014.

224 V. Gessner further draws a distinction between efficiency of law and legal certainty: "[...] Interactions between state institutions and citizens are (in western democracies) defined by Rechtsstaat or rule of law principles and are to a certain degree independent of characteristics on the actors' levels. The law attempts to define the situation with more or less success; that is, it is more or less efficient. Horizontal relations between citizens (or business undertakings and corporations) on the other hand are very much defined by the actors. They create themselves and, eventually, with the help of support structures, the necessary legal certainty", 'Globalization and Legal Certainty', *in* V. Gessner & A. C. Budak (Eds.), *Emerging Legal Certainty: Empirical Studies on the Globalization of Law*, Ashgate Publishing Limited, Aldershot, 1998, pp. 248.

225 The learning costs, or costs to become familiar with the CISG are further explored in Section 3.4 and Chapter 5.

226 Survey Question 4 *supra* Section 1.2.4.2.

with the CISG, driven primarily by emotion and non-rational factors, in addition to cases of professional negligence.[227]

It could well be that 'fear of the unknown' is actually the leading cause of CISG opt-outs, responding to 35% of the total reasons. Therefore, in such a case the primary reason for excluding the CISG would not be due to rational elements by rather non-rational factors, such as emotion and heuristics. Nevertheless, this number could even increase if we take into account the percentages of 'case by case' basis (5%) and 'client's request' (7%).

One important caveat to the 'predictability/legal certainty' consideration is the role attributed to the fear of some respondents that the CISG provisions would be unknown to state court judges, which could lead to unwanted results and costly mistakes. This is confirmed by the following quotes: 'excluded the CISG only in cases where the client prefers to have arbitration in common law jurisdictions as lawyers and arbitrators in these jurisdictions are familiar with common law'; 'risk of different interpretation of same rules in different jurisdictions'; and 'uncertain outcome of application in particular by State courts'.

Some respondents may also have opted out of the CISG because they felt that the outcome from a state court judgment arising out of the interpretation of a domestic civil code is more predictable than that of the CISG. Thus, for these respondents 'predictability' was linked to the foreseeability of the state court judgment outcome rather than any particular provision of the CISG. The following quote confirms this suggestion: 'if a national courts has jurisdiction, application of domestic civil code is more predictable'. These respondents might have been reluctant to have the CISG govern their deals due to possibly different interpretation of the CISG by these courts.

Some of the responses categorized as 'lawyer's strategy' may also encompass scenarios such as that described above, *i.e.* a strategy mentioned by some respondents adopted to avoid the application of the CISG by state court judges who would perhaps be unfamiliar with CISG provisions and could deliver unwanted results. In order to avoid this scenario, these respondents attempted to mitigate potential losses by opting out of the CISG. This seems to be in line with some of the respondents' answers to other Survey questions: 'independent and corruption-free judiciary'[228]; 'state of administration of justice in applicable jurisdiction'[229]; 'level of education of the judges'[230]; and 'difficult enforcement in the country'[231].

It is also possible that arbitration might reduce these fears and uncertainties concerning the application of the CISG. The following quotes endorse this view: 'forum for dis-

227 See, in this sense, U. Schroeter, *supra* note 164, p. 651; and L. Spagnolo, *supra* note 118, pp. 185-187.
228 Survey Question 5 *supra* Section 1.2.4.2.
229 Survey Question 3 *supra* Section 1.2.4.1.
230 Survey Question 4 *supra* Section 1.2.4.2.
231 Survey Question 6 *supra* Section 1.2.4.2.

pute resolution';[232] 'arbitration know-how available';[233] 'quality of available arbitrators';[234] 'if arbitration is chosen, then this consideration is of minor importance';[235] 'lack of qualified and impartial arbitrators in the relevant jurisdiction'.[236]

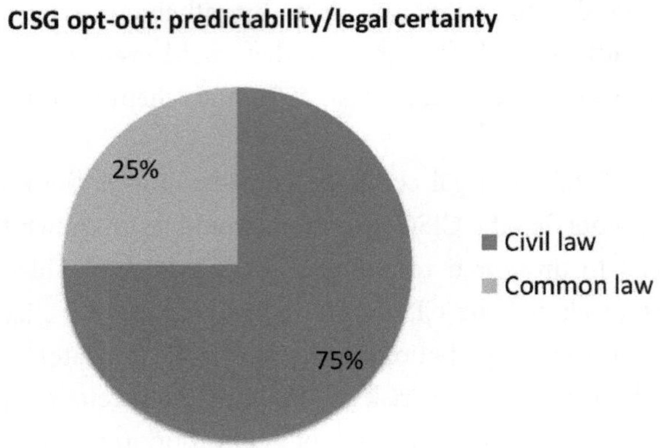

'Unfamiliarity' (11%) has also been cited as a reason for CISG opt-out in the following proportion:

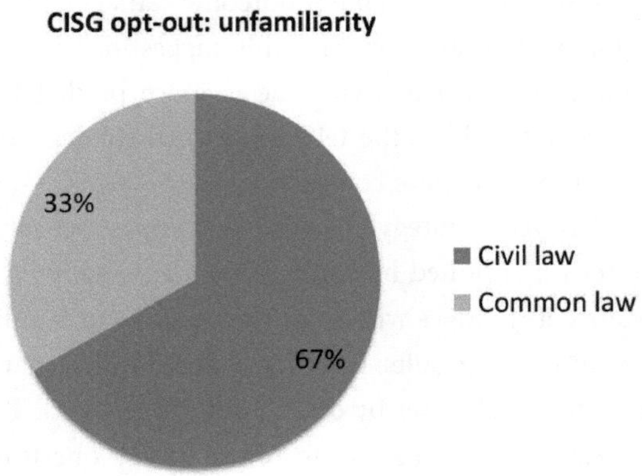

In the author's view, while this percentage generally reflects the respondents' knowledge of the CISG, some may also have indicated 'unfamiliarity' in relation to the decision-maker who would need to apply the CISG provisions. In such a scenario, the respondents might have preferred to opt out of the CISG in order to avoid an unpredictable outcome.

232 Survey Question 1 *supra* Section 1.2.4.1.
233 *Id.*
234 Survey Question 2, *supra* Section 1.2.4.1.
235 Survey Question 4, *supra* Section 1.2.4.2.
236 Survey Question 3, *supra* Section 1.2.4.1.

'Lack of case law' (9%) might have been linked to unfamiliarity with the CISG, either that of the respondents or the state court judge. This following comment endorses this possibility: 'lack of knowledge of particular body of law and its consequences on (*sic*) contract performance and avoidance'.

'Lack of case law' could be understood as the absence of CISG jurisprudence in a given jurisdiction, and not of CISG decisions worldwide. In other words, the 'lack of case law' would be linked to the fact that a given jurisdiction had not ruled on CISG matters to the satisfaction of some of the respondents, which led them to avoid the risk of a CISG case being decided by a given state court. For these respondents, therefore, this particular jurisdiction has not had sufficient experience on CISG matters so as to form a solid case law. Because of this lack of experience with CISG provisions, these respondents may have indicated 'lack of case law' as the main reason for the opting out of the CISG, when they could have indicated 'unfamiliarity' as some of them did for apparently the same reasons.

CISG opt-out: lack of case law

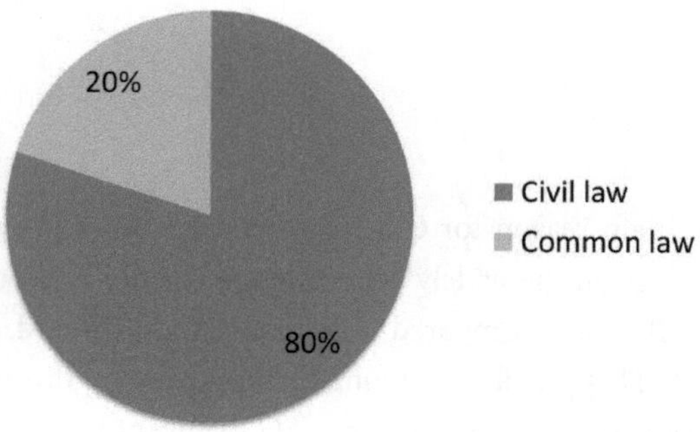

It calls particular attention that 80% of the CISG opt-outs due to 'lack of case law' were of civil law respondents. One would have thought the opposite, given the civil tradition of non-binding precedent. However, once more this could be linked to a 'fear of the unknown', translated into 'unfamiliarity', factors which will be discussed in further detail in the next chapters.[237] On the flip side, this result is also in line with Question 7, where 'solid case law' was indicated by a higher number of civil law respondents as a most desirable attribute in governing contract law.

Another way to read this percentage is to regard these respondents as having indicated 'lack of case law' on CISG matters in a given jurisdiction. Thus, the absence of CISG cases or jurisprudence in a particular jurisdiction could have prompted these respondents to avoid the CISG and therefore unwanted surprises. However, this is arguably more a cause

237 See, in this sense, *infra* Chapter 2 and Section 3.4.

of 'unfamiliarity' of the decision-maker with the CISG rather than CISG jurisprudence worldwide or the CISG provisions tested in contract litigation.

As regards 'client's request' (7%), this reason was higher among common law respondents. We have seen earlier that this reason carries a level of vagueness as it is not entirely clear why the client requested that the CISG be avoided. Whilst it could be that some CISG provisions were not sufficiently appealing to these clients, it could also be that these exclusions were the product of bias[238] and perhaps not even minimally taken on a rational level.

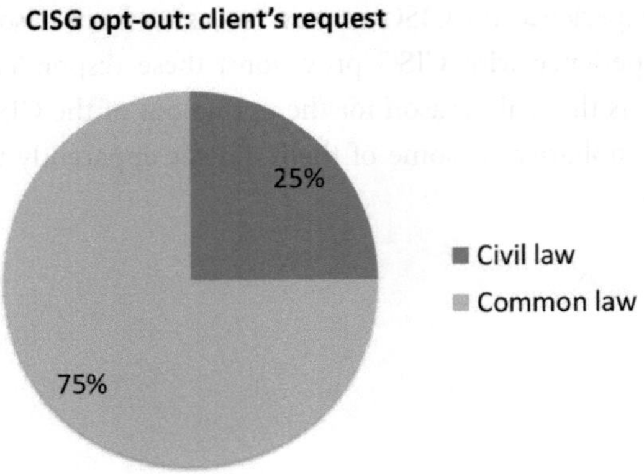

'Flexibility' (6%) was also cited as the main reason for CISG opt-outs by 6% of the respondents. This rate came as a surprise, given the widely acknowledged flexibility of the CISG.[239] However, it could be that the CISG was compared with certain state law and, on balance, the parties opted for the latter. This possibility might be supported by this answer: 'it is a question of balance. If I want balance, I go for the CISG. If I want to enforce obligations strictly, I go for specific national state laws'.

238 The topic 'heuristics and cognitive biases' is explored in fine detail in *infra* Chapter 2.

239 See, in this sense, Article 6 of the CISG; U. Schroeter, 'Freedom of Contract: Comparing CISG and PECL Provisions', *The Vindobona Journal of International Commercial Law and Arbitration*, Vol. 6, 2002, p. 261; CISG Advisory Council, Opinion no. 16, available at [www.cisgac.com/cisgac-opinion-no16/].

The following proportion was indicated by the Survey respondents:

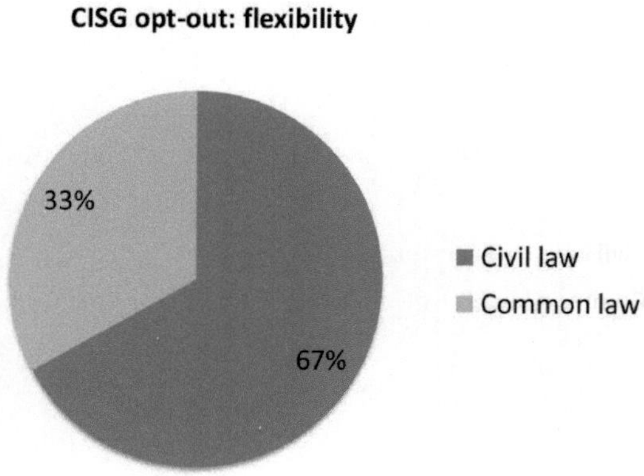

The reason 'Case by case' (5%) leaves the reader with more questions than answers, which it is hoped will be clarified in subsequent chapters. However, it may indicate that for these respondents, the CISG was not the adequate governing contract law for that particular cross-border contract. We should not exclude circumstances where 'good experience(s)'[240] with certain law may have blurred this opt-out rate.

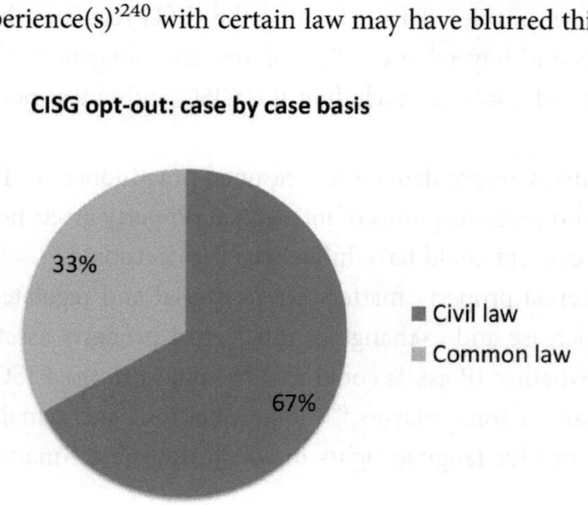

240 This and further cognitive biases are discussed in *infra* Chapter 2.

Finally, the reason 'IP matters' was cited by 5% of the respondents:

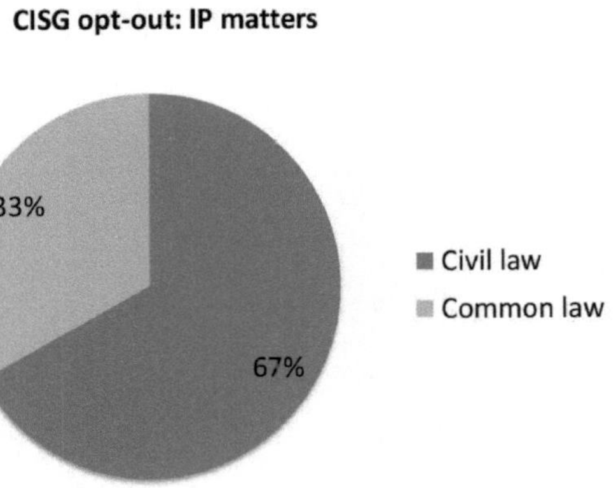

In this category, regard has to be given to contracts involving not only the sale of goods but also services. In such a case the CISG would apply if the value of the goods outweighs that of the services.[241] Another possibility here is that the exclusion was a product of a bargain *ex ante* on the provisions on validity of the agreement and the parties found it more convenient to elect one single set of rules. This is because the CISG regulates the contract formation of sales of goods and buyers' and sellers' duties and obligations.[242] Other reasons might include the use of contracts excluding the CISG without a more substantiated reason.

We should not forget that few Survey respondents were seasoned practitioners in IP matters[243] and therefore ignorance and preconceptions of intellectual property assets not being 'tangible' in a more orthodox concept could have influenced the decision.

As readers may be aware, intellectual property matters are territorial and regulated domestically. However, the rapid increase and exchange of intellectual property assets worldwide[244] poses questions as to whether IP assets could also be subject to the CISG. Whilst there is resistance on the part of some players,[245] some questions still remain open: do international IP contracts involve tangible rights in which the subject matter

241 Article 4 of the CISG: This Convention governs only the formation of the contract of sale and the rights and obligations of the seller and the buyer arising from such a contract. In particular, except as otherwise expressly provided in this Convention, it is not concerned with:
a. the validity of the contract or of any of its provisions or of any usage;
b. the effect which the contract may have on the property in the goods sold.

242 I. Schwenzer & P. Hachem, *supra* note 106, pp. 76-86, paras. 7-28.

243 There are no data produced on this matter, *i.e.* responses by areas of law.

244 See, *e.g.*, World Intellectual Property Indicators 2016, available at [www.wipo.int/edocs/pubdocs/en/wipo_pub_941_2016.pdf].

245 See B. Zeller, 'Intellectual Property Rights & the CISG Article 42', *Vindobona Journal of International Commercial Law and Arbitration*, Vol. 15, No. 2, 2011, pp. 289-302; S. Green & D. Saidov, 'Software as Goods', *Journal of Business Law*, 2007, pp. 161-181.

may be regarded as 'goods' and therefore eligible to be governed by the CISG?[246] If yes, to what extent? What should be considered 'sales transactions' and 'goods' within the wording of the CISG and in light of the sophisticated transfer of software rights?[247]

Firstly, on a close reading of the CISG, a software sales transaction, for instance, is classified as a 'sale of goods', albeit the CISG does not contain a definition of 'sale' and 'goods'. It is true that Articles 2 and 3 of the CISG expressly exclude certain transactions as sales of goods, though transactions in computer software are not specifically excluded. Moreover, under Article 3(2) of the CISG, even if the value of the labour and services involved exceeds the value of the raw material needed to manufacture the goods concerned, the transaction may still constitute a CISG sale.[248] Therefore the fact that the value of software is mainly attributed to the intellectual efforts of software developers does not render the transaction ineligible as a CISG sale of goods.[249] Assuming that computer software can be compared with a book, for example, property in the physical copy of the book is transferred to the buyer because of the sales contract but not the right to copy and publish the entire or part of its content.[250]

That said, it is worth noting that the CISG continues to face unpopular reactions among intellectual property players, in particular with respect to software contracts and research & development (R&D) agreements.[251]

Lastly, the author also acknowledges that a minor percentage of the respondents may have excluded the CISG for reasons not entirely identified and thus not categorized as above. This would include, for example, the following quotes: "international conventions, especially UN conventions, embody political compromises between a large number of countries, representing different interests. Therefore these compromise solutions do not

---

246 See Appellate Court Köln decision, Germany 26 August 1994, available at [http://cisgw3.law.pace.edu/cases / 940826 g1.html].

247 In relation to this, J. Ziegel remarks that the position of sale of software as sale of goods is difficult to sustain where the software is not imbedded in a tangible thing at the time of sale, *e.g.*, a disk or as part of a computer, cell phone, or other accessory or piece of equipment, in 'The Scope of the Convention: Reaching out to Article One and Beyond', *Journal of Law & Commerce*, Vol. 25, 2005-2006, p. 61.

248 See J. M. Lookosfy, 'In dubio pro conventione? Some thoughts about opt-outs, computer programs and preemption under the 1980 Vienna Sales Convention CISG', *Duke Journal of Comparative and International Law,* Vol. 13, Special Issue, 2003, pp. 263-289.

249 F. Diedrich, 'The CISG and Computer Software Revisited', *Vindobona Journal of International Commercial Law and Arbitration, Supplement,* Vol. 6, 2002, pp. 55-75; F. Diedrich, 'Maintaining Uniformity in International Uniform Law Via Autonomous Interpretation: Software Contracts and the CISG', *Pace International Law Review,* Vol. 8, 1996, pp. 303-338.

250 F. Diedrich, 'The CISG and Computer Software Revisited', *supra* note 249, p. 56. See also I. Schwenzer & P. Hachem, *supra* note 106, arguing that "if the software is permanently transferred to the other party in all respects except for the copyright and restrictions to its use by third parties and becoming part of the other party's property – as opposed to mere agreements on temporary use against payment of royalties – the contract is a sales contract for the purposes of the CISG", pp. 34-35, para. 18.

251 See, *e.g.* IPAG (Intellectual Property Agreement Guide) Model Agreements, available at [www.wipo.int/ amc/en/center/specific-sectors/rd/ipag/].

always fit the interests of specific parties in international sale contract"[252] and "clients do not like the CISG because people exclude it".[253] While the first quote may raise doubts as to the respondents' perception of the CISG as a balanced instrument,[254] this perception may also have been influenced by other factors and experience rather than substantive concerns about this legal framework, all of which will be further explored in this book.[255]

1.2.4.6 National Law or the CISG: What Is the Most Legally and Economically Advantageous Solution?

As we have seen thus far, legal and economic considerations appear to walk hand-in-hand in the choice of governing contract law, with some variations, depending on the legal family to which the respondent belongs. We have also discussed the reasons why certain laws, including the CISG, have been avoided by Survey participants and have attempted to reveal the underlying causes.

Now, can we safely enquire what is the most legally and economically advantageous solution: national law or the CISG?[256] What about choosing between a third country's law (regarded by some as 'neutral law') and the CISG? Which alternative provides a better legal toolkit and why?

We shall attempt to answer this question in this book[257] and we shall start with a comparison of the Survey answers to Question 8:

252 Response to Survey Question 8 *supra* Section 1.2.4.3.

253 *Id.*

254 See C. P. Gillette & R. E. Scott, 'The Political Economy of International Sales Law', *International Review of Law and Economics,* Vol. 25, 2005, pp. 446-486, arguing that, "Drafters of Uniform International Sales Law (ISL) must deal with political as well as commercial issues because they must meld different legal, governmental, and economic interests. The theory of uniform law that we elaborate predicts that efforts to accommodate these diverse political considerations will cause the law to be drafted at a high level of abstraction, explicitly to authorize numerous exceptions to the law's uniform application, and implicitly to tolerate significant variation in the interpretation of the (formally) uniform law. Commercial interests, however, require legal certainty and predictability so that parties involved in international trade are able to price the risks, including legal risks, that their contracts entail…Our analysis reveals, however, that the process of drafting ISL has been dominated by individuals concerned with political, rather than commercial interests. As a result, where commercial and political interests conflict, the ISL-creation process has subordinated the former to political concerns" (p. 447).

255 In this connection, please refer to *infra* Chapter 2.

256 It is important to note that the CISG, once it fulfills internal requirements, becomes domestic law of the contracting State. Therefore the question relates to national law solutions and CISG solutions.

257 In this connection, please refer to *infra* Chapter 5.

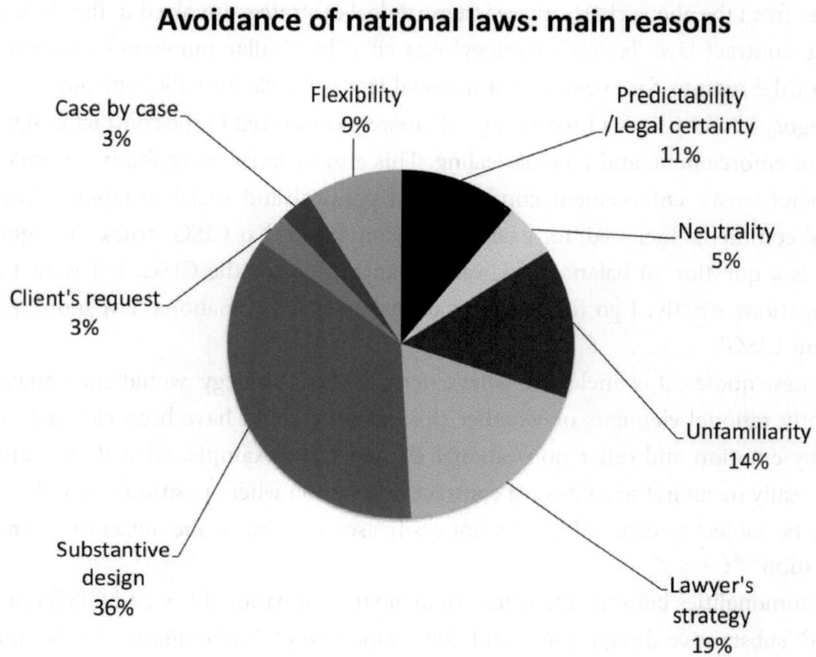
Avoidance of national laws: main reasons
Case by case
3%
Flexibility
9%
Predictability
/Legal certainty
11%
Neutrality
5%
Client's request
3%
Unfamiliarity
14%
Substantive
design
36%
Lawyer's
strategy
19%

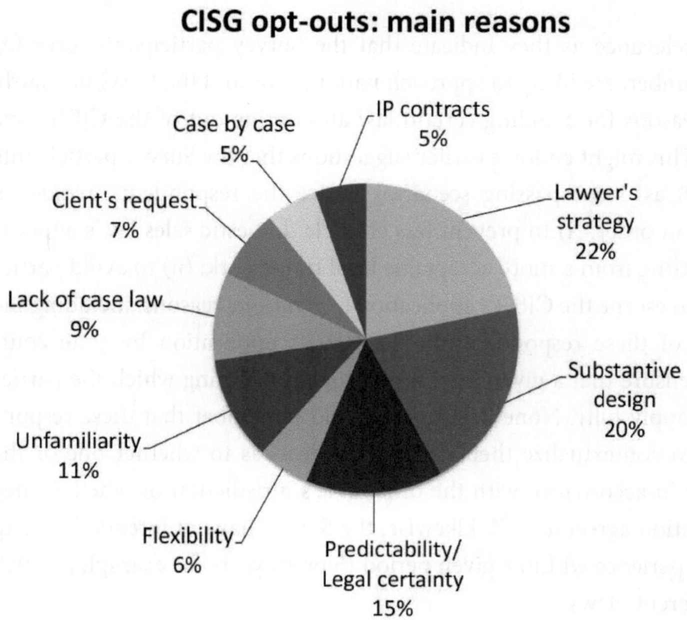
CISG opt-outs: main reasons
Case by case
5%
IP contracts
5%
Cient's request
7%
Lawyer's
strategy
22%
Lack of case law
9%
Substantive
design
20%
Unfamiliarity
11%
Flexibility
6%
Predictability/
Legal certainty
15%

As we can see from the above charts, there is a great deal of strategy involved in the choice of governing contract law: 'lawyer's strategy' was cited by similar numbers of respondents: 19% of the reasons for avoidance of national law and 22% for CISG opt-out.

This category encompasses a broad range of answers connected to the contract design itself, place of enforcement, and type of dealing. This also includes accessibility, international character, costs, enforcement concerns, and political and social instability. The respondents' comments included, for example: 'unconvinced that CISG struck the right balance'; 'it is a question of balance. If I want balance, I go for the CISG. If I want to enforce obligations strictly, I go for specific national state laws'; 'national law more favourable than CISG'.

Despite these quotes, it is unclear to what extent 'lawyer's strategy' would encompass predominantly rational elements or whether this category could have been clouded or influenced by emotion and other non-rational elements: for example, what does more 'favourable' really mean in the context of contract negotiation where positions are not yet set and may be subject to external factors not easily ascertainable at the outset of a contract negotiation[258]?

Other commonalities between the causes of avoidance of national law and CISG opt-out included 'substantive design' (36% and 20% respectively), 'unfamiliarity' (14% and 11% respectively), 'flexibility' (9% and 6% respectively) and 'predictability' (11% and 15% respectively).

These data are of relevance as they indicate that the Survey participants, save for minor differences in number, are likely to approach national law and the CISG in a fairly similar manner. The reasons for avoiding certain law and opting out of the CISG have thus clear similarities. This might endorse earlier suggestions that the Survey participants understood Question 8 as encompassing scenarios where the respondents avoided a particular national law in order: (i) to prevent less credible domestic sales law's application and parties' benefitting from a more acceptable legal framework; (ii) to avoid particular national law so as to escape the CISG's application (for various reasons, including the lack of trust of some of these respondents in the CISG's application by state court judges[259]); and (iii) to ensure that a given legal framework concerning which the parties have bargained would apply fully. Nonetheless, we should remember that these respondents were not asked to contextualize their negotiation deals as to whether one or the other choice was made in accordance with the other side's jurisdiction or whether they had included an arbitration agreement.[260] Likewise, the Survey has not intended to map out the respondents' experience within a given period (5 or 10 years for example), which could have elicited different views.

What then is the message the Survey participants have intended to deliver?

---

258 These variables are further explored in *infra* Chapter 2.

259 See reasons of CISG opt-outs *supra* Section 1.2.4.5.

260 See Survey instructions *supra* Section 1.2.3.

Firstly, this coincidence of causes shows, on the one hand, that there are some set standards by which the respondents approach the choice-of-law decision; *i.e.* there are given features and attributes that rank high in their order of preference and which the respondents would look for when deciding on governing contract law. On the other hand, this coincidence of causes revealed that, while certain rational elements were present, the approach to choice-of-law decisions is also influenced by non-rational factors, which may have led Survey participants to choose less than the best available option at the negotiation table: the high rates of exclusion under 'lawyer's strategy' may indicate as much. Reasons like 'case by case basis' and 'client's request' may also endorse this view.

While the analysis of avoidance of certain national law does not reveal specific trends, the data collected allow us to conclude that the CISG has progressed on certain fronts of common criticism: 'lack of case law', for example, was cited by 9%, and 'unfamiliarity', 11%.[261] Whilst these factors are of great importance, the rates are not alarming and attest to a gradually improving awareness of the existence and provisions of the CISG.

On the flip side, opt-out reasons such as 'predictability /legal certainty' (15%) and 'substantive design' (20%) are matters that still need further reflection and may be seen as the 'Gordian tie' of the CISG, inasmuch as they raise a red flag in connection with the degree of attractiveness of the CISG and its resulting popularity and use. However, by way of reminder, we should not disregard the possibility that the comments in these categories could also have been blurred by non-rational elements, thereby obscuring the real causes of and factors informing the respondents' opting out of the CISG.

All in all, the factors that guide the parties' choices appear to be disclosed in the Survey results, although their true meaning and extension are not entirely clear, drafters of international sales contracts seek a legal framework that provides freedom of contract and flexibility to design the duties, rights and obligations of parties to a contract. They also look for an ascertainable and intelligible legal framework that facilitates the transactions. Neutrality[262] and international character[263] were indicated as features most desired in governing contract law for a significant number of the respondents.

The respondents also demonstrated a tendency to jointly analyze the law applicable, jurisdiction (state courts or private adjudication) and enforcement[264] mechanisms (the

261 L. Spagnolo reported that lawyer unfamiliarity with the CISG also seems to vary depending on jurisdiction: from around 44% in the US, to much lower rate in Germany, Austria, and in Switzerland, where it was reported that less than 2% of lawyers were unaware of the CISG. See L. Spagnolo, *supra* note 118, pp. 152-153.

262 Survey Question 7, *supra* Section 1.2.4.3, neutrality was selected by 42.29% of the respondents.

263 Survey Question 7, *supra* Section 1.2.4.3, international character was selected by 42.29% of the respondents.

264 Douglass C. North notes that the costs of enforcing contractual arrangements are part of the total costliness of measuring valued attributed in the exchange process. The author also remakes that "[...]It is costly to measure performance and people's behavior and therefore performance can be influenced by their conviction about the fairness or justice of contracts", D. C. North, *supra* note 181, p. 10.

threshold predictability, cost and time), in order to anticipate the risks and legal measures to be taken in the course of a potential litigation.[265]

The respondents also cited choice of forum, including its adequacy and predictability, as an important consideration in their negotiation and decision-making process. The additional comments provided by the respondents suggest a fear of unwanted results, inefficient coercive mechanisms and biased decisions of state courts.[266] Arbitration was cited as a dispute resolution method that would minimize concerns of predictability of the application of rules, award made and enforcement.[267] Links between the choice of forum (courts or arbitration) have been identified from the Survey and will be further explored in this book.[268]

Emphasis was added with respect to specific provisions of a governing law, and the relevant choice varied according to the parties' position in the transaction. Additionally, experience – positive or negative – with the counterparty and the law chosen were also indicated as factors that influence a party's choice-of-law decision. We have seen that non-rational factors, for better or for worse, are likely to play a role in the choice of governing contract law. Whilst one may think that these elements are part of the decision-making processes, we shall discuss how to identify and control these factors to the party's best interest in the transaction.[269]

Some readers may be surprised at some of the Survey outcomes, which revealed incongruities between theory and practice – that is, a mismatch between parties' wishes and parties' actual choices. As a matter of fact, in contract negotiations, parties may frequently choose governing contract law in light of prior dealings, positive and negative experience of the trading partner and/or transaction.[270] Parties in the choice-of-law process may also use deductive reasoning. However, we should not overlook the fact that individual preferences are highly idiosyncratic and subject to subliminal influences, leading to scenarios where the choices taken are not always rational. For example, some parties might just choose to follow in another parties' decision-making footsteps;[271] others might be completely unaware of, uninterested or not sufficiently sophisticated to appreciate the importance of governing contract law, either because they were not instructed by lawyers or due to the lawyers' misbehaviour, which could raise issues of malpractice.[272]

265 L. G. Meira Moser, *supra* note 3, p. 33.

266 *Id.*. Survey Question 1 (Section 1.2.4.1); Survey Question 2 (Section 1.2.4.1); Survey Question 3 (Section 1.2.4.1); Survey Question 4 (Section 1.2.4.2); Survey Question 5 (Section 1.2.4.2); Survey Question 6 (Section 1.2.4.2); and Survey Question 7 (Section 1.2.4.3).

267 See, *e.g.*, Survey Question 1 (Section 1.2.4.1); Survey Question 2 (Section 1.2.4.1); Survey Question 3 (Section 1.2.4.1); Survey Question 4 (Section 1.2.4.2).

268 See, in this sense, *infra* Chapter 4.

269 See, in this sense, *infra* Chapter 2.

270 L. G. Meira Moser, *supra* note 3, p. 54.

271 *Id.*

272 See *supra* notes 170 and 172.

Accordingly, in some instances, we may not always know the reasons for parties' choices: the underlying motive could be momentary gain or need, affective valences,[273] instincts, or other suggestible factors. Awareness of the factors that influence decision-making choices, rational or otherwise, may assist contracting parties in taking advanced precautions and implementing strategies in an attempt to obtain mutual benefit from the transaction.[274] And this is precisely what we intend to develop in the following chapters: firstly, learn and appreciate the wide array of parties' wishes and the factors that influence decision-making processes; secondly, elaborate and discuss the various ways of attaining better results by filtering unwanted cognitive traps and errors, in addition to focusing on contract rationality and how to get the best of the deal by choosing the most suitable governing contract law.

It is safe to say that the Survey was one of the first of its kind to use various approaches to reveal decision-making processes. In so doing the Survey, which encompassed a large number of jurisdictions, disclosed key elements of contracting parties' discussion at the bargaining table. However, there is certainly room for improvement for a future edition of the Survey, in particular the method and respondent profile, *e.g.* giving greater clarity to the type of profile sought (in-house counsel, practitioners, academics or decision-makers), degree of experience, period of contract surveyed, enlarging representativeness of jurisdictions, offering respondents an opportunity to propose amendments and therefore providing readers with a well-rounded tool for assessing parties' preferences in cross-border sales.

To conclude, the Survey results were also instrumental in triggering further areas of study relating to the decision-making processes, including, but not limited to, the various additional-legal (or otherwise) factors that influence choice-of-law decisions and which will be further explored in this book.

1.3 Comparative Analysis

1.3.1 Summary of the Findings

Previous studies and surveys have certainly been helpful in consolidating the position of arbitration as the preferred dispute-resolution forum worldwide. They were instrumental in revealing the advantages of arbitration over state court proceedings. The studies have also indicated preferences and general reasons for choice of law to govern their transactions. Familiarity, 'home turf', 'fear of the unknown', and 'resemblance' to their own law are the main reasons for which parties choose governing contract law.

273 M. I. Fraidin, *supra* note 182, p. 921, noting that a choice among options is sometimes rooted in whether one option generates in us more welcome emotions.

274 L. G. Meira Moser, *supra* note 3, p. 54.

Inclinations regarding certain law and interplay with the forum were also acknowledged by respondents, in the sense that respondents understand that the forum play a certain role in this choice. In this regard, responses such as 'neutrality',[275] 'political and economic stability'[276] in the relevant jurisdiction and 'reliable court system'[277] support this statement. Preferred governing contract law was revealed and ranked by these previous studies.[278]

Previous surveys indicated that choice-of-law decisions were mostly driven by parties' familiarity with the chosen legal regimes – with a preference in respondents for their home law and forum – and neutrality of the law.[279] These studies are recognized as pioneering in relation to a party's main concerns in a choice-of-law and forum decision. However, we should interpret the results obtained in these previous surveys and studies with caution and realism.

This caveat is important because the scope of most of the studies mentioned above had a limited sample – of countries or regions – or were restricted to specific contract types or even data provided by a single arbitral institution. The author believes that the previous studies are not sufficient to draw generalizations around the topic of choice of law nor do they allow for a further analysis of the decision-making processes in cross-border transactions, for three main reasons. Firstly, as mentioned earlier, the scope of these studies was mostly confined to regions and specific contract types. For example, some of the studies focused exclusively on CISG opt-outs rather than the reasons for such behaviour or alternatives to change this scenario. Secondly, the focus of the questions in the earlier surveys was rather general and primarily driven by statistics. Thirdly, the surveys did not appear to be dedicated to the particulars of the law chosen, but rather to general tendencies regarding the choice of law.

The internal and external factors that prompted the respondents' choices in the earlier surveys remain unknown. The parties' main concerns were unexplored and likewise the alternatives for contracting parties to improve their decisions were not discussed. As no such data were made available in the earlier surveys, contracting parties might have been repeating the same mistakes. Indeed, as noted above, previous efforts undertaken were primarily focused on statistics and general preferences and not on the underlying causes. This failed to identify common errors in respondents' decision-making processes and therefore mechanisms to improve these processes.

---

275 See, *e.g.*, Survey Question 1 (Section 1.2.4.1); Cuniberti' 2013 study on most attractive laws (Section 1.1.2); and 2010 Queen Mary Survey (Section 1.1.2).

276 Survey Question 4 *supra* Section 1.2.4.2.

277 See *supra* note 266.

278 See, *e.g, supra* Section 1.1.2: The 2005 Oxford Institute of European and Comparative Law in partnership with Clifford Chance; S. Voigt's 2008 study; the 2008 Oxford Civil Justice Survey, jointly conducted by the Oxford Institute of European and Comparative Law and the Oxford Center for Socio-Legal Studies; the 2010 the Law Society of England and Wales conducted telephone interviews; the 2010 Queen Mary Survey; and Cuniberti's 2013 study on most attractive laws.

279 S. Vogenauer, *supra* note 17, pp. 39-60.

1.3.2 Weighting of Practical and Legal Considerations and the 'Black Box'

Despite the acknowledged importance of previous studies, setting the scene and fostering further research, there was seemingly a gap in the study of contracting parties' decision-making processes: the available data seemed unable to shed light onto the particulars behind the choice-of-law decision – the main features and standards of a governing law remained unmapped, and possible interplay with a law's substantive design and choice of forum concerns were uncharted. Moreover, considerations from an economic standpoint were not investigated. Above all, it seemed that previous studies did not ask 'how and why' contracting parties opt for one law over another or why parties exclude certain laws.

The Survey has the merit of bringing an interdisciplinary approach: 'flavours' of law, economics and psychology were part of the 'recipe' of this Survey, all in an attempt to investigate and reveal, to the furthest extent possible, the multiple driving forces that guide a party's choice. The Survey did not limit its boundaries to 'reveal' only the driving forces. The aims were two-fold and we also sought to analyze these driving forces in order to assist readers to think 'out of the box' in international contexts.

The Survey stands out because it reveals mechanisms to improve the efficiency of contracting parties' decisions. This is in contrast to earlier studies, which have been more statistic-driven. By unveiling legal and economic concerns, influenced by psychological factors, the Survey enhances contracting parties' knowledge of the 'rules of the game' in a negotiation context. This allows parties to identify and quantify the controllable factors and, subsequently, tackle, better manage, and minimize the effects of less controllable factors. All of this will result in parties' making more efficient decisions.

In addition to its pragmatic value, the Survey hopefully and to an extent, successfully addresses the main legal and economic considerations of parties negotiating the governing contract law of cross-border sales. It therefore aims to serve as a practical toolkit for parties to an agreement, party advisors, decision-makers, legal practitioners and other interested individuals, to better understand the mechanics behind the choice of governing contract law.

The Survey also provides insight into the cost-benefit analysis exercised by those involved in cross-border sales, including negotiation tactics and strategic behaviour at the bargaining table of the governing contract law in cross-border sales. Finally, the Survey aims further to reveal the presence of heuristics and cognitive biases in the choice of law of cross-border sales.[280] By exposing possible 'cognitive flaws' in decision-making processes, it offers readers alternatives to improve their choice.

In the subsequent chapters, supported by evidence, we shall reveal the common psychological triggers that influence the decision-making processes, non-rational factors that routinely influence the way parties approach this topic and the resulting consequences of

280 This topic will be discussed in detail in *supra* Chapter 2.

their choices. From this, there will be a discussion on how to identify and better control these common psychological triggers in a party's best interest and map out market costs and risks to which parties are (consciously or not) routinely exposed. We shall furthermore shed light on the idiosyncratic contract design and the mechanisms to manage this properly in an international context in an attempt to make better decisions and obtain more efficient outcomes. Finally, we shall present alternatives to escape the 'arm-wrestling' in cross-border sales and test their effectiveness, aiming to equip legal practitioners will additional tools in facilitating transactions worldwide.

We have seen thus far that parties to a contract have legal and economic preferences and inclinations to certain aspects of governing contract law and are likely to choose one law instead of another for myriad of reasons. However, as mentioned, the questions we seek to answer in this book are why parties decide the way they do; what are the main triggers and how much rational effort is put into the process of deciding on governing contract law. In addressing these questions we also aim to find out how much of this choice is based on feelings or emotion.

This topic, by critically discussing empirical studies of choice of law, will hopefully cement the structure of the next chapters, allowing readers to better understand the processes underneath the decision-making process while appreciating the theoretical flavours of the contract actors and the market, their interaction and the best options available for the maximization of gains. In the next chapter we shall therefore explore the fascinating and yet unexplored world of 'contracting parties' minds'.

2 The Unexplored World of Contracting Parties' Minds

As we have argued at the outset, academics have dedicated a substantial amount of time in a bid to explain choice of law, including the decisions that lead to a governing contract law, or in some cases to multiple laws.

However, few legal sources have been able to identify and reveal in empirical terms parties' choices and preferences in cross-border contracts. The factors and underlying motives that trigger certain decisions are often unavailable to market players and laymen in general. Therefore a few practical questions are routinely left unanswered: how do contracting parties make decisions in real-world environments? What determines key contractual choices such as the governing contract law of a cross-border sale? Is it part of a rational process or primarily intuitive-based? How much weight is attributed to rationality and how much to intuition and why? Can we control these variables? Can we improve this choice?[1]

To answer these questions, in the first chapter of this section readers are invited to consider a theoretical discussion on rational and intuitive decision-making processes. In the second and final chapter we highlight the results of the Survey[2] in another light. As discussed earlier, the Survey encompassed a large spectrum of questions,[3] so the final chapter of this section will focus on the results pertinent to the topic of this discourse: 'decision-making processes'.

We shall argue that decision-making processes are routinely influenced by cognitive biases or errors in estimations or odds, leading to irrationalities and scenarios in which the contracting parties may simply 'pass over' the better deal. We further argue that emotions may cloud better decisions in the business context.

Accordingly, by revealing contracting parties' inabilities to estimate odds and values we shed light on possible techniques to improve the rationality of these decisions and obtain more worthwhile results from the transaction. We also attempt to uncover methods to assist in identifying situations where we know parties may lean towards cognitive shortcuts, intervene in such circumstances and possibly influence or even change behaviour and outcome.

---

1 A similar analysis of the Survey was first published in L. G. Meira Moser, 'Inside Contracting Parties' Minds: The Decision-making Processes in Cross-border Sales', *Journal of International Dispute Settlement*, Vol. 8, Issue 2, 2017, pp. 250-279.

2 See more of the Survey in *supra* Section 1.2.

3 L. G. Meira Moser, *supra* note 3 in Chapter 1.

2.1 Rational Choices

Daniel Kahneman, a psychologist and 2002 Nobel prize winner in Economic Sciences, distinguishes between two systems in the mind for decision-making: System 1 – the subconscious, which operates quickly and efficiently; and System 2 – conscious and directed thought, which nevertheless operates in a rather slow and inefficient fashion. System 1 originates the impressions and feelings that serve as the main source of the beliefs and choices articulated by System 2.

Kahneman continues: "System 1 excels at constructing the best possible story that incorporates ideas currently activated, but it does not (cannot) allow for information it does not have. The measure of success for System 1 is the coherence of the story it manages to create. The amount and quality of the data on which the story is based are largely irrelevant... The combination of a coherence-seeking System 1 with a lazy System 2 implies that System 2 will endorse many intuitive beliefs, which closely reflect the impressions generated by System 1".[4]

In this section we shall focus on Kahneman's System 2, *i.e.*, the deliberative and effortful system that executes rational choices. Through a rational perspective individuals make decisions using a compensatory strategy. They identify and evaluate all available options, assess and weigh all of the relevant attributes of each option, and then select the option they evaluate most favourably.[5]

In this regard, decision-makers would assess and compare all available possibilities and decide on those that maximize their welfare. This is because rationality is expressed as internal coherence and logical consistency within a system of beliefs and preferences.[6] Richard Posner defined rationality in a fairly simple way: 'rationality is choosing the best means to the chooser's ends'.[7] Naturally, this process requires actors to infer facts by applying principles of deductive logic to all known and relevant information. A rational choice entails internal coherence; beliefs and choices must make sense and be logically connected.

Tversky & Kahneman assert that decision-making under risk follows an expected utility model. This model is based on a set of axioms (*e.g.* transitivity of preferences) which provide(s) the criteria for the rationality of choices. The choices of an individual who conforms to the axioms can be described in terms of the utilities of various outcomes

4 D. Kahneman, *Thinking, F., & Slow*, Straus and Giroux, New York, NY, 2011, pp. 85-86.

5 C. Guthrie, *supra* note 179 in Chapter 1, p. 427.

6 B. A. Mellers, A. Schwartz & A. D. J. Cooke, 'Judgment and Decision Making', *Annual Review of Psychology*, Vol. 49, 1998, pp. 449-450. In this connection, see also A. Tversky & D. Kahneman, for whom "The common conception of rationality also requires that preferences or utilities for particular outcomes should be predictive of the experiences of satisfaction or displeasure associated with their occurrences..." A. Tversky & D. Kahneman, *supra* note 31 in Chapter 1, p. 458.

7 R. A. Posner, 'Rational Choice, Behavioral Economics, and the Law', *Stanford Law Review*, Vol. 50, 1998, p. 1551.

for that individual. The utility of a risk prospect is equal to the expected utility of its outcomes, obtained by weighing the utility of each possible outcome by its probability. When faced with a choice a rational decision-maker will prefer the prospect that offers the highest expected utility.[8]

2.1.1 *Compensatory Strategy and Maximization of Benefits*

In light of the above theoretical discussion, it follows that in choosing a governing contract law parties would process all available information, make choices, and execute behaviour(s) in a way that is calculated to maximize their expected utility, *i.e.*, maximize the differential between expected benefits and expected costs.[9] In other words, contracting parties make decisions utilizing a cost-benefit analysis to achieve Pareto-efficient results.[10] A scenario is considered Pareto-efficient if it is impossible to change it so as to make at least one person better off (in their own estimation) without making another worse off (again, in their own estimation).[11] The idea is that both parties enjoy mutual benefits from the transaction.

As a practical example, imagine a scenario in which the sales contract – time being of the essence – states that the seller should deliver the goods on day X, receiving Y as payment. An alternative contract states that if the seller delivers the goods one day before day X, he would receive as payment Y+. In theory the latter contract would be mutually beneficial: as time is of the essence, earlier arrival of the goods would benefit the buyer and the seller would enjoy a higher payment.

2.1.2 *Deductive Logic and Cognitive Limitations*

As mentioned, traders are rational and self-interested players in the market so they will typically behave in a way that maximizes their welfare. Therefore, when faced with a list of options, contracting parties would, using the device of deductive logic, identify and select the options which possess attributes[12] to produce the best or most efficient results,

---

8 A. Tversky & D. Kahneman, *supra* note 6, p. 453.

9 R. B. Korobkin, *supra* note 180 in Chapter 1, available at [https://ssrn.com/abstract=496462].

10 See R. Cooter & T. Ulen, *supra* note 1 in Introduction, p. 44. In addition, see B. E. Hermalin, A. W. Katz & R. Craswell, 'The Law and Economics of Contracts', *in* A. M. Polinsky & S. Shavell (Eds.), *Handbook of Law and Economics*, Elsevier, New York, 2007, p. 16 (noting that as a welfare criterion, Pareto-efficiency evaluates a proposed allocation among a set of actors by asking whether there exists a second allocation that (i) none of the actors prefer less than the proposed allocation and (ii) at least one of the actors actually prefers to the proposed allocation. If no such second allocation exists, the proposed allocation is deemed efficient).

11 R. Cooter & T. Ulen, *supra* note 1 in Introduction, p. 44.

12 However, as D. C. North advises "To the degree that any valued attribute is too costly to be able to measure perfectly then, we have some dissipation of income as a result of a failure to be able to measure it", *supra* note 181 in Chapter 1, p. 9.

i.e. generate the maximum profit. To execute this action they would make accurate and logical inferences from the available information.

However, assessment and comparison of all available options would only be possible with an extraordinary amount of energy and time. This may be unattainable in certain decision-making settings, in addition to a human being's limited computational skills.[13] Accordingly, in these scenarios it would seemingly be inappropriate for decisions to be made under Kahneman's System 2, where the mind is slower, rule-based, analytic and controlled and where reason dominates. Decisions made under System 2 demand a level of cognitive capacity that may not be available in certain contexts, such as decisions concerning a governing contract law.

Therefore, when deciding on the governing contract law, parties likely seldom evaluate the intricacies of a certain law. Instead they may simply follow what others, when confronted with the same situation, have decided to do. This might explain why certain laws may be selected in accordance with political neutrality, *e.g.* Swiss law.[14]

The underlying reasoning may also be understood through the work of Korobkin, who states "…individuals are understood not as ruthless optimizers, but as boundedly rational human beings who have a limited supply of cognitive energy and attention and rely on a cacophony of heuristic cues".[15] In the same line of thought, Zajonc synthetizes: "We sometimes delude ourselves that we proceed in a rational manner and weigh all the pros and cons of the various alternatives. But this is probably seldom the case. Most of the time, information collected about alternatives serves us less for making a decision than for justifying it afterward."[16]

These cognitive limitations are due to our 'bounded rationality', a concept first introduced by Herbert Simon.[17] This refers to the fact that our cognitive abilities are not infinite. As mentioned, Kahneman distinguished between two systems in the mind for decision-making. The above has been focused on System 2, which deals with conscious and directed thought. Kahneman states that the difference in effort provides the most useful indicator of whether a given mental process should be assigned to System 1 or 2.

---

13 J. A. Maule & G. P. Hodgkinson, *supra* note 29 in Chapter 1, p. 68. See also M. I. Fraidin, referring to heuristic decision-making as 'inductive, speedy, and instinctive, and requires minimal effort', *supra* note 182 in Chapter 1, p. 919. For a deeper analysis of cognitive limitations, see also B. E. Hermalin, A. W. Katz & R. Craswell, *supra* note 10, p. 70, arguing that 'the simplest "model" of bounded rationality is that people make mistakes. They fail to foresee all possible contingencies and, thus, their contracts suffer from unforeseen contingencies'.

14 See empirical efforts in connection with choice of law in cross-border contracts: S. Voigt, *supra* note 62 in Chapter 1; S. Vogenauer, *supra* note 63 in Chapter 1.

15 R. Korobkin, 'What Comes After Victory for Behavioral Law End Economics', *University of Illinois Law Review*, No. 5, 2011, p. 1660.

16 R. B. Zajonc, 'Feeling and Thinking: Preferences Need No Inferences', *American psychologist*, Vol. 35, Issue 2, 1980, p. 155. See also J. Plamper, *The History of Emotions: An Introduction*. Oxford University Press, Oxford, 2015.

17 H. A. Simon, 'A Behavioral Model of Rational Choice', *Quarterly Journal of Economics*, Vol. 69, 1955, pp. 99-118.

Hence, in situations where there are time, financial and energy constraints, such as in decisions involving a governing contract law, a decision may have to be taken under System 1, although it may not be a conscious decision on the part of the contracting party.

Kahneman explains that this is because "we respond to the world in ways that we're not conscious of, that we don't control. The operations of System 1 are fast, effortless, associative, and often emotionally charged; they're also governed by habit, so they're difficult either to modify or to control".[18] System 1 has learned associations between ideas (*e.g.* an individual's associating Swiss law with a good choice in governing contract law because a colleague had a recent successful experience in a case where Swiss law was applied, or associating English law in a governing contract law as being efficient because of numerous published reports about the efficiency of English courts); it has also learned skills such as reading and understanding nuances of social situations. This knowledge is stored in memory and accessed without intention or effort. In our example above, the association of Swiss law with success equals not the idea of success.

As mentioned earlier, mental actions that are governed by System 1 are completely involuntary; *e.g.*, the same individual's thus concluding without further thought in a governing contract law decision that English courts are efficient. System 1 is fast and efficient, but Kahneman postulates that it is unable to estimate the values and probabilities associated with each available option. Therefore, to run System 1 and execute decisions in a timely fashion we rely on intuition.[19]

2.2 INTUITION

Under an intuitive decision-making process[20] individuals use mental shortcuts to make decisions when faced with limited data. In such a scenario the decision would be taken relying on their success or failure in a real-world environment and not according to logical and/or mathematical rules.[21] It is a simplified cognitive process of making decisions in light of uncertainties.

---

18 Interview available at [www.strategy-business.com/article/03409?gko=7a903].

19 R. Korobkin & C. Guthrie, *supra* note 30 in Chapter 1, p. 798.

20 *Id.* In this connection, *see* also M. I. Fraidin, *supra* note 182 in Chapter 1, noting that "[...] heuristics devices include 'availability' and 'representativeness', among other 'mental shortcuts' [...] The availability heuristic allows a decision-maker to reach a decision by immediate, reflexive reference to a different situation that comes readily to mind [...] The 'representativeness' heuristic similarly reflects a decision-maker's substitution of one item for another. A decision-maker who relies on the representativeness heuristic assesses a probability 'by the degree to which A is representative of B, that is, by the degree to which A resembles B' [...] 'Affect' or the good or bad feelings generated by a person or event, is another heuristic that sometimes drives decision-making". (pp. 919-920).

21 For further discussion on heuristics and choice of law processes, *see* L. Spagnolo, 'Green Eggs and Ham', *supra* note 124 in Chapter 1 and L. Spagnolo, *supra* note 118 in Chapter 1. For a study about heuristics and international arbitration, see L. Reed, 'The 2013 Hong Kong International Arbitration Centre Kaplan Lec-

Heuristics are channels through which intuition flows freely. One of the advantages of using these channels, or mental shortcuts, is that they take less time to decide than with conventional processing. Accordingly, it is particularly appropriate in time-pressure situations.[22]

For example, in a business context where traders operate under pressure, deadlines and busy schedules, the choice of governing contract law may be deferred to the last phase of negotiation. This choice is not infrequently – yet equivocally – treated as the 'last minute' clause, being the final 'detail' in the design of the contract.

2.2.1 Heuristics

Heuristics may be defined as mental shortcuts that the mind uses in decision-making processes. Tversky & Kahneman identified common heuristic mechanisms that we rely on to make decisions: 'availability' and 'representativeness'. Other studies have also identified mental shortcuts that trigger decisions in a similar manner, such as 'reliance of the affect', or 'feelings generated in the decision-maker by the person or argument'.[23]

With respect to the mechanics of these shortcuts, Kahneman argues that the central concept of intuitive judgments and preferences is accessibility – the ease (or effort) with which particular mental content comes to our minds. Kahneman further explains that the accessibility of a thought is determined jointly by the characteristics of the cognitive mechanisms that produce it and by the characteristics of the stimuli and events that evoke it.[24]

---

ture – Arbitral Decision-Making: Art, Science or Sport?', *Journal of International Arbitration*, Vol. 30, Issue 2, 2013, pp. 85-99. In the same vein, although shifting the focus to law and economics aspects, Thomas Schultz identifies extra-legal factors that are likely to influence arbitral decision-making. See more in T. Schultz, 'Arbitral Decision-Making: Legal Realism and Law & Economics', *Journal of International Dispute Settlement*, Vol. 6, Issue 2, 2015, pp. 231-151. Finally, discussing behavioral approach(es) to arbitral decision-making, see S. Brekoulakis, 'Systemic Bias and the Institution of International Arbitration: A New Approach to Arbitral Decision-Making', *Journal of International Dispute Settlement*, Vol. 4, Issue 3, 2013, pp. 553-585.

22 J. A. Maule & G. P. Hodgkinson, *supra* note 30 in Chapter 1, p. 70. In this connection see also K. Hall, 'Why Good Intentions are Often Not Enough: The Potential for Ethical Blindness in Legal Decision-Making (November 4, 2009)', *in* R. Mortensen, et al. (Eds.), *Alternative Perspectives on Lawyers and Legal Ethics: Reimagining the Profession*, Routledge, London, 2010, available at [http://ssrn.com/abstract=1500137], where it is argued that, "in the context of developing models of the ways in which people comprehend language, process information, utilize memory, develop judgments, make decisions and evaluate behavior, it has become increasingly clear that large parts of these mental processes occur outside of the view of the individuals involved" (p. 3).

23 M. I. Fraidin, *supra* note 182 in Chapter 1, p. 919.

24 D. Kahneman, 'A Perspective on Judgment and Choice: Mapping Bounded Rationality', *American Psychologist*, Vol. 58, Issue 9, 2003, p. 699.

It is arguable that the different (substantive) aspects of, or impressions of a certain governing contract law, as well as their attributes, can be explained through their accessibility. Moreover, the determinants of accessibility subsume the notions of stimulus salience, selective attention, specific training, associative activation, and priming.[25]

Below is a non-exhaustive list of relevant heuristics:[26]

Representativeness heuristic: representativeness involves judging the likelihood of an event according to the similarity of that event to other occurrences.

Anchoring-and-adjustment heuristic: we evaluate a problem by starting from an initial reference point – often one suggested to us – but we then make insufficient adjustments from it. Anchoring-and-adjustment refers to a tendency for judgments to be biased towards an initial value arrived at from partial or no computation.

Availability heuristic: decision-making is often based on what is most easily remembered at a given moment. It refers to the way in which probability or frequency judgments are influenced by the ease with which past examples are recalled.

Reliance on heuristics routinely produces cognitive biases, which lead individuals to reality distortions. Therefore individuals will make assumptions and generalize on topics in accordance with misrepresented facts and data. Some of these biases are reproduced below:

Framing effect: differences in the way a question is posed may generate very different answers. Tversky & Kahneman argue that we use the term 'decision frame' to refer to the decision-maker's conception of the acts, outcomes and contingencies associated with a particular choice. The frame that a decision-maker adopts is controlled partly by the formulation of the problem and partly by the norms, habits and personal characteristics of the decision-maker.[27]

Halo effect: once a good or bad impression is formed, that impression is often extended more generally and exaggerated.[28]

'Status quo' bias: individuals will tend to prefer an option consistent with the current state of affairs.[29]

Having briefly presented the above non-exhaustive list of heuristics, it is worth mentioning that they are influenced by real-life experience, shaped to a great extent by affect.

---

25 *Id.*

26 A. Tversky & D. Kahneman, *supra* note 32 in Chapter 1. See also J. A. Maule & G. P. Hodgkinson, *supra* note 29 in Chapter 1, p. 69. Three heuristics of judgment, labeled representatives, availability and anchoring were described in the 1974 review, along with a dozen systematic biases, including non-regressive prediction, neglect of base-rate information, overconfidence, and overestimates of the frequency of events that are easy to recall. Some of the biases were identified by systematic errors in estimates of known quantities and statistical facts. Other biases were identified by systematic discrepancies between the regularities of intuitive judgments and the principles of probability theory, Bayesian inference, or regression analysis. See D. Kahneman, *supra* note 24, p. 710.

27 A. Tversky & D. Kahneman, *supra* note 6, p. 453.

28 J. A. Maule & G. P. Hodgkinson, *supra* note 29 in Chapter 1, p. 69.

29 R. Korobkin & C. Guthrie, *supra* note 30 in Chapter 1, p. 805.

2.2.2 *Affect*

Preferences are not created in a vacuum: they depend on the stimulus context. This context might include the environment or local context. It might also include a larger context based on the decision-maker's past and present experience.[30]

The mechanics of heuristics demonstrate that we are influenced by (past) experience and by our attempts to modify present situations. Individuals are likely to make judgments concerning existing facts and future probabilities in ways that confirm pre-existing belief structures.[31]

However, perception is selective and memory is subject to external variables; therefore, the results typically attributed to certain alternatives might be wrongly assessed.[32] This is so because decisions are generally made without full knowledge of their consequences. Additionally, decisions taken in uncertainty call for the evaluation of two attributes: the desirability of the possible outcomes and their likelihood of occurrence.[33]

In this regard, contracting parties may have sympathies, antipathies and sensitiveness towards or better disposal of a particular law. Included in this 'weighing scale' are likes, dislikes, predilections and prejudices, preferences, attitudes, impressions, external appearances and inward feelings. All of these are important gauges of contracting parties' perceptions. Certainly, many of these perceptions are a result of experience of success or failure.

In a discussion concerning decision-making processes, affective reactions play a key role. This is because overall preferences are not simply a matter of calculating the combination of weighted component preferences. Attitudes consist of information units that have affect or utilities attached to them.[34] According to prevalent models of affect, an

30 K. Hall, *supra* note 22, arguing that "because we are not able to consult a memory of our decision making processes, we unconsciously draw upon theories that are based on cultural or sub-cultural explanations of events, experience and observation to explain our actions" (p. 5). For a discussion around cultural aspects, see V. Gessner, *supra* note 22 in Chapter 1.

31 R. Korobkin & C. Guthrie, *supra* note 30 in Chapter 1, p. 800, arguing that 'this tendency will often result in judgments compromised by what is called the "self-serving" or "egocentric" bias'.

32 Cooter et al. further discuss another bias, called false consensus effect, which happens when "an individual who projects his own behavior onto society overestimates how many others behave like he does. This bias is closely related to what the psychology literature calls the false consensus effect (FCE), which refers to a situation where people mistakenly think that others agree with them. According to the FCE, people tend to overestimate the social support of their own views and underestimate the social support for people who hold opposing views. Evidence suggests that social observers tend to form a false consensus with respect to the relative commonness of their own behavior. Several psychological mechanisms could cause just-like-me bias. One such mechanism is cognitive: a person may attend to positions with which he agrees and dismiss positions with which he disagrees. Selective attention allows his preferred position to dominate his consciousness. People also tend to associate with others who share their general beliefs, attitudes, and values." R. D. Cooter, M. Feldman & Y. Feldman, 'The Misperception of Norms: The Psychology of Bias and the Economics of Equilibrium', *Review of Law & Economics*, Vol. 4, Issue 3, 2008, pp. 897-898.

33 A. Tversky & C. R. Fox, 'Weighing Risk and Uncertainty', *Psychological Review*, Vol. 102, Issue. 2, 1995, p. 269.

34 R. B. Zajonc, *supra* note 16, p. 158.

affective reaction such as liking, disliking, preferences, evaluations, or experience of pleasure or displeasure, is based on a prior cognitive process. In this process a variety of content discriminations are made and features identified, examined for their value, and weighted for their contribution. Once this analytic task has been completed a computation of the components can generate an overall affective judgment.[35]

In the same vein, before a contracting party can appreciate a certain governing law, that party must have some knowledge of this governing law and, at the very least, must have learned some of its distinctive traits. Hence these affective reactions, and the retrieval of affect, occur without effort. Affective reactions to a stimulus may be acquired by virtue of experience with that stimulus, even if the affective reactions are not accompanied by conscious recognition.[36]

Similarly, Kahneman argues that affective valence is a natural assessment and therefore a candidate for substitution in the numerous responses that express attitudes. The author further states that there is compelling evidence for the proposition that every stimulus evokes an affective evaluation, which is not always conscious.[37] 'Valence' is what psychology terms the degree of attraction or aversion that an individual feels towards a specific object or event.

In this connection positive feelings can promote variety-seeking behaviour, an overestimation of the likelihood of favourable events, and an underestimation of the likelihood of unfavourable events. On the other hand, negative affect can produce a narrowing of attention and a failure to search for new alternatives. Framing effects, stimulus contexts, environments and response modes can profoundly shape decisions and preferences can vary depending on each of these factors.[38]

As we have seen thus far, there is a clear interplay between affect and cognition. Images which are marked by positive and negative feelings guide judgments and decision-making processes. People use an affect heuristic to make judgments; that is, representations of objects and events in people's minds are tagged to varying degrees with affect.[39]

In psychology, 'salience' refers to the ease of recalling events that are vivid and recent. Psychologists have found that people tend to overestimate the probability of salient events and underestimate the probability of non-salient events.[40]

---

35 R. B. Zajonc, *supra* note 16, further argues that affective judgments may be fairly independent of and precede the sorts of perceptual and cognitive operations commonly assumed to be the basis of these affective judgments (p. 151).

36 R. B. Zajonc, *supra* note 16, p. 163.

37 D. Kahneman, *supra* note 24, p. 710. There have also been studies of risk perceptions in individual preference. One approach takes risk to be a multidimensional construct with dimensions labeled dread, lack of familiarity and lack of controllability; see in this regard B. A. Mellers, A. Schwartz & A. D. J. Cooke, *supra* note 6, p. 451.

38 B. A. Mellers, A. Schwartz & A. D. J. Cooke, *supra* note 6, pp. 454-455.

39 R. D. Cooter, M. Feldman & Y. Feldman, *supra* note 32, p. 896.

40 *Id.*

Additionally, in the process of making a judgment or decision, people consult or refer to an 'affect pool'[41] containing all the positive and negative tags consciously or unconsciously associated with the representations. Just as imaginability, memorability and similarity serve as cues for probability judgments (*e.g.* the availability and representativeness heuristics), affect may serve as a cue for many important judgments. Readily available affective impression can be far easier and more efficient than weighing up the pros and cons or retrieving from memory many relevant examples, especially when the required judgment or decision is complex or mental resources are limited.[42]

Individuals might also be influenced by the 'status quo' bias, whereby they will tend to prefer an option consistent with the current state of affairs.[43] This could also explain why contracting parties will likely keep a certain practice such as opting-out of certain laws or using standard contracts where governing contract laws are already defined without further consideration.[44]

2.2.3 The 'Ice Cream Flavour' Dilemma

The above theoretical analysis can be applied to parties' choices in a governing law using *ice cream* as an analogy.[45] Assuming an individual generally likes ice cream, a question that arises (for the reader) is whether they have ever thought about how someone chooses a particular ice-cream flavour over another? It could be the consistency, the colour, the calories, the nutrients or it may even be a part of a certain diet. Alternatively, an individual may choose a flavour because they have (or have not) chosen that particular flavour before, or they were taught to choose one over the others; a third party once recommended a particular flavour, or because the individual simply enjoyed that particular flavour the last time they had it. Perhaps one has absolutely no idea what the thought processes behind ice-cream flavour choices are at all.

Readers may be questioning at this point: what, and to what extent, does this analogy have to do with choices in international sales contracts? The answer (which is found in the discussion to follow) may be surprising.

41 P. Slovic *et al.*, 'The Affect Heuristic', *in* T. Gilovich, D. Griffin & Daniel Kahneman (Eds.), *Heuristics and Biases: The Psychology of Intuitive Judgment*, Cambridge University Press, Cambridge, 2002, pp. 400-401.

42 *Id.*

43 R. Korobkin & C. Guthrie, *supra* note 30 in Chapter 1, p. 805.

44 See, in relation to CISG exclusion. See L. Spagnolo, *supra* note 118 in Chapter 1, pp. 191-192.

45 This analogy was first used by the author on the occasion of his presentation at the 35-year celebratory conference of the CISG in Basel in 2015, '35 Years and Beyond'.

2.3 GLOBAL EMPIRICAL SURVEY ON CHOICE OF LAW

The Survey[46] aims to provide a complete diagnosis of parties' preferences in the international contract negotiation context. It focuses on a party's strategies and choices when they decided on and assessed the governing contract law in international sales. The Survey also takes into account the advanced precautions taken by parties, and the legal and economic considerations and concerns of contracting parties in these negotiations.

2.3.1 *Highlights of the Survey Results*

How are key contractual choices, such as the governing contract law of a cross-border sale, taken? What triggers this decision? Is it construed according to rational processes or is it based on intuition? How much weight is attributed to rationality and how much to intuition and why? How can we influence this choice? There does not appear to be a single answer to these questions. A few respondents' 'peculiarities' will be investigated in further detail below.

2.3.1.1 Rational Choices

The first observation lies in the method of the Survey.

In the Survey Questions in which the respondents were served with a well-structured and logical list of options, the results appeared to indicate that the respondents made their governing-law decisions in reliance on a compensatory strategy, *i.e.* respondents weighed the pros and cons and chose the responses that were able to (theoretically speaking) maximize their welfare in a transaction.

In this regard, there is evidence of an internally coherent, laborious and effortful decision by some of the respondents. In these circumstances, the respondents' beliefs and choices were logically connected, for example when they expressed their views on (un)attractive legal features of (a) governing contract law. As the three main attractive legal features,[47] the respondents indicated: commitment to freedom of contract (66.36%); remedies available (61.75%); and provisions on damages (40.55%). On the hand, as unattractive features,[48] the respondents indicated: mandatory provisions (55.51%); complexity of structure (50.66%); and limited coverage (32.60%). It seems plausible that Kahneman's System 2 played a role in these decision-making processes and rational decisions were taken, inasmuch as the respondents attempted consciously to choose the options that were able to maximize their welfare.

46 The Survey was first published in L. G. Meira Moser, *supra* note 3 in Chapter 1.

47 Survey Question n. 2 *supra* Section 1.2.4.1.

48 Survey Question n. 3 *supra* Section 1.2.4.1.

We have explained that System 1 is characterized by speed. It runs our lives due to its efficiency, but routinely presents errors in its execution. System 2 is slow and can be defined as an investment of attention and time because it is deliberative and effortful.

While it is not possible completely to discard the role of intuitive-based processes in (at least some of) these choices (as unconscious mental processes account for a significant majority of mental acts[49]), it is probably safe to say that the respondents, in cases where they were served with a well-structured and logical list of options, conducted a fairly rational analysis of the available list, evaluated the benefits and risks of the options and then chose the options that best suited their requirements.

This is corroborated by the logical inferences made by the respondents. For example, they expressed concerns as to a specific set of provisions of potential governing contract law as well as to the enforcement of both legal rules and decisions. This demonstrates that respondents underwent some sort of laborious effort in their decision-making processes by anticipating legal strategies and possible scenarios where certain provisions could serve their interests;. *e.g.* concerns about remedies available and provisions on damages (Responses to Survey Question 2[50]).

Some of the comments and additional answers provided by the respondents confirmed that traders are self-interested players who aim to maximize their benefits from a transaction. In order to illustrate this, we selected the following quotes:

- 'home turf' advantage where possible;
- depends on whether one is representing seller or buyer;
- too favourable to the counterparty;
- for a sale on credit basis, law of the buyer's jurisdiction;
- from seller's perspective: the more protective of the buyer, the more reason against;
- predictability of outcome coupled with law's recognition of freedom of parties to a contract;
- cost/convenience of resolving disputes; and
  enforceability of resulting judgment or award.

The quotes listed above seem to indicate that the respondents undertook mental work to indicate their main legal and economic considerations when choosing governing contract law. They thought strategically and set out their preferences in order to minimize risks and maximize gains from the transaction. It appears that the respondents used System 2 in their decision-making process.

49 K. Hall, *supra* note 22, p. 4.
50 Survey Question n. 2 *supra* Section 1.2.4.1.

2.3.1.2 Intuitive Responses

The last of the Survey Questions simply required a 'yes or no' and (optional) 'why' answer. In such situation, without the support of ready-made answers, the data collected would suggest that the respondents would have needed to rely more on their intuition in deciding on an appropriate answer, including tapping into their success or failure experience, or their 'gut feeling'.

A few incongruities are apparent between parties' preferences and actual choices – there appeared to be a distortion of preferences reflected in the respondent answers to the Survey Questions. These inconsistencies will be further explored. In addition, in the section below, we aim to demonstrate that extraneous factors can distort preferences. We shall then explore why contracting parties make certain decisions and then evaluate whether the choices they made were indeed efficient in light of the contracting parties' justification.

The following selected quotes extracted from the different Survey Questions will serve as a basis for a further investigation of the above matters:

- level of development of the proposed governing law;
- positive effects on the party who seeks advice;
- counsel's and client's favourable experience;
- similarity of chosen law to law of the client;
- it is considered a 'weak law';
- the limitations of the substantive law of many under-developed countries;
- substantive law not sufficiently developed to govern the main aspects of the contractual matters;
- law not developed within the energy sector;
- 'exotic' laws that we always advise against applying;
- undesirable solutions;
- clients do not like the CISG because people exclude it;
- no experience; and
- use of precedent contract that excluded CISG.

These quotes carry multiple meanings and will certainly be of assistance to readers who wish to understand decision-making processes.

As a preliminary comment, we contend that these quotes are the product of cognitive biases or errors in estimation or odds, leading to irrationalities. Consequently, in the scenarios contemplated by these quotes, the contracting parties may simply 'pass over' the better deal because of their cognitive biases. We further argue that emotions may cloud better decisions in the business context. Accordingly, the following analysis aims to provide readers with alternatives to tackle, control or minimize the effects of cognitive error in the choice of law of cross-border sales, as well as to influence and optimize these decisions.

For methodological purposes, we shall arrange the above quotes into groups and then analyze the drives and cognitive idiosyncrasies behind these choices, noting our theoretical discussions at the outset of this chapter.

2.3.1.2.1 (Pre)judgmental Followers

We shall call the first group the '(Pre)judgmental followers'.

The first group encompasses the following quotes: 'level of development of the proposed governing law', 'the limitations of the substantive law of many under-developed countries', 'substantive law not sufficiently developed to govern the main aspects of the contractual matters', 'law not developed in the energy sector', 'weak law' and 'exotic law'.

a Profile

This group comprises an array of quotes that contain (pre-) judgments, arguably related to the substantive design or specific features of governing contract law. In this group potential governing contract laws were labelled 'exotic', 'weak', and 'substantially limited'. But what do these adjectives mean in the legal sense? This may be the first question that comes to our minds.

Do they refer to laws that have not been sufficiently 'tested' or 'used', in general or in specific contexts? Or, rather, do they refer to laws that have not produced 'desirable' or 'efficient' results? In both cases, are they based on collective perceptions? How has this been measured or quantified by the respondents? For example, a respondent who analyzed a country's putative governing contract law in relation to a specific context stated 'law not developed within the energy sector' – it appears that this individual limited valuation of the law in terms of a specific industry.

In addition, it remains unclear whether these potentially governing contract laws were perceived as sales law provisions or in a more holistic sense. The Survey approach focused on the former but we cannot discard the possibility that (un)fortunate experience with a given law in other areas could influence the choice of governing contract law in cross-border sales.

Alternatively these quotes may somehow be linked to a law's 'predisposition', *i.e.* buyer or seller-friendly.[51] If so, it should be borne in mind that contracting parties play diverse roles in the course of an international sales contract. Therefore certain provisions originally seen as unfavourable might suddenly become appealing.

Stefan Vogenauer has asserted that neither party knows in advance whether it will be better off under one or another regime.[52] Gary Born advocates that the parties' efforts in bargaining over the application of a law that will be more advantageous is often chimeri-

51 See, in this sense, a discussion of this apparent contradiction as parties refer to the CISG as both 'buyer-' and 'seller-' friendly, *supra* notes 219 and 220 in Chapter 1.

52 S. Vogenauer, *supra* note 17 in Chapter 1, p. 21.

cal because of the difficulty in predicting in advance what issues will arise in some future dispute and on what side of these issues a party may be.[53]

Hence, in addition to the explanations offered above, it may be that these '(Pre)judgmental followers' quotes should also be understood in conjunction with the level of a country of origin's development.

It is likely that this first set of quotes appears to be the product of cognitive biases or errors. As such, the decisions that have been taken as a result of these cognitive biases may not be a choice that was anticipated by the respondents when they made their decision.

As discussed at the outset of this chapter, when choosing governing contract law, contracting parties sometimes consult their 'affect pool', where positive and negative tags or identifiers, consciously or unconsciously associated with certain options, reside. In this consultation with the 'affect pool', associative operations are readily made and the result is the valence attributed to the particular identifier. This operation can be far easier than weighing the pros and cons or retrieving experience from memory, especially when the decision is complex or mental resources are limited.[54]

However, as Kahneman warns, although every stimulus evokes an affective evaluation, this is not always conscious.[55] Therefore, in laborious contexts that require deliberative work from the decision-maker, such as choosing governing contract law, consultation of the 'affect pool' might lead to systematic evaluation errors.

In this regard, these specific '(Pre)judgmental followers' respondent quotes may have been driven by 'affective valences'.[56] In this case, this will be in relation to a certain governing contract law. This may explain, for example, the 37.35% of respondents who did not inform or disclose the relevant reasons for avoiding a particular national law.[57]

b Practical Notes

Importantly, from a practical point of view, is there a way to control or minimize the effects of a contracting party's reliance on this particular cognitive bias?

---

53 In this regard, see G. Born, *International Commercial Arbitration*, Kluwer Law International, Alphen aan den Rijn, 2014, p. 2645, noting that private parties want a stable substantive legal regime and a single, neutral procedural framework. Born elaborates further, explaining that these objectives are particularly important in international commercial matters, where differences between national law and procedures can be great, where the need for predictability and stability is particularly important and where the risk of arbitrary or discriminatory legislative or judicial action is especially acute. In the same vein, I. Schwenzer states that, by agreeing on arbitration many of the imponderables regarding choice of law and application of foreign law may be circumvented. See I. Schwenzer, *supra* note 195 in Chapter 1, p. 724.

54 P. Slovic *et al.*, *supra* note 41, pp. 400-401.

55 D. Kahneman, *supra* note 24, p. 710.

56 M. I. Fraidin, *supra* note 182 in Chapter 1, p. 921, noting that a choice among options is sometimes rooted in whether one option generates in us more welcome emotions.

57 For further information, please refer to Section 1.2.4.3.

The unpopularity of certain laws is seldom rationally explained. Studies suggest that a greater exposure to the law, combined with a broader access to the particulars of the law, might assist in answering this question. Zajonc explained in his seminal article that exposure may generate a 'liking feeling'.[58] The author advanced evidence where melodies presented five times were liked better than those the participants had never heard of before, even though the persons could not distinguish the former from the latter in terms of familiarity. Hence greater exposure to putative governing contract law may overcome a 'fear of the unknown'.[59]

One additional point should be raised regarding the popularity of certain laws connected with a politically neutral state. Christiana Fountoulakis argues that it is a popular fallacy[60] to designate the law of a politically neutral state to govern an international contract whose terms have been carefully drafted and negotiated under another law, perhaps in quite a different way from the law of the politically neutral state. Hence another way of minimizing the effects of this cognitive bias is further to investigate the underlying reasons for the opt-in or opt-out, as certain exclusions and negative tags associated with putative governing contract law might be the product of cognitive imperfection.

As a final remark, the presence of anchoring-and-adjustment heuristic in these quotes should not be overlooked. According to this heuristic device, we evaluate a choice by starting from an initial reference point – often suggested to us – but we then make insufficient adjustments from it. A mundane example of anchor can be found in restaurant menus, where pricy items are offered to make the others look reasonable.

In the case at hand, although we have limited data provided by these respondents, it is likely that contracting parties could have suggested other possible governing contract law at the negotiation table. The respondents may have evaluated the different law from an initial reference point – probably one or a set of certain laws – resulting in wrong or insufficient adjustment. These may have translated into the labels given to the above

58 R. B. Zajonc, *supra* note 16, p. 163.

59 In relation to this, please refer to *supra* Section 1.2.4.3, discussing this 'fear of unknown' and its interplay with CISG opt-outs.

60 C. Fountoulakis, *supra* note 195 in Chapter 1, p. 306 *et seq.* In this line of thought, Schwenzer and Hachem state that parties, 'by resorting to what they believe is a 'neutral law, often confuse political neutrality with suitability of the chosen law for international transactions'. According to the authors, 'if the parties choose such a third (neutral) law, they may be even worse off than if they had chosen one of their home laws. To begin with, they have to investigate this foreign law. Furthermore, the trouble and costs in proving it are even more burdensome.' I. Schwenzer & P. Hachem, *supra* note 220 in Chapter 1, p. 465. To illustrate that domestic sales law can be unpredictable and not suitable to international contracts, the authors give, as a way of example, Swiss Law: "First, if the seller does not deliver goods in conformity with the contract, the Swiss Supreme Court distinguishes between *peius* (inferior goods) and *aliud* (different goods). In case of the former, the buyer must give prompt notice to the seller (according to Article 201 of the Swiss Code of Obligations (CO)) to preserve any remedies for breach of contract with a one year limitation period (Art. 201 CO); in case of the latter, the buyer can demand performance for ten years after the conclusion of the contract regardless whether it gave notice of nonperformance or not. And it can be extremely difficult to predict where the line between *peius* and *aliud* will be drawn in a particular case" (p. 465).

quotes. This may be so because comparison frequently leads to inconsistencies, given the different variables at play, which are not always easily identifiable.

As an alternative, to tackle or better control this bias, a two-fold approach may assist. Firstly, it is important to remind contracting parties that, due to time and cognitive limitations, insufficient adjustments may be performed in the course of a choice. Awareness is thus a 'cognitive-bias mitigator' and militates in favour of rationalization. It has been argued that this conscious mental process can be affected by repeated use: the more we develop and use particular rationalizations, the more they become habitual and seemingly part of our thinking processes.[61] Secondly, contracting parties should understand that adjustment requires laborious and effortful work, which cannot be clouded by mental shortcuts. It is thus advisable to establish an elaborate framework for making business decisions, taking into consideration the ideas discussed in this chapter, aiming to increase the changes of eliminating cognitive biases.

All in all, it seems that the respondents of the group '(Pre-)judgmental followers' made decisions based on System 1, although believing that System 2 was in operation. It is arguable that laborious contexts such as the governing contract law demand performance of the deliberative and thoughtful System 2, without which inefficient outcomes may likely result. Nonetheless, although decisions can be taken under System 1 instead, due to constraints, there may be ways to curtail or challenge the cognitive biases that originate from decisions made under System 1.

2.3.1.2.2 Experiential Followers

We shall call the second group to be discussed the 'Experiential followers'. The second group encompasses the following quotes: 'positive effects on the party who seeks advice', 'undesirable solutions', and 'counsel and client's favourable experience'.

These quotes fall within a category that could also be named 'experiential perceptions'. In other words, respondents may have used certain laws in their contracts in the past and attributed a 'grade' or 'rate' to this experience.

a Profile

These responses of individuals falling in this group seem to indicate that these decisions have been derived from real-life occurrences. In this group, experience in connection with governing contract law was labelled 'positive', 'undesirable', and 'favourable'.

While the 'grades' or 'rates' attributed to this experience are easily identifiable, it remains unclear whether the individual experiences relate to the end result or features of the law itself. For example, 'undesirable solutions' may be labelled as such because a decision-maker denied a request, a court case or arbitral award result was unfavourable or, alternatively, because of a gap in a legal framework.

61 K. Hall, *supra* note 22, p. 8.

It appears that common heuristic devices may also have guided these choices. The heuristic devices' 'representativeness' and 'availability' may assist in explaining these quotes. For ease of reference:

Representativeness: involves judging the likelihood of an event based on the similarity between that event and knowledge of similar occurrences.

Availability: a decision-making is often based on what is most easily remembered at a given moment. It refers to the way in which probability or frequency judgments are influenced by the ease with which past examples are recalled.

> In this regard, Mellers *et al.* have argued that
> we base many of our decision on rules or heuristics that convey information about who we are and how we interact with others. These decisions may have involved tradeoffs at one point, but they have become 'generic' applications of rules to situations. Regardless of the function of the rule, this process minimizes effort and allows us to turn our attention to other matters.[62]

For example, a positive or negative experience with certain governing contract law may be readily available in a contracting party's mind to immediately trigger and guide the choice. In addition, the judgment of a likelihood of success or failure of a contract may be based on a similar case where that same law was chosen.

A caveat to this is that whilst the function of these devices can minimize effort, it frequently leads to irrationalities – contracting parties, due to error in odds, estimation or even the comparison with previous experience, may routinely pass over a better deal.

b *Practical Notes*

How can we then minimize or control the effects of these heuristic devices? It is probably safe to say that knowing that these heuristic devices exist and may influence choice is a start. Contracting parties should be able to foresee this and attempt to correct or exploit them as appropriate.

This can be achieved firstly by noting that good and bad past experiences are subject to different outlooks and inward feelings that shape a contracting party's perceptions. In addition, perception is selective and memory is subject to external variables, such as the context of that experience. Nonetheless, it is important to note that an undesirable result or solution provided by certain governing contract law in the past may turn out to be attractive in a different business context. Contracting parties should be made aware of this ideal.

62 B. A. Mellers, A. Schwartz & A. D. J. Cooke, *supra* note 6, pp. 459-460.

Kahneman and Riis, while interpreting happiness, allude to two selves.[63] This may also help us to understand some of the quotes rated as 'good' or 'bad' experiences. They assert that there is the 'experience self', the one who does the living and for whom time is vital; and the 'remembering-evaluating self', the one who grades the experience, keeps scores and maintains records.

Kahneman and Riis further assert,

> The principal finding of this line of research was that episodes are scored by the value of a representative moment, which can be the feeling associated with its end or a weighted average of the ending moment – the most intense one-this has been called the peak/end rule. As implied by the peak/end rule, the evaluation of episodes is remarkably insensitive to their durations-this phenomenon has been called duration neglect.[64]

It appears that a whole event will usually be represented by a single memory and we tend to score events at the very end. However, this can lead to inappropriate choices. For instance, an unpleasant memory of a complex negotiation of certain governing contract law may lead the party to avoid an entire future deal, composed of different variables which cannot be anticipated at the moment of choice. As Kahneman and Riis explain, evaluation of this episode is insensitive to its duration and guided by the value attributed to it.[65]

Shifting now to the context of execution of certain governing contract law, we could think of a fairly straightforward example. Let us assume certain law has been chosen to govern a cross-border contract. A dispute has arisen and one party has claimed damages for breach of contract. The respondent has contended that the claim for damages should be denied or, alternatively, reduced, as claimant did not mitigate its loss. The claimant was unaware of the mitigation of losses principle in the relevant law nor was he aware of the case law. The claimant's unawareness may influence the outcome of the case; however, the parties will have to prepare their arguments and collect relevant evidence. Overall, although we are working on limited data here, the governing contract law should not be seen as a 'bad choice' at all. However, because evaluation of events is insensitive to its

63 D. Kahneman & J. Riis, 'Living, and Thinking About It: Two Perspectives on Life', *in* F. A. Huppert, N. Baylis & B. Keverne (Eds.), *The Science of Well-Being*, Oxford University Press, Oxford, 2005, pp. 285-304. In order to illustrate the biases that result from the dominance of the remembering self the authors state: "…consider a music lover who listens raptly to a long symphony on a disk that is scratched near the end, producing a shocking sound. Such incidents are often described by the statement that the bad ending 'ruined the whole experience'. But, in fact, the experience was not ruined, only the memory of it. The experience of the symphony was almost entirely good, and the bad end did not undo the pleasure of the preceding half hour. The confusion of experience with memory that makes us believe a past experience can be ruined is a compelling cognitive illusion. The remembering self is sometimes simply wrong." (p. 285).

64 D. Kahneman & J. Riis, *supra* note 63, p. 286.

65 *Id.*

duration, and possibly to its intensity, this choice might be seen as 'bad' by the claimant.[66]

'Bad experiences'[67] in relation to a certain law will likely be scored by momentary episodes of frustration of expectations in relation to its execution, and yet might not be an overall 'bad experience' or bad choice. In addition, differences in the way a question is posed may also generate very different answers (note: the framing effect). The same applies with regard to the way a certain experience is remembered and evaluated by a contracting party.

Let us suppose a party advisor engages in discussion with a contracting party on the choice of law that has been used in a past case. The party advisor might use different questions to approach this topic, for example: 'In our last case, this law's provisions on damages played against us. Shall we avoid this law?' or 'The last time we used this law our claim for damages was denied. Shall we avoid it this time?' In the former, the advisor offers elements to evaluate the context, allowing the party to undertake more laborious mental work. In the latter, on the other hand, the question is rather rhetorical and focused primarily on the result, the 'denial', reminding the contracting party of the end result.

As seen, the use of different frames, translated into words, tones and language construction may engage or deviate a contracting party from a thoughtful process of evaluation. This can intervene, and not always positively, in the choice of governing contract law.

2.3.1.2.3 Herd Followers

We shall call this final group the 'Herd followers'. The third and final group encompasses the following quotes: 'clients do not like the CISG because people exclude it', 'no experience', 'similarity of chosen law to law of the client', and 'use of precedent contract that excluded CISG'.

a Profile

As discussed, preferences are not created in a vacuum; they depend on the stimulus context. This context might include the external environment at large or a more local stimulus. It might also include an even broader context based on a decision-maker's past and present experience. Thus, the quotes in this group appear to reaffirm the earlier assumptions that we are highly influenced by our 'habitat', in this case by the legal and commercial environments.

66 Other examples might include provisions amended, recent judgements and other 'surprises' which may not militate against the party in the long run, but may, at first sight, be perceived as such by the party.

67 The quote "Undesirable solution" could likewise have been prompted by a provision that appeared to be more favorable and ended up being less or not favorable at all. See Survey Question n. 8 *supra* Section 1.2.4.3. For the reasons given by the respondents, please consult *supra* Section 1.2.4.3.

For example, the quote 'clients do not like the CISG because people exclude it' provides a glimpse into a contracting party's mind: some individuals are highly influenced by a created perception or generalization that may not even correspond to reality. In such situations these parties will opt simply (and dangerously) to follow in another's footsteps.

Likewise, 'no experience', 'similarity of chosen law to law of the client', and 'use of precedent contract that excluded the CISG' also demonstrate the thought processes behind the 'herd followers'. These individuals will likely not investigate further the available options or question the reasons for prior decisions. Rather, for convenience, they may simply choose law that resembles that of the client's location.

Nonetheless, in some instances the percentage of this 'herd' perception may not be as high as people initially think. In one of his influential articles on decision-making processes Kahneman identified and described a dozen system biases, including overestimates of the frequency of events that are easy to recall. As the author explains, this bias was identified by 'systematic errors in estimates of known quantities and statistical facts'.[68] Hence, although contracting parties may believe they are following a certain statistical trend in a decision, this may not be the case.

b Practical Notes

Kahneman's above-cited overestimation of an event might explain at least some of the quotes of this group. The halo effect may also apply in this instance when analyzing the quotes of this group: once a good or bad impression is formed, that impression is often extended more generally and exaggerated.[69] For example, one exclusion regarding a specific governing contract law, or discussion of it, may suffice for a contracting party to form an inclination not to use a specific contracting law.

In the same vein, another aspect of the decision-making process is the 'status quo' bias. This means that individuals will tend to prefer an option if it is consistent with the current state of affairs.[70] This may explain the quote 'no experience' and might also clarify why contracting parties will tend to use standard contracts where certain governing contract laws are already defined.

Contracting parties may also refer the decision to those whom they deem to have greater status than they (the 'one reason' heuristic).[71] In this connection the quote 'Use of precedent contract that excluded CISG' might be explained.

The quote 'similarity of chosen law to law of the client' proves that similarity serves as a cue for these judgments, and contracting parties will tend, by the device of representativeness, to identify features similar to their own law and then choose them.

---

68 D. Kahneman, *supra* note 24, p. 710.

69 J. A. Maule & G. P. Hodgkinson, *supra* note 29 in Chapter 1, p. 69.

70 R. Korobkin & C. Guthrie, *supra* note 30 in Chapter 1, p. 805.

71 See C. Guthrie, *supra* note 179 in Chapter 1, p. 431.

Finally, we should not overlook the effect of the 'availability'[72] heuristic in the quote 'clients do not like the CISG because people exclude it'. According to this heuristic, the frequency of exclusion might have been assessed by the ease with which it comes to one's mind, typically by recalling such occurrence among one's acquaintance.[73] This mental operation of retrieval[74] might capture earlier events.

The availability heuristic seems to fit in this quote, where the 'bad feeling' generated by a previous opt-out influenced the decision-making process.[75] In other words, this respondent mimicked the decision made by others (what the doctrine calls 'imitation' heuristic), by opting out of the CISG. Therefore, recent experience of exclusion, or pre-negotiation of it, could have meant that this respondent regarded that scenario as a 'standard practice'.

The above assumptions could lead us to the conclusion that these respondents might also have overestimated the frequency of exclusion of the CISG. The same claim could apply to the use of a precedent contract's opting-out of the CISG. Furthermore, contracting parties are typically risk-averse[76] and will thus tend to follow the 'herd' – whatever 'herd' they belong (or wish) to. Accordingly, the quote 'no experience' could be translated into 'unknown territory! Better to be safe than sorry'. Unsurprisingly, we should not disregard the possibility that contracting parties may have sympathies and antipathies towards certain laws, sensitiveness, and be better disposed to a particular law. All of these could have been built up by personal perception, either in practice or in abstract.

What are the available mechanisms to tackle these biases? Firstly, being aware of the 'herd', or at least of its direction or drives, might enable control the effects of this bias. As discussed earlier, 'awareness' is vital in the process of optimization of decisions, given its 'cognitive-bias mitigation' function.

As a further tool to minimize this cognitive bias, we could use a collaborative approach in identifying these biases in the 'herd' followers. When we are aware of the cognitive biases present in the other side of contractual negotiation, we are able more easily to avoid them in our own approach to decision-making or ensure the other side is aware and informed of this. This is because, due to bias blindness,[77] it may be easier to identify cognitive flaws in someone other than ourselves. This process may prove to be more efficient than identifying our own cognitive biases. Moreover, the establishment of a clear and consistent framework within which to make business decisions – taking into

72 See *supra* note 32 in Chapter 1, at p. 21.

73 A. Tversky & D. Kahneman, *supra* note 32 in Chapter 1, p. 1127, stating that the reliance on availability leads to some biases, relating to retrievability of instances, effectiveness of a search set, imaginability and illusory correlation.

74 A. Tversky & D. Kahneman, *supra* note 32 in Chapter 1, p. 1128.

75 See M. I. Fraidin, *supra* note 182 in Chapter 1, pp. 919-920.

76 R. Cooter & T. Ulen, *supra* note 1 in Introduction, p. 46.

77 See D. Kahneman, 'Bias, Blindness and How We Truly Think', available at [www.bloombergview.com/articles/2011-10-24/bias-blindness-and-how-we-truly-think-part-1-daniel-kahneman].

consideration the ideas discussed above – may enhance knowledge of the rational elements at play, thereby avoiding the interference of cognitive biases.

All of these above processes may assist in attempting to improve the rationality of a decision; or alternatively, to use a certain decision in a contracting party's best interests.

As a final note, the analysis of these selected quotes may also serve as a warning to contracting parties who daily interact in the market. This is because, on the one hand, contracting parties can and should make decisions using rational processes, *i.e.* a laborious analysis of the available options and attempting to obtain the best results from the transaction. On the other hand, contracting parties may have trouble making decisions about future events and they are generally quite impatient and risk-averse while doing so.

The empirical data adduced in this chapter suggests that, while parties may and should execute a cost-benefit analysis in cross-border sales – by anticipating behaviour, advanced tactics, and possible legal battles – cognitive errors are likely to play a significant role in the decision-making processes. We have seen that contracting parties do not always fully reflect on the all the options available while opting out or choosing certain governing contract law. Such behaviour may lead to unpleasant surprises and inefficient decisions.

Nonetheless, this enquiry has demonstrated that there are practical benefits in understanding a contracting party's choices which are subject to these 'imponderables'. Firstly, knowledge of heuristics and cognitive biases certainly assists contracting parties in better understanding the risks to which they are routinely exposed in decision-making contexts. In addition to these risks, this 'awareness alert' serves to signal to contracting parties that they might be passing over a 'better deal' in certain business contexts.

A better knowledge of the mechanics of these judgment processes may also help contracting parties to create channels by which to intervene in these situations, anticipate a counterparty's behaviour and re-orientate its own behaviour so that it is aligned with the contractual interests at stake.

Mapping out, quantifying and understanding these cognitive flaws and idiosyncratic decision-making processes may lead contracting parties to improve the rationality of their decisions. This in turn allows contracting parties to appreciate the strengths and weaknesses of both contracting parties. From this, the decisions taken can lead to optimized results whilst at the same time assisting contracting parties to prevent surprising outcomes and costly mistakes.[78]

In the next chapter we shall explore the 'backstage costs', *i.e.*, the wide array of costs incurred for those who use the market. Discussion will be dedicated to the details of the interplay between the market and players in that market: from the interaction and friction arising from cultural and linguistic obstacles, to the intricacies of asymmetric information concerning the contract and the market; noting cognitive limitations, and the bargaining power and learning costs faced by contracting parties.

78 See also L. G. Meira Moser, *supra* note 1.

3 MARKET DISTORTIONS AND IMPERFECTIONS: THE 'STAGE' OF THE ART

Contracts have historically been conceived as instruments of exchange and distribution of welfare.[1] By assisting in the execution of these processes, contracts have been positioned at the forefront of the development of markets worldwide.

In modern times contracts assume an even more instrumental role in a market where diversity of legal and cultural[2] backgrounds is the rule. In fact, a volatile financial climate, coupled with heterogeneous actors who have idiosyncratic preferences, mean that market players need to rely on efficient tools to regulate and facilitate transactions worldwide. How can parties develop and manage these tools effectively? How many obstacles are down the road to be chanced upon? How can we properly identify and control them? How much cost is involved in this process? We aim to address these questions in the discussion to follow.

First and foremost, in order to design and use a framework that rightfully outlines parties' duties, rights and obligations, it is necessary to ponder the costs involved. In addition, distortions and imperfections of the market will also need to be examined.[3]

The first part of this chapter will therefore examine the particulars of the market as the playing field on which parties interact via contracts. The market failures that are likely to influence the choice-of-law clauses in cross-border sales will be further explored. In this

1 For an analysis of the evolution of the notions of the contract, see generally Joan Miquel, *Derecho privado romano*, Marcial Pons Ediciones Jurídicas, Madrid, 1992; Michel Villey, *Le Droit Romain*, Presses Universitaires de France, Paris, 1949; Juan de Churruca, *Introducción histórica al Derecho Romano*, Universidad de Deusto, Bilbao, 1994.

2 See, in this connection, V. Gessner, *supra* note 22 in Chapter 1, also arguing that "[…] Another crucial difference is to be found in communication where Far Eastern cultures are at one end and Western cultures at the other end of the continuum. Japanese and Chinese verbal interaction very much relies on the context of the speech situation and very little has to be made explicit. The opposite position is held by cultures like the German or Scandinavian tradition where very little seems to be assumed and all the rest must therefore be linguistically expressed -leading to the so-called Teutonic style of discussion where a critical statement is not perceived as an offense but rather the rule of the game. High context cultures are necessarily static whereas low context cultures facilitate rapid changes in private, economic and political life." (p. 133).

3 There are other market distortions that will not be the subject of this chapter, *e.g.*, externalities, moral hazard and market power. It is worth mentioning that externalities are the third-party effects and the question lies in whether the parties internalize the incurring costs. In international sales contracts, while choosing law or using forum clauses, the parties internalize the costs as they may need to prove facts and legal rules before jurisdictions less or more familiar with the applicable law. Therefore, in situations where the law chosen differs from the law of the forum, although at a first glance it could be seen as an externality inasmuch as decision-makers would need to ascertain new legal rules, the parties do internalize these costs by providing certified translations, legal opinion, and so on. As regards externalities, see B. E. Hermalin, A. W. Katz & R. Craswell, *supra* note 10 in Chapter 2, p. 24 *et seq.*

regard, readers will be served with alternatives on how to avoid some market distortions – or at the very least minimize their effects – and, in consequence, become more efficient decision-makers. In the second part of the chapter, readers are invited to consider the legal and economic choices that contracting parties are likely to encounter while deciding on choice-of-law clauses, based upon empirical evidence. In so doing, readers will enjoy practical insights into and overall awareness of the contracting parties' principal concerns at the bargaining table in cross-border sales.

The regulation of contracts involving parties coming (or not) from different legal systems imposes difficulties because of the rules of private international law and the distinct forms of international conflict-resolution methods, in combination with cultural, linguistic and geographical barriers. At first sight, these latter factors might be regarded as the primary obstacles contracting parties encounter when negotiating cross-border transactions. All these aspects are highly sensitive and may interfere with the success of a deal.

Firstly, geographical distance is a reality that parties will inevitably face. Naturally, distance may pose hindrances, such as the great difficulty of having an in-person 'meeting of minds' to negotiate a contract. This prevents the building up of a more solid relationship and rapport with the other side as well as a feeling of empathy with the potential business partner, which is sometimes acknowledged and used as leverage in business contexts. However, cross-border deals across jurisdictions are routinely concluded and geographical distances are often overcome or mitigated through technological advancements, such as the Internet and, particularly, videoconferences, conference calls, and online database facilities that allow parties to interact, share information and store and exchange documents.

Cultural and linguistic aspects are arguably harder to manage, since the way a contracting party behaves may vary according to cultural and pre-existing behavioural standards. For example, certain gestures, words, and mannerisms may cloud a deal or be rightly or wrongly interpreted by the potential business partner. This may also include a contracting party's behaviour in pre-negotiation meetings and during the contract's execution. Similarly, linguistic differences may translate into misrepresentations and misunderstandings, thereby resulting in wrong, miscommunicated and inefficient decisions.

If the parties anticipate these early on, the above-mentioned primary obstacles can be effectively overcome or, at the very least, better controlled. In fact, in this multi-faceted and evolving environment the choice-of-law mechanisms play a paramount role. Stating the choice of law may be regarded as highly complex when parties have to analyze a multitude of criteria.[4] This can include: connections to a foreign law, substantial connec-

4 In relation to the topic, L. Spagnolo advocates that "Improvements in predictability of the identity of the law to be applied and its correct application enables more accurate risk allocation within contracts, reduces wasteful precautionary investments, and decreases anticipated litigation costs since there will be less post-contractual 'wriggle room' for argument about the identity of the applicable law in the event of litigation." See L. Spagnolo, *supra* note 118 in Chapter 1, p. 122.

tion with the proposed or applicable law, restrictions on party autonomy where the choice of law touches upon mandatory provisions, substantial connection with the parties or the transaction, and unknown, confusing or hermetic conflict-of-law rules. All the above elements interrelate and have a role to play in the same place: the market.

The market is the stage on which actors interact via contracts governed by legal frameworks. As with any stage, the market has distortions and imperfections. Accordingly, parties will need firstly to identify and subsequently make use of efficient tools to enjoy benefits from the transactions. In the following discussion we shall focus on the market distortions and imperfections that should be taken into consideration by parties involved in cross-border deals if they intend to reach efficient results.

3.1 Bounded Rationality

It is undisputed that traders, as market players who intend to maximize their gains from a transaction, wish their contracts to be governed by a legal framework that is comprehensive, predictable, accessible and commercially focused.[5] Nevertheless, inherent limitations – or so-called bounded rationality – may impair the maximization of gains. This is one of the market failures that will be further analyzed in this chapter.

Bounded rationality is a concept first introduced by Herbert Simon.[6] It conveys the idea that human beings have limited computational abilities to anticipate events and record these in writing. People make mistakes all the time; fail to foresee and ponder all available options, as well as possible alternatives and solutions to daily questions and mundane contingencies. This naturally applies to contract negotiation contexts as well. Moreover, people are generally quite impatient when it comes to drafting a contract and exploring rational decision-making solutions. Therefore people simply fail to identify or predict risks – a failure that routinely results in bad choices and costly mistakes.

Mistakes of such nature are made because 'cognitive traps' prevent people from seeing, seeking, using, or sharing relevant, accessible and perceivable information during decision-making.[7] However, the truth is that even if people were to have more or different information, they would not be able to process them all due to inherent limitations.[8]

Apart from cognitive limitations, market players are also heterogeneous and complex; they have inclinations and idiosyncratic preferences, which are often unavailable to anybody else, and are constantly influenced by exogenous factors.[9]

5 In this sense, see G. Born, *supra* note 53 in Chapter 2, p. 2746.
6 H. A. Simon, *supra* note 17 in Chapter 2, p. 69.
7 Further information available at [www.12manage.com/description_bounded_rationality.html#rs1], p. 1.
8 *Id.*
9 The driving forces behind these choices are discussed in detail in *supra* Chapter 2.

3.1.1 Market Players

With foundations in mutual agreement, a contract is an instrument of trade,[10] developed to generate and distribute welfare. From an economic perspective, contracts are formed by market players, who are rational maximizers of their own welfare. From a legal standpoint, a contract typically follows an extended set of communications[11] that can include offers, counter-offers and other exchanges of information and communications, all governed by an elaborate framework of legal rules that determine when, how, and on what terms contractual obligations are created.[12] Consequently, the law chosen plays an important role in interpreting and enforcing the terms contractually agreed and those the parties leave out (un)intentionally.

In this connection it is argued that the rules of contract law formation aim to promote clear channels of communication so that the parties may know where they stand.[13] The authors Hermalin, Katz and Craswell explain that the law of contract formation pursues this task in two distinct ways. Firstly, it establishes authoritative forms and terms of art that the parties can use when negotiating their agreements. Secondly, it allocates the risk of miscommunication so as to encourage parties to take optimal precautions to prevent and insure against misunderstanding.[14]

Contracting parties make decisions using a cost-benefit analysis to achieve Pareto-efficient results.[15] The idea is that both parties enjoy mutual benefits from the transaction. This is a sort of 'weighing scale' approach, where pros and cons are measured – and the heavier prevail. For example, let us suppose a company is willing to implement new technologies to capture potential clients worldwide. This will imply direct costs, such as the price of the new technology device, *e.g.* a software, in addition to installation and training costs. However, with this new technology, the company will improve the end results by communicating faster with potential clients and develop sophisticated channels to choose the right business partners. This might also have a positive effect on current employees who will regard the company's behaviour as an indication of business acumen and the progress of the business.

---

10 See E. A. Farnsworth, *Contracts*, 4th edn., Aspen, New York, 2004, p. 5, arguing that the exchange between individuals allocates the resources according to the bargains between them.

11 See A. W. Katz, *supra* note 178 in Chapter 1, arguing that perhaps more important than any substantive legal entitlements is the extensive body of doctrine that governs the procedural mechanics of exchange and that determines when and how the parties' communications interact to create a binding obligation (p. 2).

12 B. E. Hermalin, A. W. Katz & R. Craswell, *supra* note 10 in Chapter 2, p. 52.

13 *Id.*, p. 57.

14 In the same way that the law of torts allocated liability for accidents to the least-cost avoider and least-cost insurer. See B. E. Hermalin, A. W. Katz & R. Craswell, *supra* note 10 in Chapter 2, p. 57.

15 See R. Cooter & T. Ulen, *supra* note 1 in Introduction, p. 44. In addition, see B. E. Hermalin, A. W. Katz & R. Craswell, *supra* note 10 in Chapter 2, p. 16 (noting that as a welfare criterion, Pareto efficiency evaluates a proposed allocation among a set of actors by asking whether there exists a second allocation that (i) none of the actors prefer less than the proposed allocation and (ii) at least one of the actors actually prefers to the proposed allocation. If no such second allocation exists, the proposed allocation is deemed efficient).

If we switch examples to choice of law in cross-border sales, we could think of a case where a company has decided to choose for the first time a particular governing contract law. Certainly, there will be direct costs involved, as we shall discuss in the next few paragraphs. In the same equation there will be 'training costs' associated with it. Nevertheless, the benefits of choosing this law can outweigh the costs. For example, the company is a seller of goods and the provision on damages for breach of contract slightly favours the seller by ascribing to the buyer certain burdens in case of a breach. As the company is willing to draft a template using this law for 100 similar contracts in the pipeline, this might turn out to be a good choice.

Endorsing this assumption, the answers and comments provided in the empirical efforts presented at the outset[16] suggest that parties, from an economic standpoint, analyze the calculated risks involved in a potential dispute at the very beginning. Parties also consider ways to finance and secure the transaction, factor in the cost of learning an unknown or less familiar law, appreciate the difficulties of enforcing a resulting decision in unfriendly or hostile jurisdictions, in addition to the procedural pitfalls that they may face, such as the evidentiary phase, deadlines, confusing or unclear payment mechanics, and recalcitrant debtors.[17] The respondents also indicated that economic choices and preferences vary according to the position in the transaction: buyer or seller; as in a game, where the priorities, choices and preferences will be defined according to the better incentives.[18]

In this ideal scenario contracting parties would ponder the costs involved in any transaction and behave in a fairly rational manner, aiming to enjoy benefits from any transaction. Regrettably this does not always happen in real-life situations. This is precisely the reason why we aim to disclose the triggers and imperfections that may prevent parties from making better decisions and avoiding costly mistakes[19] at the negotiation stage.

Firstly, irrational decisions are made partially because parties have idiosyncratic preferences not easily appreciated or understood by another party. In other words, not everyone likes the same thing, the same way. For example, parties usually include terms in their contracts that describe the object of the agreement or govern the principal risks affecting the value of the agreed obligations. The terms can describe the goods to be delivered, date, price and means of delivery, or identify the party who will bear the risks arising from the agreement. The terms can also release the seller from his obligations if a strike or similar event – unforeseeable circumstance or force majeure – occurs, or even allow for renegotiation of the agreement under certain conditions (hardship clause, for example).

16 For further details, please refer to *supra* Chapter 1.

17 L. G. Meira Moser, *supra* note 3 in Chapter 1, p. 38.

18 *Id.*

19 This is discussed in fine detail in *supra* Chapter 2.

Parties' preferences are highly idiosyncratic and subject to external factors not readily accessible to the other party during the period of negotiation. In addition, parties' judgments, among other things, are often blurred by cognitive limitations. As discussed earlier, parties have limited cognitive skills both to anticipate facts and events, and translate them into contractual provisions. As a result, contracts are naturally incomplete. However, is it prejudicial to leave out contractual flaws or gaps? After all, are there only disadvantages in taking this approach?

3.1.2 *Opportunistic Behaviour*

Parties might leave out contractual flaws or gaps in a contract due to opportunistic behaviour. Opportunistic behaviour is one of the foundations of bounded rationality. It has been defined as '...self-interest seeking with guile',[20] meaning that, given the circumstances, market actors may serve their own interest rather than those of the other contracting party. Oliver Williamson argues that it is not necessary that all agents be regarded as opportunistic to identical degree: it suffices that those who are less opportunistic than others are difficult to ascertain *ex ante* and that, even among the less opportunistic, most have their price.[21]

In law of contract theory, opportunistic behaviour is often associated with the performance of acts guided by motives in a deceptive way, often in disaccord with a party's normal state of mind, who aims simply to obtain an advantage of a certain situation. In scenarios such as that described, parties may behave inconsistently with their pre-existing beliefs and intentions in order to benefit from a situational position in the contractual game. Another way to see this is as a party who adapts in a highly flexible fashion to changing circumstances, due to self-interested purposes.[22]

There are different types of opportunistic behaviour. One is called '*ex ante* opportunism' or upfront, where a party will explore pre-contractual information asymmetries, as we shall discuss in further detail in one of the subchapters to follow.[23] The other type of opportunistic behaviour, 'ex post opportunism', refers to the exploitation of information asymmetries by not bearing their full consequences (also called moral hazard).[24] Let us use examples of 'ex post opportunism' to clarify this definition.

A health insurance policy states that the policyholder can claim back expenses relating to medicine for healthcare purposes up to a certain amount. The policyholder, noting that

20 O. E. Williamson, 'Transaction-Cost Economics: The Governance of Contractual Relations', *The Journal of Law and Economics*, Vol. 22, Issue 2, 1979, p. 234.

21 *Id.*, For a complete discussion on opportunism, see O. E. Williamson, *Market and Hierarchies: Analysis and Antitrust Implications*, Free Press, New York, 1975, pp. 7-10; pp. 26-30.

22 Further information available at [www.12manage.com/description_bounded_rationality.html#rs1], p. 2.

23 See *infra* Section 3.2.2.

24 Further information on moral hazard, available in R. Cooter & T. Ulen, *supra* note 1 in Introduction, p. 48.

his claim is significantly lower than the allowance, decides to include in the claim an inexpensive beauty product, assuming the insurer would not investigate.

Another example: a person rents a car and pays full insurance in case of damage, meaning that someone else will pay for whatever happens with the car. During the entire rental period this person drives faster and behaves less prudently than normal because they know that someone else will bear the consequences, and in this example, pay the loss.

If we use an example of behaviour relating to the choice of governing contract law, one could think of a party who has more knowledge of similar cases to that being handled, or has had similar experience using the same law and in similar circumstances. The consequence of this is that parties will not trust each other to the fullest extent possible, fearing that the other party, who has experience, might be in possession of more information on a certain contractual circumstance or governing contract law. From this, the chance that parties will maximize gains from the transaction is reduced.[25]

A way to avoid or perhaps minimize the effects of such behaviour is to choose efficient legal tools when interacting with the counterparty. What does this entail?

Efficient tools are legal instruments that are able to reduce potential asymmetries by providing a balanced legal framework, such as the use of neutral legal standards. It is noted, however, that an even balance between buyer and seller might not be achievable, nor perhaps desirable. This is so because, as discussed earlier, parties who enter into international transactions might have inclinations towards certain law. At first sight a party might believe that a more buyer- or seller-friendly law would assist. However, as the contract is performed, there may be variables not contractible[26] which may play a role in the fate of the contract. For example, there may be circumstances revealed during the performance of a contract, such as onerous obstacles to the delivery of the goods (unexpected late delivery due to carriage problems or administrative matters) or payment of the price for the goods. Therefore, on balance, parties would ideally opt for law that equally weighs some key provisions between buyers and sellers.[27]

---

25 In relation to opportunistic behavior, see also the 'prisoner's dilemma' and the 'free-rider problem', available at R. Cooter & T. Ulen, *supra* note 1 in Introduction, p. 48.

26 See, in this sense, J. Flood & F. Sosa arguing that "[...] The basic problem of any exchange lies in the insecurity that characterizes any interaction. Most institutional approaches view the problem of opportunism as the central problem in any exchange situation. There is always the danger that parties will not behave in cooperative ways, because they prefer to do what renders the highest profit to them. Thus, mechanisms are necessary to develop stable expectations with regard to the behavior of interaction partners", 'Lawyers, Law Firms, and the Stabilization of Transnational Business', *Northwestern Journal of International Law & Business*, Vol. 28, Issue 3, 2007, p. 490 The authors continue "[...] Interaction between two human beings involves the problem of double contingency: in order to coordinate interaction, ego has to be able to expect the behavior of alter as well as the expectations alter has with regard to ego's behavior. It is therefore at the reflexive level of 'expectations of expectations' that the problem of orientation of behavior, as well as the strategies for handling disappointments, has to be defined and solved" (p. 450).

27 L. G. Meira Moser, *supra* note 3 in Chapter 1, p. 37.

3.1.3 *Contractual Incompleteness*

3.1.3.1 Why a Complete Contract Can Be Costly

Theoretically speaking, a complete contract would not only take into account all possible risks, but also the transaction costs[28] – including costs for negotiating and drafting[29] the contract, especially with an international perspective[30] and for predicting unlikely events. This means that all contracts are incomplete. Moreover, parties may choose or avoid certain terms and provisions for strategic reasons, *e.g.* in an attempt to explore a higher bargaining power[31] or avail themselves of an asymmetry of information.[32] Therefore, as a rule and as illustrated in the earlier chapter, contracts are incomplete.

One cannot forget the sophisticated international arena in which the agreements celebrated may require technical and multi-disciplinary knowledge. Added to this is the possibility that an international contract can involve multiple variables: language and cultural barriers, and foreign law likely to be unrelated to one (or both) parties.[33] Any non-contractible variable generates transaction costs.[34] Accordingly, careful consideration should be given to the choice of law methods and conflict-of-law rules, where applicable, in order to avoid uncertainty, potential disputes and unwanted outcomes.

28 See R. Coase, 'The Problem of Social Cost', *Journal of Law and Economics*, Vol. 3, 1960. pp. 1-44. Scholars have developed the 'Coase Theorem', a scenario in which a situation in which (i) the parties are rational in terms of their individual self-interest; (ii) there are zero transaction costs; and (iii) there is a market for all goods, involving well-specified property rights, market transactions will lead to an efficient allocation (maximizing total welfare), regardless of the initial assignment of entitlements.

29 The final version of the contract may be subject to a number of variables, which G. Cordero-Moss observes to be "a mixture of legal analysis, the exercise of bargaining power, deference to widespread contract practice, reliance on one's own drafting experience, the need for standardisation, the need for efficiency and the assumption of risk. The proportion of the various components may vary, and in some situations, the assumed risk is well considered, whereas in other situations, it may remind one more of recklessness than of the assumption of calculated risk", G. Cordero-Moss, *International Commercial Contracts: Applicable Sources and Enforceability*, Cambridge University Press, Cambridge, 2014, p. 25.

30 J. Basedow, 'Lex Mercatoria and the Private International Law of Contracts in Economic Perspective', *Uniform Law Review*, Vol. 12, Issue 4, 2007, pp. 697-713, "[...] It has to be recalled that the primary objective of the regulation of cross-border contracts is the reduction of transaction costs generated by the constitutional uncertainty of foreign trade. These costs have various reasons: uncertainty about the applicable law, the fragmentary nature of that law, in particular the absence of rules on certain issues relevant for the contract at hand, difficult access to legal literature of the applicable law, language problems, the lack of precision inherent in the foreign legal language relevant to the case at hand, the difficulty of obtaining advice on the foreign law, etc. In cases linked to several legal systems, these costs may be multiplied" (p. 710).

31 The topic of bargaining power is further explored *infra* Section 3.3.

32 For further information and practical examples, see *infra* Section 3.2.

33 The costs of investigating foreign law and proving it are even more burdensome. See I. Schwenzer & P. Hachem, *supra* note 220 in Chapter 1, p. 465.

34 L. G. Meira Moser, *supra* note 3 in Chapter 1, p. 21.

3.1.3.2 When Less Is More?

In contract drafting, one should reflect, besides costs, on the consequences of a provision, once a dispute concerning contract provision arises. For strategic reasons, it might not be a bad idea to have fewer elements in a contract or leave indeterminacies to be interpreted and decided by an adjudicator, *i.e.*, a judge or arbitrator. For example, this approach might be regarded as positive for certain types of contract more exposed to exogenous factors in its performance; alternatively, this approach may benefit parties with less experience in a particular industry.

The following subchapters will focus on two additional market distortions or imperfections that interfere with Pareto-efficiency,[35] namely information asymmetry and bargaining power. These failures, if successfully identified and tackled, guide parties towards their intention, thus rendering efficient results and, to the extent possible, mutual benefit.

3.2 ASYMMETRIC INFORMATION

We have seen that market players may use asymmetric information to behave opportunistically.[36] What is asymmetric information? It appears whenever a datum of information is either unobservable or unverifiable in a contract.[37] In contract negotiation, one could think of a myriad of scenarios where key information might be considered asymmetric, either in the view of both parties; one party in relation to the other; or both parties in relation to the decision-maker. There might also be instances where the party who possesses the information does not want fully to disclose it for strategic reasons, or is simply unaware of its full content. Different scenarios will be discussed below in detail.

3.2.1 Contractual Gaps

As we have discussed in earlier chapters, a contract represents a tool that enables an exchange between individuals. It equips the contracting parties with stimuli to act towards the performance of the agreement. A contract can vary in efficiency[38] according to the incentives at play to facilitate the achievement of contract goals. In this connection, A. Katz advocates that the most important effect of contract law may lie in the incentives

35 A scenario is considered Pareto-efficient if it is impossible to change it so as to make at least one person better off (in his own estimation) without making another worse off (again, in his own estimation). See R. Cooter & T. Ulen, *supra* note 1 in Introduction, p. 44 *et seq.*

36 See, for example, J. Flood & F. Sosa, *supra* note 26, pp. 490-491.

37 See A. Schwartz & R. E. Scott, 'Contract Theory and the Limits of Contract Law', *Yale Law Journal*, Vol. 113, 2003, p. 556.

38 The ideas on efficiency were first developed by Adam Smith, indicating that division of labor creates efficiency and brings economic growth. See A. Smith, *The Wealth of Nations*, 5th edition, Methuen & Co., Ltd., London, 1904, available at [www.econlib.org/library/Smith/smWN.html].

it provides for information acquisition and disclosure. The mechanical procedures of contract law regulate such behaviour in two ways. Firstly, they condition the existence of an enforceable contract on whether and how much information is disclosed; secondly, they make the parties' informational perspective relevant to interpreting their agreement's specific terms.[39]

There is no doubt that contractual terms depend on what the parties intend to achieve, shared information about the business, transaction costs, the general characteristics of their industry, knowledge interactions, such as asymmetric information and unequal bargaining power, and the legal system in force.[40] These information asymmetries are closely connected to contractual incompleteness.[41] The legal literature explains this as a failure to predict or anticipate events which parties might wish were contingencies, but which cannot serve as such because they are not verifiable or ascertainable by a third-party adjudicator of any contract dispute.[42] There are different sets of information asymmetry, which will be explored in further depth below.

3.2.1.1 Costs of Anticipating Events

One of the most common information asymmetries concerns contractual incompleteness and is linked to cognitive limitations in writing down and recording all contingencies and probabilities surrounding a given contract.[43] Anticipating events may be costly and will not always be accurate, as most of the time one event triggers another not foreseen in the contract.

For example, let us suppose that a marketing campaign is in the process of being concluded. According to the relevant contract, the marketing campaign involves, among other obligations, the organization of outdoor events. One of the contractual provisions states: 'subject to favourable weather conditions, a weekly outdoor event shall be organized by contractor A during the month of August in city X'. With respect to this clause and its execution, nothing else has been agreed but 'favourable weather conditions'.

In light of the above, multiple questions arise; for example, can these events take place in case of light rain or if the weather is overcast, or if it rained in the morning but it is

---

39 See A. W. Katz, *supra* note 178 in Chapter 1, p. 7.

40 See E. A. Posner, 'Economic Analysis of Contract Law after Three Decades: Success or Failure?' *University of Chicago Law & Economics, Olin Working Paper No. 14,* 2002, available at [http://ssrn.com/abstract_id=304977].

41 Contractual incompleteness is also explained by bounded rationality, *i.e.*, our cognitive limitation in foreseeing (or if so, wrongly) all possible contingencies affecting a contract. For reference to bounded rationality as the idea that human cognitive abilities are not infinite, see H. A. Simon, *supra* note 17 in Chapter 2, pp. 99-118; and C. Jolls, C. R. Sunstein & R. Thaler, 'A Behavioral Approach to Law and Economics', *Stanford Law Review*, Vol. 50, Issue 5, 1998, p. 1477.

42 See B. E. Hermalin, A. W. Katz & R. Craswell, *supra* note 10 in Chapter 2, p. 64; L. G. Meira Moser, *supra* note 3 in Chapter 1, p. 20.

43 See B. E. Hermalin, A. W. Katz & R. Craswell, *supra* note 10 in Chapter 2, p. 64.

sunny in the afternoon or if it is a sunny day but the ground is still wet after two days of severe rain, or if the rain starts during the event?

As we can see from the above, several questions may derive from one undetermined (or less determined) condition when the contract was drawn up. However, it is unlikely – and perhaps impracticable in many instances – that parties anticipate all possible contingencies that may affect a contract due to, description costs, which apply in addition to cognitive limitations.

3.2.1.2 Description Costs

Description costs are those arising out of a complete report of a certain fact or event and the consequences attached to it. Describing events may not always be an easy task and descriptions in contracts are seldom accurate. An example of this complexity is outlined below and may assist readers in understanding this concept.

Let us use a fairly trivial example that could serve as a parameter for other contracts. Party A orders from Party B dark chocolate bars. The contract stated 'Party B should deliver N dark chocolate bars on date X'. No additional details have been provided. What initially seems a straightforward task can suddenly become a puzzle in these circumstances: Party B is faced with multiple questions: in terms of the chocolate description '60, 70, 85, 90…; which percentage is the "right" darkness sought by party A?'; in terms of consistency, 'does Party A like creamy dark chocolate or plain?', 'sugar-free or standard dark?', 'with or without added flavour?'; in terms of source, 'branded or not branded?', 'less or more affordable?', 'any preference in terms of country of origin?', 'any allergy free?', and the list continues.

This example shows that we are seldom precise because we fail to stipulate all possible alternatives. Indeed, descriptions are time-consuming, require strenuous mental work and are, therefore, costly.

How then do parties deal with these daily situations? They will rely on the reasonable skills and judgment of those assigned the task, yet pondering the costs of enforcement it if the assigner fails to deliver the expected result. Consequently, parties will endeavour to elect the most suitable 'audience',[44] *i.e.*, the forum to hear potential disputes.

3.2.1.3 Costs of Enforcing Provisions and the 'Would Have Wanted' Approach

The costs of enforcing provisions are those of having the contractual provisions as well as the governing contract law duly applied. In the example earlier it is likely that party A pondered the costs of 'enforcing' a flawed description. Party A may have simply relied on Party B's reasonable judgment (who may use mental shortcuts to make the series of decisions referred to in the above example[45]). Accordingly, when it comes to more com-

44 Discussion of forum options is available in *infra* Chapter 4.
45 The topic of heuristics is explored in detail in *supra* Chapter 2.

plex contracts, the cost of enforcing provisions assumes a rather instrumental role. It will determine who will hear and decide potential disputes regarding the execution or interpretation of a particular contractual divergence.

In the calculation of costs of enforcing provisions, evaluation and expertise play a key role. This will likely be paramount, as parties will tend to assign a contractual dispute to an interpreter able to verify and evaluate facts and events with great accuracy of detail. The interpreter will need to investigate whether such an event or fact occurred and then attribute or attach a consequence to it based upon the contractual provisions agreed by the parties, including the governing contract law.

Evaluation and expertise costs may extend their effects beyond the boundaries of the legal aspects of a particular dispute. For example, in a dispute regarding conformity of goods, it is expected that the adjudicator will be well versed in the particular industry and therefore able to identify or verify the alleged event – conformity or non-conformity of goods – and then rule on the consequences of it. If the adjudicator does not hold such expertise, there is a strong possibility of increased enforcement costs due to the necessity of additional effort and time to demonstrate, in our example, (non-)conformity.

It thus becomes imperative to consider and evaluate expertise costs when parties decide upon a dispute-resolution clause and, in its absence, the choice of forum rules. Once this has been pondered, parties will be able to act towards 'lowering their arms' and focus more on other aspects of the deal.

Alternatively, contracting parties may use a 'would have wanted' approach. This is when parties rely on the skill and judgment of a third party, a judge or private adjudicator (in case of arbitration) as interpreter, *i.e.*, the interlocutor between the parties. This may require sufficient expertise of the interpreter to read the facts before her and apply the legal commands available.

As earlier discussed, one of the advantages of having contractual gaps is the indeterminacy of the contractual triggers. It may happen that a 'would have wanted' approach may benefit one party, especially as the parties' positions in the course of a contract may change. Hence a certain provision that appeared to be advantageous may turn out to be less appealing.

3.2.2 *Asymmetry Inter Partes*

3.2.2.1 Particular Knowledge or Expertise of the Party Regarding the Goods

A set of information asymmetries can be considered *inter partes*:[46] particular knowledge or expertise of the seller or buyer regarding the goods traded. For example, the seller may

46 According to S. Shavell, a prototypical example is where a contracting party chooses an inefficient term in order to masquerade as another kind of party and thereby gain a price advantage. The optimal assessment of the term might be to override it to obtain efficient action, even though that interpretation is not best on

be aware of the specifics regarding the efficiency or the depreciation value of a certain machine being sold, through internal reports or previous inspection, but this information would be unavailable to the buyer.

One could also think of another example of asymmetry where one of the contracting parties has more experience in, or better knowledge of, the chosen or applicable law. In such a scenario the party with greater knowledge has an advantage and will likely explore this to the extent that he/she can enjoy efficient results.[47] This can include, for instance, the contracting party's behaviour, a decision to perform certain obligations or breach the contract, to remain silent or inactive or to take action or refrain. In other cases the asymmetry lies only between the two parties on the one hand and a third-party enforcer, such as a court, on the other (*e.g.* when an experienced trader can tell that his supplier has delivered nonconforming goods, but the non-conformity is not apparent to a non-specialist).[48]

3.2.2.2 Counterparty's Knowledge of the Potential Governing Contract Law

The counterparty's superior knowledge in relation to potential governing contract law certainly imposes challenges on the other party. Although knowledge has various degrees of proficiency, this must surely represent an advantage to the party who possesses it. It is likely the party will behave in such a way as to maximize the benefits from the transaction. Here we should also note the possibility of a party's having knowledge of similar law or a similar legal family; for example, in a contract between parties from civil and common law jurisdictions, with third-party law chosen from civil or common law origins.

3.2.2.3 Strategic Informational Asymmetry

Finally, one could think of 'strategic informational asymmetry',[49] a scenario in which a party decides tactically to withhold information in order to avoid less beneficial terms that would result from disclosure of the information.[50] Typically, the legal regime chosen will assist in lowering the level of information asymmetry by imposing rules on disclosure

average for the set of individuals who write the observed contract. For example, some individuals who obtain mortgage loans with rates that fluctuate uncapped with the market rate of interest might underestimate the likelihood of a large increase in the market rate. By signing an opt-out clause, they prevent courts from interpreting their mortgage contracts so as to protect them from extreme variation in the market. See S. Shavell, 'On the Writing and the Interpretation of Contracts', *Journal of Law, Economics and Organizations – JLEO*, Vol. 2, Issue 2, 2006. p. 310.

47 L. G. Meira Moser, *supra* note 3 in Chapter 1, pp. 20-21.

48 See A. W. Katz, 'Contractual Incompleteness: A Transactional Perspective', *Case Western Reserve Law Review*, Vol. 56, Issue 1, 2005, pp. 169-186, p. 174; L. G. Meira Moser, *supra* note 3 in Chapter 1, pp. 20-21.

49 See L. A. DiMatteo & D. Ostas, 'Comparative Efficiency in International Sales Law', *American University International Law Journal*, Vol. 26, Issue 2, 2011, p. 409.

50 L. G. Meira Moser, *supra* note 3 in Chapter 1, p. 21.

and parties' duties. It may also place the burden on the party who is in an advanced position at a later stage of the contract, or, in the example of the goods traded, legal rules on the duty of inspection phase, all in an attempt to equalize the imbalance between seller and buyer.[51]

According to Avery Katz, majoritarian default rules help to address at least some problems of asymmetric information. Buyers without bargaining power will be reluctant to spend resources reading and evaluating unfamiliar contract terms, as such expenditure is relation-specific and can be expropriated by the seller *ex post*. If all provisions of the contract are interpreted literally, sellers who wish to offer high-quality terms will have no credible way to promise not to add disclaimers in the fine print.[52] It should be noted here that, although they may not be regarded as deal-breakers, 'default rules' have been cited as relevant features in governing contract law.[53]

In addition to information asymmetries in cross-border sales, parties will also come across bargaining power, another market distortion to be tackled if parties intend to achieve efficient results and avoid wrong decisions.

3.3 Bargaining Power

The bargaining power is the contracting parties' ability to negotiate deals, to dictate conditions and impose their own preferences and choices over the other contracting party. In international contexts, the bargaining power will certainly come into play in relation to applicable law issues. This is why choice of law processes are of great relevance and requires empirical analysis for a deeper discussion.[54]

---

51 One could read Article 35(3) of the CISG as an incentive for the seller to disclose information which otherwise would render him liable for providing non-confirming goods. Article 35(3) of the CISG reads as follows:

1. The seller must deliver goods which are of the quantity, quality and description required by the contract and which are contained or packaged in the manner required by the contract.
2. Except where the parties have agreed otherwise, the goods do not conform with the contract unless they:
   a. are fit for the purposes for which goods of the same description would ordinarily be used;
   b. are fit for any particular purpose expressly or impliedly made known to the seller at the time of the conclusion of the contract, except where the circumstances show that the buyer did not rely, or that it was unreasonable for him to rely, on the seller's skill and judgement;
   c. possess the qualities of goods which the seller has held out to the buyer as a sample or model;
   d. are contained or packaged in the manner usual for such goods or, where there is no such manner, in a manner adequate to preserve and protect the goods.
3. The seller is not liable under subparagraphs (a) to (d) of the preceding paragraph for any lack of conformity of the goods if at the time of the conclusion of the contract the buyer knew or could not have been unaware of such lack of conformity.

52 See A. W. Katz, *supra* note 178 in Chapter 1, p. 9.

53 For example, 26.27% of the respondents in the Survey see 'default rules' as positive legal features, as opposed to 18.94% who regard them as negative. These percentages lead us to believe that 'default rules', although not of vital importance, certainly play a role in deciding governing contract law. See *supra* Section 1.2.4.1.

54 See, in this sense, *supra* Chapter 1.

3.3.1 *Playing 'at Home', Playing 'at the Opponent's Home' or Playing at a 'Neutral Field': The So-Called 'Arm-Wrestling'*

Traders, as rational and self-interested players in the market, are often unwilling, for several reasons, to subject themselves to the law of the counterparty.[55] These include the counterparty's knowledge of the law (which may influence the case outcome and unbalance the parity of arms in a potential legal battle), seller-/buyer-friendly national law tailored-made to regulate domestic transactions, or a fear of a partial and biased judicial system (along with inefficient coercive mechanisms), which could lead to opportunistic behaviour and enforcement difficulties.

As a matter of fact, contracting parties frequently face the conundrum: 'playing at home', 'playing at the opponent's home' or playing on a 'neutral field'[56]?

Exercise of bargaining power is like arm wrestling: a contracting party who has more means – or strength – is likely to have his voice heard (or arm less injured) at the bargaining table. This obviously does not mean that the outcome of a potential dispute will be favourable to this party. This might indicate, however, that this party has sufficient tools, or is sufficiently equipped with the means to persuade the counterparty and impose certain contractual provisions.

3.3.2 *Substantial Relationship to the Parties or the Transaction*

If the context permits, contracting parties will likely choose law that has a substantial relationship to them or the transaction. This assumption finds support in empirical evi-

---

55 As C. Fountoulakis explains, the parties are familiar with their own law and are convinced that they will save considerable costs in not being required to investigate the intricacies of foreign law. Moreover, if they have their own law applied, they do not have to consult external experts, but rather can rely on their usual, well-acquainted legal advisors. The author goes further and states that the parties to an international contract will strive towards an application of their own law, even if that law is less suitable for the transaction at hand than other law might be. See C. Fountoulakis, *supra* note 195 in Chapter 1, p. 304.

56 For further reference on neutrality and freedom of non-national arbitral tribunals, see O. Lando, 'The Law Applicable to the Merits of the Dispute', *Kluwer Law International,* Vol. 2, Issue 2, 1986, pp. 104-115. O. Lando delves into the particulars of choices of law, including '[t]he choice of lex mercatoria as the system of law to govern the contract.' (p. 107); see also J. D. M. Lew QC, advocating for 'principles of the *lex mercatoria* detached from any legal system' (p. 144), 'The Law Applicable to the Form and Substance of the Arbitration Clause', *in* Albert Jan van den Berg (Ed.), *Improving the Efficiency of Arbitration Agreements and Awards: 40 Years of Application of the New York Convention,* ICCA Congress Series, Volume 9, Kluwer Law International, Alphen aan den Rijn, 1999, pp. 114-145. *A contrario sensu,* Lord Mustill, showing skepticism, defined *lex mercatoria* "[T]hus, so the theory runs, those appointed to decide international commercial disputes ought to apply, not any one domestic law of contract or sale of goods or carriage by sea, chosen in accordance with recognised theories of the conflicts of laws, but a single law which is the law of the international trading community as a whole." (p. 51). See Lord Mustill, 'Arbitration: History and Background', *Journal of International Arbitration,* Vol. 6, Issue 2, 1989, pp. 43-56. For further reference on the topic, see F. Galgano, *Lex mercatoria.* Il mulino, Bologna 2001; and P. Fouchard, E. Gaillard & B. Goldman, *Traité de l'arbitrage commercial international,* Litec, Paris, 1996. 7

dence discussed earlier[57] and falls within the category of 'familiarity'. In fact what is often agreed in daily/routine deals is the choice of 'neutral law' from a 'third jurisdiction'. Yet, how 'neutral' is a third jurisdiction's law?

3.3.2.1 The Resort to a Third Jurisdiction's Law – A Trojan Horse?

'Arm wrestling' (or so-called bargaining power) aside, parties may feel tempted to resort to a third jurisdiction's law in an attempt to balance power. However, a third jurisdiction's sales law, agreed by the parties as applicable, or through forum clauses,[58] may still lead to unpredictable and undesirable results.[59] These include a foreign law to be applied by a tribunal unfamiliar with that law, or a law that classifies contracts and imposes a set of or ready-made contractual terms as a mandatory rule, or whose non-application requires from the contracting parties express consent. These factors can end up conflicting with or modifying some of the negotiated contractual provisions. There could even be a scenario in which one party is aware of the provisions of a particular third law (and that it is advantageous to its own interests) and may suggest to the other party that the law strikes a neutral compromise – such a choice can turn out to be a 'Trojan horse'.[60]

It is important to draw a line here in order to differentiate between neutral rules that refer to 'rules of a third jurisdiction' and neutral rules that also refer to 'uniform rules'.[61]

As mentioned, a third jurisdiction's sales law may still lead to unpredictable and undesirable results.[62] This is because of the transaction costs incurred, coupled with uncertainties and the domestic law's 'physiology' – that is, a vocation to regulate contracts within national boundaries.

3.3.2.2 Uniform Contract Laws – A Way Out?

Uniform contract laws were created to promote and facilitate international transactions worldwide and are generated by a conciliatory approach from different legal families. They are neutral laws in the sense that neither party is directly associated or identified with them and, therefore, neither party has a particular advantage when applying it, the parties are thus said to be *quasi* on the same 'level playing field'.[63]

57 See, in this sense, *supra* Section 1.1.2.

58 As L. Spagnolo exemplifies, if a choice of forum clause fails to attain the intended result, it may affect the efficacy of the choice of law. The chosen law may unexpectedly become a foreign law to be proven as fact and applied by a tribunal unfamiliar with that law; both a costly and risky exercise. See L. Spagnolo, *CISG Exclusion and Legal Efficiency,* Wolters Kluwer, Alphen aan den Rijn, 2014, pp. 191-192 and p. 437.

59 For additional examples, see also C. Fountoulakis, *supra* note 195 in Chapter 1, p. 308, noting that the Swiss sales law differentiates meticulously between 'delivery' and 'non-delivery' of the ordered goods.

60 C. Fountoulakis, *supra* note 195 in Chapter 1, p. 312.

61 See, in this sense, L. G. Meira Moser, *supra* note 3 in Chapter 1, p. 28.

62 I. Schwenzer & P. Hachem, *supra* note 220 in Chapter 1, p. 464.

63 C. Fountoulakis, *supra* note 195 in Chapter 1, p. 314; L. G. Meira Moser, *supra* note 3 in Chapter 1, p. 28.

In order to avoid concerns regarding the applicable law,[64] and deter parties from adopting strategies that may impair the transaction, uniform laws, such as the United Nations Convention on Contracts for the International Sales of Goods (CISG),[65] provide default provisions on key contractual aspects,[66] which are tailored to tackle some of the market[67] distortions or failures – precisely the legal risks and the transaction costs[68] associated with the governing law in cross-border sales. This subsequently allows parties to maximize their gains from the transaction.

For those parties whose states have adopted uniform laws,[69] the transaction costs resulting from uncertainty as to which law is applicable to the dispute or the potential battle over the choice of private international law rules may be considerably reduced.[70] In the first place, the race for an applicable law no longer exists and thus there is no need for

64 For further reference on this matter, see E. Muñoz & L. G. Meira Moser, *'Brazil's Adhesion to the CISG – Consequences for Trade in China and Latin-America'*, *in* I. Schwenzer & L. Spagnolo (Eds.), *Globalization versus Regionalization – 4th Annual MAA Schlechtriem CISG Conference*, Eleven International Publishing, the Hague, 2013, pp. 79-96.

65 To promote uniformity in this area of law the CISG was created under the auspices of the United Nations Commission on International Trade Law (UNCITRAL), the United Nations body responsible for drafting model laws for the standardization and /or harmonization of international trade. See *1980-United Nations Convention on Contracts for the International Sale of Goods*, United Nations Commission on International Trade Law, available at [www.uncitral.org/uncitral/uncitral_texts/sale_goods/1980CISG.html].

66 As L. A. DiMatteo & D. Ostas argue, employing the common core and better rules approaches resulted in an interesting amalgam of common and civil law rules. The CISG consists of rules that can be characterized as: (1) rules consistent with both common and civil law legal traditions, (2) rules that recognize the superiority of a given common or civil-law rule – at least for the sake of transborder transactions, (3) rules that are fabricated to be national-system neutral, (4) rules that abdicate to national law by expressly refusing to cover certain topics, and (5) rules that fit in one of the first three categories but are subject to modification by the CISG's preference for original or autonomous interpretation of its rules (pp. 376-377). See L. A. DiMatteo & D. Ostas, *supra* note 49, pp. 371-439.

67 According to R. Coase, 'market' may be understood as an institution that exists to facilitate the exchange of goods and services, thereby reducing costs when exchange operations are conducted. See R. Coase, *The Firm, the Market and the Law*, University of Chicago Press, Chicago, 1998, p. 7.

68 See, in this sense, F. de Ly, remarking cross-cultural, transaction costs and contract management as advantages of the CISG 'The Relevance of the Vienna Convention for International Sales Contracts – Should We Stop Contracting it Out?', *Business Law International*, Issue 3, 2003, pp. 241-249, 241, 246.

69 The CISG extracts models of civil law and common law elements capable of harmonizing trade between countries of different legal traditions. See C. Samson, 'L'harmonisation du droit de la vente internationale de merchandises entre pays de droit civil et pays de common law', *Contemporary Law: Canadian Reports to the 1990 International Congress of Comparative Law*, 1990, pp. 100-125; B. Goldman, 'Frontières du droit et lex mercatoria', *Archives de philosophie du droit*, Vol. 9, 1964, p. 177 *et seq.*; E. Gaillard, 'Trente ans de lex mercatoria. Pour une application sélective de la méthode des principes généraux du droit', *Journal du Droit International*, No. I, 1995, pp. 5-30; B. Oppetit, 'La notion de source du droit et le droit du commerce international', *Archives de philosophie du droit*, Vol. 27, 1982, pp. 43-53; B. Oppetit, 'Autour du contrat international', *Droits*, Vol. 12, 1990, pp. 107-115; P. Schlechriem & C. Witz, *Convention de Vienne sur les Contrats de Vente Internationale de Marchandises*, Dalloz, Paris 2008; I. Schwenzer (Ed.), *supra* note 106 in Chapter 1.

70 See A. W. Katz, 'The Strategic Structure of Offer and Acceptance: Game Theory and the Law of Contract Formation', *Michigan Law Review*, Vol. 89, Issue 2, 1990, pp. 215-295.

determination on this matter[71] – costs of bargaining are saved. Secondly, the applicable law is not foreign to any of the parties, eliminating the costs of learning.[72]

In the empirical efforts undertaken and discussed above,[73] the respondents' preference for legal neutrality supports the cost-benefit analysis. This is opposed to the option for a party's domestic set of rules, which may generate more transaction costs and information asymmetries between the parties. By choosing a neutral law parties, in theory, depart from the same starting points and, while this will not invariably happen, it tends to result in greater mutually beneficial results.

Finally, uniform laws are prepared to respond to economic concerns in a rather effective way: costs, political instability and unfamiliarity would be minimized by the use of uniform law, as both parties will depart from rules not identified or closely connected to any of the contracting parties (most likely reducing to zero the imbalance regarding costs and unfamiliarity). With respect to political stability, the same reasoning applies. Political stability may result in legislative changes and drawbacks, a scenario of uncertainty that parties will definitely try to avoid by all means (for example, 74.89% of respondents selected legal certainty in the Survey results[74]).

3.4 Transaction Costs

Another market distortion that parties will come across is transaction costs. These reflect the burden that parties bear when they use the market, *e.g.*, costs incurred in negotiating, drafting and enforcing a contract.[75] One of the most intricate concerns of such costs relates to the amount spent on negotiating, predicting behaviour, choice of partners, preparation and management of agreement,[76] in addition to legal fees, drafting and print-

71 See, in this sense, O. Lando, remarking that "when foreign law is applicable, it must be ascertained. This ascertainment is manageable when the parties or the court have good access to reliable sources of information on the foreign law. In general, the law of a country which belongs to the same family of laws and which is expressed in the same or a related language can be ascertained… Even if you have good access to a foreign legal system it may be a task to learn exactly what the rule is", and adds that "It is also difficult to get information on the law of a country which belongs to an alien family of laws. Obtaining reliable information about the contents of such a foreign law is often cumbersome, time-consuming and costly. The difficulties increase when the language is unknown, and become almost insurmountable when the foreign law is uncertain, as for instance when the relevant case law is obscure and contradictory. So far as is known no country has managed to develop rules and procedures for the ascertainment of foreign law which are at the same time efficient, fast and inexpensive", 'Some Features of the Law of Contract in the Third Millennium', *Scandinavian Studies in Law*, Vol. 40, 2000, p. 347.

72 G. Cuniberti, *supra* note 55 in Chapter 1, p. 10.

73 See *supra* Chapter 1.

74 In this connection, please refer to *supra* Section 1.2.4.1 *et seq.*

75 D. C. North, *supra* note 181 in Chapter 1, p. 9.

76 See A. Schwartz & R. E. Scott, *supra* note 37, pp. 562-568. The search for contractual partners involves advertising, correspondence, travel and the parties' time; acquiring and disclosing information about the value of exchange: the costs of disclosure will include communication costs – the time that it takes buyers to read and process the information or the potential cost of being distracted from other, more important

ing costs, costs of researching the effects and probability of a contingency, and the costs to the parties and courts of verifying whether a contingency occurred.[77] One cannot forget that a cross-border sale may involve multiple additional variables: language and cultural barriers, foreign law most often unfamiliar to one (or both) parties,[78] and any non-contractible variable that can generate transaction costs.

This equation[79] of variables also takes into account: the efforts of the parties in looking for the goods in the market, the comparative analysis of price and quality desired and the compliance of due performance, guarantees in any default, and working on the drafting of contractual instruments which clearly outline the rights, duties and obligations of the parties.[80]

Consequently, if the legal system does not provide an adequate degree of certainty and predictability,[81] it becomes difficult to achieve economic transactions because such implementation may involve consuming more resources due to the increased risk. Thus it follows that an increased degree of legal predictability may lead to decreased transaction costs. A domestic law, for example, may not sufficiently reduce the transaction costs[82] of international contracts due to distinctions between the contract rules that govern the particular matter in different states. If the rules are dissimilar in trading partners' juris-

---

information. See B. E. Hermalin, A. W. Katz & R. Craswell, *supra* note 10 in Chapter 2, pp. 53-54; L. G. Meira Moser, *supra* note 3 in Chapter 1, p. 21. As regards management of agreements, see also J. Gordley, 'Mistake in Contract Formation', *The American Journal of Comparative Law*, Vol. 52, Issue 2, 2004, pp. 433-468.

77 See I. Ayres & R. Gertner, 'Filing Gaps in Incomplete Contracts: An Economic Theory of Default Rules.' *Yale Law Journal*, Vol. 99, 1989-1990, p. 93.

78 The costs of investigating a foreign law and proving it are even more burdensome. See I. Schwenzer & P. Hachem, *supra* note 220 in Chapter 1, p. 465.

79 See R. Sefton-Green, citing Helmut Wanger, for whom the list of potential costs shows more than those of transaction: (i) collecting information; (ii) legal disputes; (iii) setting incentives for pushing through legal claims; and (iv) other *e.g.*, consumers' rights of redress and complaint, including in cross-border contracts, travel, time (opportunity costs), postage, bank charges and costs linked to transferring payment from the eurozone to the non-euro zone (or vice versa), annoyance costs (negative utility), and translation costs. In addition, R. Sefton-Green queries whether the costs of legal uncertainty are actually measurable and argues that the 'cost of reducing the costs should also be considered', R. Sefton-Green, 'Choice, Certainty and Diversity: Why More is Less', *European Review of Contract Law*, Vol. 7, Issue 2, 2011, p. 139.

80 Legal measures, when considered inevitable to satisfy the claim, enter in this equation. See A. Schwartz & R. E. Scott, *supra* note 37, pp. 565-568.

81 See R. Posner, arguing that the most important function of contract law is to provide a legal remedy for breach in order to enhance the utility of contracting as a method of organizing economic activity, and this function is independent of whether there is any uncertainty about the terms. See R. Posner, 'The Law and Economics of Contract Interpretation', *University of Chicago Law & Economics, Olin Working Paper No. 229*, 2004, available at [http://ssrn.com/abstract=610983].

82 The expression 'transaction costs' is referred to by R. Coase as costs of market transactions, *supra* note 28. See also R. Coase, 'The Nature of the Firm', *Economica*, Vol. 4, Issue 16, 1937, pp. 390-391: "[t]he costs of negotiating and concluding a separate contract for each exchange transaction which takes place on a market must also be taken into account".

dictions, parties cannot rely on a common legal framework to govern their contracts.[83] Therefore they will have to bargain and consequently increase the transaction costs.[84]

Additionally, sensitive concerns about costs, for example the amount spent on predicting results arising from the application of unknown or less familiar domestic law, will affect the parties' behaviour in the course of contract negotiation and performance, and the preparation and management of the relevant legal instruments. Uncertainties of this nature are translated into transaction costs. Naturally, greater uncertainty surrounding the success of a transaction translates into higher costs.

3.4.1 *Unknown or Less Familiar Governing Contract Law*

As previously stated, contracts are naturally incomplete. The effort and cost of anticipating possible contingencies, bargaining over their resolution (assuming they are anticipated), and then describing them adequately in contracts may not be proportionate to the benefits arising out of the contracts.[85] Moreover, the costs of enforcing provisions, even if the contingency can be drafted efficiently, may outweigh the benefits of the transaction, making a complete contract ultimately inefficient. Contract default rules[86] exist thus to help fill the gaps.[87]

In the first instance, emphasis is given to the accessibility and intelligibility aspects of governing contract law. In relation to accessibility, language considerations represent a hindrance that deserves some reflection.[88] This could be elucidated by information asymmetries between the parties and the resulting cost of learning (assuming that one of the contracting party is familiar with that language). However, it is unclear whether this consideration would also include the choice of forum (if so, in case of state courts, language would be a barrier to possible dispute resolution and resulting decision and enforcement, in addition to the overall costs included. If private adjudication were cho-

83 For argument that differing domestic laws are perceived as an obstacle to international trade, see I. Schwenzer, *supra* note 195 in Chapter 1, pp. 723-732.

84 In this connection, see G. Born, *supra* note 53 in Chapter 2, p. 2616, noting that 'giving the significant divergences in the treatments of many issues between different national legal systems, choice-of-law issues are not only important, but sometimes decisive in international commercial disputes'. Born further elaborates on the matter, stating that "[...] if an undeveloped law is potentially applicable, if a transaction involves a state that may be subject to significant political changes, or if there are particular needs for certainty or enforceability, then an express choice-of-law clause will often be an essential prerequisite for proceeding with a transaction", p. 2745.

85 See S. Shavell, 'Economic Analysis of Contract Law', *Harvard Law and Economics Discussion Paper No. 403*, 2003, p. 6, available at [http://ssrn.com/abstract=382040].

86 See L. A. DiMatteo & D. Ostas, *supra* note 49, p. 375, arguing that, generally speaking, one of the most important functions of any system of contract law is to offer to the parties default rules that do not require bargaining.

87 See S. Shavell, *supra* note 85, pp. 6-7.

88 For example, some of the respondents of the 2014 Survey selected 'language considerations' as a positive legal feature of governing contract law. By the same token, some respondents cited 'language' as an additional feature to be noted in a most desirable governing contract law. See Survey results *supra* Section 1.2.4.1.

sen, this concern would be minimized as the private adjudicator(s) appointed would be familiar with that language, in addition to the language of the other contracting party).[89]

In any event, with regard to this particular concern (noting that this does not include the law itself but only the language of the law), in departing from a third jurisdiction's law, parties would in theory reduce potential information asymmetry relating to language. If parties decide to elect a third jurisdiction's sales law, this does not necessarily mean that there will be no information asymmetry in the matter: languages have phonetic and grammatical similarities and the party's geographical proximity to the third jurisdiction's sales law itself should not be overlooked.[90]

Uniform laws – neutral by nature and not identified with any of the contracting parties – would best correct this market distortion by providing parties with the respective set of rules in several authoritative languages, facilitating access to law.[91]

On the matter of uniform contract law and language aspects, I. Schwenzer explains that there are three scenarios of contracting parties. In the first group the parties come from countries where the same language is spoken and therefore, in general, these countries would belong to the same legal family (with minor differences which may be negligible). In this group there would hardly be a need for a unification of contract law, as the parties would still prefer the law that is more familiar to them than any unified law.

In the second group a company with overwhelming bargaining power concludes a contract with an economically weaker party. In such a scenario the powerful company will usually be able to impose anything it wants on its contract partner. However, in this case problems of ascertaining and proving the chosen law can be encountered.

Finally, the third group consists of parties from countries where different languages are spoken, or parties are either from a common law and civil law jurisdiction or from two civil law jurisdictions. In such a scenario, if neither party has the economic power to impose its own law upon the other, they will often agree on a third law.[92] I. Schwenzer explains that this third law might be a system that could familiar to both parties and may have influenced the law of both parties' countries in a certain way. However, if no such common background exists, parties will most likely resort to 'neutral law', thereby often confusing political neutrality with suitability of the chosen law to international transactions.[93]

Endorsing the same observation, C. Fountoulakis concludes that it is a popular fallacy to designate the law of a politically neutral state to an international contract whose terms have been carefully drafted and negotiated under another law, perhaps quite different from the law of that politically neutral state.[94]

89 L. G. Meira Moser, *supra* note 3 in Chapter 1, p. 34.
90 *Id.*
91 L. G. Meira Moser, *supra* note 3 in Chapter 1, p. 34.
92 See I. Schwenzer, *supra* note 195 in Chapter 1, p. 724.
93 *Id.*, p. 725.
94 See C. Fountoulakis, *supra* note 195 in Chapter 1, p. 306 *et seq.*; L. G. Meira Moser, *supra* note 3 in Chapter 1, p. 35.

A contrario sensu, the expected consequences of an incomplete contract may not be so harmful to contracting parties, as they may wish to delegate it to the decision-marker's interpretation and discretion on certain variables and aspects of the contract,[95] the so-called 'would have wanted' approach.[96]

Therefore, all systems of contract law must provide default terms to cover the issues over which the parties do not specifically bargain.[97] In this regard, if a certain law is accompanied by legally-implied provisions or ready-made contract terms, parties may prefer to use the standard terms, where the reduction in their transaction costs is likely to exceed the increased costs incurred, as compared with those who would prefer other implied terms, and would have to contract out of the regime to which they will otherwise be legally subject.[98]

3.4.2 Cost of Learning

On balance, probably the greatest expected costs are those necessary for the very wording of the clauses. Although this may not always be confirmed in practice, parties need to ventilate hypotheses, calculate probabilities, imagine possible benefits and costs, negotiate changes, draft the contract and submit it to the scrutiny of lawyers. Thus the cost of drafting contractual terms will always be greater than zero, so that contracts are never complete. Only some provisions will be written – precisely the provisions where the expected benefit exceeds its expected cost. In any event, the more carefully drafted the contract, the easier it will be for the parties to resolve a dispute over its meaning.[99]

In the equation concerning the 'cost of learning', we should not overlook the cost of predicting results. This sort of 'guessing game' is highly undesirable in any contractual

95 The policy of leaving out eventualities uncovered by the contract may justify the *raison d'être* of renegotiation clauses cumulated with arbitration, inasmuch as parties leave uncertainties and contingencies not foreseen to be ascertained by arbitrators, experts in the subject matter. For a deeper analysis on renegotiation clauses, see R. Fabre, 'Les clauses d'adaptation dans les contrats', *Revue Trimestrielle de Droit Civil*, Vol. 82, 1983, pp. 1-30; B. Oppetit, 'L'adaptation des contrats internationaux aux changements de circonstances: la clause de hardship', *Journal du Droit International*, No. 4, 1974. p. 797; H. Ullmann, 'Droit et Pratique des clauses de hardship dans le système juridique américain', *Revue de Droit et des Affaires Internationaux*, No. 7, 1988, pp. 889-904; and M. Sornarajah, 'Supremacy of the Renegotiation Clause in International Contracts', *Journal of International Arbitration*, Vol. 5, Issue 2, 1988, pp. 97-114.

96 See I. Ayres & R. Gertner, *supra* note 77, noting that strategy is a source of contractual incompleteness, inasmuch as one party might tactically withhold information that would increase the total gains from contracting (the 'size of the pie') in order to increase her private share of the gains from contracting (her 'share of the pie') (pp. 93-94); see also B. E. Hermalin, A. W. Katz & R. Craswell, *supra* note 10 in Chapter 2, p. 65, noting that courts are most likely to react to a gap by trying to fill it with either an objectively reasonable term, or with their best guess as to what the parties would have wished, had they negotiated over the contingency in question.

97 See B. E. Hermalin, A. W. Katz & R. Craswell, *supra* note 10 in Chapter 2, p. 15.

98 See A. Kronman, 'Paternalism and the Law of Contracts', *Yale Law Journal*, Vol. 92, Issue 5, 1983, p. 766.

99 See R. Posner, *supra* note 81, p. 42.

context and is likely to generate more uncertainties, increasing costs both of performance and enforcement at a later stage. In fact, as we have seen at the outset, empirical efforts indicated an overall appreciation of familiarity with respect to the proposed law. This can be associated with the main economic consideration 'cost of learning', in addition to whether the law is more buyer- or seller-friendly and the applicable forum.

The cost of becoming proficient in a certain system of law may well pose obstacles.[100] Proficiency does not come easily; there are different levels of knowledge and understanding of law, which should be noted by contracting parties. The various studies and surveys undertaken and explored in Chapter 1[101] assist us in concluding that uniform law would be better suited to the scenarios described above. This is particularly so, noting the flexibility and accessibility of uniform law, which aims to promote uniformity of application and facilitate international transaction worldwide.

We have discussed thus far the theoretical aspects of market distortion and failure. Emphasis was also added to the interplay between parties and market via contracts, and the risks to which parties are routinely exposed while negotiating cross-border deals.

It is vital to understand and appreciate the risks which can endanger a contractual relationship and it is hoped that this chapter has offered insight into this topical issue. Another matter of great concern in a contract design, which may not fall within the choice-of-law 'bracket', but nonetheless plays a vital part in the decision, is the choice of forum, *i.e.*, the jurisdiction (state court or arbitration) best equipped to hear the contractual claims of disputing parties. It is hoped that the following chapter will shed light on these questions, as well as provide insight into the interplay of choice of law and choice of forum.

---

100 As L. Spagnolo notes, information costs prompt exclusions, despite the fact that the alternative requirement of familiarity with multiple foreign sales laws inherently carries an equal or probably greater information cost. What drives exclusions is the perception of information costs, which bear some connection with actual costs but can be distorted by psychological biases. See L. Spagnolo, *supra* note 118 in Chapter 1, p. 155. An analysis of these psychological biases can be found in *supra* Chapter 2.

101 See *supra* Chapter 1.

4 Choosing the Right Audience, or the Jurisdictional Conundrum

How do parties choose their audience in a cross-border negotiation sale? How do they decide on the adequacy of the forum[1] to hear potential disputes and why? What are the main forces that influence this choice? Is there any connection between the forum and choice of governing law of which we should be aware? What conclusions are to be drawn from these hypotheses? How can we improve this choice?

To answer these questions this chapter will examine theoretical discussions and empirical evidence. Readers will recall that in Chapter 1 they were invited to appreciate studies on choice of law worldwide, including the Global Empirical Survey on Choice of Law (hereinafter the Survey).[2] As we have seen in earlier chapters, this Survey aimed to identify the main legal and economic considerations arising at the bargaining table of international sales contracts. Since the Survey encompassed a large spectrum of questions – and the focus was not on choice of forum preferences but rather on choice of law, this chapter will discuss the answers and additional quotes that refer to choice of forum. Other evidentiary sources will be discussed in the first part of this chapter. In the second and final part of this chapter readers are invited to engage in a theoretical analysis of choice of court and arbitration agreements, with the aim of assessing the popularity of the two main forms of international dispute resolution, namely international litigation and international arbitration. We also discuss the common concerns and the alternatives to overcome obstacles that prevent parties from making better choices. This embraces the main concerns and driving forces behind this choice, relied on the evidence discussed at the outset of this discourse.

4.1 Studies on Choice of Forum

Examining studies discussed thus far,[3] a few more questions may come to mind: how much weight is attributed to this choice in cross-border sales? Is there any connection between choice of forum (court or arbitration) and choice of law? If so, are parties entirely aware of what this entails? If not, are they aware of the available alternatives to

1 'Forum' here means arbitration or state court.

2 See *supra* Section 1.2.4.1 *et seq.*

3 For methodological purposes, the studies on choice of forum discussed here are part of the studies selected in Chapter 1. Likewise, these are not meant to be exhaustive but rather to be restricted to the studies researched in Chapter 1.

complement and approximate these choices? Possible answers to, and reflections on, these questions will be investigated in detail in this chapter.[4]

In the following paragraphs we shall examine the data on jurisdictional choice in international transactions, aiming to reveal main concerns and approaches generally taken in choosing an international dispute resolution mechanism. The discussion also asks whether there is interplay between forum selection choice and governing contract law and, if so, what are the underlying reasons. We shall start with the studies conducted by the School of International Arbitration (SIA), Queen Mary, University of London.

4.1.1 SIA International Arbitration Studies

Queen Mary, University of London undertook its first empirical study on international arbitration in 2006, in partnership with Pricewatercoopers Company (PWC). The aim of the first research project, '2006 International Arbitration Study: Corporate Attitudes and Practices',[5] was to reveal corporate attitudes to international arbitration as a means to resolving cross-border dispute. The results suggested that arbitration had reached a considerable degree of popularity among market players.

For example, asked to disclose the preferred mechanism(s) for resolving cross-border dispute, respondents answered: 44% International arbitration & ADR; 29% International arbitration; 16% International mediation & other ADR; and 11% transnational litigation.[6] At that time 73% of the respondents already preferred to use international rather than state court litigation to resolve cross-border disputes.[7] Unsurprisingly, the advantages included flexibility, enforceability and privacy.[8] Disadvantages, on the other hand, included time and cost.[9]

In 2008 Queen Mary, University of London and Pricewatercoopers Company (PWC) undertook another survey involving companies doing business internationally (International Arbitration: Corporate Attitudes and Practices 2008), in order to index data on the use of arbitration as a mechanism of dispute resolution.[10] The results revealed a very high level of voluntary compliance with arbitral award (84% of respondents indicated that the opposing party had complied in full in more than 76% of cases[11]), and demonstrated that

4 An analysis of this interaction was first published in L. G. Meira Moser, 'Arbitration and Choice of Law in Cross-Border Transactions: A Potential Interplay?', *ASA Bulletin*, Vol. 34, Issue 1, 2016, pp. 95-111.

5 The Survey's data are available at [www.arbitration.qmul.ac.uk/docs/123295.pdf].

6 2006 International Arbitration Study: Corporate Attitudes and Practices, p. 5, Chart 2.

7 *Id.*, 73% being the total of 'international arbitration' preference alone (29%) or in combination with other ADR mechanisms (44%).

8 2006 International Arbitration Study: Corporate Attitudes and Practices, p. 6, Chart 3.

9 *Id.*, p. 7, Chart 4.

10 The Survey's data are available at [www.pwc.co.uk/assets/pdf/pwc-international-arbitration-2008.pdf].

11 International Arbitration: Corporate attitudes and practices 2008, p. 8, Chart 6.

parties attempt to avoid receiving a decision because of a desire to preserve good commercial relations. 86% of the respondents said they were 'satisfied' with arbitration.[12]

The study is undoubtedly useful as it allows us to recognize an 'arbitration culture' in cross-border transactions – arbitration is a mechanism used by sophisticated parties who prefer a specialized forum to resolve contractual dispute with their trading partners. As we shall see later, this is so because arbitration tends to create a level playing field for the maintenance of business relations, providing an efficient and cost-effective dispute resolution platform, which is often unavailable through the state court. The survey findings reinforced the idea of arbitration as an efficient dispute-resolution mechanism.

The data also demonstrate that only 6%[13] of the respondents resorted to the courts to enforce the arbitral award. This confirms the disciplining force of extra-legal sanctions,[14] and the parties' desire to preserve business relations (27%[15]). These vectors guide the behaviour of market players. Furthermore, as the greatest motive to avoid an arbitral award and reach a settlement was precisely the preservation of business relations, the results reinforce the notion that arbitration encourages the preservation of commercial ties. Additionally, in 43%[16] of cases, the dispute ended before the first hearing, endorsing the inference that arbitration tends to encourage agreement between the parties, or incentivize early settlement. There might be several reasons for this: as parties proceed to a hearing they will need to advance costs and are likely to invest time and money in preparation of pleadings, engage counsel, expert witness, incur out-of-pocket costs, etc. The risk of imposition of an award (interim or otherwise), which means a binding decision, might also influence and encourage settlement before the first hearing.

Besides offering a dispute-settlement mechanism capable of preserving business relations between parties, arbitration tends to speed resolution of dispute and, most importantly, enforce what has been agreed by the parties. The expertise of arbitrators in the matter in dispute, procedural flexibility and the possibility of confidential information also reduce transaction costs.

Following on the 2008 Survey, in 2010, Queen Mary, University of London conducted another International Survey on 'Choices in International Arbitration', sponsored by White & Case LLP.[17] This time, however, the survey aimed to consider the key factors that influence corporate choice in international arbitration. The survey revealed corporate attitudes to and policies on dispute resolution matters, including maximization of effectiveness of arbitration proceedings and confidentiality perceptions.

The data collected in this survey confirmed some of the propositions made earlier, in particular those concerning the frequent use of arbitration in cross-border transactions

---

12 *Id.*, p. 5, Chart 2.
13 *Id.*, p. 5, Chart 3.
14 This topic is further explored *infra* Section 4.3.1.
15 International Arbitration: Corporate attitudes and practices 2008, p. 7, Chart 5.
16 *Id.*, p. 7, Chart 4.
17 The Survey's data are available at [www.arbitration.qmul.ac.uk/docs/123290.pdf].

and the underscoring advantages *vis-à-vis* state court litigation. In this regard it is worth mentioning the number of corporations that have a dispute resolution policy (68%[18]) and the importance of confidentiality in international arbitration (for 62% of respondents 'very important', followed by 24% 'quite important'[19]). Once more, the survey revealed arbitration as a method widely used for the resolution of international dispute.

In 2013 Queen Mary, University of London and PricewaterhouseCoopers Company (PWC) undertook another survey, called 'Corporate Choices in International Arbitration: Industry Perspectives'.[20] It focused on industry's perceptions of arbitration in major sectors of the economy, namely Energy, Construction and Financial Services. The results indicated that, in line with previous findings, 52%[21] of respondents favoured arbitration as the best dispute resolution mechanism. The survey findings have the merit of offering an overview of the level of popularity of arbitration by industry sector. For example, in the Energy and Construction sectors, according to the 2013 survey, arbitration was clearly the preferred dispute-resolution mechanism.[22]

Finally, as to the disadvantages of arbitration, the list of factors revealed in the 2013 survey included: cost and delays, followed by a perceived lack of clear-cut decisions and a shortage of arbitrators with the requisite expertise.[23]

In conclusion, the data gathered in this survey showed that, generally speaking, arbitration continued to be the preferred dispute-resolution method yet concerns remained as to the cost of arbitration and delay.

The preference for arbitration in cross-border dispute has also been recently recognized. In 2015, Queen Mary, University of London conducted another international survey on 'Improvements and Innovations in International Arbitration', sponsored by White & Case LLP.[24] The survey sought to ascertain the view of the arbitration community as a whole on improvements and innovations in the arbitration process.

The survey results indicated that arbitration is the preferred dispute resolution method for 90% of respondents.[25] As to the best and worst features of international arbitration, there were no surprises: enforceability of awards (65%), avoidance of specific legal systems/national courts (64%) and a tie flexibility (38%) and selection of arbitrators (38%) completed the 'top 3' list. Other relevant considerations included confidentiality and privacy (33%) and neutrality (25%).[26] The 3 worst features of international arbitration cited were cost (68%), lack of effective sanctions during the arbitral process (46%)

18 Choices in International Arbitration 2010, p. 5, Chart 1.
19 *Id.*, p. 29, Chart 25.
20 The Survey's data are available at [www.arbitration.qmul.ac.uk/docs/123282.pdf].
21 Corporate choices in International Arbitration – Industry perspectives 2013, p. 6, Chart 1.
22 *Id.*, p. 7, Chart 3.
23 *Id.*, p. 9, Chart 6.
24 The Survey's data are available at [www.arbitration.qmul.ac.uk/docs/164761.pdf].
25 2015 Improvements and Innovations in International Arbitration, p. 5, Chart 1.
26 *Id.*, p. 6, Chart 2.

and lack of insight into arbitrators' efficiency (39%). Respondents also noted lack of speed (36%) and national court intervention (25%).[27]

In 2016 Queen Mary, University of London and Pinsent Masons LLP undertook another survey, the largest industry-sector survey of international arbitration, called 'Pre-empting and Resolving Technology, Media and Telecoms disputes'.[28] It focused on industry's perceptions of ADR in these sectors. In line with previous findings, 92% of respondents indicated that international arbitration is well suited to TMT dispute, 43% of respondents ranking arbitration as the most preferred dispute resolution mechanism. The survey findings further confirmed that the popularity of arbitration depends upon the industry concerned. For example, in the IT sector 50% of in-house counsel reported that litigation was the most encouraged dispute resolution mechanism (arbitration scored 27%). By contrast, respondents from the Energy, Construction and Manufacturing industries all rated arbitration the most encouraged DR mechanism.[29]

In view of the data presented above, it seems unquestionable that arbitration is the preferred dispute resolution method worldwide for cross-border matters,[30] albeit some criticism and suggestions for improvement, in particular regarding speed and cost have consistently been mentioned. Whilst we have seen sufficient evidence that arbitration is a popular choice in international transactions, how popular is it in cross-border sales disputes? In order to answer this question we shall discuss the Pace Law School CISG Database.

4.1.2 *Pace Law School CISG Database*

The late Albert Kritzer,[31] Associate Professor at Pace University School of Law and founder of the Institute of International Commercial Law, created an autonomous network of CISG websites as well as the Pace Law School CISG Database (CISG database)[32] in addition to the most successful legal academic competition worldwide, the Willem C. Vis International Commercial Arbitration Moot.[33]

27 *Id.*, p. 7, Chart 3.

28 The Survey's data are available at [www.arbitration.qmul.ac.uk/docs/189659.pdf].

29 A summary of the findings can be found in G. Moser, '2016 Queen Mary International Dispute Resolution Survey: Unveiling Technology, Media and Telecoms (TMT) Disputes', *Kluwer Arbitration Blog*, 15 December 2016, available at [http://kluwerarbitrationblog.com/2016/12/15/post-queen-mary-ip-survey/].

30 See J. D. M. Lew QC, 'Achieving the Dream: Autonomous Arbitration', *Arbitration International*, Vol. 22, Issue 2, 2006, p. 185, remarking that "[…] International arbitration, before neutral arbitrators, in a third country, with non-national or international procedures being followed, has become the essential mechanism for the settlement of all kinds of international business disputes".

31 *Remembering our Colleague Professor Albert H. Kritzer*, available at [www.cisg.law.pace.edu/cisg/Albert_Kritzer.html%5D].

32 *Id.*

33 Details of the Vis Moot, including history and further information are available at [https://vismoot.pace.edu]. See also E. E. Bergsten, 'The Willem C. Vis International Commercial Arbitration Moot and the

The CISG database compiles international doctrine and commentary on topical issues relating to private international law, the CISG and uniform international sales law.[34] It maintains an archive of judicial and arbitration decisions collected in some seventy countries where dispute arising from contracts for the international sale of goods has resulted in an application of the CISG, making these decisions, notably, available in English.[35]

The CISG database has received the approval of many scholars worldwide and compiles more than 3,000 decisions translated into English.[36] An inexhaustible source for research, the network serves as a consultative body for judicial decisions involving issues posed by the CISG.[37]

The CISG Database[38] presents evidence that arbitration is the preferred dispute resolution mechanism in cross-border sales. As at January 2018,[39] it contains links to 3,152 court decisions and arbitral awards on the CISG. Of this total number (3,152), 891 were arbitral awards, totalling c. 28% of the total in the CISG Database. Further, it has been submitted, on an assessment on CISG Database, Unilex,[40] and CISG online,[41] that 26% of CISG cases are decided by arbitral tribunal.[42] While the percentage may not, at a first sight, be impressive, one observation is in order: arbitral awards are typically confidential and therefore the number published on these databases allows us to assume that the effective incidence of CISG application in arbitration cases worldwide is significantly higher.[43] This may attest to the popularity of arbitration in CISG-based contracts and may suggest that it is more frequently used than international litigation.[44]

Teaching of International Commercial Arbitration,' *Arbitration International*, Vol. 22, Issue 2, 2006, pp. 309-314; E. E. Bergsten, 'Experimental Education through the Vis Moot', *Journal of Law & Commerce*, Vol. 34, No. 1, 2015, pp. 1-15; L. G. Meira Moser, 'Albert H. Kritzer, the 1980 UN Convention (CISG), and the Vis Moot: An Inseparable Relationship', *Pace International Law Review*, Vol. 24, 2012, pp. 258-265.

34 Albert H. Kritzer, CISG Database, available at [www.cisg.law.pace.edu].

35 L. G. Meira Moser, *supra* note 33, p. 262.

36 Albert H. Kritzer, *supra* note 34.

37 F. Ferrari (Ed.), *supra* note 34 in Chapter 1.

38 Albert H. Kritzer, *supra* note 34.

39 Consultation carried out on 5 January 2018.

40 Unilex database available at [www.unilex.info].

41 CISG-online database available at [www.cisg-online.ch].

42 N. Schmidt-Ahrendts, 'CISG and Arbitration', *Belgrade Law Review*, No. 3, Year LIX (2011), pp. 212-213. See also, in this sense, L. Mistelis, *supra* note 119 in Chapter 1, pp. 387-388, who has reached the same conclusion for awards rendered prior to 2008, remarking that "if it is true that significantly less than 5% of arbitration awards get published then one could assume that there are between 4250 and 5000 awards on the CISG... That makes arbitration the main forum for the resolution of disputes arising out of international sales contracts under the CISG".

43 See N. Schmidt-Ahrendts, *supra* note 42, p. 213, reporting that in an enquiry made with the ICC, out of 3000 cases randomly selected, in 155 of them the CISG was applied, which the author considered surprisingly high given that the search involved all kinds of disputes and not only sale of goods.

44 D. Taylor, 'Reflections on a Critical Aspect of CISG-Governed International Sale of Goods Transactions: The Impact of the Hague Convention on Choice of Court Agreements on Forum Selection', *International Trade and Business Law Review*, Vol. 15, 2012, p. 49.

Having discussed parties' preferences and perceptions, with a particular focus on arbitration, we shall now explore the detail of the Survey. Participants in the Survey were not asked to disclose whether their decisions were made in the context of contracts subject to arbitration or courts.[45] Therefore we aim to reveal key triggers in the choice of a certain jurisdiction (whether court or arbitration), all in an attempt to determine whether parties make efficient choices. Is there a way to improve their choices? To this end, we invite the readers to explore some intricacies of the Survey.[46]

4.1.3 *The Global Empirical Survey on Choice of Law*

As indicated at the start of this chapter, answers and additional comments of the respondents to the Survey Questions (with the exception of questions 7 and 8[47]) will be discussed below.

The Survey Questions 1 to 3[48] sought to identify – explore and discuss – the importance of legal considerations in choosing governing contract law.

As mentioned in Chapter 1,[49] the Survey did not aim to and thus did not ask the respondents to draw a distinction between the negotiation of contracts with arbitration agreements and those with choice of court agreements. Therefore, whilst we can certainly make inferences based on the answers and additional comments provided by the respondents, it might not be possible to obtain clear data on the approach (or different approach) to these choices depending on the dispute resolution clause chosen by the respondents.

Despite this, as we have seen, the respondents pointed out that the choice of jurisdiction, including its adequacy and predictability, is an important factor in their contract negotiation decision-making process. This is confirmed by additional comments in which the respondents disclosed a fear of unwanted results, in addition to concerns of inefficient coercive mechanisms and biased decisions of state courts.[50] Arbitration was also cited as a forum that would minimize concerns of predictability of the application of rules, award made and its enforcement.[51]

45 See Survey instructions *supra* Section 1.2.3.

46 A thorough analysis of the Survey is present *supra* Section 1.2.4.1.

47 Question 7 of the Survey concerns the most desirable governing contract law and Question 8 deals with opting-out. Further information is available in *supra* Section 1.2.4.3.

48 A detailed breakdown of answers and percentages are available in *supra* Section 1.2.4.1.

49 See *supra* Section 1.2.4.1.

50 See, *e.g.*, Survey Question 3 (Section 1.2.4.1); Survey Question 4 (Section 1.2.4.2); Survey Question 5 (Section 1.2.4.2); Survey Question 6 (Section 1.2.4.2); and Survey Question 7 (Section 1.2.4.3).

51 See, *e.g.*, Survey Question 1 (Section 1.2.4.1); Survey Question 2 (Section 1.2.4.1); Survey Question 3 (Section 1.2.4.1); Survey Question 4 (Section 1.2.4.2).

That said, in Questions 1 to 3 the respondents were asked first to indicate the three (3) main legal considerations and then, positive and negative features associated with the governing contract law.

The answers that call for particular attention and bear on our discussion of jurisdictional matters are as follows:
- for a sale on credit basis, law of the buyer's jurisdiction;
- 'home turf' advantage where possible;
- enforceability;
- forum for dispute resolution;
- independent and corruption-free judiciary;
- enforceability of resulting judgment or award;
- cost/convenience of resolving disputes;
- whether the jurisdiction has ratified the UN Convention on Contracts for the International Sale of Goods (CISG);
- quality of available arbitrators;
- state of administration of justice in applicable jurisdiction;
- lack of qualified and impartial arbitrators in the relevant jurisdiction;
- independence and impartiality (or lack thereof) of judiciary; and
- potential enforcement issues.

The 2014 Survey Questions 4 to 6,[52] in their turn, aimed at identifying, exploring and discussing the respondents' economic considerations in deciding which law should govern a cross-border sale. The 2014 Survey also aimed at revealing whether there were overlaps in legal and economic considerations and, if so, what this could represent in practice. The respondents were asked first to indicate the three (3) main economic considerations and then positive and negative features of the governing contract law.

The three main economic considerations cited were cost of enforcement of legal rules (75.77%), political stability in the relevant jurisdiction (57.27%) and unfamiliarity and cost of learning (47.58%).

The answers that call particular attention and bear on our discussion on jurisdiction matters are as follows:
- level of education of judges;
- what courts will decide on potential disputes;
- if arbitration is chosen, then this consideration is of minor importance;
- enforceability;
- predictability of approach or interpretation to be adopted (respectable system, settled case law);
- independent and corruption-free judiciary;

52 A detailed breakdown of answers and percentages are available *supra* Section 1.2.4.2.

- average speed of legal enforcement processes;
- difficulty of enforcement in the jurisdiction; and
- corrupt judiciary.

The Survey answers and additional comments above confirm that, in choosing a governing contract law due consideration is given to choice of forum. Thus, these choices are indeed complementary and in some instances taken concomitantly. However, as mentioned earlier, whether these choices have been thought through in the context of potential claim to be heard by a state court judge or by an arbitrator has not been fully explored in the Survey. Nevertheless, answers and additional comments may hint that for some respondents a choice-of-law decision may carry different weight if an arbitration agreement is also a matter for discussion at the bargaining table. What that would entail may not yet be entirely clear, but we shall discuss how parties can make more efficient choice-of-law decisions by more rational thinking on the choice of the forum (courts or arbitration).

While it is not possible to estimate the number of respondents who answered these questions in light of contracts subject to arbitration agreements,[53] some did express their views on the matter in stating that 'if arbitration is chosen, then this consideration is of minor importance'.[54] This indicates that considerations could be more or less relevant depending on whether a choice-of-court or an arbitration clause had been inserted in the agreement. In support of this view, the above comments show that there is a general fear among some respondents that the forum chosen may not be independent or corruption-free, in their approach to a choice-of-law clause in the agreement or even to apply the law by default. It seems that some respondents understand that the option for arbitration would increase enforcement of choice-of-law clauses and application of the law.[55]

The respondents' concerns as to the appropriate forum to hear a potential dispute is translated into uncertainty as to the outcome (time, cost and enforcement barriers) and also whether the courts would act independently and impartially. This could be summarized by the following response: 'what courts will decide on potential disputes'.[56]

Conversely, litigating in a given court may not be seen as a deal-breaker by some respondents as long as there is certainty regarding the law applicable. This assumption is confirmed by the following responses: 'whether the jurisdiction has ratified the UN Convention on Contracts for the International Sale of Goods (CISG)'[57] and 'for a sale on credit basis, law of the buyer's jurisdiction'.[58]

53 See note 50 *supra*.

54 Response to Survey Question 4, *supra* Section 1.2.4.2.

55 See I. Schwenzer, *supra* note 195 in Chapter 1, p. 724, arguing, *inter alia*, that by agreeing on arbitration many of the imponderables of choice-of-law and forum selection clauses would be 'circumvented'.

56 Response to Survey Question 4, *supra* Section 1.2.4.2.

57 Response to Survey Question 2, *supra* Section 1.2.4.1.

58 Response to Survey Question 1, *supra* Section 1.2.4.1.

Some respondents may decide to litigate in a particular jurisdiction for tactical reasons: 'average speed of legal enforcement processes';[59] 'for a sale on credit basis, law of the buyer's jurisdiction';[60] and "'home turf' advantage where possible".[61]

The respondents' fears and concerns might signal that for some the certainty of enforcement of a choice-of-court agreement[62] might mitigate enforcement concerns, inasmuch as the court chosen would not decline jurisdiction but rather assign it and apply its conflict of law rules or uphold a choice of law clause decided by the parties as the case may be. This legal certainty could likewise increase the use of the CISG, by default, and decrease instances where parties would opt out of the CISG for fear that another court, not that chosen by the parties, would retain jurisdiction to hear the case.

All in all, it comes as a no surprise that some jurisdictions may be, or at least be perceived to be, more popular than others due to adjudicative attractions, as not all courts will accept jurisdiction on the basis of the parties' choice. Therefore, jurisdictional choices are no doubt of relevance in deciding on governing contract law. If respondents fear that certain state courts may not be fully equipped to deal with complex matters, or may perhaps not be fully impartial or independent in upholding contractual choices, what would be the game changer? How could market players take more efficient decisions?

In order to answers these questions we shall now shift the discourse to a theoretical consideration of choice of court agreements, albeit one that is supported by the evidence presented in the above discussions. The purpose of the following paragraphs is to explore synergies between choice of court and choice of law agreements. We shall subsequently outline the main differences between choice of court and arbitration agreements, aiming to disclose, among other features, any interplay these processes may have with the choice of law.

4.2 Choice of Court Agreements

A choice of a court agreement entails that a given country's courts will have jurisdiction over any dispute arising out of the contract that binds the parties. The agreement confers power on one jurisdiction, that chosen by the parties, to hear a dispute. This is of utmost importance as parties can spend time and resources litigating jurisdictional matters, thereby delaying the resolution of dispute. However, enforcing a choice of court agreement may be a hurdle that parties would come across once a dispute arises. Why do parties still opt for a choice of court agreement?

---

59 Response to Survey Question 6, *supra* Section 1.2.4.2.

60 Response to Survey Question 1, *supra* Section 1.2.4.1.

61 *Id.*

62 The Hague Convention on Choice of Court is discussed *infra* Section 4.2.3.

While arbitration has been consistently cited as a 'go to' option in cross-border matters, we should not forget that not all market players are likely to use arbitration. And this is so for various reasons including sophistication of players, cost and convenience of dispute, legal culture, type of contract, relationship to the contract and the parties. Therefore it is also necessary to consider how parties who might not use arbitration approach the choice of law and whether they see this choice from a different perspective. We should also ask whether these players make rational choices.

4.2.1 *The Hurdles of Choosing a State Court Jurisdiction*

Contracting parties are often concerned with the adequacy of a forum of a potential dispute, in addition to the enforcement of the legal rules chosen and the resulting decision. Parties are generally aware of the risks involved if litigation becomes the sole recourse in seeking enforcement of a contract. They will likely anticipate the opponent's behaviour, including recalcitrant or delaying tactics, possible biased judgment of state courts and enforcement concerns.[63]

The appropriate forum to hear potential disputes was indicated as a source of apprehension by a number of respondents in the Survey. Their concerns ranged from lack of impartiality and independence of judgment, to doubts about the effectiveness of coercive mechanisms.

Concern regarding adequacy of forum can be explained by the following premise: contracts are naturally incomplete.[64] As they are incomplete, the role of the applicable law will be to interpret the terms on which the parties agreed, fill the gaps left and complete the terms of the contract according to its legal framework, case law, uses and practice. But the application of the law will be exercised by the decision-maker that belongs to the forum assigned to hear the dispute. Parties tend to ensure that a forum that is most receptive and responsive[65] to their business preferences and concerns hears their dispute.[66]

---

63 L. G. Meira Moser, *supra* note 3 in Chapter 1, p. 28.

64 See S. Shavell, *supra* note 85 in Chapter 3.

65 A. Katz, arguing that "[…]In the arena of international sales contracts, it is relatively easy for the parties for the parties to opt out of substantive interpretative regimes if they wish, either through explicit choice of governing law, or through forum clauses that will ensure that any dispute is heard by a tribunal that is more responsive to their business concerns. The rules and culture of international private law have long taken a liberal attitude toward the parties' contractual choice of applicable law; and the CISG follows in this tradition, specifically authorizing parties in Article 6 to exclude the application of the entire convention from their contract, or, less drastically, to derogate from or vary the effect of any of its provisions, including the trade usage provision of Article 9(2).." 'The Relative Costs of Incorporating Trade Usage into Domestic versus International Sales Contracts: Comments on Clayton Gillette, Institutional Design and International Usages under the CISG', *Chicago Journal of International Law*, Vol. 5, Issue 1, 2004, pp. 183-184.

66 Studies suggest that arbitrators are viewed as experts who are better able to verify dimensions of commercial contracts than court judges. See, for example, A. Dixit, 'Arbitration and Information', Working Paper, Princeton University, Princeton, NJ, 2003.

The awareness and, to a certain degree, uncertainty in relation to jurisdiction is apparent in the following matters mentioned by the respondents in the Survey:
- enforceability;
- forum for dispute resolution;
- independent and corruption-free judiciary;
- arbitration know-how available;
- enforceability of resulting judgment or award;
- predictability;
- enforcement rules and procedure;
- familiarity with the law of the jurisdiction by the parties;
- cost/convenience of resolving disputes;
- quality of available arbitrators;
- state of administration of justice in applicable jurisdiction;
- lack of qualified and impartial arbitrators in the relevant jurisdiction;
- independence and impartiality (or lack thereof) of judiciary;
- potential enforcement issues;
- level of education of the judges;
- what courts will decide on potential disputes;
- if arbitration is chosen, then this consideration is of minor importance;
- predictability of approach or interpretation to be taken (respectable system, settled case law);
- unpredictable approach/interpretation;
- average speed of legal enforcement processes;
- difficult enforcement in the country;
- corrupt judiciary.

It is undisputed that forum selection has long been a favourite topic of academic investigation. The main advantages of private adjudication over state court litigation have certainly been extensively explored, yet the topic still fascinates and intrigues lay readers, practitioners and scholars worldwide. As evidence above demonstrates, it is arguable that arbitration, a popular choice for private adjudication, has become the preferred method of dispute resolution in international settings. Nevertheless, we aim to investigate this subject in more detail in order to provide answers to the following questions: which requisites define the popularity of a state court jurisdiction? What triggers the option for one jurisdiction over the other? What could improve the use of choice of court agreements? We shall start by exploring the main concerns and driving forces of choice of court agreements.

4.2.1.1 Cost and Convenience

Given that parties (as rational actors) will tend to agree deals securing mutual benefit, we shall outline cost and convenience arising from recourse to state courts for the resolution of cross-border dispute. In deciding the most efficient dispute resolution method, it is essential that parties consider forum convenience and 'contract enforcement costs', *i.e.*, the costs of enforcing what has been contractually agreed. In other words, when opting for a given state court, parties should evaluate the costs incurred in having their duties, rights and obligations outlined in the contract duly observed. This is not an equation as straightforward as one would have thought, but from a legal and economic perspective, regard should be given to the costs of enforcing the contract.

In certain jurisdictions there is a lack of expeditious remedies or measures, coupled with a 'judicial activism', *i.e.*, hermetic procedural mechanisms that allow the judge to influence the substantive law.[67] This includes entrusting the judiciary to perform functions that are not merely adjudicatory, thereby departing from the paradigm that justice is reactive, neutral, technical and programmed.[68]

In such scenarios judges might adopt an interventionist approach based on political ideology or a wish to redress inequality of bargaining power. State court judges may exempt a party from performing certain contractual obligations or even modify and adapt the contract in order to align it with a particular policy. Accordingly, parties should reflect and ponder on their choices in potential litigation, using cost-benefit analysis in a realistic (and rational) approach to procedural conduct.

Particularly in the context of choice of law agreements, these jurisdictions may not, for these reasons, be willing to uphold an agreed choice of law, thereby leaving parties in a state of legal uncertainty, highly undesirable and costly in business environments. Therefore, regard should always be given to the 'receptivity' of the jurisdiction to a party's business preferences and concerns.[69] Parties should be aware of the risks involved in choosing a court system with which they are unfamiliar. This ensures parties can attempt to avoid unpleasant surprises and costly mistakes.

4.2.1.2 Risk of Bias or Partiality

A further important aspect that should be taken into account when considering state courts is the fear of favouritism. It is an unspoken rule that judges in certain jurisdictions will tend to favour the weaker party in the name of justice, national policy, ideology and

67 N. Garoupa, 'A análise econômica do direito como instrumento de reforço da independência do Judiciário', *Revista de Direito Bancário e do Mercado de Capitais*, No. 37, 2007, p. 84.

68 J. E. Faria, 'O judiciário e seus dilemas', *Revista do Advogado, Associação dos Advogados de São Paulo*, No. 56, 1999, p. 66; C. M. da Silva Velloso, 'Problemas e soluções na prestação da Justiça', *Revista dos Tribunais*, Vol. 664, 1991, pp. 215-235; J. E. Faria, 'A crise do poder judiciário no Brasil', *Justiça e Democracia*, No. 1, 1996, pp. 18-64.

69 See, in this sense, empirical efforts discussed *supra* Chapter 1.

even personal inclination. If one of the parties belongs to the jurisdiction, the fear of favouritism may increase.

This fear is understandable and we could use an ordinary example to illustrate: a football match between teams from different countries. It would be inconceivable to have a referee from either. In some national leagues and tournaments (*e.g.*, Brazil), referees may be chosen from different states or regions of the same country in order to avoid bias and lift the fear of favouritism.[70]

In the same vein, William Park notes that the greater reliability often found in arbitral awards, as contrasted with court judgments, derives from different notions of 'law' in commercial transactions. The calculus of duty is simply not the same as between judges and arbitrators: "(...) Bearing obligations to the citizenry as a whole, judges may seek to implement societal values that sometimes trump private agreements. Although responsible judges will master existing authority before taking the law in new directions, many traditions allow appellate judges to overrule precedent".[71]

W. Park continues, "as creatures of the parties' consent, arbitrators must show special fidelity to shared expectations expressed in contract or treaty, fixing their eyes on existing norms rather than proposals for the law as it should be... the arbitrator may look to enhance shared *ex ante* expectations or the parties themselves, applying the law on an 'as is' basis. By contrast, appellate judge might explore principles that push law into new directions, so as to promote certainty from the perspective of emerging policy".[72]

Another facet of state court jurisdiction is the risk of bias and partiality at the point when the national legal system is chosen. For example, in an international contract, the primacy of parties' agreement may lead arbitrators to conclude that the litigants intended to invoke only part of a national legal system. By contrast, a judge may feel inclined to apply the norms of his or her own state more broadly, perhaps tweaked by an impulse to shape those norms to reflect the forum's changing policy concerns.[73]

Last but certainly not least, there are also enforcement concerns at the level of choice of court agreements, for the very same reasons stated above and which could undermine parties' agreements and lead to more costs and inefficient results. In these cases the state court elected by the parties would decline jurisdiction, leaving them in a state of uncertainty as to which court will have jurisdiction to hear a dispute and whether this court would uphold parties' contractual choices. As we have seen, these uncertainties generate costs.[74]

70 For philosophical reflections on being and appearing good, see J. Driver, 'Caesar's Wife: On the Moral Significance of Appearing Good', *The Journal of Philosophy*, Vol. 89, No. 7, 1992, pp. 331-343.

71 W. W. Park, 'The Predictability Paradox – Arbitrators and Applicable Law', *Dossier XI of the ICC Institute of World Business Law: The Application of Substantive Law by International Arbitrators*, 2014, pp. 60-61.

72 *Id.*

73 W. W. Park, *supra* note 72, p. 65.

74 See S. Shavell, *supra* note 85 in Chapter 3.

4.2.1.3 Political and Economic Uncertainties

Political and economic instability in certain jurisdictions tend to impose hindrances for the use of the respective state courts and, in consequence, their domestic law. These uncertainties are routinely regarded as a sort of 'underdevelopment' of the court system,[75] or a lack of consistency and, therefore, adequacy for international contracts.

Much of this suspicion has its origin in legislative change. In certain jurisdictions, the legislative bodies constantly passes new law, undertake legal reforms and amendments; they regularly approve new codes and regulations, which requires users to be constantly up-to-date and subject to a level of uncertainty often not tolerated in the business context. This also applies to procedural regulations, the provisions of which may be revoked and changed in a short space of time. As we have seen, uncertainties can mean costs. International contexts are complex and adding this uncertainty might render their entire operation impractical.

Another point of concern lies in financial stability. Economic drawbacks in certain jurisdictions serve as a warning to parties not to choose that court system. Economic instability may lead to undesirable change and affect the legislative and judicial bodies of a given jurisdiction. As discussed earlier, uncertainties generate costs, and contracting parties are (or should be) rational players (despite heuristics and cognitive biases[76]) and, more often than not, risk-averse.[77] Hence, parties will likely avoid jurisdictions that have been under economic sanction and have witnessed recent economic drawbacks.

We have seen that the parties' main concern generally lies in uncertainty as to whether state courts would uphold a choice of court agreement and, in consequence, whether a substantive law will be applied in accordance with the parties' agreement or by default. In light of this, some questions may arise: are certain laws not used as a result of a fear that a given state court would not enforce contractual choices? Are certain courts avoided simply because of a lack of mechanisms to empower jurisdiction? How can we ascertain that a choice of court agreement be duly observed? What would be a game changer for these players? Are there winds of change approaching?

4.2.2 *The Hague Convention on Choice of Court*

When an international dispute is in prospect, a question that often arises is: where should I bring a legal action? What are the risks and costs involved if a court declines jurisdiction? What is the fate of the contract in case of parallel proceedings? And what if the courts do not enforce a choice of court agreement? These questions refer to the conflict of

75 For a deeper explanation of the factors that trigger these choices, cognitive limitations and heuristics, please refer to *supra* Chapter 2.

76 *Id.*

77 L. G. Meira Moser, *supra* note 3 in Chapter 1, p. 27.

jurisdiction rules that are regulated by Civil Procedure Codes, Acts and Regulations,[78] and added complexity is seen when this goes beyond the borders of a country's own rules.[79]

There are a number of reasons for which parties initiate proceedings in the courts of a given State, which include but are not limited to differences in procedure and rules of evidence, efficacy and speed of judicial proceedings, familiarity with a given system, the language to be used,[80] the court's reputation, the 'quality and ability of the judiciary and the legal profession', the cost of court proceedings, ease of enforcement of judgment, the 'legal climate' and differences in conflict of law rules.[81] These are matters of concern since the law of the forum will impose upon the parties a legal framework that provides for certain rules to be followed,[82] which may limit party autonomy in a contractual dispute. It has also been argued elsewhere[83] that parties tend to prefer courts when the governing national law is clear and when emergency relief is likely to be important in resolving disputes.[84]

It should be clear that if a contract does not contain a choice of forum clause, the question of which court has jurisdiction will be regulated by the private international law in each jurisdiction where the party attempts to sue the counterparty.[85] Generally, a party may always be sued in the country where it has its registered office or where it undertakes its main business, and even in the country where the main performance was to be carried out. The courts may also retain jurisdiction if, in their estimation, there is sufficient connection with the transaction.[86] This creates an atmosphere of uncertainty, no doubt undesirable for market players, resulting in higher transaction costs.[87]

78 In the European Union, the Brussels Council Regulation on Jurisdiction and the Recognition of Judgements in Civil and Commercial Matters (Brussels II) and the Lugano Convention of 2007 ratified by the EU, Denmark, Iceland, Norway and Switzerland. Further information available at [http://eur-lex.europa.eu].

79 See, in this sense, L. G. Meira Moser, 'CISG in Brazilian Courts: A Promising Start – Case Commentary on Inversiones Metalmecánicas I.C.A. v. Voges Metalurgia Ltda.', *Internationales Handelsrecht*, Vol. 16, Issue 4, 2016, pp. 133-136.

80 This consideration is not exclusive to choice of court agreements. The importance of language in contracts subject to arbitration, and its interplay with parties' due process, is discussed by S. Tung, 'The Importance of Languages in International Arbitration and How They Impact Parties' Due Process Rights', *Contemporary Asia Arbitration Journal*, Vol. 10, Issue 1, 2017, pp. 113-132.

81 L. Silberman & F. Ferrari, 'Getting to the Law Applicable to the Merits in International Arbitration and the Consequences of Getting It Wrong', *NYU Law and Economics Research Paper No. 10-40*, 2010, pp. 1-34.

82 *Id.*

83 C. R. Drahozal, 'Private Ordering and International Commercial Arbitration', *Penn State Law Review*, Vol. 113, p. 1050.

84 Despite this, the busiest arbitration institutions in the world have now set of rules intended to expedite procedure, including emergency arbitrators. See *e.g.*, the London Court of International Arbitration (LCIA) [www.lcia.org] and the International Court of Arbitration of the International Chamber of Commerce (ICC) [https://iccwbo.org].

85 G. Cordero-Moss, *supra* note 29 in Chapter 3, p. 157.

86 *Id.*

87 See discussion about transaction costs *supra* Section 3.4.

A game changer[88] for concerns regarding choice of court agreements could certainly be the Hague Convention on Choice of Court (hereinafter the Hague Convention), concluded in 2005 and which came into force on 1 October 2015.[89] Under the Hague Convention, parties' choice of court agreements are upheld[90] and resulting judgments are enforceable by all contracting parties. The intention of the Hague Convention is that parties from contracting States should feel more confident in trading with each other and making use of each other's courts.[91]

4.2.2.1 Main Features

The Hague Convention has three main pillars: Article 5,[92] which provides that the chosen court must hear the dispute; Article 6,[93] which prevents any court not chosen by the parties from proceeding with a hearing (the court must suspend or dismiss proceedings), thus the other contracting State must abstain from asserting jurisdiction over the claim; and Article 8,[94] in accordance with which judgment given by the chosen court must be recognized and enforced by the courts of the contracting States.[95]

To illustrate, let us suppose that a Mexican buyer and a German supplier have entered into a sales contract.[96] The parties have elected the courts of Mexico to hear any contrac-

88 Some authors argue that "The real game-changer could be the Judgments Convention. By providing for the mutual enforcement of court judgments not limited to exclusive jurisdiction clauses, the Judgments Convention, if ratified by a large number of States, could have a wide-ranging impact on the world of international disputes as we know it. If States recognize the value in ratifying the Judgments Convention, it could undoubtedly give international arbitration – and the New York Convention – a run for their money, as it would provide an alternative global instrument that meets the practical needs of international litigation", S. Jhangiani & R. Amin, 'The Hague Convention on Choice of Court Agreements: A Rival to the New York Convention and a "Game-Changer" for International Disputes?', *Kluwer Arbitration Blog*, 23 September 2016, available at [http://kluwerarbitrationblog.com/2016/09/23/the-hague-convention-on-choice-of-court-agreements-a-rival-to-the-new-york-convention-and-a-game-changer-for-international-disputes/%5D].

89 Further information is available on the website of the Hague Conference on Private International Law [https://www.hcch.net/en/home].

90 The full text of the Convention is available at [https://www.hcch.net/en/instruments/conventions/full-text/?cid=98].

91 G. Rowan *et al.*, 'Hague Choice of Court Convention: Gaining Momentum', available at [https://uk.practicallaw.thomsonreuters.com/7-619-7898?transitionType=Default&contextData=(sc.Default)&firstPage=true&bhcp=1].

92 The full text of the Convention is available at [https://www.hcch.net/en/instruments/conventions/full-text/?cid=98].

93 *Id.*

94 *Id.*

95 There might be some friction if the member state made a declaration under Article 19 of the Hague Convention, which allows a court of a contracting State to decline to hear the dispute if it has no connection with the dispute or the parties. In the author's view, this is a most unfortunate provision and one that contradicts the nature of cross-border contracts and cross-border litigation to that effect, *i.e.*, the search for a neutral forum to hear disputes. That said, none of the member states has made such declaration. Nevertheless, Article 32 of the Hague Convention authorizes member states to make (and modify) an Article 19 declaration at any time.

96 In this example both Germany and Mexico are contracting States.

tual dispute but the German party has initiated proceedings in Germany. In this case German courts will be obliged either to suspend or dismiss those proceedings in accordance with its obligations under the Hague Convention. Therefore, once the Mexican court renders a judgment the German court will be bound to enforce it.

Now, let us suppose that the same Mexican buyer has entered into a sales contract with a Brazilian[97] supplier. The parties have elected the courts of Mexico to hear any contractual dispute. If a dispute arises, the Hague Convention will apply to the agreement and will require the Mexican court to take jurisdiction. Nevertheless, unless and until Brazil becomes a contracting State, the Hague Convention will not prevent a Brazilian court from taking jurisdiction nor will it require the Brazilian court to enforce a judgment of the Mexican court.

Let us suppose that Brazil had acceded to the Hague Convention and that the Brazilian party's main assets were located in African countries. The Mexican party obtained a favourable ruling before the Mexican court and seeks to enforce the judgment in Africa. If the country where the Mexican party seeks enforcement has not acceded to the Hague Convention at the time of the enforcement, domestic law will apply to determine whether the judgment can be enforced.

The long-term goal of the Hague Convention, some authors argue,[98] is to build an international legal regime for choice of court agreements similar [99] to that established for arbitration agreements by the New York Convention on the Recognition and Enforcement of Foreign Arbitral Awards (1958 NY Convention[100]). This would, in turn, place court judgments on an equal footing with arbitral awards when it comes to worldwide enforcement.[101] While enforcement is indeed one of the main advantages professed by enthusiasts of arbitration and their users generally,[102] some authors are sceptical[103] as to whether the Hague Convention would gain momentum and perhaps represent a threat to

97 Brazil is currently not a contracting State.

98 C. T. Kotuby Jr. *et al.*, 'The Hague Choice of Court Convention Takes Effect, and With It Greater Certainty for International Transactions', Jones Day Publications, 2015, available at [www.jonesday.com/the-hague-choice-of-court-convention-takes-effect-and-with-it-greater-certainty-for-international-transactions-10-29-2015/].

99 M. Hwang SC described the Hague Convention as 'a sort of mini version of the New York Convention for the enforcement of court judgments', M. Hwang SC, 'Commercial Courts and International Arbitration – Competitors or Partners?', *Arbitration International*, Vol. 31, Issue 2, 2015, pp. 193-212.

100 The text of the 1958 NY Convention is available at [www.uncitral.org/pdf/english/texts/arbitration/NY-conv/New-York-Convention-E.pdf].

101 Chief Justice Sundaresh Menon of Singapore described the Hague Convention as a 'game-changer in the international enforceability of court judgments', speech available at [www.supremecourt.gov.sg/docs/default-source/default-document-library/media-room/opening-lecture—difc-lecture-series-2015.PDF].

102 See, *e.g.*, 2015 Queen Mary, University of London Survey, 'Improvements and Innovations in International Arbitration', *supra* note 25.

103 D. Taylor, *supra* note 44, p. 59, arguing that "international arbitration needs to retain an identity and features separate and distinct from international litigation, with clear advantages such as flexibility of procedure, privacy, neutrality and, when possible, lower cost and greater speed".

the popularity of arbitration, while also acknowledging that this would be dictated by the path that international arbitration takes.[104]

Although the number or signatory States is still modest,[105] any party can take advantage of the Hague Convention. If a party chooses to have a contractual dispute heard in a court of a signatory State, this choice will be given full effect and the resulting judgment will be enforceable in all other signatory States.[106] This affords parties greater certainty and flexibility as to their 'audience' and the possible results of this choice. In addition, Article 3(a) of the Hague Convention provides that a choice of court agreement may be drafted for the purpose of deciding disputes which 'have arisen or may arise',[107] suggesting that an exclusive choice of court agreement may also be concluded after a dispute arises.

What would be the implications of the Hague Convention in a choice of law decision-making process?

4.2.2.2 A Synergy with Choice of Law?

One of the hurdles of using a choice of court agreement is that of bargaining over and choosing a court which is thought convenient to both parties. We have seen that 'arm-wrestling'[108] would drive this choice but that often parties decide to choose a third country's court to resolve potential disputes, one that may not always be the best option and which may also be subject to jurisdictional matters once a dispute arises.

The Hague Convention, however, ensures the necessary legal certainty for the parties that their choice of court will be respected and that the resulting judgment will produce legal effects in any of the contracting States. This is a welcoming development in cross-border sales and one that, in the author's view, is capable of increasing the synergy with and the rationality of the choice of governing contract law.

For example, if parties to both the Hague Convention[109] and the CISG[110] decide to litigate in one of their jurisdictions, the CISG will by default apply as the governing

104 M. Rea & M. C. Marotti, 'What Is All the Fuss? The Potential Impact of the Hague Convention on the Choice of Court Agreement on International Arbitration', *Kluwer Arbitration Blog*, 16 June 2017, available at [http://kluwerarbitrationblog.com/2017/06/16/fuss-potential-impact-hague-convention-choice-court-agreement-international-arbitration/].

105 The Hague Convention counts 30 members bound to it to date. Further information is available at [https://www.hcch.net/en/instruments/conventions/status-table/?cid=98].

106 'The Hague Choice of Court Convention Takes Effect, and With It Greater Certainty for International Transactions', available at [www.jonesday.com/the-hague-choice-of-court-convention-takes-effect-and-with-it-greater-certainty-for-international-transactions-10-29-2015].

107 Article 3 of the Hague Convention.

108 See *supra* note 25 in Chapter 1.

109 The list of contracting States of the Hague Choice of Court Convention is available at [https://www.hcch.net/en/instruments/conventions/status-table/?cid=98].

110 The list of contracting States of the CISG is available at [www.uncitral.org/uncitral/en/uncitral_texts/sale_goods/1980CISG_status.html].

contract law.[111] In such a scenario, in addition to avoiding litigation on unsettled jurisdictional issues, parties would need not to bargain over the governing contract law, thereby decreasing transaction costs. Even if one of the Hague Convention parties' signatories is not a signatory to the CISG, if the parties wish the CISG to govern the contract, they may obtain such result by virtue of the benefits offered by the Hague Convention, *i.e.*, enforcement of the choice of court agreement and the advantages that it entails: the application of the rules of the given court system, including its conflict of law rules. These parties are likely to select a forum more receptive to their contractual wishes. This in turn may increase awareness of the parties of the potential synergy with choice of law decisions.

We could also think of the clear advantage of using a neutral legal framework such as the CISG to govern a cross-border sales dispute heard in a State signatory to the Hague Convention, resulting in a judgment enforceable in all signatory States.

The Hague Convention will increase predictability and efficiency of the choice of forum by reducing the irrational race to courts and parallel proceedings, which often generate more costs and uncertainties exhaustively disclosed by evidentiary sources.[112] Enforceability issues, a source of concern among market players,[113] will also be significantly minimized.[114] From this, parties are likely to make more rational decisions as to forum. Given that attention will no longer be focused on forum concerns, parties will be granted room to make more rational choice of law decisions, as there will be a safer harbour or platform for their reliance on the courts to apply the governing contract law chosen or applied by the courts by default.

By way of caveat, let us remember that the Survey, for chronological reasons, unfortunately did not capture the impact of the Hague Convention on the choice of law decision-making processes, as the Convention came into force in 2015. Ratification of the Hague Convention could, however, reveal other perceptions from market players, including potential links and synergies with the choice of law.[115]

---

111 The application of the CISG may occur independently (Article 1(1)(a)) or by rules of private international law Article 1(1)(b)).

112 See, generally, Queen Mary International Arbitration Studies *supra* Section 4.1.1.

113 See, for example, in the Survey, where this has constantly been cited by the respondents as a sort of apprehension. Further analysis of the Survey results is available in Chapter 1 *supra* pp. 50 *et seq.*

114 See a comparison drawn by R. A. Brand between the Hague Convention and the 1958 New York Convention, 'Arbitration or Litigation? Choice of Forum After the 2005 Hague Convention on Choice of Court Agreements', *University of Pittsburgh Legal Studies*, Research Paper No. 2009-14, p. 15 *et seq.*, available at [https://ssrn.com/abstract=1397646]. A further analysis is conducted by M. Ahmen & P. R. Beaumont in UK Post-Brexit, 'Exclusive Choice of Court Agreements: Some Issues on the Hague Convention on Choice of Court Agreements and Its Relationship with the Brussels I Recast Especially Anti-Suit Injunctions, Concurrent Proceedings and the Implications of Brexit', *Journal of Private International Law*, Vol. 13, 2017; same source, *Centre for Private International Law Aberdeen Working Paper Series*, Working Paper No. 2016/5, available at [https://ssrn.com/abstract=2824703].

115 The future research, anticipated in *infra* Section 5.2, will aim to capture interactions and potential links.

Although market incentives still militate in favour of arbitration agreements for reasons that will be discussed below, this scenario could change with the gain in popularity of the Hague Convention.[116] Even if it is still premature to make exhaustive predictions and assess the real consequences thereof, the author believes that the more States – CISG parties/signatories or otherwise – accede to the Hague Convention, the more the CISG will stand out as a neutral legal framework tailored to govern deals between contracting parties.

4.3 Arbitration Agreements

As we have seen, arbitration was indicated by a number of respondents as a 'safety measure' in international highways.[117] Forum concerns were always associated with questions of choice of law, which might suggest that choice of forum, in certain instances, would guide the choice of law.

Even when asked about the positive legal features of a governing contract law, respondents consistently cited arbitration and enforceability concerns. One respondent, answering the question about main economic considerations of governing contract law, actually indicated 'if arbitration is chosen, then this consideration is of minor importance'.[118]

While this of course cannot be taken as a rule, it might endorse the view that parties will take costs and convenience into account when choosing their 'audience', translating into enforcement concerns. This is confirmed by the following responses: 'cost of enforcement of legal rules'[119] (75.77%) and 'political stability in the relevant jurisdiction'[120] (57.27%), indicated as the two main economic considerations when choosing governing contract law.

4.3.1 A 'Go to' Option in Cross-Border Sales

It might be argued that arbitration tends to tone down a confrontational party-counterparty hearing, or 'Manichean dichotomy', by allowing greater flexibility and creative alternatives to keep the relationship alive, to explore potential future deals and early settlement, or even to mitigate losses at an equal level for all parties involved.[121] Others may argue that the greater

116 For example, in November 2016, the Australian Parliament's Joint Standing Committee on Treaties recommended accession to the Convention on Choice of Court Agreements. See more details at [www.aph.gov.au/Parliamentary_Business/Committees/Joint/Treaties/Airworthiness-USA/Report_166/section?id=committees%2Freportjnt%2F024013%2F24043].

117 See, *e.g.*, Response to Survey Question 1 (Section 1.2.4.1); Response to Survey Question 2 (Section 1.2.4.1); Response to Survey Question 3 (Section 1.2.4.1); and Response to Survey Question 4 (Section 1.2.4.2).

118 Response to Survey Question 4 (Section 1.2.4.2).

119 *Id.*

120 *Id.*

121 See, generally, evidentiary sources from Queen Mary International Arbitration Studies, *supra* note 112.

flexibility in arbitration proceedings tends to give parties leeway to collaborate further as the service provided is expensive and sanctions may be applied to those who 'behave badly'.[122]

Naturally, we should not deceive ourselves into a romantic view that arbitration is a 'friendly' process where actors play fair. They may not do so at all. As in a game, parties are self-interested players who set strategies and preferences to maximize their gains from any transaction. After all, arbitration is a procedural option by which parties submit their disputes for a neutral to determine, with clear adjudicative intentions.

It is thus understandable that both parties want to make their case and win the dispute. Arbitration differs, however, from state court litigation because incentives are distinct and the 'costs of use' are directly and immediately borne by users,[123] thereby potentially reducing recalcitrant behaviour, encouraging early settlement[124] and promoting commercial and business-focused decisions.[125]

4.3.1.1 The Application of the Law on an 'As Is' Basis

As we have seen, arbitration was indicated by a number of respondents in the Survey as a 'safety measure' in international highways. Forum concerns were associated with questions regarding choice of law, which might suggest that choice of forum, in certain instances, would guide the choice of law.

Before exploring this interplay, one question (perhaps rather straightforward) should be considered: what makes arbitration so attractive in cross-border transactions?

Arbitration tends to attract less frivolous or groundless argument than do court proceedings because parties have to pay to test them, and the cost, unlike court proceedings fees in most jurisdictions, can be considerable.[126] Accordingly, parties may eventually suffer the setback of a groundless argument or recalcitrance in compliance with arbitral award of what had been decided in an arbitration process or resistance to participation in arbitration proceedings, since there is no externalization of costs.[127] For these reasons,

122 By way of examples, some institutions will publish the name of the parties who have not voluntary complied with the decision. Commodity trade associations adopt such procedure, see, among others, International Cotton Association [www.ica-ltd.org/safe-trading/loua-part-one/].

123 As opposed to courts, where litigants are at the same time taxpayers.

124 For example, the rate of settlement of arbitration cases at the WIPO Arbitration and Mediation Center (WIPO Center) is 40%. Further information available at [www.wipo.int/amc/en/center/caseload.html].

125 Although there is no evidentiary source to attest to this pattern of conduct, *i.e.* less occurrences of recalcitrant behaviours in comparison to court rooms, this inference is drawn upon by the author's own experiences.

126 Costs are understood here to include: institutional charges (as the case may be); arbitrators' fees; legal and arbitration costs; and reputational costs, *i.e.* costs of tainting a name in the market, the figure of which may not be easily quantified. While this behaviour could also happen in court cases, the cost would then be diluted, given the lesser publicity *vis-à-vis* arbitration cases, which tend to be monitored closely by institutions and media vehicles, for example Global Arbitration Review (GAR) [www.globalarbitrationreview.com]. In addition, players who resort to arbitration are likely to be more exposed to extra-legal sanctions and risk of banishment of trade and loss of additional contracts, in addition to opportunity costs.

127 Unlike litigation costs, where taxpayers contribute to the development and maintenance of the court system.

and given the 'business outlook' of arbitration, parties tend voluntarily to comply with an arbitration award and, in some cases, in order to preserve (good) business relations, settle the dispute even before a decision is rendered.[128]

As stated earlier, W. Park understands that the greater reliability often found in arbitral awards, as contrasted with court judgments, derives from different notions of 'law' in commercial transactions. The calculus of duty is simply not the same as between judges and arbitrators: "(...) Bearing obligations to the citizenry as a whole, judges may seek to implement societal values that sometimes trump private agreements. Although responsible judges will master existing authority before taking the law in new directions, many traditions allow appellate judges to overrule precedent..."[129]

Another point that is certainly of great interest is the approach of arbitrators, as opposed to state court judges, to the governing contract law.[130] In this connection, we should not forget the expertise of the decision-maker in arbitral proceedings, who has practical experience in the business environment.[131] While we acknowledge that there are state court judges who possess business acumen, and courts are generally well acquainted with commercial matters, such attributes are not required of judges, who are rather bound by a different set of rules and trained to cover a broader spectrum of cases, not always having expertise and background in the field in dispute. As Richard Posner[132] observes: 'judges in interpreting contracts are guided by rules, arbitrators by their knowledge of the commercial context'. The recognition of arbitration clauses and enforceability of awards may stand out as most important characteristics.[133]

Other features of arbitration include flexibility, procedural simplicity and accessibility of rules; confidentiality, and the assessment of the costs of enforcing the contract[134] (noting the arbitral awards are unappealable on the merits (unless otherwise agreed by the parties), susceptible though to annulment, where applicable). The neutrality of the venue, the ability of parties to control procedure and ease of enforcement complete the list of advantages of the use of arbitration to resolve international sales disputes.[135]

In this regard, according to S. Shavell,[136] arbitration is an example of a 'private adjudication' mechanism that reduces the transaction costs since it provides broader access to the contractual information in relation to court litigation, in addition to the arbitrator's expertise and flexibility of the rules.

128 See *supra* note 95 in Chapter 3.

129 W. W. Park, *supra* note 71, pp. 60-61.

130 See *supra* note 39 in Chapter 3.

131 B. Oppetit, *Théorie de l'Arbitrage*, Press Universitaires de France, Paris, 1998. p. 28 *et seq*.

132 R. Posner, *supra* note 81 in Chapter 3, p. 38.

133 J. D. M. Lew QC, *supra* note 30, p. 189.

134 E. Mackaay & S. Rosseau, *Analyse Économique du Droit*, Dalloz, Paris, 2008, pp. 362-400.

135 See more in L. G. Meira Moser, 'Arbitragem em contratos empresariais: redução de custos e eficiência da transação', *Revista de Direito Empresarial (RDE)*, No. 13, 2010, pp. 33-55.

136 S. Shavell, *supra* note 85 in Chapter 3, p. 22.

In his outline of the great flexibility parties enjoy in arbitration, McConnaughay[137] contends that "a principal virtue of international commercial arbitration is its lawlessness, its ability because of its unrestrained flexibility to accommodate the enormous procedural, presentational, and decisional standard differences that typically exist among parties to multinational transactions".

An additional motive for including arbitration clauses in a contract could be what Richard Posner has termed the 'middle of the road' propensity of arbitrators: the party that expects to be sued, rather than to sue, in the event of a breakdown of the contractual relationship, will want such a clause because it will reduce the party's expected liability.[138] In international settings, where a myriad of variables are present, parties are likely to include an arbitration clause to mitigate their expected liability.

4.3.1.2 The 'Middle of the Road' Archetype

In an environment of uncertainty, particularly in cross-border transactions, private adjudication mechanisms play a major role.[139] This is so much so that arbitration has been considered the most efficient out-of-court dispute resolution method worldwide. A reason for this is the expertise of the decision-maker, who has practical experience in the business environment.[140]

Private methods of conflict resolution may be preferred not only because they may be faster – or ought to be – *vis-à-vis* court litigation, but also because arbitrators are more prepared to interpret the facts and resolve the matter in dispute: the parties give the arbitration panel considerable discretion to design the process; the arbitrator, who is familiar with business negotiation and complex commercial disputes, should therefore develop and implement the framework within which resolution is to be achieved and, whenever possible, encourage the parties to resolve the dispute by settlement.[141]

An additional motive for including arbitration clauses in a contract could be what Richard Posner has termed the 'middle of the road' propensity of arbitrators: the party that expects to be sued, rather than to sue, in the event of a breakdown of the contractual relationship, will want such a clause because it may reduce potential losses. Posner gives the example of a brokerage firm which would want to have an arbitration clause because it is much more likely to be sued by than to sue a customer. Posner explains that one might think along these lines if including an arbitration clause would favour one party over the other, or the other party would object, or demand compensation. Nonetheless, unfortunately, some parties, in deciding whether to include an arbitration clause might

137 P. J. McConnaughay, 'Risks and Virtues of Lawlessness: A Second Look at International Commercial Arbitration', *Northwestern University Law Review*, Vol. 93, 1998, p. 522.

138 R. Posner, *supra* note 81 in Chapter 3, p. 19.

139 See, in this sense, *supra* note 120.

140 See B. Oppetit, *supra* note 131.

141 See S. Shavell, *supra* note 85 in Chapter 3, p. 22.

not bother to do so because the expected cost of so doing would be difficult to estimate but probably slight when measured against the probability of a breach of contract that would lead to actual suit.[142] This can be put in the context both of domestic and international arbitration. It might well be that, depending on a balance of probability of breach – from a supplier's or buyer's point of view – including an arbitration clause could reduce a party's expected liability.

Similarly, in opting for arbitration, parties should also carefully consider the choice of the seat, which determines the procedural law applicable to the extent that the parties have not agreed otherwise, including grounds for setting aside an award.[143]

In reliance on evidentiary sources we have argued that, if arbitration is chosen, the choice of law tends to have less weight, as parties are more aware of what to expect.[144] Naturally, we should not overlook the fact that arbitral awards have to be enforced by state courts in case of recalcitrance of the losing party.[145] Nonetheless, these proceedings tend to be simpler than enforcement of a domestic decision,[146] which is subject, *inter alia*, to jurisprudential inclination, which is not always easy to ascertain and frequently requires parties complete understanding of the legal system.

In most countries domestic courts adopt a policy of minimal intervention when it comes to judicial review in arbitration-related matters. In this connection there are, of course, jurisdictions notable for their pro-arbitration stance, but generally a minimalist approach is adopted. In addition to this, if the jurisdiction has acceded to the 1958 New York Convention (1958 NYC),[147] then certainty is added to the arbitration outcome. In this regard, Julian Lew observes that the 1958 NYC establishes three fundamental standards for international arbitration: (i) it must conform with or come within the terms of the arbitration agreement; (ii) the parties must be treated fairly and with equality (*i.e.*, international due process); and (iii) the award must respect international public policy both with respect to its content and its subject matter.[148]

---

142 See R. Posner, *supra* note 81 in Chapter 3, p. 19.

143 J. D. M. Lew QC, L. Mistelis & S. Kroll, *Comparative International Commercial Arbitration*, Kluwer, Alphen aan den Rijn, 2003, pp. 693-732; R. Goode, 'The Role of the Lex Loci Arbitri in International Commercial Arbitration', *Arbitration International*, Vol. 17, Issue 1, 2001, pp. 19-40; W. W. Park, 'The Lex Loci Arbitri and International Commercial Arbitration', *International and Comparative Law Quarterly*, Vol. 32, Issue 1, 1983, pp. 21-52.

144 L. G. Meira Moser, *supra* note 4, pp. 95-111.

145 See P. Sanders, 'New York Convention on the Recognition and Enforcement of Foreign Arbitral Awards', *Netherlands International Law Review*, Vol. 6, 1959, pp. 43-55.

146 See, in this sense, the New York Convention 1958 Database available at [http://newyorkconvention1958.org]; see also, D. M. Lew QC, L. Mistelis & S. Kroll, *supra* note 143, pp. 703-706.

147 Convention on Recognition and Enforcement of Foreign Arbitral Awards, 7 ILM 1046 (1968) [New York Convention]. Ratified by 159 States, the New York Convention is available at [www.uncitral.org/uncitral/en/uncitral_texts/arbitration/NYConvention.html%5D].

148 J. D. M. Lew QC, *supra* note 30, p. 189. See also, J. D. M. Lew QC, L. Mistelis & S. Kroll, *supra* note 143, pp. 687-732.

We have examined, at both theoretical and empirical levels, the advantages and challenges of international arbitration as an adjudicative process of dispute resolution. We have acknowledged the worldwide popularity of international arbitration in cross-border sale disputes and how this has for centuries shaped international trade. Now, one question still remains: what is the correlation – if any – between arbitration agreements and choice of law? Is there some sort of interaction of which we should be aware?

4.3.2 *Arbitration Agreements and Choice of Law: Potential Interplay*

We have seen thus far the main concerns of parties regarding forum selection, as well as the driving factors informing this choice. Arbitration has been repeatedly cited as the preferred dispute resolution mechanisms in cross-border transactions. Is there any relationship between choice of forum and choice of law? Does one choice inform or in any way determine the other? To answer this question, we should look back to the empirical studies.

The Queen Mary, University of London results in 2010,[149] for example, being limited to contracts that contain an arbitration clause, cannot provide data on a putative relationship of choice of law and choice of court clauses. However, an indication of the respondents' position with regard to this relationship might be found in their attitude to the choice of the seat of arbitration (which determines the procedural law applicable to proceedings to the extent that the parties have not agreed otherwise[150]): 51% of the respondents decided on the governing law before they selected a seat of arbitration: conversely, the choice of the seat did not weigh heavily on the choice of law.[151] In support of this evidence, the 2014 Survey results show that parties to international sales contracts tend to look for 'business common-sense' solutions, with greater accuracy of determination of fact, which is what is generally sought by those who opt for arbitration.

Might choice of forum be determinative of choice of law? The Survey results suggest that, in some instances, the choice of arbitration may assist parties in avoiding enforcement concerns typically associated with state courts. Therefore, in scenarios such as these, the governing contract law might be given less consideration at the negotiation table, and would therefore play a somewhat ancillary role. Two observations might support this hypothesis.

Firstly, parties may resort to arbitration if they are willing to obtain a decision based upon the facts of the case, primarily on the contract that binds them, irrespective of the intricacies of the law chosen. An arbitrator should apply the law chosen by the parties and

149 Results available *in supra* Section 4.1.1.

150 S. Vogenauer, *supra* note 17 in Chapter 1, pp. 48-49.

151 2010 International Arbitration Survey: Choices in International Arbitration, p. 9, Chart 5, see *supra* Section 4.1.1.

if such law imposes certain constraints, then the arbitrator must abide by them, provided, of course, that such constraints really apply to the concrete situation.[152] However, certain constraints resulting from a rule of the applicable law might not prevent the arbitrator from seeking the most appropriate solution consistent with the parties' legitimate expectations.[153]

Therefore, for some players, arbitration is seen as a fact-finding-and-resolution procedure, where decision-makers base their determinations on the available record, guided by the contract *inter partes*, These parties seek a commercially reasonable and fair outcome that primarily takes into account the concerned industry usage and their behaviour in the course of a contractual relationship.

Secondly, parties see arbitration as an alternative or a way out, to mitigate a lack of knowledge or asymmetric information[154] regarding certain governing contract law, which has been (perhaps inadvertently) chosen or imposed (*e.g.* bargaining power) by the counterparty. In this scenario parties may believe that use of arbitration increases their chances of a successful outcome – be it right or wrong – given the 'middle of the road' propensity of arbitrators, as opposed to the 'imponderability' frequently associated with state court judges.

Does the above mean that the governing contract law is of no relevance? This author does not believe so. What this might indicate is that parties who use arbitration wish to obtain a decision based on the provisions of the contract itself and the practice and usages of the particular industry, in addition to observation of the parties' conduct in the course of the contractual relationship.

Are parties then indifferent to the governing law's provisions? This author does not believe so. Parties, it is important to say, want a lawful and not legally vitiated contract. As a matter of fact, one caveat is in order here. A greater business-like attachment does not mean that the law chosen should be disregarded.[155] Naturally, the law is of utmost im-

152 F. Perret, 'Resolving Conflicts between Contractual Clauses and Specific Rules of the Governing Law – Strict Application of the Law or Flexible Approach', *Dossier of the ICC Institute of World Business Law: The Application of Substantive Law by International Arbitrators*, 2014, p. 109.

153 F. Perret, *supra* note 152, p. 109.

154 The topic of asymmetric information is explored in detail in *supra* Section 3.2.

155 In relation to this topic, see M. Savare, 'Clauses in Conflict: Can an Arbitration Provision Eviscerate a Choice-of-Law Clause', *Seton Hall Law Review*, Vol. 35, 2004, pp. 597-611, who warns that "(...) although arbitrators afford substantive law a certain degree of deference when rendering their decisions, they feel empowered to deviate from the law in the interests of justice..." (p. 606). The author further argues that "in any given arbitration, it is unclear to what extent arbitrators will apply the substantive laws selected by the parties or whether they are bound to apply any substantive law at all..." (p. 611). Debating the same topic, the author G. Cordero-Moss alerts that the freedom that arbitral tribunal typically enjoys in relation to the applicable laws has some limitations, "(...) the *ordre public* of the court that exercises judicial control may not be violated by the award and the tribunal may not render a decision in equity without having been empowered to do so by the parties. Between these two borders there are a wide range of possibilities to disregard the parties' instructions, particularly by applying various rules of private international law...". See G. Cordero-Moss, 'Can an Arbitral Tribunal Disregard the Choice of Law Made by the Parties?', *Stockholm International Arbitration Review*, 2005, pp. 8-20, p. 20; and G. Cordero-Moss, *supra* 389, pp. 283-284.

portance, as it will determine when, how, and on what terms contractual obligations are created.[156] Parties acknowledge this and certainly have a 'wish list' of key principles they want to see governing their contract and will try to find law that corresponds to it, subjecting themselves to a forum that will appreciate and apply this set of chosen commands.[157] It is also safe to say that an arbitration agreement, in addition to lowering transaction costs in the short and long run, confers efficiency on the operation, as the arbitrator acts as an interlocutor between parties and market.

The data presented in this chapter indicate that, despite users' complaints relating to costs and time, arbitration continues to be the preferred method of dispute resolution in cross-border disputes.

Evidentiary sources also attest to a correlation between choice of law and arbitration. It is suggested that, once arbitration is chosen, the governing contract law is likely to follow through: arbitration would give parties a feeling of 'comfort' which does not appear to be available in state courtrooms.[158]

In the author's view, this feeling of 'comfort' is a two-edged sword. On the one hand, it could encourage parties to make better governing contract law choices: parties ultimately rely on the arbitrator's skills and judgement in applying the law chosen or determining it in the underlying contract. However, and on the other hand, this feeling might blur rational decisions by a mistaken perception that a choice of a law is of 'minor relevance' – an equivocal and dangerous belief that the arbitrators will master it after all, irrespective of the law chosen or otherwise determined by the arbitrators.

That said, the Hague Convention, with its gradual increase of adhesions, may bring 'winds of change' to current resolution of dispute in cross-border sales, depending on the incentives in play, including the potential amount at stake, the nature of the dispute, in addition to the relationship established between the parties and the type of contract.[159] As the case may be, these variables could militate in favour of the use of courts in cross-border sales.

Some of the attractive features generally associated with arbitration may be eclipsed by the Hague Convention: in the first place, enforceability of the court judgment – cited as one of the causes of the unpopularity of litigation – will no longer be a disadvantage of

156 See B. E. Hermalin, A. W. Katz & R. Craswell, *supra* 10 in Chapter 2, p. 52.

157 See J. D. M. Lew QC, who observes that "[…] in international arbitration, as with the absence of the forum's conflict of law rules, there are no rules expressed as to how a tribunal should determine the content to the relevant law and the specific rules it should apply. However, the expectation is that a tribunal will correctly apply the substantive rules to issues presented by the facts in each case. The need to ascertain the content of the applicable law is an essential task of the international arbitral tribunal." J. D. M. Lew QC, 'Iura Novit Curia and Due Process', *Queen Mary School of Law Legal Studies Research Paper No. 72/2010*, 2011, p. 2, available at [https://ssrn.com/abstract=1733531].

158 L. G. Meira Moser, *supra* note 4, p. 111.

159 As seen, the relationships with the parties and the transaction rank high in contracting parties' decision-making processes. See, in this sense, the Survey results in *supra* Section 1.2.4.1 *et seq.*

international litigation,[160] although the finality of arbitral awards remains, unlike appeal options in court instances.[161] In addition, the possibility of avoiding a given legal system, an advantage linked to international arbitration, could now likewise be related to international litigation as parties may be able to choose a forum more convenient to their business interests, more efficient and neutral. Last but not least, cost, which as we have seen is a recurrent complaint of arbitration-users,[162] could now militate in favour of international litigation,[163] given the possibility of choosing efficient courts and/or less onerous courts fees, which would allow judgement to be enforced in any of the contracting States.[164] Evidentiary sources discussed in the preceding chapters suggest that 'enforcement concerns'[165] remain a vital preoccupation in negotiating choice of law clauses and can be a deal-breaker. The author wonders whether, in the change of climate that the Hague Convention may produce, parties would be more willing to choose other governing contract law or be less resistant to attempting the use of other laws.

160 Article 8 – Recognition and Enforcement

1. A judgment given by a court of a contracting State designated in an exclusive choice of court agreement shall be recognised and enforced in other contracting States in accordance with this Chapter. Recognition or enforcement may be refused only on the grounds specified in this Convention.
2. Without prejudice to such review as is necessary for the application of the provisions of this Chapter, there shall be no review of the merits of the judgment given by the court of origin. The court addressed shall be bound by the findings of fact on which the court of origin based its jurisdiction, unless the judgment was given by default.
3. A judgment shall be recognised only if it has effect in the State of origin, and shall be enforced only if it is enforceable in the State of origin.
4. Recognition or enforcement may be postponed or refused if the judgment is the subject of review in the State of origin or if the time limit for seeking ordinary review has not expired. A refusal does not prevent a subsequent application for recognition or enforcement of the judgment.
5. This Article shall also apply to a judgment given by a court of a contracting State pursuant to a transfer of the case from the chosen court in that contracting State as permitted by Article 5, paragraph 3. However, where the chosen court had discretion as to whether to transfer the case to another court, recognition or enforcement of the judgment may be refused against a party who objected to the transfer in a timely manner in the State of origin.

161 D. Taylor, *supra* note 44, pp. 56-57.

162 See, *e.g.*, *supra* Section 4.1.1: 2015 Queen Mary, University of London Survey 'Improvements and Innovations in International Arbitration'; 2016 Queen Mary, University of London Survey 'Pre-empting and Resolving Technology, Media and Telecoms Disputes'.

163 See *supra* note 144.

164 The Hague Conference of Private International Law has made progress with the 'Judgments Project', which refers to two aspects of private international law in cross-border litigation in civil and commercial matters: the international jurisdiction of courts and the recognition and enforcement of their judgments abroad. As regards the international jurisdiction of courts, it led to the 2005 Hague Convention. A draft Convention for recognition and enforcement of their judgments abroad has been drafted and further detail is available at [https://www.hcch.net/en/projects/legislative-projects/judgments].

165 See, *e.g.*, *supra* Section 4.1.1: Queen Mary, University of London first empirical study on international arbitration, '2006 International Arbitration Study: Corporate Attitudes and Practices'; Queen Mary, University of London Survey, 'International Arbitration: Corporate Attitudes and Practices 2008'; 2015 Queen Mary, University of London Survey 'Improvements and Innovations in International Arbitration'; the Global Empirical Survey on Choice of Law; and L. G. Meira Moser, *supra* note 3 in Chapter 1, p. 28.

With cross-border negotiation and forum options and concerns now discussed, some questions still remain unanswered: does national law effectively respond to the intentions of the parties? Is it to be called neutral? Does it ultimately deliver effective outcomes? We aim to answer these questions in the next and final chapter.

5 Parties' Main Concerns and the Efficiency of Transnational Legal Standards

Contracting parties typically have a wish list of topical rules or guidelines that they want to see governing their contracts. What are these rules, guidelines or legal standards? How relevant are they and to what extent can they effectively influence and determine the choice of governing contract law?

This chapter will examine parties' main choices and assess the efficiency of transnational legal rules to meet them. This will require some light review and assessment of the CISG as a neutral transnational legal framework.[1] The chapter is intended to shed light on some of the core concerns of contracting parties, in choosing governing contract law. Hence, readers should not expect to encounter an exhaustive analysis of the 101 articles of the CISG,[2] but rather a cursory overview of its appealing features. The purpose of the chapter is to remind contracting parties of the elements in the CISG, and warn of the cognitive biases we have discussed above,[3] which may have clouded some perceptions of the use and practical advantages of the CISG as governing contract law.

One caveat is in order at this point. The chapter does not aim either to recommend the CISG as a *panacea* for all the worries attending cross-border sales. Whilst the CISG, as does any other governing contract law, has limitations which will be discussed in the following sections, we intend to give clarity to some of the common confusions encountered in consideration of the CISG. It is hoped that this will show how CISG provisions are economically efficient in cross-border sales.

5.1 Legal and Economic Considerations: Choices – Who's Who?

The 'rising action' in literary drama is often associated with the 'greatest moment', the most expected and desirable performance on stage. By analogy, in cross-border transactions, the 'rising action' is where parties have to evaluate legal and economic considera-

1 Although aware of their existence, the author does not consider other transnational legal frameworks or compare them with the CISG, which is the focus of the chapter.

2 The CISG is divided into four parts: a general part on definitions, sphere of application and rules of construction (Articles 1-13); a second part on contract formation (Articles 14-24); a third part on general provisions and rights and obligations of the parties to an international sales contract (Articles 25-88); and a final part on how states may formally adopt the CISG, including reservations (Articles 89-101). The full text of the CISG is available at [https://www.cisg.law.pace.edu/cisg/text/treaty.html].

3 See *supra* Chapter 2.

tions in order to choose the ideal governing contract law. As in literary contexts, this is certainly the most delicate and critical part of the process as it contemplates the end result and all that it entails. In cross-border transactions the final product sought is a balanced contract, which takes into account various market failures, parties' limitations and idiosyncratic preferences.

Studies discussed earlier suggest that choice of forum (courts or arbitration), degree of familiarity with the law and cost and convenience of resolving disputes play a decisive role in the choice of governing contract law. Parties evaluate the adequacy of rules that best suit their interests in the transaction and calculate legal risks they may run and have to tackle or minimize before the chosen forum.[4]

What are these contracting parties' main considerations?[5] Are there legal standards that they wish to see govern their deals? If so, what are the features of a most desirable governing contract law? Does domestic law respond to contracting parties' intentions? We shall explore the core principles of an ideal legal framework for cross-border sales, founded on empirical data and theoretical analysis. From this we attempt to gain understanding of what contracting parties appreciate when analyzing putative governing contract law. We shall also investigate these substantive considerations and assess how transnational rules are equipped to govern such deals.

A legal framework should have substantive features that make it appealing to parties, or particular industry-sector contracts and even negotiation contexts. In the following sections we shall break down and explain the core substantive considerations that parties tend to consider when assessing the pros and cons of any legal framework.

5.1.1 *Predictability of Rules*

Contracting parties will likely prefer law with which they are familiar, composed of rules with a degree of certainty and predictability. In cross-border transactions, where a myriad of laws may intersect, what is the most efficient[6] law to govern such contracts? Is there one after all?

---

4 L. G. Meira Moser, *supra* note 3 in Chapter 1, p. 32.

5 For example, it has been suggested that in international arbitration the factors to consider in the choice of substantive law would include: accessibility (parties, counsel and arbitrators can examine it and ascertain its merits with a minimum of difficulty); predictability (the legal system chosen should have clear statements on the issues which are most likely to arise); effect given to the parties' agreement; and public policy. See, in this sense, J. B. Tieder, 'Factors to Consider in the Choice of Procedural and Substantive Law in International Arbitration', *Journal of International Arbitration*, Vol. 20, Issue 4, 2003, p. 405; M. Blessing, 'Choice of Substantive Law in International Arbitration', *Journal of International Arbitration*, Vol. 14, Issue 2, 1997, pp. 39-66; O. Lando, *supra* 416, pp. 104-115; see also J. D. M. Lew QC, *supra* note 56 in Chapter 3, pp. 114-145.

6 For a discussion on efficiency and law and its intersection with economics, please refer to *supra* Section 3.1.1, notes 17 and 21 in Chapter 3.

Take as an example negotiation of a sale of granulated iron ore between England (buyer) and Iran (seller). English and Iranian parties will both be tempted to propose their domestic law,[7] for reasons exhaustively discussed in previous chapters. It is indisputable that the law applicable should be readily accessible and intelligible to the parties, their counsel and the decision-makers. Predictability is a vital feature of a market. Players wish to avoid unpleasant surprises. The truth is that national laws are typically not written in 'black-and-white', there are certainly shades involved, which the parties' lawyers may not be aware of until they find themselves in a situation where they are forced to access the law for a contract dispute. As acknowledged by scholars, domestic laws are often shortsighted, drafted to govern domestic affairs[8] and seldom, if ever, fit in a large international context.

The CISG, on the other hand, tackles this gloomy scenario by setting time frames and limiting liabilities. For example, the CISG sets limits losses and damages recoverable due to default (Article 74[9]), according to which the parties undertake to indemnify only for damages foreseeable at the time of conclusion of the contract. This enables them to calculate potential risks and avoid unforeseen liabilities. Article 35[10] also provides predictability by levelling asymmetry of information[11] between the parties, by limiting the seller's obligation to how objectively informed he/she was at the time the contract was concluded.

It should also be noted that the courts[12] of a member state to the CISG are obliged to regard its international character and the need to promote uniformity in its interpretation.[13] This militates in favour of the increasing predictability of its rules.

One additional example is the reference to 'at the time of the conclusion of the contract', which is present in the vital phases of a CISG contract: sphere of application (Articles 1 and 2); general provisions (Article 10); obligations of the seller (Article 31; 35; 38;

7 As we have discussed in Chapter 1, 'home law' is typically associated with 'familiarity', and generally represents one of the 'go to' options of the parties in decision-making processes. See more *supra* Chapter 1. *A contrario sensu*, see analysis of cognitive biases, including 'familiarity', which explains how decisions based upon 'familiarity' may blur or influence this process negatively. See, in this sense, *supra* Chapter 2.

8 M. Blessing, *supra* note 5, p. 41.

9 Art. 74 CISG: "Damages for breach of contract by one party consist of a sum equal to the loss, including loss of profit, suffered by the other party as a consequence of the breach. Such damages may not exceed the loss which the party in breach foresaw or ought to have foreseen at the time of the conclusion of the contract, in the light of the facts and matters of which he then knew or ought to have known, as a possible consequence of the breach of contract." For a thorough analysis about the topic, see I. Saidov, *The Law of Damages in International Sales – the CISG and Other International Instruments,* Hart Publishing, Oxford, 2008.

10 Art. 35 (1)(b) CISG: "1) The seller must deliver goods which are of the quantity, quality and description required by the contract and which are contained or packaged in the manner required by the contract. (…) (b) are fit for any particular purpose expressly or impliedly made known to the seller at the time of the conclusion of the contract, except where the circumstances show that the buyer did not rely, or that it was unreasonable for him to rely, on the seller's skill and judgement".

11 The topic of asymmetric information is explored in detail *supra* Section 3.2.

12 Article 7(1) of the CISG.

13 I. Schwenzer, *supra* note 195 in Chapter 1, p. 728.

and 42); obligations of the buyer (Article 55); passing of risk (Article 68); provisions common to the obligations of the seller and buyer (Article 73; 74 and 79). This reference of time is highly commendable in cross-border deals and increases predictability.

The CISG operates by means of harmonious and uniform rules, notably in the areas of greater divergence of legal systems, namely the formation (and burden of proof) of the contract, the interpretation of the parties' previous (and current) dealings and conduct, obligations of buyer and seller, reciprocal obligations, in addition to the consequences arising from breach of the relationship, default, termination of contract and damages.

Lisa Spagnolo, investigating the reasons for, and 'measuring' the efficiency of, the CISG exclusion, divides her analysis between substantive and non-substantive features, advantages and disadvantages,[14] which will be mentioned in the next section.

5.1.1.1 Degree of Certainty

Decision-makers should ideally be able to understand and apply the law with little or no difficulty. In this connection, predictability and flexibility are characteristics of significance in governing contract law. It is hoped that the law will provide gateways to optimal results, allowing parties to avoid conflict and their resolution via litigation or arbitration. Therefore it is of utmost importance that the law chosen is clear on issues commonly known to generate dispute. In addition, accessibility of the law and a solid body of case law fall within the degree of certainty sought by contracting parties.[15]

Lord Mansfield once defined certainty "In all mercantile contracts the great object should be certainty. And therefore, it is of more consequence that a rule should be certain, than whether it is established one way or the other. Because speculators in trade then know what ground to go upon".[16]

Studies discussed at the outset have shown that legal certainty ranked first in a contracting parties' list of concerns.[17] In the 2014 Survey, respondent's references to 'favourable experi-

14 L. Spagnolo, *supra* note 118 in Chapter 1, pp. 47-148.

15 L. G. Meira Moser, *supra* note 3 in Chapter 1, p. 32.

16 *Vallejo v. Wheeler* (1774) 98 ER 1012, 1017. See also M. Bridge, 'Good Faith, the Common Law, and the CISG', *Uniform Law Review*, Vol. 22, Issue 1, 1 March 2017, pp. 98-115, p. 101, remarking that "the conventional view is that certainty encourages investment in, and commitment to, contractual ventures. For example, a rule that requires a documentary presentation to be closely or exactly compliant with the demands of a documentary letter of credit is designed to do this, though whether it fulfills the design in practice, given that the majority of documentary presentations made are, in fact, in one or more particular ways, non-complaint, is perhaps a moot point".

17 See, for example, Queen Mary, University of London Survey (2010 edition), *supra* Section 1.1.2 and the Global Empirical Survey on Choice of Law, *supra* Section 1.2; L. G. Meira Moser, *supra* note 3 in Chapter 1, pp. 27-28.

ence and use of standard contracts',[18] 'positive effects of the party who seeks advice'[19] and 'habit – use of standard contracts'[20] endorse preferences for legal certainty and familiarity.

The empirical studies on choice of law demonstrate that, in contractual contexts and relationships with trading partners, parties may be inclined to adopt a conservative approach, being risk-averse,[21] unless there are market incentives to make them choose other laws or where bargaining power has played a role. This could include, for example, a new set of contracts, or new party advisors more experienced in international sales law, or new trading partners, including those from countries more or less familiarized with cross-border matters. A greater degree of knowledge of other sets of rules and bad experience of old ones might also be added to the list.[22] Would the CISG meet the requirement 'degree of certainty'[23]?

Evidentiary sources discussed in Chapter 1[24] showed that there is an element of indeterminacy in the consideration of 'legal certainty'. It is unclear what parties consider 'certainty' to be, let alone 'legal certainty' and what this would entail in the assessment of law.

In an attempt to better understand the studies discussed, we have argued in Chapter 1[25] that 'legal certainty', 'predictability', 'familiarity' and 'solid body of case law' are all intertwined – they show that the respondents may simply be unaware or afraid of the 'unknown'. This inference may explain why respondents selected 'body of case law that facilitates interpretation of legal rules' as the second most appealing feature of the 'most desirable substantive law' in the Survey.[26] These respondents seek predictable outcomes and the obvious attitude would be to choose a law with which they are 'familiar', or, if not available, a law easily accessible. This would thus give them a sense of 'certainty'.

How certain can law possibly be to qualify as certain? Does it mean that law has been tested in courts and produced case law? Would not exposure to that law that generates the feeling of knowing its legal framework and, by consequence, making use of it?

18 Response to Survey Question 1, *supra* Section 1.2.4.1.

19 *Id.*

20 *Id.*

21 In connection with this, C. Fountoulakis argues that if parties have their own law applied, they do not have to consult external experts, but rather, can rely on their usual, well-acquainted legal advisors. Parties to an international contract will strive towards an application of their own law, even if that is less suitable for the transaction at hand than other law might be. See C. Fountoulakis, *supra* note 195 in Chapter 1, p. 304.

22 As discussed in *supra* Chapter 2, there are biases and other non-rational factors which may cloud and blur decision-making processes.

23 Against this background, as we have acknowledged in Chapter 1, 'lower degree of certainty' has been one of the causes for the exclusion of the CISG by some of the respondents. In addition, 'degree of level certainty' falls within the broad category 'substantive concerns' elected by the respondents who opted-out the CISG. The full list of factors disclosed by the respondents is available in *supra* Section 1.2.4.3.

24 See *supra* Chapter 1.

25 See *supra* Chapter 1 *et seq.*

26 Responses to Survey Question 7, *supra* Section 1.2.4.3.

All the above considerations are connected and form species of 'fear of the unknown', *i.e.*, a 'mask' of ignorance worn by some parties to hide emotions and non-rational factors,[27] leading to decisions hardly driven by rational considerations.[28] A. Farnsworth, remarking on fears of common lawyers of the CISG, states: "Fundamental breach - OK, but strange; Nachfrist - We don't understand it, we never heard of it, but we like it; Price reduction – We don't understand it, and we don't like it; Specific Performance – We hope your courts will not resort to it as much as they may".[29]

We also argue that domestic law, no matter how developed are their courts, contains elements of indeterminacy not even thought through rationally by some contracting parties. The author also wonders whether if it is rather the means and the ease with which the parties access law that matter most.

5.1.1.2 Accessibility

Accessibility of law embraces the mechanisms publicly available to those wishing to familiarize themselves with it. Accessibility concerns the ease with which a user can search for a set of legal rules, including legal authorities, acts, translations and case-law materials.

As we have seen, contracting parties may encounter language barriers in negotiating governing contract law. This can be overcome, or at least controlled, by trustworthy translations, case law and legal authorities available in other languages.

Uniform contract law has the advantage of offering authoritative translations in several languages, in addition to access to online databases. CISG users can *e.g.* access over 3,000 cases reports online,[30] in addition to more than 10,000 bibliography citations and 1,600 full texts of commentaries, monographs and books on the CISG and related subjects, plus the UNCITRAL Digest, the CLOUT[31] and other bodies[32] that thrive on its uniformity of application.[33] It has also been submitted that the persuasive value of adequate and consistent decisions from member States could substantially promote the in-

27 See further discussion on this topic in *supra* Chapter 2.

28 See V. Gessner, *supra* note 22 in Chapter 1, pp. 132-145.

29 E. A. Farnsworth, *Lausanne Colloquium*, '1980 Vienna Convention on the International Sale of Goods', Schulthess Polygraphischer Verlag, 1985, p. 105.

30 See CISG Database, Pace Law School, available at [www.cisg.law.pace.edu/]. See also CISG-online database, Global Sales Law, available at [www.globalsaleslaw.org/index.cfm?pageID=29].

31 CLOUT stands for Case Law on UNCITRAL Texts. Available at www.uncitral.org/uncitral/en/case_law.html.

32 *Inter alia*, the CISG Advisory Council. Further information is available at [www.cisgac.com/].

33 It is important to note that both a judicial and arbitral interpreter have to interpret CISG rules with regard to its international character and to the need to promote uniformity of its application. As L. A. DiMatteo & D. Ostas argue, this requires a search of original interpretations and rejects homeward trend bias in which national rules and jurisprudence are used to fill in interpretive gaps. See L. A. DiMatteo & D. Ostas, *supra* note 49 in Chapter 3, p. 381.

ternational character and uniform interpretation[34] mandated by Article 7 of the CISG.[35]

No matter how 'advanced' or 'developed' a national law is (or ought to be in the eyes of some players[36]), their legal frameworks are not freely accessible for search of case law and legal authorities. The CISG online platforms thus arguably represent an unrivalled advantage *vis-à-vis* national law.

5.1.1.3 Intelligibility

Intelligibility of law is generally associated with ease of its determinacy. Parties tend to seek law that is easy to ascertain and will likely avoid the myriad legal vagaries that present obstacles to clear interpretation of the rules. In fact, the studies undertaken suggest a preference for flexibility and freedom of contract governed by easy-to-ascertain and neutral rules.[37] Respondents were inclined towards a law that was easy to ascertain,[38] that facilitated the transactions and was accompanied by a body of case law, of assistance in interpretation[39] of legal rules.

In international settings accessibility of law is also paramount. The law applicable in a cross-border sale will not always be readily available or accessible to practitioners and laymen in general. The consequences are well known: greater costs of engaging local counsel and or translation. In this regard the CISG offers an unrivalled advantage to its users.

As seen, the CISG's search engines provide access to in a given jurisdiction. This modern, user-friendly platform sets an unparalleled standard for the CISG as body to

34 See, in this connection, Camilla Baasch Andersen, advocating the use of a global jurisconsultorium in the pursuit of autonomy of terms under the CISG (p. 181 *et seq.*), defining as "an obligation to refer to what others are doing in other jurisdictions when sharing law, requiring scholars to refer to the work of scholars from other member states and requesting judges and legal counsel to find inspirational authority in CISG precedents from other member states" (p. 181), 'Uniformity and Harmonization by Case Law: The CISG and the Global Jurisconsultorium', pp. 175-189, p. 181, *in* Morten M. Fagot (Ed.), *Unification and Harmonization of International Commercial Law - Interaction of Deharmonization*, Wolters Kluwer, Alphen aan den Rijn, 2012. Camilla reported an increase in the number of jurisconsultorium cases.

35 A. S. Komarov, 'Internationality, Uniformity and Observance of Good Faith as Criteria in Interpretation of CISG: Some Remarks on Article 7 (1)', *Journal of Law & Commerce*, Vol. 25, 2005-06, pp. 75-85, p. 81. See also generally L. A. DiMatteo, et al., 'The Interpretive Turn in International Sales Law: An Analysis of Fifteen Years of CISG Jurisprudence', *Northwestern Journal of International Law & Business*, Vol. 24, Vol. 24, Issue 2, 2003, pp. 314-319. See J. Felemegas, 'The United Nations Convention on Contracts for the International Sale of Goods: Article 7 and Uniform Interpretation', *CISG Database,* available at [https://www.cisg.law.pace.edu/cisg/biblio/felemegas.html]

36 A discussion on cognitive biases is addressed in *supra* Chapter 2.

37 L. G. Meira Moser, *supra* note 3 in Chapter 1, p. 44.

38 As argued by Schwartz and Scott, a court cannot enforce contracts without a theory of interpretation that 'maps' from the syntactic content of the parties' writing to the writing's legal implications. See A. Schwartz & R. E. Scott, *supra* note 37 in Chapter 3, p. 547.

39 In connection with this, Schwartz and Scott assert that when dealing with this topic one should begin by clarifying two interpretive issues: What does the language of the contract mean; and in what language was the contract written? See more in A. Schwartz & R. E. Scott, *supra* note 37 in Chapter 3, p. 570 *et seq.*

govern cross-border sales. In addition to user-friendly search engines and databases, the CISG rules are available in several authoritative languages, with translations available in languages of member states,[40] thereby increasing accessibility and lowering transaction costs. This makes CISG readily available in court and arbitral proceedings rendering costly translations and expert testimony superfluous.[41] Although English was used to discuss the CISG at its inception, having authoritative languages as opposed to an official language is certainly another advantage of the CISG over national law. Indeed, translations of national law are seldom available and their accuracy may not be clearly known. This is a particular handicap for companies in developing and small and medium countries which may also lack the resources for specialized advice on a foreign law, as the party who pleads foreign law will often have to prove that it provides what the party asserts.[42]

As we have seen above, the CISG attracts academic bodies that work towards uniformity of the CISG's application.[43] In compiling and translating case law, sharing knowledge and information, users become aware of how provisions are been applied, which in turn increases the so-called 'certainty' that players may be looking for. It is also acknowledged that a certain degree of imprecision[44] is found in uniform laws, which allows for greater flexibility and adaptation.[45] On this matter John Honnold asserts that uniform words in themselves will not guarantee uniform results,[46] inasmuch as legal practitioners are required to use unreliable and imperfect tools, *i.e.*, words, which will never be able to craft the perfect law.[47] John Honnold remarks that even a simple phrase, such as 'home sweet home' presents the French translator with a challenge, let alone common law concepts such as 'consideration' and 'trust'. However, John Honnold raises these questions to enlighten the difficulties encountered in quests for the international unification of law and concludes that 'We cannot expect perfect uniformity in applying the Convention – or for that matter, any other statute'.[48]

Ole Lando argues that the English courts, while developing principles and rules which provide certainty,[49] have eroded the doctrine of consideration by conferring very limited

40 CISG translations are available at [www.cisg.law.pace.edu/cisg/text/text.html].

41 I. Schwenzer, *supra* note 195 in Chapter 1, p. 731.

42 O. Lando, *supra* note 71 in Chapter 3, p. 348.

43 I. Schwenzer & P. Hachem, *supra* note 220 in Chapter 1, p. 466.

44 In this connection, Ole Lando asserts, "[…] predictability is only one of several legal values. Rules which create certainty also tend to bring about rigidity. They do not consider special circumstances and changing conditions. The legal process is not and can never be a mere syllogism. It is above all an effort to reach the most fair and appropriate decision", in *The Law Applicable to the Merits of the Dispute,* LCIA; Kluwer Law International 1986, Volume 2, Issue 2, pp. 104-115 (p. 112).

45 I. Schwenzer & P. Hachem, *supra* note 220 in Chapter 1, p. 466.

46 J. Honnold, 'The Sales Convention in Action – Uniform International Words: Uniform Application?', *Journal of Law & Commerce,* Vol. 8, 1988, p. 207.

47 P. J. Mazzacano, 'Harmonizing Values, Not Laws: The CISG and the Benefits of a Neo-Realist Perspective', *Nordic Journal of Commercial Law*, Issue 1, 2008, p. 6, available at [https://ssrn.com/abstract=1434174].

48 J. Honnold, *supra* note 46, p. 212.

49 Whilst this is not the place to compare English law and the CISG, Michael Bridge identified three categories of these differences: "First, there are rules in the Vienna Convention which have no counterpart in English

effect on each precedent.[50] Ole Lando points out that the fact that English law consists of thousands of rules laid down in cases, some of which date back to the 19th century or much earlier, make it difficult to find these sources, an inference confirmed by Roy Goode "The major weakness of the judge-made law is its immense diffusion and the consequent difficulty of access to it".[51]

Another factor to be taken into account when choosing law is the level of complexity of its terminology. The language of the CISG is plain, not hermetic and free of niceties. This corresponds to an economic rationality: the CISG rules are destined for traders, who are more concerned about the functionality of such rules than to the complexity of the terms. The CISG is undoubtedly a source of outstanding legal certainty for market players and for all those who interact with cross-border traders and explore international trade. *Lingua franca*[52] of the international trade, the CISG favours a flexible model: it is composed of rules that are adaptable and sensitive to the contingencies of international commerce, autonomous and focused on concepts that are mouldable and subsumed by the case's factual background. The CISG is a complete and self-sufficient set of rules within its scope of application, which seek uniformity of interpretation, to be carried out in an autonomous way by its interpreters, without the interference of a given law.

The CISG uses simple terms that observe an economic rationality of the contract.[53] By enshrining the good faith principle[54] in interpreting its rules, the aim of the CISG is to promote the implementation and maintenance of contractual relations between the parties. This, in turn, demonstrates that the CISG is more suited to international trade than is national law, which is never thought of as facilitating cross-border transactions as an underlying aim, but rather focused on protecting the interests of nationals.

---

law, such as those on the remedy of price reduction, on cure, on giving notice to the seller of the lack of conformity of the goods and on the preservation of rejected goods. Second, there are rules of the Convention which appear at face value to differ from the provisions of English law and which might or might not lead to the same outcome on the facts. Bridge gives the example of Article 79 on exemption, which 'is structured very differently from its English counterpart dealing with frustration and impossibility of performance'. Third, there are Convention rules which appear at first sight to be similar to those of English law but which in fact differ significantly. An example is the duty to supply goods in conformity with the contractual description under Article 35 of the Convention." Michael Bridge, *in* M. Bridge, J. J. Fawcett & J. M. Harris, *International Sale of Goods in the Conflict of Laws*, Oxford University Press, 2005, pp. 639-640.

50 L. Goff, 'The Future of the Common Law', *International and Comparative Law Quarterly*, Vol. 46, 1997, pp. 745-748.

51 R. Goode, *Commercial Law*, Butterworth, London, 2004, p. 1205 *et seq.*

52 This term appeared as early as in J. Honnold, *supra* note 46, pp. 207-212, p. 212.

53 L. Spagnolo, *supra* note 118 in Chapter 1, pp. 47-148.

54 *A contrario sensu*, it is sometimes argued that the good faith principle may play against the CISG and encourages some players to opt-out of its application. As we have acknowledged in *supra* Chapter 1, 'principle of good faith' was cited by some of the respondents as a reason for the CISG's exclusion; however, this reason does not seem to be prevalent and the vagueness of answer provided by these respondents does not allow this author to elaborate further on this cause.

As we shall discuss in the following section, the CISG rules were intended and designed to generate efficiency and facilitate trade worldwide. This is proved by the terms of its preamble, which state that the CISG aimed at contributing to "the removal of legal barriers in international trade and promote the development of international trade".[55]

5.1.1.4 Complexity of Structure

Complexity of structure is inherently linked to the cost of learning, including the resources spent on revealing the intricacies of the legal framework. This can encompass, for example, case law that is not easy to understand, or layers of a legal system which may cloud a straightforward interpretation of the rules. One could also argue that 'limited coverage' falls under the heading 'complexity of structure', given the cost of learning and overall expenses, in addition to those associated with its unpredictability and uncertainty regarding the matters not covered.

'Limited coverage' was cited by some respondents as a reason for opting out of the CISG.[56] Naturally, as we know, the CISG covers only the formation of the contract of sale and the rights and obligations of the seller and the buyer arising from such a contract.[57] Whilst the CISG does not regulate the validity and effect a contract may have on the property,[58] we argue that the provisions covered by the CISG are the key provisions to market players after all, and that the uncovered provisions are subject to a myriad of vagaries in national law.

All in all, parties will often elect a set of rules which they find accessible and intelligible, which parties, party advisors and decision-makers have little difficulty in understanding and in applying its provisions.[59]

5.1.2 Legal Neutrality

Neutrality ranks high as a deal-breaker in international settings and it might be linked to several factors explored earlier, but principally to the fact that the transaction is essentially 'trans-' 'national', beyond borders.

In business transactions parties will often trade with counterparties of very different legal traditions and yet may be willing to establish a relationship and rely upon trade usage and practice. When negotiating governing contract law, imposition of one of the

55 The preamble of the CISG states, *inter alia* "[…] BEING OF THE OPINION that the adoption of uniform rules which govern contracts for the international sale of goods and take into account the different social, economic and legal systems would contribute to the removal of legal barriers in international trade and promote the development of international trade…".

56 See, in this sense, *supra* Section 1.2.4.3.

57 Article 4 of the CISG. See also *supra* 226.

58 See generally I. Schwenzer & P. Hachem, *supra* note 106 in Chapter 1, pp. 73-94.

59 L. G. Meira Moser, *supra* note 3 in Chapter 1, p. 44.

contracting party's law or (perhaps) a third party's, may not be welcomed by the other party, could cause disruption in their relations and threaten other deals.

5.1.2.1 Rules Not Identified or Associated with the Contracting Parties

Parties will, unless circumstances dictate otherwise, choose neutral law to govern their deals, be it a law of a third country or a soft law or a set of principles. Perhaps the first real question is: what is 'neutral' in an international contract? If a contract for sale of 7,000 cbm of steam coal involves a buyer from Switzerland and a seller from Indonesia, is English law considered 'neutral'? The answer has different facets, which we are principally concerned with the meaning of 'neutral'. From a purely territorial point of view, yes, in our hypothetical case English law would be perceived as 'neutral'. However, the way 'neutrality' in law might be read is through a rather 'purist' approach.

In our example, 'legal neutrality'[60] involves no links to any of the contracting parties, a literal 'fair game'. How is this possible when a third country law is chosen? The answer may be negative. As elaborated earlier,[61] laws also have a DNA, they were thought, planned and conceived to a specific system and to govern a given territory, are exposed to external factors, and suffer 'mutations' from time to time. They are not neutral in the meaning of 'legal neutrality'. What is neutral then? The answer is: the law that was meant to be neutral in the first place.

A preference for legal neutrality supports the cost-benefit analysis, as opposed to the option for a party's domestic set of rules that may generate more transaction costs and information asymmetry between the parties. By choosing neutral law, parties – theoretically speaking – depart from identical starting points and this may result in greater mutually beneficial results. With this in mind, we should further explore the CISG and its role to play in the concept of 'neutrality'. Before doing so, it is worth noting the percentages around parties' concerns with legal neutrality (33.48%[62]) and international character (31.28%[63]) in the Survey.

The CISG was at its inception first conceived to be neutral.[64] It is part of the CISG's DNA and will always be. Naturally, in order to be neutral, a conciliatory approach from different legal families was necessary.[65] As stated above, a law cannot be neutral if it was not meant to be. It might be used as such, with the idea that it can assume such a role, and

60 In Truong's study, in only 13% of the 108 contracts surveyed did parties choose a neutral law, *supra* note 23 in Chapter 1. On the other hand, in the 2010 Queen Mary, University of London Survey, the respondents' choices were mostly influenced by the perceived neutrality and impartiality of the chosen legal system with regard to the parties and their contract (66%), see more in Chapter 1 *supra* note 73 in Chapter 1.

61 See *supra* note 177 in Chapter 1 and general discussions in *supra* Chapter 1.

62 Response to Survey Question 1, *supra* Section 1.2.4.1.

63 *Id.*

64 For background of discussions about the Project of unification, see *supra* note 47.

65 For references to pre-CISG discussions, please consult I. Schwenzer, 'Commentary on the United Nations Convention on the International Sale of Goods (CISG)', Introduction, pp. 1-12.

perhaps even operate in a rather neutral way towards certain aspects of the legal life of a contract, but such law was never meant to be neutral; it has and will always have links to, and influences from, a specific legal family.

Before delving into the particulars of the CISG's core principles, readers are reminded that the CISG is a product of a compromise[66] (*compromis*) obtained from 62 countries that participated at the outset of its discussions.[67] Given the degree of legal diversity among the participants, the only way to harmonize substantive rules of contract law was to compromise. From this, participating States would thus be required to abandon the idea that the CISG rules reflect their own legal system.

Given the above context, one can integrate different concepts, principles and ideas in an independent system of rules, operational and adapted to the needs of international trade. Hence, in interpreting the principles of the CISG, one must always be guided by the international character of the contract and its circumstances, and not necessarily by a certain hermeneutics already devoted to a certain rule or concept in a given State.[68] To this end, Article 7(1) reinforces the importance of having due regard to the CISG's international character as well as the need to promote uniformity across all member states.[69] This requires courts to avoid recourse to domestic legal concepts unless they are required to do so. It has been submitted elsewhere that the four main policies underlying the rules of the CISG are: (i) freedom of contract, (ii) cooperation and reasonableness, (iii) success-

---

66 As it happens, the process of drafting the CISG has not been welcomed by everyone. Gillete & Scott brought forward a criticism suggesting that "[...]the structure of the ISL [CISG] drafting process would produce a treaty (1) that contained many vague and ambiguous provisions resulting in formal uniformity without substantive uniformity; (2) that allowed nations otherwise bound by CISG provisions to contract out with relative ease; and (3) that would generate divergent interpretations undermining even the initial benefits of formal uniformity", p. 473, C. P. Gillette & R. E. Scott, *supra* note 254 in Chapter 1, p. 473.

67 For a historical recap of the CISG, see C. M. Bianca & M. J. Bonell, *Commentary on the International Sales Law – The 1980 Vienna Sales Convention*, Giuffrè, Milan, 1987, pp. 3-7; P. Schlechtriem, *Uniform Sales Law, The UN-Convention on Contracts for the International Sale of Goods*, Manzsche Verlags – und Universitats-buchhandlung, Vienna, 1986, pp. 17-23.

68 Art. 7(1) of the CISG states: "(1) In the interpretation of this Convention, regard is to be had to its international character and to the need to promote uniformity in its application and the observance of good faith in international trade."

69 The goal of uniformity has been a source of criticism of the CISG's mandate yet most of these criticisms had their inception in the 1990s when there were still suspicious revolving around the application of the CISG. For a read on the criticisms of the CISG's goal of uniformity, which dates back to 1990s, see, among others, C. Sheaffer, 'The Failure of the United Nations Convention on Contracts for the International Sale of Goods and a Proposal for a New Uniform Global Code in International Sales Law', *Cardozo Journal of International and Comparative Law,* Vol. 15, 2007, pp. 461-495; P. B. Stephan, 'The Futility of Unification and Harmonization in International Commercial Law', *Virginia Journal of International Law*, Vol. 39, 1999, pp. 743-797; Philip Hackney, 'Is the United Nations Convention on the International Sale of Goods Achieving Uniformity?', *Louisiana Law Review,* Vol. 61, 2001, pp. 473-486; and J. E. Bailey, 'Facing the Truth: Seeing the Convention on Contracts for the International Sale of Goods as an Obstacle to a Uniform Law of International Sales', *Cornell International Law Journal,* Vol. 32, 1999, pp. 273-317.

ful completion of exchange and (iv) compensating injured parties for breach.[70] We shall now examine these policies, interplay and challenges.

5.1.2.2 Commercially-Focused 'Physiology'

On the basis of its legal neutrality the CISG emerges as a legal alternative in an environment where uncertainties are generally great and a dose of distrust between players may also cloud the choice of the law to govern their deals. The CISG sought to adopt essentially practical solutions to rule on cross-border sales, using plain language, thereby greatly facilitating its comprehension and functionality among traders, the real participants and protagonists of the trade. The CISG incorporates a set of norms for international merchants, including principles which evolved from the *lex mercatoria*:[71] commercial usage, practice and custom being given regard rather than unified black letter law.[72]

In a number of market transactions, parties would wish to continue trading under the same practices and *modus operandi* already in course and this is so likewise for economic reasons. Whilst national laws could address their trade practice concerns, a 'cross-border commercially-focused' feature is not part of a national law's DNA, and in fact many domestic laws are driven by consumer protection.[73] This reinforces the advantage of the CISG as a framework tailored for cross-border sales, where 'commercially intelligible' rules are needed.

5.1.3 Legal Flexibility

Legal flexibility is understood as how 'mouldable' or 'adaptable' the legal framework is in accommodating the parties' needs on a case by case basis. For example, how one can modify, revoke or withdraw an offer? What are the timelines and processes to alter certain contractual conditions? What are the consequences attached to these questions?

---

70 See Robert A. Hillman, *Cross-reference and Editorial Analysis of Convention Article 7*, available at [https://www.cisg.law.pace.edu/cisg/text/hillman.html]; see also A. M. Garro, 'La formación del contrato em la convención de Viena sobre compraventas internacionales y en el proyecto de unificación', *Revista Jurídica de Buenos Aires*, Vol. III, 1987, pp. 12-58.

71 For a historic overview of the *lex mercatoria*, see *supra* note 56 in Chapter 3.

72 P. J. Mazzacano, *supra* note 47, p. 19. See, on the dynamics of the various sources of the *lex mercatoria* and their harmonisation, Filip de Ly, 'De Facto Harmonization by Means of Party Autonomy and Model Contract Clauses (*Lex Mercatoria*)', *in* Morten M. Fagot (Ed.), *Unification and Harmonization of International Commercial Law – Interaction of Deharmonization*, Wolters Kluwer, Alphen aan den Rijn, 2012, pp. 151-160.

73 In many civil law countries consumer protection is governed by acts and codes which invariably interact, not always in a constructive fashion, with commercial contracts. There are also examples in common law countries, such as the UK where the Consumer Rights Act was enacted in 2015 and has replaced provisions of the 1979 Sale of Goods Act.

It goes without saying that traders appreciate freedom and flexibility in their negotiations. They may wish to have their deals concluded in writing or orally (as the case may be). They may also wish to rely on practices already established between themselves or market practices and usages. The question at this point is what are the main elements that determine legal flexibility?

5.1.3.1 Commitment to Freedom of Contract

The principle of freedom of contract, which is well known worldwide, acknowledges the binding effect of parties' consent. In the CISG it is adopted in Article 6[74] and is common in most, if not all, legal systems as a guiding principle of contract law. Therefore, little needs to be said in relation to such principle, apart from noting that the CISG, unsurprisingly, is committed to freedom of contract.[75]

As the Chief Justice Sundaresh Menon reminds us, Article 6 reflects the CISG's aim of striking a balance between the interest of commercial actors, national governments and the project of legal unification as it clearly signals that the CISG is intended to provide commercial actors with a choice rather than to coerce them into a mandatory regime.[76] Article 6 does provide for gateways for parties to shape the CISG to their particular needs, allowing them to derogate or vary provisions which could otherwise interfere in their deals in a manner not desirable to the deal at stake.[77]

It is noteworthy that the economic rationality of parties' autonomy is evident since rational economic agents (despite their limitations, as we have seen) will know best how to achieve what it most advantageous to them.[78] There might be cases where both parties may wish to continue trading under the same conditions they had established in prior dealings: using emails and amendments made orally, for example. The CISG strongly supports such intention and goes even further by allowing parties to derogate or vary the effects of CISG provisions, as we shall discuss shortly.

---

74 Article 6 of the CISG provides that "the parties may exclude the application of this Convention or, subject to article 12, derogate from or vary the effect of any of its provisions".

75 U. Schroeter, *supra* note 239 in Chapter 1, pp. 257-266; I. Schwenzer & P. Hachem, *supra* note 106 in Chapter 1, pp. 101-118. See also CISG Advisory Council, Opinion no. 16, available at [www.cisgac.com/cisgac-opinion-no16].

76 Speech delivered on the occasion of the 35th Anniversary of the Convention on Contracts for the International Sale of Goods ('CISG') 'Roadmaps for the Transnational Convergence of Commercial law: Lessons learnt from the CISG', 23 April 2015, available at [www.supremecourt.gov.sg/docs/default-source/default-document-library/media-room/cisg-speech-(final—230415).pdf].

77 A thorough analysis of Article 6 of the CISG is available in T. M. Maureen, 'United Nations Convention on Contracts for the International Sale of Goods: Creating Uniformity of International Sales Law', *Fordham International Law Journal*, Vol. 12, 1989, pp. 727-729. See also F. Ferrari, 'Remarks on the UNCITRAL Digest's Comments on Article 6 CISG', *Journal of Law & Commerce*, Vol. 25, 2005, pp. 13-37.

78 For insights into the drafting of CISG contracts, see J. P. McMahon, 'Drafting CISG Contracts and Documents and Compliance Tips for Traders – Guide for Managers and Counsel' (2004), available at [www.cisg.law.pace.edu/cisg/contracts.html].

The CISG alludes to the general principles on which it is based, embodied in Article 7, but does not define them properly. For Anglo-Saxon scholars, these principles would be summed up in three implicit postulates: the obligation to compensate the expenses in which one of the parties is illegitimately taken by the other to incur; the reciprocal obligation to communicate any important information; and the obligation to mitigate loss resulting from breach of the contract.[79] On the other hand, civil law scholars consider that the inspiring principles of the CISG are the parties' autonomy, internationality, the validity of international practice, the gap-filling nature of the CISG rules and reasonableness.[80]

For example, the CISG provides in Article 11 that a contract does not need to be concluded or evidenced in writing.[81] This freedom of form to conclude a sales contract is nevertheless subject to reservation[82] defined in the CISG.[83] The possibility of the deal being concluded orally is consecrated and its existence can be proven by any legitimate means. Therefore, both a letter or e-mail containing the details of the negotiation between the parties or an invoice issued by the seller are instruments capable of justifying the existence of a commercial contract. However, in order for the contract to be deemed formed, the parties must comply with the requirements of offer and acceptance.

As seen, the CISG provides parties with great freedom to design their deals as they see fit and this also attends a rational efficiency, according to which parties are best placed to maximize their interests and will concentrate efforts to reach such goal. It is worth noting though, that Article 11 is controlled by Article 12 of the CISG, which imposes certain

---

79 J. Honnold, & H. Flechtner, *Uniform Law for International Sales under the 1980 United Nations Convention*, 4th edn., 2009, Kluwer, Amsterdam, 2009, pp. 142-148.

80 C. Witz, 'L'interprétation de la CVIM: divergences dans l'interprétation de la Convention de Vienne', *in* F. Ferrari (Ed.), *The 1980 Uniform Sales Law. Old Issues Revisited in the Light of Recent Experiences*, Sellier, European Law Publishers, Munich, 2003, pp. 279-333; C. Witz, 'CVIM: interprétation et questions non couvertes', *RDAI*, No. 3/4, 2001, pp. 253-275; V. Heuzé, 'La formation du contrat selon la CVIM: quelques difficultés', *RDAI*, No. 3/4, 2001, pp. 277-291; and F. Ferrari, 'Interprétation uniforme de la Convention de Vienne de 1980 sur la vente internationale', *Revue Internationale de Droit Comparé*, Vol. 48, Issue 4, 1996, p. 827; see also V. Heuzé, *La vente internationale de marchandises - Droit Uniforme*, GLN Joly éditions, Paris, 1992, pp. 85-102.

81 Art. 11: A contract of sale need not be concluded in or evidenced by writing and is not subject to any other requirement as to form. It may be proved by any means, including witnesses.

82 Current Reservation States under Article 96 of the CISG include: Argentina, Armenia, Belarus, Chile, Paraguay, the Russian Federation, Ukraine and Vietnam. Three other contracting States recently withdrew their declarations: China, Latvia and Lithuania - but they remain regarded as reservations States for contracts concluded before the withdrawal took effect, as per Article 97(4) CISG. See also in this sense, U. Schroeter, 'The Cross-border Freedom of Form Principle Under Reservation: The Role of Articles 12 and 96 CISG in Theory and Practice', *Journal of Law & Commerce*, Vol. 33, No. 1, 2014, p. 87. See also I. Schwenzer & P. Hachem, *supra* note 106 in Chapter 1, pp. 1264-1266.

83 See, in this sense, U. Schroeter, remarking in relation to the CISG that "[...] a decision was eventually reached in favor of the freedom of form principle (or principle of 'informality') becoming the basic rule in the uniform law. This general principle was incorporated into the Convention through Articles 11 and 29(1) CISG", U. Schroeter, *supra* note 82, p. 83. For an explanation regarding the treatment to forms in civil and common law jurisdictions, see the same reference on pp. 81-82.

restrictions on this freedom if the contracting State made a declaration under Article 96 of the CISG.[84]

Another aspect of the CISG which falls within the category of 'freedom' to conclude contracts is flexibility of proof, which is nevertheless subject to the absence of reservations[85] defined in Articles 12[86] and 96 of the CISG. As we have seen, parties do not want to feel tied up with legal formalities, which may compromise their deals. The same applies to the form to conclude a contract, which should also accompany an economic rationality.[87] Therefore, the CISG once more attends to this rationality by allowing a contract to be '...proved by any means, including witnesses'[88]. For completeness, it should be mentioned that Article 11 may be bound by restrictions in its reach by Article 12 of the CISG.

On the issue of contract formation the rule adopted by the CISG[89] is the reception rule: the contract is concluded when acceptance reaches the offeror.[90] The reception rule makes sense for international sales since it aims at ensuring that all parties are aware of the time of the contract's conclusion. This avoids unnecessary performance expenses by an offeree who acts in reliance on an acceptance that has been dispatched but may never reach the offeror.[91]

---

84 Art. 96 of the CISG: A Contracting State whose legislation requires contracts of sale to be concluded in or evidenced by writing may at any time make a declaration in accordance with article 12 that any provision of article 11, article 29, or Part II of this Convention, that allows a contract of sale or its modification or termination by agreement or any offer, acceptance, or other indication of intention to be made in any form other than in writing, does not apply where any party has his place of business in that State. A list of Reservation States is available at [www.uncitral.org/uncitral/en/uncitral_texts/sale_goods/1980CISG_status.html].

85 See U. Schroeter, *supra* note 82, p. 35, arguing that the freedom of form principle, while it represents an important policy decision, came subject to a compromise, *i.e.*, reservation of Articles 12 and 96 of the CISG.

86 Article 12 of the CISG: Any provision of article 11, article 29 or Part II of this Convention that allows a contract of sale or its modification or termination by agreement or any offer, acceptance or other indication of intention to be made in any form other than in writing does not apply where any party has his place of business in a Contracting State which has made a declaration under article 96 of this Convention. The parties may not derogate from or vary the effect or this article.

87 See commentary of Article 11 of the CISG by Schmidt-Kessel, *in* I. Schwenzer (Ed.), *supra* note 106 in Chapter 1, pp. 203-213.

88 See *supra* note 82.

89 A valid offer must have all essential elements of the type of contract: goods, price and quantity or a way to determine them. CISG Arts. 14(1), 55: a valid offer shall reflect the offeror's intention to be bound by its offer. Under the CISG an offer becomes effective when it reaches the offeree, so that withdrawal is also possible before that moment. *See* CISG Art. 15(1)(2); Likewise, revocation is possible before dispatch of acceptance: CISG Art. 16(1), unless the offeror has obliged himself to uphold its offer, for example by fixing a period for acceptance. *See* Brazil Art. 428(III) Civil Code; Art. 19 PRC CL; CISG Art. 16(1)(a). See also generally L. G. Meira Moser, 'A formação do contrato de compra e venda entre ausentes: a interlocução entre a Convenção de Viena (CISG) e o direito brasileiro', *in* V. Fradera & L. G. Meira Moser (Eds.), *A Compra e Venda Internacional de Mercadorias: estudos sobre a Convenção de Viena de 1980*, Atlas, São Paulo, 2010, p. 108 *et seq.*

90 CISG Art. 18(2).

91 E. Muñoz & L. G. Meira Moser, *supra* note 64 in Chapter 3, pp. 89-90.

Another example of economic efficiency is the alterations between the offer and acceptance,[92] in which the CISG departs from the strict mirror-image-rule by distinguishing between material and immaterial alterations[93] of the offer by the acceptance.[94] Article 19(2)[95] of the CISG seeks to relax the mirror-image-rule by making a reply, which contains additional or different terms that do not materially alter the offer, a valid acceptance. The policy, to promote uniformity and preserve agreements, should lead to a restrictive interpretation of what constitutes a material alteration.[96] The extent to which an alteration is considered material may also interact with the course of dealings and trade usage,[97] in addition to previous negotiation and other elements of informing intent[98] under the CISG.[99] This rule seems fit for cross-border sales as it seeks to avoid the minor

---

92 On this topic, U. Schroeter argues that Article 19 has not proved to be an ideal solution given the numerous cases of merger of the issues of formation and content of a contract. U. Schroeter further argues that the divergences in 'offer' and 'acceptance' frequently cause problems, in particular if standard forms are used by both parties, see commentary of Article 19 of the CISG by U. Schroeter, *in* I. Schwenzer (Ed.), *supra* note 106 in Chapter 1, p. 351, para. 2.

93 U. Schroeter, while commenting Article 19, remarks that "[...] the distinction between materially and immaterially different terms from the outset depends on the circumstances of the individual case (ie the significance which particular modifications have for the contract and the parties, having regard to the content of the contract, the size of the order, the relationship between the parties, the economic position, etc)", *supra* note 93, p. 358, para. 17.

94 See CISG Art. 19, which provides that only variations concerning the subject matter, quantity, quality, price or payment, time of performance, place and manner of performance, liability for breach of contract and dispute resolution is a material discrepancy and may render the acceptance a counter-offer.

95 Article 19(2) of the CISG: (2) However, a reply to an offer which purports to be an acceptance but contains additional or different terms which do not materially alter the terms of the offer constitutes an acceptance, unless the offeror, without undue delay, objects orally to the discrepancy or dispatches a notice to that effect. If he does not so object, the terms of the contract are the terms of the offer with the modifications contained in the acceptance.

96 M. del Pilar Viscasillas, 'Contract Conclusion under the CISG', *Journal of Law & Commerce*, Vol. 16, 1997, p. 337.

97 Article 9 of the CISG. See also U. Schroeter, arguing that changes to matters mentioned in Article 19(3) of the CISG may be considered immaterial on account of the particular circumstances of the case, the practices of the parties, preliminary negotiations, or usage. U. Schroeter concludes that "Article 19(3) therefore merely contains a rebuttable presumption that the parties intend to regard the matters listed as 'material'", *supra* note 93, p. 356, para. 15. In this connection, but discussing arbitration clauses as potential changes, see I. Schwenzer & D. Tebel, 'The Word is not Enough – Arbitration, Choice of Forum and Choice of Law Clauses under the CISG', *ASA Bulletin*, Vol. 31, Issue 4, 2013, pp. 740-755, arguing that "the mentioning of dispute resolution clauses in Art. 19(3) CISG evidences that the CISG generally governs dispute resolution clauses", p. 745. See also P. Schlechtriem, for whom Article 19(3) "attempts to alleviate the difficulties in distinguishing between material and immaterial modifications by listing the contractual provisions to which any modifications are presumed to be material", P. Schlechtriem, *supra* note 67, p. 55.

98 Article 8 of the CISG.

99 M. del Pilar Viscasillas, *supra* note 96, pp. 337-338.

differences that do not alter the *essentialia negotti*,[100] a concept that can be raised by one of the parties to refute the existence of a cross-border sale at performance phase.[101]

5.1.3.2 Degree of Flexibility: How Far Can We Go?

Parties' autonomy reaches its apex of exercise in Article 6 of the CISG,[102] which allows for parties to exclude the application of provisions of the CISG in whole or in part, and to change the effects of any provision. This article without doubt confers an important trade-off on parties to international trade, who may use it to leverage deals and reduce transaction costs.[103] This also accompanies the idea of the CISG as aligned with market expectations and the freedom that is generally sought.

Article 6 of the CISG might be seen as a bargaining chip, allowing players to sit down and examine the provisions which might not be advantageous to buyer or seller. Alternatively, this provision has the merit of allowing parties to vary the effect of the rule, for example by reducing or extending deadlines, or dispensing with certain practices, limiting liabilities. However, attention is drawn to the exceptions to Article 6 of the CISG, which are found in Article 12.[104]

5.1.4 Mandatory Provisions: Unwelcome Surprises?

Mandatory provisions are regarded as rules that may curtail a party's autonomy freely to design their rights, duties and obligations of certain deals. They are often treated with suspicion as they may interact (not always in a positive way) with the negotiated terms of a contract. In some instances they may also restrict the freedom of contract generally

100 U. Schroeter, discussing materially different terms, sustain that the 'additions' of an acceptance must first be examined via Article 8(3) of the CISG, *i.e.*, in light of the negotiations between the parties and the practices established between them, *supra* note 93, p. 353, para. 8.

101 See U. Schroeter, *supra* note 93, p. 351, para. 1; E. Muñoz & L. G. Meira Moser, *supra* note 64 in Chapter 3, p. 90.

102 Art. 6 of the CISG: "The parties may exclude the application of this Convention or, subject to article 12, derogate from or vary the effect of any of its provisions."

103 See, *e.g.*, CLOUT case n°. 106, in which the Austrian Supreme Court concluded that Art. 57 of the CISGmay be excluded by the parties. In another case (Landgericht Giessen, Germany, 5.07.1994), the Court considered it possible to exclude the application of art. 39 of the CISG (notice requirement), according to the will of the parties; CLOUT case n°. 1305, in which a Polish court reasoned that the parties were entitled under Article 6 CISG to shape the contract as they saw fit, which *inter alia* allowed them to introduce a provision for an automatic termination of the contract within a certain period of time.

104 Art. 12 CISG: "Any provision of article 11, article 29 or Part II of this Convention that allows a contract of sale or its modification or termination by agreement or any offer, acceptance or other indication of intention to be made in any form other than in writing does not apply where any party has his place of business in a Contracting State which has made a declaration under article 96 of this Convention. The parties may not derogate from or vary the effect or this article."

sought by parties. At other times mandatory provisions may also bring about unwelcome surprises.[105]

Freedom of contract ranks first in contracting parties' preferences list.[106] The empirical results discussed at the outset of this book showed that parties wish to enjoy great flexibility to design the contract.[107] Friction between freedom of contract and mandatory provisions are discussed below.

Mandatory provisions may contain unwelcome surprises which could curtail the freedom of contract sought. They may hinder the course of a contract and threaten the core of the agreement. This makes mandatory provisions undesirable for parties who wish to be able to design their rights, duties and obligations as freely as possible without the intervention of rules that generate inefficient results.[108] Mandatory provisions of national origin are those enacted by the states and are a matter of public policy because they are imperative. Examples of public law provisions include: provisions on antitrust, tax law and environmental protection laws.[109] Private law provisions of public policy would also include protection of one of the parties, *i.e.*, limitations to penalties or exclusions of liability, particular form requirements for specific types of contract, and licensing requirements.

Naturally, awareness of the existing mandatory provisions – as well as potential interactions with the negotiated terms in the contract – is a key consideration in the process of electing the most suitable governing contract law.

5.1.5 *Legal Interpretation*

Interpretation of rules is certainly a key factor in any decision and is also linked to Chapter 1, inasmuch as the degree of predictability and ease with which a rule is ascertained will dictate how a decision-maker will interpret and apply a legal rule. Now, in this exercise, governing principles will play a key role, as we shall see below.

105 In this connection, R. Michaels advises that "[...] Economists named two limits to party autonomy: negative third-party externalities and information asymmetries, which are mirrored in the international mandatory rules and relate to specific kinds of contracts with structurally weaker parties: consumer contracts, employment contracts, and insurance contracts", 'Economics of Law as Choice of Law', *Law and Contemporary Problems*, Vol. 71, No. 3, 2008, p. 95.

106 In this sense, see empirical data discussed *supra* Chapter 1.

107 *Id.*

108 L. G. Meira Moser, *supra* note 3 in Chapter 1, p. 36.

109 See D. Hochstrasser, 'Choice of Law and "Foreign" Mandatory Rules in International Arbitration', *Journal of International Arbitration*, Vol. 11, Issue 1, 1994, p. 67.

5.1.5.1 Hermeneutic Tools

In an attempt to contribute to the 'removal of legal barriers in international trade and promote the development of international trade',[110] the CISG's mandate finds support in the principle of good faith, which is enshrined in Article 7.[111] Readers should not, however, confuse it with the principle of subjective good faith, meaning the state of awareness of compliance or not with the law.

As Justice Sundaresh Menon advises, 'good faith is a protean term susceptible to many variations of meaning in different jurisdictions'.[112] However, the UNCITRAL Commission decided that while good faith ought not to be limited just to contract formation, it should equally not be elevated to a freestanding principle.[113] Therefore this approach was to employ good faith as a principle of contract interpretation leaving some discretion to national courts in applying the CISG.[114]

B. Sheehy submits that Article 7 of the CISG can be read as referring to good faith in three ways: (i) good faith in interpreting the CISG itself; (ii) promoting good faith in international trade; and (iii) good faith as a governing principle for contracts falling under its control.[115]

I. Schwenzer and P. Hachem acknowledge that the meaning of 'good faith' is controversial and lists three main issues[116] relating to the requirement to observe 'good faith in international trade' when interpreting the CISG. Firstly, whether it applies only to the interpretation of the CISG or also directly to the contractual relationship between the parties. Secondly, the difficulty of determining the standard of 'good faith'. Thirdly, it is unclear whether and to what extent the interpretation of particular concepts or provisions of the Convention can result in their modification in order to conform with the required standard.[117] With this, the requirement to observe good faith in international trade may – in conjunction with Article 7(2) – finally be of relevance in the context of gap-filling.[118]

---

110 CISG preamble, available at [www.cisg.law.pace.edu/cisg/text/treaty.html].

111 Article 7 of the CISG: "(1) In the interpretation of this Convention, regard is to be had to its international character and to the need to promote uniformity in its application and the *observance of good faith in international trade.*" (emphasis added).

112 Justice Sundaresh Menon's speech, available at [www.supremecourt.gov.sg/docs/default-source/default-document-library/media-room/cisg-speech-(final—230415).pdf].

113 Report of the Working Group on the International Sale of goods on the work of its ninth session (Geneva, 19-30 September 1977), available at [www.uncitral.org/pdf/english/yearbooks/yb-1978-e/vol9-p61-85-e.pdf].

114 Justice Sundaresh Menon's speech, *supra* note 112, p. 19.

115 B. Sheehy, 'Good Faith in the CISG: The Interpretation Problems of Article 7', *Review of the Convention on Contracts for the International Sale of Goods (CISG) ed. by Pace International Law* Review, 2007, p. 11, available at [https://ssrn.com/abstract=777105].

116 I. Schwenzer & P. Hachem, *supra* note 106 in Chapter 1, Article 7, p. 126, para. 16.

117 *Id.*

118 *Id.*

As regards the first aspect, Schwenzer and Hachem contend that good faith is a general clause serving to interpret the CISG only and not individual contracts. However, "it may influence the reading of individual communications under Article 8… it also influences indirectly the contractual relationship between the parties, as it may be used to concretize rights and obligations established by the provisions of the CISG".[119]

With respect to the second aspect, Schwenzer and Hachem submit that there is no independent and autonomous source producing express principles of good faith in international trade other than those embodied in the conventions and used as applicable under Article 9 of the CISG.[120] In addition, the authors submit that it is then a matter for the courts and arbitral tribunal to decide and to characterize such rules as containing or amounting to standards of good faith in international trade. And the authors conclude on this point, stating that "the more often courts and tribunals refer to such standards as standards of good faith in international trade when applying Article 7(1), the more concrete the requirements of this provision becomes".[121]

As to the third and final aspect,[122] Schwenzer and Hachem remark that one has to distinguish concretizing rights and obligations of the parties under provisions of the CISG and the actual modifications of CISG provisions. Schwenzer and Hachem give as example the concretization of the obligation to mitigate losses under Article 77[123] of the CISG: observing 'good faith' may under certain circumstances lead to an obligation of the aggrieved party to re-negotiate with the party in breach as a reasonable measure to mitigate loss.

While the term 'good faith' is present in some CISG rules: 27, 32, 35, 38 (1), 46 (1), 54, 62, 68, 77 and 79 (4),[124] in this author's view the CISG does not explicitly provide for a

119 I. Schwenzer & P. Hachem, *supra* note 106 in Chapter 1, Article 7, p. 127, para. 17.

120 See also M. Schmidt-Kessel, 'Commentary on the UN Convention for the International Sale of Goods (CISG)', *supra* note 106 in Chapter 1, Article 9, pp. 181-196.

121 *Id.*, pp. 127-128, para. 18.

122 M. Schmidt-Kessel, 'Commentary on the UN Convention for the International Sale of Goods (CISG)', *supra* note 106 in Chapter 1, Article 9, p. 128, para. 19.

123 Article 77 of the CISG: A party who relies on a breach of contract must take such measures as are reasonable in the circumstances to mitigate the loss, including loss of profit, resulting from the breach. If he fails to take such measures, the party in breach may claim a reduction in the damages in the amount by which the loss should have been mitigated.

124 While it is highly disputed, some authors maintain that the relevance of the principle of good faith is not limited to interpretation of the Convention. In this connection, C. M. Bianca & M. J. Bonell argue that "There are a number of provisions that makes reference to, Article 14(2)(b), 19(2), 27(2), 35 and 44, 38, 45(2), 60(2) and 67, and 74 to 77, which constitute a particular application of this principle, thus confirming that good faith is also one of the 'general principles' underlying the Convention as a whole. As such it may even impose on the parties additional obligations of a positive character. This will be the case, if during the negotiating process or in the course of the performance of the contract a question arises for which the Convention does not contain any specific provision and the solution is ground in applying, in accordance with Article 7(2), the principle of good faith", *supra* note 67, p. 85.

duty to act in good faith[125]– as would be the case in certain jurisdictions[126] – and it thus seems that good faith is limited to the interpretation of the contract of sale while not imposing a duty on the contracting parties themselves.[127]

In this regard, Michael Bridge states that the claim that Article 7(1) of the CISG should be interpreted on the basis as giving rise to a duty of good faith on the contracting parties themselves is 'seriously at odds with the rule of law'[128] and wonders "How are contracting parties to plan for the future and assess risk if their efforts are to be subjected to an occult, broad standard that has never been subjected to a rigorous definition or, so far as I can see, any real attempt to answer hard questions? In what sense are they trusting their fate to the law if there is no predictability in its application?".[129]

To understand the roots of this principle further, Ole Lando, while citing Paul Legrand,[130] points out that the courts in England regard the general principle that the parties to a contract must act in good faith as incompatible with the adversarial nature of contract. Paul Legrand observes that the historical explanation of the English attitude appears to be that the law of contract was framed in cases of charterparty and sale of commodities, which were concluded between parties who typically had no lasting relationship, and who regarded themselves as adversaries.[131] However, Ole Lando further states that:

> many of the results which in the Continental systems are achieved by requiring good faith have been reached in English law by more specific rules, and these

125 The principle of objective good faith is applied to legal affairs, referring to the standard duties attached to the contractual obligations imposed on the contractors in order to act with honesty, loyalty, probity, before, during and after contracting, regardless of any express contractual provision. Nothing has to do, therefore, with psychological prediction of the contractors or intentions; for example, the application of this principle is not by subsumption, nor is its content filled abstractly, but only casuistically. It is, therefore, an express authorization to the judge to seek in the morals the basis for decision of a specific case. Two meanings are generally attributed to objective good faith: principle or standard. As a standard, objective good faith can receive varied meanings according to the matter where it is applied, since the standard established a socially accepted pattern of conduct, capable of adapting to the peculiarities of the case. In some legal systems objective good faith is interpreted as a principle, and as such is called upon to perform three relevant functions: interpretation, concretization and control. As far as the concretizing role is concerned, a more concrete determination of its content is made by reference to usage and customs. Such function is more clear in the context of international trade, where usage and custom play a rather pivotal role. With respect to the control role, it is generally understood as a directive to the parties' behavior.

126 The principle of objective good faith is expressly stated in para. 242 of the BGB, sec. 1-103 of the UCC and in para. 231 of the Restatement (Second) of Contracts. Also in art. 1134 of the Code Civil and in arts. 1337-8, 1366, 1375 of the Codice Civile.

127 See also commentary to Article 7 of the CISG by I. Schwenzer & P. Hachem, *supra* note 106 in Chapter 1, pp. 119-142.

128 M. Bridge, *supra* note 16, p. 109.

129 *Id.*, pp. 109-110.

130 P. Legrand, 'On the Unbearable Localness of the Law, Academic Fallacies and Unseasonable Observations', *European Review of Private Law*, Vol. 10, Issue 1, p. 64.

131 O. Lando, 'Culture and Contract Laws', *European Review of Contract Law*, Vol. 3, Issue 1, 2007, p. 10.

> rules are becoming more and more numerous. Thus the courts have imposed a strict moral code in the fiduciary relationships; and good faith is required in contracts which are characterised as uberrimae fidei. Furthermore, the courts have on occasion limited the right of a party who is the victim of a slight breach of contract to terminate the contract on that ground, when the real motive was to escape a bad bargain. And the victim of a wrongful repudiation of a contract is not permitted to ignore the repudiation, complete his own performance and claim the contract price unless the victim has a legitimate interest in doing so.[132]

Despite the above, good faith principle finds less enthusiastic followers among Anglo-Saxon traders. In common law jurisdictions, the doctrine of estoppel,[133] which does not differ essentially in its ultimate ethical foundation, is much more accepted yet has a restricted dimension. This is because it was developed to mitigate the rule of consideration (promissory estoppel is the situation in which, for reasons of equity, the party who in good faith has relied on the promise of another, making a change in legal or economic position, may find a remedy in court to protect herself).

On this matter, Peter Schlechtriem remarks that the function of Article 7 of the CISG can probably be fulfilled by the rule that the parties must conduct themselves according to the standard of the 'reasonable person'[134] which is expressly described in a number of provisions and, therefore, according to Article 7(2),[135] must be regarded as a general principle of the CISG.[136]

Michael Bridge, in a bid to attain success for the guide of its application to CISG contracts, remarks that "Article 7(1) is expressly in the passive voice and does not indicate exactly who or what should be paying regard to good faith. However, since contracting parties make and perform contracts, and courts and tribunal interpret and enforce those contracts, the bearers of the duty can only be courts and arbitrators".[137]

In fact, the CISG achieves greater accuracy of results by upholding the principle of reasonableness as the standard of a reasonable person. Although not expressly enshrined

132 O. Lando, *supra* note 71 in Chapter 3, p. 397.

133 B. Fauvarque-Cosson, 'La confiance legitime et l'estoppel'. *Electronic Journal of International Law*, Vol. 11, Issue 3, 2007, available at [www.ejcl.org/113/article113-8.pdf]; D. Mazeaud, 'La confiance légitime et l'estoppel', *Revue Internationale de Droit Comparé*, No. 2, 2006, pp. 362-392.

134 Article 8 of the CISG.

135 In the same line of thought, I. Schwenzer & P. Hachem argue that "The maxim of 'observance of good faith in international trade' as established by Article 7(1), therefore, concerns the interpretation of the Convention only and cannot be applied directly to individual contracts. However, it may influence the reading of individual communications under Article 8. It also influences indirectly the contractual relationship between the parties, as it may be used to concretize rights and obligations established by the provisions of the CISG 'Commentary on the UN Convention for the International Sale of Goods (CISG)'", *supra* note 106 in Chapter 1, p. 127, para 17.

136 P. Schlechtriem, *supra* note 67, p. 39.

137 M. Bridge, *supra* note 16, p. 108.

in the CISG, it is implicit in several of its rules.[138] Reasonableness relates to common sense, that is, what is held in certain circumstance, at a certain moment, in a certain community as rational, balanced, prudent and sensible. It is also a concept that must be fulfilled from the case circumstances,[139] thereby also facilitating transactions.

The CISG also incorporates a practical approach via Article 8(3), according to which "in determining the intent of a party or the understanding of a reasonable person would have had, due consideration is to be given to all relevant circumstances of the case including the negotiations, any practices which the parties have establishes between themselves, usages and any subsequent conduct of the parties". As the author Peter Mazzacano remarks, this provision uses trade usage as a factor for interpreting the will of the parties as it lends an interpretative value to the usages.[140] In this author's view, this approach likewise follows an economic rationality, by increasing both legal certainty and commercial predictability in international trade.

Michael Bridge further concludes in relation Article 7(1) of the CISG that good faith has played a rather ancillary and meaningless role in the case law and that 'those fearful of the disruptive effect of good faith should perhaps stop worrying'.[141]

As to gap-fillers, Article 7(2) of the CISG provides for a subsidiary mechanism for filling contractual gaps, in the event that there is no specific tool to resolve the controversy or by applying the principles that inspire the CISG. In other words, questions relating to matters governed by the CISG, which are not expressly covered, shall be settled in the first place in accordance with CISG's underlying general principles,[142] or 'internal gaps', failing which by the applicable law under the rules of private international law or 'external gaps'.[143] Article 7(2) of the CISG reaffirms the commitment to interpret the

---

138 Arts. 14, 16 (2) (b), 18 (formation of the contract); art. 25 (general provisions); arts. 33, 34, 35, 37, 38, 39, 43, 44, 46, 47, 48, 49 (obligations of the seller); arts. 63, 64, 65 (obligations of the buyer); arts. 72, 73, 74, 75, 76, 77, 79, 85, 86, 87, 88 (provisions common to the obligations of the seller and of the buyer).

139 See, in this sense, Landgericht Zwickau, Germany, 19.03.1999; CLOUT case nº 189 (Oberster Gerichtshof, Áustria, 20.03.1997); Hoge Raad, Netherlands, 7.11.1997; CLOUT case nº 215 (Bezirksgericht St. Gallen, Switzerland, 3.07.1997); CLOUT case nº 166 (Arbitration – Schiedsgericht der Handelskammer Hamburg, 21.03, 21.06.1996); CLOUT case nº 308 (Federal Court of Australia, 28.04.1995); CLOUT case nº 106 (Oberster Gerichtshof, Austria, 10.11.1994); CLOUT case nº 273 (Oberlandesgericht München, Germany, 09.07.1997).

140 P. J. Mazzacano, *supra* note 47, p. 22.

141 M. Bridge, *supra* note 16, p. 115.

142 See U. Magnus, arguing that "general principles are safeguards which, at a rather high level of abstraction, try to secure just results in the application of the law" (pp. 166-167) and about art. 7(2) of the CISG "[...] the underlying general principles serve as guidelines and aids to interpretation in the application of the concrete provisions of the respective convention. And because they necessitate being first discovered and inferred from the entire contents of the respective convention, they also serve to verify the basis structure and the policy and value judgments of that convention", U. Magnus, 'Harmonization and Unification of Law by Means of General Principles', *in* Morten M. Fagot (Ed.), *Unification and Harmonization of International Commercial Law – Interaction of Deharmonization*, Wolters Kluwer, Alphen aan den Rijn, 2012, p. 167.

143 See I. Schwenzer, *supra* note 106 in Chapter 1, p. 132, p. 27.

CISG in an autonomous and systemic manner, so that any zones of indeterminacy or gaps are filled by the very principles that support it, and only as a last sort via the applicable law under the rules of private international law.

By way of examples, judicial decisions have determined the application of domestic law in time-bar claims,[144] agency relationships,[145] validity matters (clause contained in the contract prohibiting transfer of licence in a software licence agreement).[146] Similarly, courts have looked at domestic laws to apply interest rates.[147] In these cases the judge applied the CISG and, in the points uncovered, either expressly or implicitly (inspiring principles), used the 'dépeçage', *i.e.*, through the conflict of law method, the judge applied national law to specific points.

As we have seen, even though a contract is naturally incomplete (rationality is limited and it would otherwise lead to high transaction costs), the CISG's gap-filling methods are certainly worth observing at the time of conclusion of the contract, in particular to avoid the application of unwanted domestic law. This degree of zeal is and should be weighed at the time of entering into cross-border sales contracts.

5.1.5.2 Conduct of the Parties and Trade Usages

The way a contracting party behaved in the past and behaves in the course of a deal is regulated by the CISG and, unless otherwise agreed by the parties, will bind them pursuant to Article 9.[148] This provision parties more responsible in international settings as their conduct will have repercussions and bind them. The same is true of trade usage (of a particular industry) which likewise (unless opted-out) will be binding. This economically efficient provision gives legal effects to customs and trade usages. Custom is the repeated

---

144 See CLOUT case n°· 1507.

145 US District Court, Southern District of New York, *Korea Trade Insurance Corporation v. Oved Apparel Corporation*, 23/3/2015.

146 Rechtbank Midden-Nederland (the Netherlands), *Corporate Web Solutions v. Dutch company and Vendorlink B.V.*, 25/3/2015; see also Court of appeal State of Rio Grande do Sul (Brazil, *Voges Metalurgia Ltda. v. Inversiones Metalmecanicas I.C.A.* – IMETAL I.C.A, 23/3/2017, discussing invalidity claims in a sales contract.

147 See, *e.g.*, US District Court, North District, Illinois, East. Div., USA, *Chicago Prime Packers, Inc., v. Northam Food Trading Co.*, 21/5/2004; US District Court, District of Kansas, *Guang Dong Light Headgear Factory Co., Ltd. v. ACI Intern.*, Inc, 28/4/2008; Gerechtshof's-Hertogenbosch, the Netherlands, *G.W.A. Bernards v. Carstenfelder Baumschulen Pflanzenhandel GmbH*; see also SCC arbitral awards examined by L. Bergman, *supra* note 94 in Chapter 1.

148 Article 9 of the CISG:
1. The parties are bound by any usage to which they have agreed and by any practices which they have established between themselves.
2. The parties are considered, unless otherwise agreed, to have impliedly made applicable to their contract or its formation a usage of which the parties knew or ought to have known and which in international trade is widely known to, and regularly observed by, parties to contracts of the type involved in the particular trade concerned.

practice, continuous and spontaneous, originating in the market, and calls for two founding elements: the use and the consciousness of market players of its observance.[149]

However, such practices assume the status of legal rules as they become legal rules by imposition of the market, through prolonged and uninterrupted use. Usage and custom, whether of legal rules or simply those that fill legal business content as elements of factual support, can be interpretative.[150] So, either they are legal rules of interpretation or they are statements that say how one understands manifestations of will.

In the case of a trade usage the presumption is that of the parties' knowledge. This is because it is socially diffused and easy to access, so asymmetry of information between the parties and the legal rule is thus low (which is certainly more efficient and reduces transaction costs when compared to a legal rule imposed by the State, the content of which often does not reflect market realities).

The rule contained in Article 9[151] of the CISG directs the interpreter of the contract to trade usage, that is, that to which both dealers had prior access.[152] Article 9 of the CISG provides that the parties are bound by any use or practice established or agreed by them, as well as trade usages applicable to the contract and its formation, which is recognized in international trade and which (unless otherwise agreed by the parties[153]) the parties knew or ought to have known.

It has been submitted that the CISG prescribes a double function to trade usage, normative[154] and interpretative.[155] Scholars have disagreed as to whether Article 9(2) establishes a normative validity of the particular trade usage. There is a view that supports the idea that Article 9(2) is concerned with contract supplementation instead, or 'with the acceptance of an implied norm from which an agreement within the meaning of para-

149 L. G. Meira Moser, 'A cláusula compromissória, a conduta das partes e a força jurígena dos usos e costumes – comentário da Sentença Estrangeira Contestada no 855', *Revista de Arbitragem e Mediação*, Vol. 35, Issue 9, 2012, pp. 317-340; See also F. Ferrari to whom the CISG grants 'normative effect' to trade usages, see F. Ferrari, 'What Sources of Law for Contracts for the International Sale of Goods? Why One Has to Look Beyond the CISG,' *International Review of Law and Economics*, Vol. 25, 2005, pp. 333-336.

150 L. G. Meira Moser & F. Pignatta, 'Campo de Aplicação e Disposições Gerais (arts. 14 a 24)', *in* L. G. Meira Moser & F. Pignatta (Eds.), *Comentários à Convenção de Viena sobre contratos internacionais de venda de mercadorias*, Atlas, São Paulo, 2015, pp. 3-33.

151 See *supra* note 149.

152 F. Ferrari, 'La rilevanza degli usi nella Convenzione di Vienna sulla vendita internationzionale di beni mobilli', *Contratto e Impresa*, anno X, No.1, 1994, pp. 239-258.

153 In this connection, A. W. Katz reminds us that "there is no apparent pattern of attempts by contracting parties to opt out of the Article 9(2)'s trade usage provision, even though such opt-out clauses are explicitly authorized by Article 6, and even though parties regularly include in their contracts merger and entire-agreement clauses that exclude pre-contractual communications from the interpretative process", *supra* note 65 in Chapter 4, pp. 183-184.

154 See, in this sense, G. Cordero-Moss, noting that the CISG not only creates binding law as an international convention that is ratified by so many states, but that even gives recognition to the spontaneous rules born out of commercial practice, *supra* note 29 in Chapter 3, p. 34.

155 Ch. Pamboukis, 'The Concept and Function of Usages in the United Nations Convention on the International Sale of Goods', *Journal of Law & Commerce*, Vol. 25, 2005-06, p. 108; F. Ferrari, *supra* note 149, pp. 314-341.

graph 1 arises'[156]. This author concurs with this later view, inasmuch as Article 9(2) is to be interpreted within the meaning of Article 9(1) and in light of the hermeneutic guidance of Article 8. However, it should also be noted that the concept of usage is autonomous and internationally uniform,[157] that is free from domestic laws' influence, thereby incorporating a variety of contextual legal standards that will be subject to ex post substantive interpretation for their content.[158] In addition, considerations of usage and practice under Article 9(1) occurs on the basis of the intent of the parties under Article 8 of the CISG and the rules contained in Article 9 are not restricted to contract content but also contract formation.[159] This is another novelty of the CISG and one that represents a 'vehicle for flexibility' as it contributes to the longevity of this legal framework and grants trade usage functions both to interpret and supplement the CISG contract.[160]

This provision allows for important reflection on ways to reduce transaction costs by entrusting the parties with ample autonomy and flexibility in the design of risks, rights and contractual obligations. In this respect, one can think of a myriad of practices established between parties where they do not detail the contract signed, either in relation to the formation of the contract, for example, specific requirements or formalities adopted, modified and or dispensed between the parties, or even in execution. These will depend on a trade-off among a variety of planning and incentive considerations. As Avery Katz remarks, these considerations would include

> the costs of writing more detailed contracts ex ante, the costs of rent-seeking both ex ante in contractual negotiations and ex post once a dispute has arisen, the principal parties' ability to provide their legal and business agents with proper incentives to enter into contracts on efficient terms, the parties' attitudes toward risk and the distribution of information among potential tribunals, the need to make specific investments whose value depends on a partic-

156 I. Schwenzer, *supra* note 106 in Chapter 1, p. 187, para. 13.

157 C. M. Bianca & M. J. Bonell, *supra* note 67, pp. 110-111.

158 A. W. Katz, *supra* note 65 in Chapter 4, p. 183, arguing that these contextual legal standards "include not just the trade usage provision of Article 9(2), but also provisions that prescribe a reasonableness test for all interpretative questions, that allow contractual liability to be imposed without any formal writing requirement, that direct tribunals to interpret the entire Convention in light of unspecified standards of good faith in international trade, that indicate that questions not expressly settled in the CISG should be settled by reference to the general principles on which it is based, and that direct tribunals to consider all relevant evidence in interpreting the parties' intentions and expectations, including even communications that would be barred as parol evidence under common law systems".

159 I. Schwenzer, *supra* note 106 in Chapter 1, p. 182, para. 3. See also, generally, L. Graffi, 'Remarks on Trade Usages and Business Practices in International Sales Law', *Journal of Law & Commerce*, Vol. 29, Issue 2, 2011, pp. 273-295.

160 In this connection, but supporting a view that Article 9(2) of the CISG establishes a normative validity of trade usage, P. Mazzacano advises that the CISG provides the foundation for the legal effect of usage, by giving it a status superior to the CISG rules itself. Usage will thus, in Mazzacano's view, prevail over articles of the CISG either by virtue of the will of the parties (Article 9(1) or objectively (Article 9(2)), *supra* note 47, p. 25.

ular contract interpretation, and the need to induce complementary investment by third parties who may have differential access to the formal and substantive aspects of the principal parties' agreement.[161]

While jurisprudence has yet to be developed more fully, it has certainly produced a variety of cases on the functionality, extension and effects of Article 9 of the CISG. For example, there are court decisions and arbitral awards that have determined that exclusionary clauses,[162] provisional price clauses,[163] and accrual of interest in case of a deferred payment[164] were incorporated into the CISG via Article 9(2) and therefore, must be observed in the performance of the contract. In other cases automatic absorption of trade usage and custom of certain negotiating areas were recognized as binding to the contract.[165] The binding effect of the commercial practice established between the parties (Article 9(1))[166] requires a pattern to be regularly, and not sporadically, observed, but with a frequency ascertainable in the established commercial relationship. Consequently, usage and practice that have become established between the parties are regarded as binding. One can think of a myriad of practices that parties may have agreed, such as the time period for delivery or for payment of goods. In long-term contractual relations these terms are often similar in subsequent dealings. Article 9(1) of the CISG thus also makes sense from a cost-benefit perspective,[167] since parties will not have to negotiate this term separately for each consecutive contract.[168]

In connection with this, it should also be recalled that the behavioural coherence of the parties (reflected in Article 9(1)) is strongly linked to the prohibition of *venire contra*

---

161 A. W. Katz, *supra* note 65 in Chapter 4, p. 185.

162 US District Court, Western District Washington at Tacoma, *Barbara Berry, S.A. de C.V. v. Ken M. Spooner Farms, Inc.*, 13/4/2006.

163 ICC Arbitration Case No. 8324/1995, available at [http://cisgw3.law.pace.edu/cases/958324i1.html].

164 Argentina, Juzgado Nacional de Primera Instancia en lo Comercial No. 7, *Elastar Sacifia v. Bettcher Industries Inc.*, 20/5/1991.

165 For example, Federal Court of Australia, *Australia, Hannaford (trading as Torrens Valley Orchards) v. Australian Farmlink Pty Ltd*, CAN 087 011 541 [2008] FCA 1591; US District Court, S.D., New York, USA, *Geneva Pharmaceuticals Technology Corp. v. Barr Laboratories, Inc. et al.*, 10/5/2002, 98 Civ. 861, 99 Civ. 3607 (citing the CISG's 'strong preference for enforcing obligations and representations customarily relied upon by others in the industry'; Spain, Audiencia Provincial, Barcelona, *X v. Y*, 13/5/2014, discussing the use of English language as 'lingua franca' and thus amounting to an international usage within the meaning of Article 9(2) of the CISG; Spain, Tribunal Supremo, *X v. Y*, 1/7/2013, discussing the trade usage of invoices in the commodity trade; Austria, Oberster Gerichtshof, *X v. Y*, 21/3/2000, applying local German usages of the wood trade.

166 Zivilgericht Kanton Basel-Stadt, Switzerland, 21/12/1992, P4 1991/238; US Court of Appeals (11th Circuit), USA, Treibacher Industrie, *A.G. v. Allegheny Technologies, Inc.*, 12/9/2006, 5-13995; Arbitral Award, ICC 8817/1997; Court of Appeal of Turku, Finland, 12/4/2002; Oberster Gerichtshof, Austria, 31/8/2005, 7 Ob 175/05v; Amtsgericht Duisburg, Germany, 13/4/2000, 49 C 502/00.

167 As we have discussed, drafting lengthy contracts is time-consuming, expensive and may not capture the parties' intention to the fullest extent possible, see L. G. Meira Moser, *supra* note 3 in Chapter 1.

168 V. Mak, 'According to Custom…? The Role of "Trade Usage" in the Proposed Common European Sales Law (CESL)', *European Review of Contract Law*, Vol. 10, Issue 1, 2014, p. 71.

factum proprium[169] and refers to the element of trust that has emerged between the parties. A contracting party, by her acts, words and gestures, awakens in the other contracting party the confidence that a business behaviour coherence will be observed. The binding force between the parties is therefore not the act itself, but rather the trust created by the parties' behaviour.

When interpreting a contract governed by the CISG one has to be concerned with interpreting the contractual statements using the complex of circumstances in which the declaration of will and the behaviour is placed. Just as an example of the systemic reading of the CISG, the circumstances mentioned in Article 18[170] (formation of the contract) represent an 'open clause' and, therefore, are subject to the determinations of both Article 9(2) and 8(3).

These circumstances are reflected in the negotiation practice entered into between the parties, especially when there is no express acceptance in previous contracts. This may also happen if there is a negotiated use already developed between the contracting parties or even in the negotiating sphere, which dispenses with the declared acceptance, or even in cases where silence is the reasonable response to acceptance.

The flexibility of contracting parties under the CISG regime is hence a key advantage to players, which generates unequivocal improvement of Pareto to the parties, who will cooperate to the extent that they enjoy the benefits provided by the contractual game. Thus a signature on an invoice, for example, showing agreement, is interpreted as acceptance.[171] Related commercial acts are to be interpreted as tending to accomplishment of the contract;[172] the dispatch of goods without the refusal of the other party, or their collection by a third party, are practices which allow us to consider that acceptance was given under the CISG.[173]

---

169 See *supra* note 100 in Chapter 3.

170 Art. 18 CISG:

1. A statement made by or other conduct of the offeree indicating assent to an offer is an acceptance. Silence or inactivity does not in itself amount to acceptance.
2. An acceptance of an offer becomes effective at the moment the indication of assent reaches the offeror. An acceptance is not effective if the indication of assent does not reach the offeror within the time he has fixed or, if no time is fixed, within a reasonable time, due account being taken of the circumstances of the transaction, including the rapidity of the means of communication employed by the offeror. An oral offer must be accepted immediately unless the circumstances indicate otherwise.
3. However, if, by virtue of the offer or as a result of practices which the parties have established between themselves or of usage, the offeree may indicate assent by performing an act, such as one relating to the dispatch of the goods or payment of the price, without notice to the offeror, the acceptance is effective at the moment the act is performed, provided that the act is performed within the period of time laid down in the preceding paragraph.

171 See, *e.g.*, *Inta S. A. v. MCS Officina Meccanica S.p.A.*; Cámara Nacional en lo Comercial, Sala E, Argentina, 14/10/1993, no 45626.

172 *Sté Calzados Magnanni v. Sarl Shoes General International – S.G.I.*, Cour d'Appel de Grenoble, 21/10/1999, no 96J/00101.

173 CLOUT case n°. 193 (Handelsgericht des Kantons Zürich, Switzerland, 10/7/1996); CLOUT case n°. 416 (Minnesota State District Court, United States, 9/3/1999); CLOUT case n°. 291 (Oberlandesgericht Frankfurt a.M., Germany, 23/5/1995).

From this we have seen that the way the CISG regulates trade usage allows for the application of rules that are adaptable and sensible to the contingencies of international trade. In certain cases, because the practices established by the parties may be detailed, and so is the industry-sector where both parties are placed, the CISG would mean reduced drafting and learning costs as there is less asymmetry of information, notably because of binding trade usage and previous practice established between parties. However, one should not forget that the parties may simply vary or annul the binding effect of these practices by virtue of Article 6 of the CISG.[174] Naturally, the existence of an agreement is necessary to that effect and this could be made by general business terms, provided that they have been validly agreed by the parties. As discussed, this article allows parties, subject to some limitations readily noted, to shape the contract as they see fit.

5.1.6 *Body of Case Law*

5.1.6.1 To Be Settled or Not?

Concerns of case law show that parties will set strategies and evaluate their chances of winning. Hence, settled case law may be regarded as highly positive if there is no need to test a new legal thesis before the appropriate forum. This is because the legal thesis on which the party wishes to rely may have already been tested and embodied in the law (rules uniformly interpreted generate predictable results).[175] Conversely, if the legal thesis needs to be tested before the (appropriate) courts, parties will need to assess costs, risks and forum convenience. Depending on the background and particulars of the case, it might be advisable to test new legal thesis before less conservative fora.[176]

5.1.6.2 Interpretation of Legal Rules

Naturally, interpretation of legal rules, as we have seen, is of utmost importance for a fair and just outcome. As S. Shavell argues, the courts' interpretation influences the way parties draft a contract: the more accurately it expresses the parties' true wishes, the more willing parties will be to leave gaps and to adopt general terms, whereas parties are more willing to make the extra effort in drafting more detailed contracts when the courts refrain from interpreting terms or interpret in ways that contradict, oppose or are inconsistent with their true intention.[177]

---

174 Article 6 of the CISG prescribes that the parties may exclude the CISG wholly or in part, save for Article 12. If the CISG has been wholly excluded, the law applicable must be determined by the general conflict rules of the forum. See C. M. Bianca & M. J. Bonell, *supra* note 67, pp. 58-59. In the scenario above, if those rules lead to the application of the law of a CISG contracting State, the domestic sales legal framework of that State will govern the contract. See J. P. McMahon, *supra* note 78, available at [www.cisg.law.pace.edu/cisg/contracts.html#a6].

175 L. G. Meira Moser, *supra* note 3 in Chapter 1, p. 41.

176 *Id.*

177 See S. Shavell, *supra* note 46 in Chapter 3, pp. 290-291.

As a way to avoid the vagaries of determination, Richard Posner argues that, to the extent that arbitrators are considered more reliable interpreters than judges, we can expect contracts containing arbitration clauses (other things being equal) to be shorter than contracts that do not.[178] In addition to the contours of the deal, parties are certainly concerned with its substantive design, how can they maximize gains, minimize losses, predict, avoid and if avoidance is impossible, tackle unpleasant surprises.

5.1.7 *Provisions on Performance*

Provisions on performance play an important role, as they will determine the extent of rigor required for a party in order to accomplish contractual duties and obligations. They will likewise determine the consequences of contractual parties' omissions or inaction in the performance phase of certain duties and obligations. Consequently, contracting parties will likely prefer governing contract law that clearly states parties' duties and obligations.

Studies discussed at the outset indicated that this topic is of concern contracting parties. For example, in the Survey 29.49% of respondents indicated provisions on performance as a positive legal feature of governing contract law.[179] 33.04% regarded 'provisions on performance' as a positive economic feature of governing contract law[180] and 22.03% as possibly being a negative legal feature.[181]

Provisions on performance, in terms of economic considerations, was their first concern, before 'broad interpretation of the legal rules' and 'gap-filling mechanisms'.[182] One could explain these results in light of the fact that provisions on performance might be seen as determinant or perhaps even part of the same package of 'remedies available' and 'damages'.

5.1.7.1 Delivery of Goods

As regards the delivery of goods, the CISG has also come up with cost-effective solutions. Article 35 contains a uniform concept of 'lack of conformity',[183] which includes differences in quality, quantity, delivery of an *aliud*, and defects in packaging. This distinguishes the CISG from most domestic law on liability for defective goods.[184]

178 See R. Posner, *supra* note 81 in Chapter 3, p. 18.
179 Global Empirical Survey, *supra* Section 1.2.4.1.
180 Global Empirical Survey, *supra* Section 1.2.4.2.
181 Global Empirical Survey, *supra* Section 1.2.4.1.
182 Global Empirical Survey, *supra* Section 1.2.4.2.
183 I. Schwenzer, *supra* note 106 in Chapter 1, Article 35, p. 593, para. 4.
184 For example, the UCC distinguishes between express and implied warranties U.C.C. §§ 2-313, 2-314 (1977). The UK Sales of Goods Act 1979 likewise distinguishes conditions and warranties (c. 54, paras. 14 and 15); and the French legal system vice caché and vice apparent. Many of the jurisdictions of Romanic legal tradition will list differences regarding non-conformity delivery.

Absent an express agreement the CISG will treat any type of discrepancy in the goods delivered under the parameters of conformity established under Article 35,[185] and the same list of remedies[186] will be available regardless of the type of non-conformity.[187] Such a uniform concept of lack of conformity displaces the concepts of 'warranty'[188] found in many domestic laws and thus reduces the risk of opportunistic claims based on grounds solely intended to reduce or extend the remedies available.[189]

In addition, the duty of examining and giving notice of any non-conformity in the goods established by the CISG brings certainty in trade. Article 38 CISG[190] provides for examination within as short a period as is practicable in the circumstances. Such circumstances include cases where the contract involves the carriage of goods, or where these are redirected in transit or redispatched by the buyer without a reasonable opportunity for examination, in which case examination could be deferred until after the goods have arrived at their destination. The article thus provides more efficient allocation of risks and transactions costs.[191] The duty to inspect 'within as short a period as is practicable in

185 Article 35 CISG:

1. The seller must deliver goods which are of the quantity, quality and description required by the contract and which are contained or packaged in the manner required by the contract.
2. Except where the parties have agreed otherwise, the goods do not conform with the contract unless they:
   a. are fit for the purposes for which goods of the same description would ordinarily be used;
   b. are fit for any particular purpose expressly or impliedly made known to the seller at the time of the conclusion of the contract, except where the circumstances show that the buyer did not rely, or that it was unreasonable for him to rely, on the seller's skill and judgement;
   c. possess the qualities of goods which the seller has held out to the buyer as a sample or model;
   d. are contained or packaged in the manner usual for such goods or, where there is no such manner, in a manner adequate to preserve and protect the goods.
3. The seller is not liable under subparagraphs (a) to (d) of the preceding paragraph for any lack of conformity of the goods if at the time of the conclusion of the contract the buyer knew or could not have been unaware of such lack of conformity.

186 In the case of non-conforming goods the buyer may resort to the usual remedies, namely specific performance, avoidance of the contract, damages and price reduction, I. Schwenzer, 'Conformity of the Goods – Physical Features on the Wane?', *in* I. Schwenzer & L. Spagnolo (Eds.), *State of Play: The 3rd Annual MAA Schlechtriem CISG Conference*, Eleven International Publishing, The Hague, 2012, p. 108.

187 I. Schwenzer, *supra* note 106 in Chapter 1, Article 35, p. 593, para. 4.

188 See UNCITRAL Digest of Case Law on the United Nations Convention on the International Sale of Goods, Art. 35, U.N. Doc. A/CN.9/SER.C/DIGEST/CISG/35; see also CLOUT Case n°. 219 and CLOUT Case n°. 256.

189 E. Muñoz & L. G. Meira Moser, *supra* note 64 in Chapter 3, p. 91.

190 Art. 38 of the CISG: "(1) The buyer must examine the goods, or cause them to be examined, within as short a period as is practicable in the circumstances.

1. If the contract involves carriage of the goods, examination may be deferred until after the goods have arrived at their destination.
2. If the goods are redirected in transit or redispatched by the buyer without a reasonable opportunity for examination by him and at the time of the conclusion of the contract the seller knew or ought to have known of the possibility of such redirection or redispatch, examination may be deferred until after the goods have arrived at the new destination."

191 L. Ratniece, while discussing Article 38 of the CISG under an economic perspective, remarks that the inspect goods would normally include: (i) costs of the inspection procedure (costs of the specialists, analysis, etc.); (ii) costs of storage of goods while they are being inspected; (iii) costs of human resources, who have to

the circumstances' tends to decrease transaction costs for the parties by making inspection more efficient through flexibility: while the seller benefits from faster examination (he will arguably be remunerated sooner), the buyer may be in a position to defend herself against an alleged breach under paragraph 1 by proving that the particular type of goods could only be inspected within a given period.[192]

The CISG sets a neutral and internationally suitable obligation regarding notice of non-conformity. Firstly, the notice should specify the nature of the non-conformity.[193] It is not sufficient that the buyer manifests its existence in a vague or ambiguous way. He must at least describe the type of non-conformity, *e.g.*, *aliud*, defects of quantity or quality.[194] This is not because it is necessary to characterize the type of defect for statutory or contractual remedial purposes, but because such information might allow the seller to take steps to cure the non-conformity or avoid further damages. The extent of the information will depend on the circumstances of the case.

Secondly, the buyer is required to give notice within a reasonable time after he has discovered or ought to have discovered the non-conformity. On this issue some courts and arbitral tribunals have rightly followed the noble month rule developed by two respected scholars, based on comparative law analysis:[195] one month after the buyer has or ought to have discovered the non-conformity is considered a flexible yardstick (and not an absolute time limit) for measuring timeliness of notice.[196]

The CISG's unified rule on examination and notice avoids the risks of opportunistic conduct of sellers' and buyers' racing to litigate before a particular court or under a particular domestic law only because this suits their interest.[197]

organise and follow the inspective procedure; and (iv) seller's costs of waiting for the expected purchase price, L. Ratniece, 'An Economic Analysis of the Duty to Inspect Goods Pursuant to the CISG and CESL', *RGSL Research Papers No. 8*, 2012, p. 45, available at [www.rgsl.edu.lv/uploads/files/RP_8_Ratniece_final.pdf].

192 L. Ratniece, *supra* note 191, p. 47.

193 Art. 39(1) CISG: "(1) The buyer loses the right to rely on a lack of conformity of the goods if he does not give notice to the seller specifying the nature of the lack of conformity within a reasonable time after he has discovered it or ought to have discovered it." See also I. Schwenzer, *supra* note 106 in Chapter 1, pp. 654-655, para. 6.

194 I. Schwenzer, *supra* note 106 in Chapter 1, pp. 654-655, para. 6; p. 656, para 7.

195 The two scholars are I. Schwenzer & C. B. Andersen; *see* generally C. B. Andersen, 'Noblesse Oblige...? Revisiting the "Noble Month" and the Expectations and Accomplishments It Has Prompted', *in* A. Büchler, & M. Müller-Chen (Eds.), *Festschrift für Ingeborg Schwenzer zum 60. Geburtstag*, Stämpfli, Bern, 2011, p. 33 *et seq.*

196 *Id.*

197 E. Muñoz & L. G. Meira Moser, *supra* note 64 in Chapter 3, p. 96.

5.1.7.2 Exemptions

Non-performance solutions are also of great importance to parties at the bargaining table since non-performance of a single obligation may amount to breach of contract, with no or varied available remedies to cure such a failure. In a less strict scenario a set of obligations must be unobserved to amount to breach of contract, which can also be cured by a list of remedies available.

5.1.8 Remedies Available: Gateways

Remedies are alternatives or gateways that assist parties to restructure an uneven contractual status. For example, it might be the case that governing contract law is excessively liberal in its provision of remedies, allowing parties to use it for non-performance of any contractual obligation. On the other hand, certain governing contract laws may adopt a less liberal approach, whereby remedies can be used in a rather limited set of circumstances.

In a defaulting party scenario remedies provide some form of alternatives. The same rationale applies here in terms of approach: liberal or more conservative. Law that is better suited to this scenario can vary greatly according to the case and chances of success. However, impractical as it may be, or perhaps impossible, this exercise of 'futurology' is highly undesirable. Therefore contracting parties will delve into law that may strike a better balance of rights, duties and obligations.

In addition, the type of remedy available is also a factor that will influence the parties' behaviour during potential litigation. Remedies can be used as means of obtaining a successful result or mitigation of loss.

As we have seen thus far, governing contract law will influence parties' intentions to cooperate and the contract, or encourage breach. If the consequences of breach outweigh the performance of a contract that may not meet the interests of one of the contracting parties, there is a high chance that a breach will occur. If the law imposes severe (monetary) penalties in case of breach, the party contemplating it will need carefully to ponder whether the gains of breach overweigh the consequences.

This is a delicate and complex decision as parties will need to anticipate potential failures beforehand. This would be the case, despite parties' likely not wishing to consider these matters during contract negotiation: the division *e.g.* of matrimonial property during divorce proceedings. Save for exceptions, couples generally do not think of the consequences of a marriage in terms of a divorce and subsequent property regimes. In certain cultures it might sound disrespectful and untrustworthy to require from the spouse a total separation of property regime.

Parties may use 'convenient standards', hoping that a breach will never happen. It is actually rare to hear of alternative property regimes that balance potential interests at stake and minimize risks. One could argue that this kind of contract is rather influenced by emotions[198] and therefore deprived of rational elements. However, the truth is that the same approach appears to be adopted in commercial dealings as well – parties will use mental shortcuts[199] to make decisions, due, among other things, to time pressures and monetary constraints.

From this, it follows that parties would ideally aim to elect governing contract law that offers a balanced set of remedies. These can include ways in which parties can overcome or cure a failure, in addition to understanding the consequences of a fatal and sometimes inevitable breach of contract.

5.1.9 *Provisions on Damages*

Contracting parties should generally have an interest in knowing the remedies available and provisions on damages should breach occur. Simple as it may be, these factors measure the amount at stake. The remedies will provide the parties with gateways, shortcuts and legal measures either to remedy (or to point out the symptoms of) default, or, for purposes of convenience, to breach the contract. Remedies will also serve to evaluate the next step: damages.[200]

The topic of damages may vary worldwide and this arguably is the reason why the topic was indicated as a positive legal feature in a survey discussed earlier.[201] Of course, parties with supposedly stronger cases (in theory, as many factual variables can determine the strength of a potential claim. The legal assessment of these variables will be a matter for the discretion of state courts or private adjudication) may be interested in electing laws – and settled case law – that have clearly stated provisions on damages. This can include an allocation of more severe burdens on the defaulting party in case of a breach of contract, or laws that have requirements in classifying a defaulting scenario, along with clear monetary consequences. One could also think of laws that adopt a literal interpretation of the contract terms, also noting that damages are typically dealt with in the contract.

On the other hand, some parties may prefer law that contains broader terms and provisions, unsettled case law, coupled with a wide interpretation of breach and its consequences, including the provisions on damages. This leads us to the parties' behaviour in bringing an action. A party might spend more on the evidentiary phase if new informa-

198 In this connection, please refer to *supra* Chapter 2.

199 A detailed analysis of these mental shortcuts is provided in *supra* Section 2.2.1.

200 L. G. Meira Moser, *supra* note 3 in Chapter 1, p. 32.

201 See Survey results *supra* Section 1.2.4.1, where, with respect to the positive legal features of governing contract law, the respondents elected commitment to freedom of contract (66.36%), remedies available (61.75%) and provisions on damages (40.55%).

tion renders the case more appealing, or abandon the endeavour if the reverse proves true.[202]

5.1.9.1 Setting out the Features of a Defaulting Scenario

As in a game, if one contracting party understands that it has a higher chance of defaulting and breaching a contract, this party will bargain to avoid certain law that would favour the other contracting party, or whose case law endorse, for example, generous claims for damages for some particular reasons.

To illustrate this behaviour, let us imagine that law X will not share equal benefits between the contracting parties, *i.e.* does not generate Pareto-efficient results. For instance, a sales law that endorses limited parties' flexibility to design the contract. In this scenario law X is worse than law Y. However, let us suppose that law X gives a benefit to a party if a certain condition is met. In this scenario a party who is likely to meet that condition might prefer to choose that law. This could be a case of being exempt from performing certain contractual obligations due to force majeure or hardship. If parties adopt uniform laws, this strategic behaviour would be moot.[203]

According to the studies presented at the outset,[204] 'remedies available' and 'provisions on damages' represented the two main positive economic features of governing law in the view of contracting parties. In the same survey 'remedies available' and 'provisions on damages' were also indicated by the respondents as the two main positive legal features of governing law.

This scenario endorses the assumption that parties will tend to make rational decisions if the situation permits, *i.e.*, if market distortions and parties' cognitive biases and heuristics[205] are identified, and tackled or controlled beforehand. If so, parties will likely approach the choice-of-law decision with rational tools, therefore increasing the chances of avoiding bad decisions and costly mistakes. This is achieved by anticipating strategies of the counterparty, outcomes and reactions to the contractual scenes.[206]

As previously stated, once the above variables are controlled – or at least identified – parties can generally predict the transaction outcome: if it does not succeed as expected, it is important to analyze the remaining choices. Therefore, remedies and damages will walk hand in hand towards the same goals: maximize the gains or minimize the losses, according to the parties' position.

202 See G. S. Geis, 'Economic as Context for Contract Law. Framing Contract Law: An Economic Perspective by Victor Goldberg', *University of Chicago Law Review*, Vol. 75, Issue 1, 2008, p. 585.

203 L. G. Meira Moser, *supra* note 3 in Chapter 1, p. 33.

204 See Survey results *supra* Section 1.2.4.2.

205 For a thorough analysis of this topic see *supra* Chapter 2.

206 L. G. Meira Moser, *supra* note 3 in Chapter 1, p. 40.

5.1.9.2 Statements and Commands on Damages and Calculation

Provisions on damages will complete the key factors that determine the amount at stake. This can assist in shedding light on alternatives to succeed in a potential dispute, for parties to adopt strategic behaviour, to request *inter alia* specific performance, to terminate or rescind the contract and its implications in terms of damages and/or mitigation of loss in certain circumstances.[207]

Studies have demonstrated that remedies and damages are decisive in guiding the behaviour of the contracting parties in face of a defaulting scenario.[208] Provisions on damages may also have a negative economic impact for the same reasons indicated before: the damages will measure the potential gain or loss; broad interpretation of legal rules may leave room for discrepancies, uncertainties, lack of uniformity, unfounded legal thesis and wrongful decision-making assessments. In such a scenario parties may need to invest resources in hiring lawyers to examine the law and experts to make a case to prove a new legal thesis.[209] This will also generally affect predictability and legal certainty.[210]

Studies have suggested that remedies and damages may be regarded negatively for the same reasons provided by the respondents. This leads us to assume that parties, who take on different roles in a contract – 'protagonists', 'villains' or mere 'actors' –, with weaker and stronger cases (roles that can vary and undergo modification even in the course of a contract's life), would ideally opt for law that equally weighs the provisions on remedies and damages between buyers and sellers.[211]

As Gary Born argues, the parties' efforts in bargaining over the application of a law that will be more advantageous are often chimerical, because of the difficulty of predicting in advance what issues will arise in some future dispute and on what side of these issues a party may be.[212] This assumption again reinforces the advantages provided by uniform laws by creating a balance between the buyer's and seller's duties and obligations in a contract.

5.1.10 Statute of Limitations: A Time-Bar Conundrum?

Statute of limitations is a factor surprisingly not always ventilated beforehand by parties while deciding on governing contract law.[213] Contracting parties will need to analyze disparities in time, which may guide the parties' course of action in case of a breach.

207 *Id.*, p. 37.

208 See Global Empirical Survey results *supra* Section 1.2.4.1 *et seq.*

209 See I. Schwenzer & P. Hachem, *supra* note 220 in Chapter 1, p. 465.

210 In the Global Empirical Survey on Choice of Law legal certainty was ranked by 74.89% of the respondents as one of the main legal considerations in the choice of law decision-making process. See Survey results to question 1 *supra* Section 1.2.4.1.

211 L. G. Meira Moser, *supra* note 3 in Chapter 1, p. 37.

212 G. Born, *supra* note 53 in Chapter 2, p. 2747.

213 See, for example, Survey results *supra* Section 1.2.4.1 and the absence of this topic in other empirical studies discussed in Section 1.1.

Parties analyze the implications of the choice if the transaction fails to produce the expected results. In such a case statute of limitations (noting that domestic limitation periods are subject to great disparity in length[214]) will determine the period within which civil claims must be brought, along with the date that the limitation period is tolled.[215]

A statute of limitations[216] may be regarded as a two-edged sword: it may be an important reference point to understand the behaviour of the defaulting party (and in certain cases this will play in its favour) and to adopt measures to avoid time-barred claims, or a way to benefit from short limitation periods. In reality a statute of limitations might turn out to be a time-bar conundrum because, as we have seen in this chapter, parties do not know in advance their positions in the course of a contract execution. It may be that suddenly a shorter limitation period will benefit a party who at the outset looked for a longer limitation period.

In the international sales context the Convention on the Limitation Period in the International Sale of Goods has been developed to establish uniform rules governing the period of time within which a party to a contract for the international sale of goods must commence legal proceedings against another party, to assert a claim arising from the contract or relating to its breach, termination or validity. By doing so, it brings clarity and predictability to an aspect of great importance for the adjudication of the claim.[217] While its adhesion it is still modest,[218] this could interact positively with the CISG, which does not have statute of limitations and may thus be in a disadvantageous position in relation to national laws in this respect. As the question of limitation of claims is not covered by the CISG, if the parties are not signatories to the Convention on the Limitation Period in the International Sale of Goods, the applicable national law is to be determined by conflict rules of the forum.

5.1.11 Gap-Filling Mechanisms: Default Rules and Safeguards

Gap-filling mechanisms operate as 'wild cards' – their function can vary according to the players who hold them. These mechanisms will come into play whenever uncovered contractual scenes arise, or whenever unforeseen circumstances require legal coverage. In such scenarios, parties will look into the extra-coverage layers anticipated or not in the

---

214 See P. Schlechtriem, 'Limitation of Actions by Prescription', available at [www.unidroit.org/english/publications/proceedings/1999/study/50/], discussing discrepancies and implications in terms of limitation period worldwide.

215 See G. Born, *supra* note 53 in Chapter 2, p. 2668.

216 See L. G. Meira Moser, *supra* note 3 in Chapter 1, p. 41.

217 The text of the Convention is available at [www.uncitral.org/uncitral/en/uncitral_texts/sale_goods/1974Convention_limitation_period.html].

218 The list of member states is available at [www.uncitral.org/uncitral/en/uncitral_texts/sale_goods/1974Convention_status.html].

contract. If the contract is silent in this respect, contracting parties will need to analyze the legal commands chosen, *i.e.*, the governing contract law.

For example, if domestic law has been elected to govern a cross-border transaction, attention should be given beforehand to the domestic provisions that allow - under what conditions and to what extent - this 'search for answers' in other legal materials. Naturally, if there is information asymmetry between the parties, gap-filling mechanisms will also be explored to the benefit of the one who possesses greater information.

Default provisions are highly desirable as they reduce the transaction costs involved in efforts and time to design each and every provision of a contract. They also tend to decrease information asymmetry. With a balanced set of default provisions, parties do not need to bargain over all contract provisions as they can rely on default 'shortcuts'. However, it is advisable that a great deal of care be devoted to analysis of this set of default rules. For example, the CISG and the UNIDROIT Principles[219] are, generally speaking, well equipped with default provisions, which tend to operate as 'deal-accelerators' inasmuch as they are more likely to provide neutral legal standards than national rules.

Default provisions may also be regarded as 'safeguards', or defences against provisions that otherwise bargained would unbalance the contract or attribute unjust onus to one or both contracting parties. This is corroborated by the studies presented earlier where, for example, in the Survey default provisions were cited by 26.27% of respondents as a positive legal feature in governing contract law.[220] Overall, gap-filling mechanisms were cited as a positive economic feature in governing contract law. All in all, suffice it to say that gap-filling mechanisms are highly desirable in a contract as they operate under the mandate of a 'negative surprise-blinder'. However, to work adequately these mechanisms have to be carefully selected beforehand.

We have explored and unveiled in this chapter the peculiarities of the contractual scene and its *entourage*: the market or 'stage', alongside the interactions with their main agents, *i.e.*, the market players or actors. We have seen that, as on any stage, the market has failures and distortions, which parties have to become aware of in order to avoid costly mistakes and therefore make better decisions. With this, readers should have familiarized themselves with the risks and costs involved in using the market.

This chapter has focused on the 'rising action', the most important scene in any play: in our case the legal and economic considerations regarding choice-of-law clauses. We have seen that, if the imponderables (market distortions, cognitive limitations and heuristics) are controlled - or at least identified, parties will be more inclined to make decisions using rational tools, thereby behaving in the course of a contract's life according to

219 The International Institute for the Unification of Private Law (UNIDROIT) is an independent intergovernmental Organisation with its seat in the Villa Aldobrandini in Rome. Its purpose is to study needs and methods for modernising, harmonising and co-ordinating private and in particular commercial law as between States and groups of States and to formulate uniform legal instruments, principles and rules to achieve those objectives. The UNIDROIT Principles and further information about the Institute are available at [www.unidroit.org/].

220 Further information is available in *supra* Section 1.2.4.1.

the script of the play, noting the decision to perform or breach the contract, to claim damages or mitigate loss, to gather evidence, to exchange and communicate information, to manage, transfer or allocate risks, to behave opportunistically, to adopt delaying tactics, or to spend resources in resolving disputes. Included in these considerations are, for example procedural strategies, enforcement pitfalls, recalcitrant debtors, arguments on invalidity, revocation and nullity of contract, request for injunctions, relief and orders.[221]

In this connection we have seen that, all things being equal, the CISG, as a neutral transnational legal framework, is better equipped to respond to the needs of cross-border players for the array or reasons outlined and discussed in this chapter. Due to both structural principles and substantive content, the CISG presents a better option for players who wish to level the playing field, avoid unnecessary hiccups and costly mistakes.

For the reasons discussed above, parties are likely to be better off with a choice of the CISG governing their deals. Having said all this though, one wonders whether, if the CISG is indeed the best (and most economically efficient) option, why it does not have the level of popularity among trade players that one would expect.

Data do still suggest that the CISG is resisted by market players. However, the reasons for such resistance, as discussed in Chapter 1,[222] are not entirely captured on a rational level and can indeed be better explained by non-rational factors.[223]

It may be apt at this juncture again to refer to the results discussed at the outset. In arbitration contexts the most recent study, conducted by Linn Bergman, has attested to the popularity of the CISG in SCC international arbitration awards.[224] We shall also refer to the results obtained in the Survey,[225] which as submitted earlier[226] had not drawn distinction between court cases and arbitration cases. In the Survey, 33% of the respondents claimed to have opted out of the CISG in previous dealings and 59.64% avoided a particular national law. Of the 60% of the respondents who had avoided a particular national law, 37% did not disclose their reasons. Of the 33% who had opted out of the CISG, 45% did not disclose the reason for exclusion of the CISG's application.

Readers may be asking themselves at this point whether such a high rate of opt outs and avoidances may suggest that the CISG is not the best alternative.[227]

221 L. G. Meira Moser, *supra* note 3 in Chapter 1, p. 43.

222 See *supra* Chapter 1.

223 See, in this sense, *supra* Chapter 2.

224 See *supra* Section 1.1.2.1, note 93 in Chapter 1.

225 See, in this connection, *supra* Section 1.2.4.1 *et seq.*

226 See *supra* Section 1.2.4.3.

227 L. Spagnolo, delving into the reasons for CISG exclusion, points out an issue of agency that may affect the rate of opt-outs: "One could cynically view the lawyer's behaviour in 'blind' opt-outs as simply a matter of self-interested behaviour by an agent. It is rational from the agent's perspective to maximize short-term gains by earning the same fee without investment in information costs. In high exclusion jurisdictions, it is possible that lawyers feel that there is little chance of clients being alerted to the inadequacy of their advice, given that so few of their peers are familiar with the CISG, making discovery unlikely unless there is sub-

The comments provided suggest that national law was avoided for several reasons: because parties sought neutrality, international character and legal certainty as the main aspects of the law to govern their contracts; cost of learning, time, unsettled or unpredictable case law – in combination with unstable political, social and legal systems, and enforcement concerns.

The comments also validated the assumptions at the outset that parties are rational maximizers of their own welfare and, as such, use bargaining power to make their choices prevail in contract negotiation. Proof is indicated by the respondents who avoided a particular national law because it was the opposing party's, or a law, on their assessment, not favourable for the particular transaction or suitable to their interests, opting for a set of neutral rules.[228]

It is worth quoting one of the additional reasons provided by the respondents for avoiding a particular national law:

> Avoided the law of the counterparty's domicile because choosing that law might encourage the counterparty to breach the contract relying on legal advice available in its own country instead of trying to cooperate in the full performance of the contract".[229]

This reason reaffirms the premise that parties do take decisions in light of legal and economic considerations. In this example the respondent opted to avoid a domestic law because it anticipated the counterparty's less cooperative behaviour (arguably, in such situations the counterparty will be better informed about ways to avoid discharge of certain contractual obligations with no or fewer (harmful) consequences or, *a contrario sensu,* tactics to present a defence or rebut an allegation of breach[230]).

The reasons provided by respondents for avoiding certain domestic laws show that parties generally analyze governing laws via a cost-benefit analysis, predicting behaviour, advanced tactics and possible litigation. However, parties may have excluded national law for reasons based purely on intuition or heuristic method.[231] This could explain, for

---

sequent litigation, itself perhaps the most expensive (and therefore most unlikely) of monitoring methods. Lawyers might therefore prefer to run the risk rather than invest in familiarity, since in the context of such a jurisdiction, there is little competitive pressure to do otherwise. Or, they might be willing, but not have the time. Either way, it is the client who unwittingly bears the detrimental effect of an inefficient choice of law." See L. Spagnolo, *supra* note 118 in Chapter 1, p. 189.

228 A distinction between neutral rules as the rules of a third jurisdiction and neutral rules as uniform rules is discussed in L. G. Meira Moser, *supra* note 3 in Chapter 1, p. 28.

229 See Survey Question 8, *supra* Section 1.2.4.3.

230 See comments to Survey results, Chapter 1, Question 2 *supra* Section 1.2.4.1.

231 See discussion about this topic in *supra* Chapter 2.

example, the 37.35% who did not or disclose their reasons for avoiding a particular national law.

The exclusions may also have been driven by 'affective valences'.[232] 'Valence' is what psychology calls the degree of attraction or aversion that an individual feels to a given object or event. This can be illustrated by the following quotations: 'exotic laws' and 'weak law'.

It is also worth quoting this additional reason provided by the respondents 'International Sales of Goods are international in essence, so particular a (*sic*) national law might bring obligations not conceived for international trade'. This comment addresses some of the topics dealt with at the outset of this book, in particular, the risks incurred when contracting parties opt for a certain domestic law just because of its arguable 'neutrality', without a thorough analysis of the provisions that may play an important role in an international contract's life.[233]

The reasons provided by the respondents for excluding the application of the CISG were overall related to the degree of familiarity with and experience of application of its provisions, and inadequacy or suitability of the CISG to certain types of contract which may touch upon national regulations or other practice areas and expertise, domestic law in such a case being more appropriate in certain instances.

A lack of solid case law,[234] the risk of non-uniform application of the CISG rules by state courts,[235] and a client's request, the latter varying according to its position in the transaction, complete the ranked-first list of reasons. Limited coverage was cited as a reason for the CISG's exclusion, although it is unclear whether the dispute (or contract) involved challenges on contract validity or effects on transfer of ownership of the goods, matters outside the scope of the CISG.[236]

Some respondents indicated that the CISG was excluded at the counterparty's request, without disclosing the reason, which leads us to conclude that multiple factors may have influenced this decision and that the choice of the CISG as governing contract law.

---

232 See M. I. Fraidin, *supra* note 182 in Chapter 1, p. 921, noting that a choice is sometimes rooted in whether one option generates in us more welcome emotions.

233 See, *inter alia, supra* note 117 in Chapter 1.

234 A *contrario sensu*, as I. Schwenzer and P. Hachem argue, greater accessibility of the CISG saves time and cost, and it makes the outcome of cases more predictable, which makes these the main advantages of the CSIG as compared with the application of domestic law. See I. Schwenzer & P. Hachem, *supra* note 220 in Chapter 1, p. 467. Furthermore, there is an obligation in courts, when applying the CISG, to have regard to its international character and the need to promote uniformity in its interpretation.

235 In this connection, see I. Schwenzer, 'Divergent Interpretations: Reasons and Solutions', *in* L. A. DiMatteo (Ed.), *International Sales Law: A Global Challenge*, Cambridge University Press, New York, 2014, arguing that the degree of familiarity with the CISG among national courts is still very low (p. 114).

236 Article 4 of the CISG: This Convention governs only the formation of the contract of sale and the rights and obligations of the seller and buyer arising from such a contract. In particular, except as otherwise expressly provided in this Convention, it is not concerned with:

a. the validity of the contract or of any of its provisions or of any usage;
b. the effect which the contract may have on the property in the goods sold.

Given the answers to the Survey questions, where respondents indicated familiarity with the law as a key factor, one could conclude that lack of awareness of the CISG, associated with the learning costs of becoming proficient,[237] might have also influenced the rate of opt-outs.

The following quote deserves some thought: "Clients do not like the CISG because people exclude it".[238] As discussed at the outset, parties' decisions may be also guided by non-rational motives or causes. This seems to apply here, where heuristic appears to have played an important role insofar as the 'bad feeling' generated by a previous opt-out influenced the decision-making process.[239] In other terms, this respondent mimicked the decision made by others (what the doctrine calls 'imitation' heuristic[240]), by opting-out of the CISG.

In some instances, under a heuristic-based approach, parties may also refer the decision to those whom they deem to have greater status than they ('one reason' heuristic).[241] In this regard, the quote 'Use of precedent contract that excluded CISG' provides an example of a case where a heuristic may have influenced this choice. The following additional answer also endorses this inference: 'It is a question of balance. If I want balance, I go for the CISG. If I want to enforce obligations strictly, I go for specific national state laws'.

Except in relation to the provision on 'consequential damages' cited, which was compared with domestic provisions (and the content of which should not be interpreted as a criticism *per se*) and 'the principle of good faith' (which has been cited as such without any further explanation), it is unclear whether other specific provisions were the cause of exclusion.

A result that calls for particular attention is that 45% of respondents did not disclose the reason for the CISG's exclusion, leaving room for interpretation as to underlying motives, which could vary from the attorney's lack of experience[242] and knowledge of this set of rules[243] to the use of bargaining power in certain instances, the convenience of use of standard contracts electing a certain national law (due to, *inter alia*, a settled case

237 As regards economic analysis and CISG, see L. Spagnolo, 'A Glimpse through the Kaleidoscope', *supra* note 124 in Chapter 1, pp. 135-156. See also L. Spagnolo, *supra* note 118 in Chapter 1.

238 Response to Survey Question 8, *supra* Section 1.2.4.3.

239 See M. I. Fraidin, *supra* note 182 in Chapter 1, pp. 919-920.

240 C. Guthrie, *supra* note 179 in Chapter 1, p. 431.

241 *Id.*

242 See I. Schwenzer & C. Kee, *supra* note 2 in Chapter 1, p. 438, noting that problems in practice still remain most notably what might be termed the domestic orientation of lawyers. This issue would arguably be a case of standard of legal education.

243 See L. Spagnolo, 'Rats in Kaleidoscope', *supra* note 124 in Chapter 1, pp. 157-178, arguing that "*...lawyers may also be very reluctant to choose the CISG due to an irrationally inflated 'far of the unknown'*. It is a case of 'green eggs and ham'. The unfamiliarity heuristic or instinct will be heightened if the lawyer never encountered the CISG in law school, or it looks very different from local domestic law, or he has never encountered it in dispute work (or all three) – so their rule of thumb is to opt out, if the other party will let them..." (p. 163).

law) and even a fear of unpredictable results in case the CISG has to be applied by national courts less familiar with its provisions.[244]

As possible causes not disclosed by the respondents of exclusion of application of the CISG, one could also think of *e.g.*, of contracts involving not only sale of goods but also services (in such a case the CISG would apply if the value of the goods outweighs that of the services[245]), or contracts that required a bargain *ex ante* on the provisions on validity[246] of the agreement and the parties found it more convenient to elect one single set of rules, noting that the CISG regulates the contract formation of sale of goods and buyers' and sellers' duties and obligations. Other reasons might include the use of contracts excluding the CISG without a more substantiated reason.[247] One should not neglect the possibility that a heuristic-based approach[248] has been taken by some of the respondents, *i.e.*, decisions may have been made founded primarily on success or failure in real-world environments rather than through rational components, and may not have resulted in the best choice.

The comments also suggest that ratification of the CISG by the jurisdiction concerned contributes to a decision in favour of the proposed governing law, following analysis of question 1,[249] where a number of the respondents indicated neutrality and international character as main legal considerations. This additional answer merits some observations: once the CISG is ratified by a certain State (and the subsequent legislative formalities are fulfilled in the respective jurisdiction), the provisions of the CISG becomes national law

---

244 In this connection, Article 7 of the CISG reads as follows:

1. In the interpretation of this Convention, regard is to be had to its international character and to the need to promote uniformity in its application and the observance of good faith in international trade.
2. Questions concerning matters governed by this Convention which are not expressly settled in it are to be settled in conformity with the general principles on which it is based or, in the absence of such principles, in conformity with the law applicable by virtue of the rules of private international law.

245 Article 3 of the CISG. See also I. Schwenzer & P. Hachem, *supra* note 106 in Chapter 1, Article 3, pp. 60-72.

246 Article 4 of the CISG. See also I. Schwenzer, & P. Hachem, *supra* note 106 in Chapter 1, Article 3, pp. 73-94.

247 As to possible reasons for the opt-outs, the author L. Spagnolo states: "…a great deal of automatic opting out occurs via general conditions in standard forms contracts drafted long ago, possibly with legal advice. Redrafting those forms with legal input for most businesses can only occur on occasional intervals, with smaller business perhaps seeking advice less frequently than larger businesses. As legal advice is a form of information cost, small-medium businesses face proportionately higher information costs, and are therefore more prone to imperfectly informed decision making and concurrent efficiency losses from less suitable choices of law". See L. Spagnolo, 'Rats in Kaleidoscope', *supra* note 124 in Chapter 1, p. 159; see also L. Spagnolo, *supra* note 118 in Chapter 1.

248 See R. B. Korobkin, *supra* note 180 in Chapter 1, p. 3, arguing that: "[…] notwithstanding its global rationality and potential for optimal results in some circumstances, heuristic reasoning is extremely problematic for law, for two related reasons. First, heuristic often will cause actors subject to the legal system to make non-optimal judgments and choices because the actors over-or underweight information concerning facts in the world of their subjective preferences relative to that information's probative value. Reliance on a heuristic implies neglect of at least some potentially relevant information, and if the heuristic is not precisely suited to the relevant problem, suboptimal outcomes will result"; see also A. Tversky & D. Kahneman, *supra* note 32 in Chapter 1; see also L. Spagnolo, *supra* note 118 in Chapter 1.

249 Question 1 of the Survey invited readers to express their views on the positive features of a governing contract law. For further information, please refer to *supra* Section 1.2.4.1.

applicable to international sale of goods. As such, in a transaction between parties from contracting States (which have not acceded with reservations[250]), the CISG will be applied in its entirety,[251] in cases where parties have not agreed on the application of other law or excluded the CISG's application,[252] provided that conflict rules of the forum endorse that choice. If the transaction does not involve both contracting States, the CISG will be the governing law when the rules of private international law lead to its application.[253]

This chapter has discussed alternatives to escape 'arm-wrestling', 'home turf', deadlock situations and other tactical scenarios in cross-border sales. We have presented and compared alternatives which can be used in international contract settings and then verified the effectiveness of their solutions in light both of the legal and economic aspects, touching upon contracting parties' concerns and preferences collected in the earlier chapters. All of this is with a view to offering to legal practitioners tools to enable them effectively to optimize, at an even level between parties, the exchange of goods worldwide.

5.2 Future Research

Further to the reach and importance of the Global Empirical Survey on Choice of Law, future research has already been discussed and the author is keen to share what future research will encompass. It should be a global survey aimed at investigating choices and preferences and assessing the popularity of the CISG and other neutral legal frameworks by industry sector. The future research intends to cover how stakeholders, by industry sector, generally approach this subject; how have been their experiences with the CISG and other neutral legal frameworks so far, and whether they want to propose changes going forward. The goal is thus to obtain a broad analysis of the use and perceptions of the CISG and other neutral legal standards by industry sector and the level of attention given to these legal frameworks in conjunction with the reasons for opt-ins and opt-outs.

---

250 CISG, Article 95, reads as follows: Any State may declare at the time of the deposit of its instrument of ratification, acceptance, approval or accession that it will not be bound by subparagraph (1)(b) of article 1 of this Convention.

251 CISG, Article 96, reads as follows: A Contracting State whose legislation requires contracts of sale to be concluded in or evidenced by writing may at any time make a declaration in accordance with article 12 that any provision of article 11, article 29, or Part II of this Convention, that allows a contract of sale or its modification or termination by agreement or any offer, acceptance, or other indication of intention to be made in any form other than in writing, does not apply where any party has his place of business in that State.

252 CISG, Article 1, reads as follows:

1. This Convention applies to contracts of sale of goods between parties whose places of business are in different States:
    a. when the States are Contracting States; or
    b. when the rules of private international law lead to the application of the law of a Contracting State.

(...)

253 See additional examples in E. Muñoz & L. G. Meira Moser, *supra* note 64 in Chapter 3, p. 88.

There will also be a distinction between court agreements and arbitration agreements and the study will also aim at revealing the level of knowledge and exposure of the CISG and other neutral legal standards among practitioners, in addition to showcasing the circumstances in which these legal frameworks are actually taken into account by the survey participants.

The research is in its inception but will also look into and analyze (un)attractive features of the CISG and other neutral legal standards, how (un)successful they have been so far and whether there are improvements to make them more appealing in certain industry sectors. The future research will serve to consolidate the 2014 Survey's findings,[254] reveal the main criticisms of the CISG and other neutral legal standards by industry sector and hopefully contribute to rethink approaches taken in choice-of-law decision-making processes, thereby making them capable of delivering efficient results in a fast moving and globalized legal world.

254 See Global Empirical Survey discussed in *supra* Section 1.2.4.1 *et seq.*

Conclusion

Contract negotiation invariably confronts situations in which one's optimal action depends upon on what the other party chooses. For example, seller1 sells 11,000 mt of anthracite (quality B) for £ 50/mt (delivery in 5 working days), whereas seller2 sells 5,000 mt of anthracite (quality A) for £ 35/mt, immediate delivery. The buyer desires anthracite in large quantity. Both quality and time are of importance. How would you evaluate the optimal action(s) here?

Our legal choices (good or bad) are frequently guided by our counterparty's behaviour, which may not be easily ascertainable. The choice of governing contract law is no different. This choice is possibly the most important in contract negotiation and the reason for this inference may be as simple as this: this decision determines the law that will govern a contract from 'back to front': it will set out duties, rights and obligations that will be observed by the contracting parties, in addition to creating scenarios for, *inter alia*, reduction of damages, exemption of performance and penalties.

In light of the relevance of this topic to a contract's life, we decided to investigate in greater depth than how scholars and practitioners had approached the topic, whether evidence has supported the theoretical discussions thus far and whether a new study could further shed light on the topic and offer practical insights. There has been little convincing data gathered to address these points, which formed the basis for the reasons behind this book.

To commence, we undertook a global survey to assess the parties' approach to this choice: how do parties decide the governing contract law in practice after all? What are their main legal and economic considerations? Are there any deal-breakers and overlaps? Have they excluded or opted out of some laws? If so, why?

The Survey was a provocative invitation to delve into the rather unexplored world of 'contracting parties' minds', the results of which have been exhaustively discussed in this book.

In order to structure this book, the first chapter sets out data on choice of law worldwide. Previous studies were discussed and contrasted so that we could extract similarities, differences and draw tendencies and conclusions. The second chapter invited readers to appreciate the theoretical concepts of rational and non-rational decision-making processes and contained an analysis of the common 'traps' contracting parties are routinely exposed to, which have been discussed based on the empirical evidence presented in the first chapter. The third chapter of this book was labelled 'Market distortions and imperfections': how market players interact in a volatile scenario of idiosyncratic preferences, and which tools they need to rely on to regulate and facilitate transactions worldwide. The fourth chapter then discussed the adequacy of the forum: who should hear the claims of the parties and why? Are there any connections between the forum (courts or arbitration) and the choice of governing contract law? The fifth and final chapter discussed parties' main legal and economic concerns and the efficiency of a-national rules *vis-à-vis* national regimes.

We have argued throughout this book that the choice of law, given its importance, should be carefully thought through, based on rational elements and free from non-rational factors. Nonetheless, we have seen that non-rational elements are likely to play a role in the decision behind the choice of law. We have thus provided data on how imperfections occur and, in order to tackle these interferences, we have proposed tools and alternatives for market players.

However, what is seldom explored is how this decision is made in real-life. What are the main drives and triggers of this decision? What we have discussed is that, as with any other decision, underlying motives should be investigated beforehand so that parties are aware of the triggers and factors that may prompt the choice of law decision.

We have argued that more attention should be given to the choice of governing contract law in cross-border sales. The reason for this was the contrasting results and discrepancies demonstrated in the empirical data, which revealed that, despite parties' believing they are making rational decisions, intuition may frequently and unconsciously blur their choices.

That said, we contend that in modern times a multi-faceted view of this choice should emerge, one that observes psychological elements in the first place: why am I making this decision? Am I being rational? Or rather, am I taking this decision based purely on emotions and earlier impressions and perceptions of this matter? This multi-faceted view also considers legal and economic considerations: is it advantageous for me (as party or party counsel) or for the case (as decision-maker) to choose this law? What protection or remedy is most likely to be needed? Is a literal interpretation of the contract sought? How much weight is to be given to the contextual evaluation of the relationship? Is this inference supported by legal and economic consequences? What is the likelihood that I shall need to rely on provisions A, B or C of the legal framework? Is there a risk attached to it, which I should be aware of?

We also contend that in this new approach to the choice of law, careful attention should be given to a-national rules, such as the CISG. We have seen, and proven this through analysis of data, that parties are likely to opt for a balanced set of rules, one that supports flexibility and parties' autonomy, tailored to regulate cross-border transactions. We have argued that national law, no matter how developed, were never conceived for such purpose (for evident reasons). In addition we have discussed some of the key CISG provisions and have shown that they are economically efficient and promote and provide rationality (which is commended in cross-border scenarios).

For all the above reasons, this study aims to equip contracting parties with efficient tools to enable them to think choice of law strategically and rationally. In a dynamic, globalized and complex world of contracts, we understand that this approach, which connects law, economics and psychology, tackles common negotiation traps and anticipates costly mistakes, thereby making contracting parties better off.

Bibliography

Adar, Y., 'The CISG in Israel', *in* L. A. DiMatteo (Ed.), *International Sales Law: A Global Challenge*, Cambridge University Press, New York, 2014, pp. 518-538.

Ahmen, M.; Beaumont, P. R., 'Exclusive Choice of Court Agreements: Some Issues on the Hague Convention on Choice of Court Agreements and its Relationship with the Brussels I Recast Especially Anti-Suit Injunctions, Concurrent Proceedings and the Implications of Brexit', *Journal of Private International Law*, Vol. 13, 2017, pp. 386-410.

Andersen, C. B., 'Noblesse Oblige…? Revisiting the "Noble Month" and the Expectations and Accomplishments it has prompted', *in* A. Büchler, & M. Müller-Chen, (Eds.), *Festschrift für Ingeborg Schwenzer zum 60. Geburtstag*, Stämpfli, Bern, 2011, pp. 33-49.

Andersen, C. B.,'Uniformity and Harmonization by Case Law: The CISG and the Global Jurisconsultorium', *in* Morten M. Fagot (Ed.), *Unification and Harmonization of International Commercial Law – Interaction of Deharmonization*, Wolters Kluwer, Alphen aan den Rijn, 2012, pp. 175-189.

Ayres, I.; Gertner, R., 'Filing Gaps in Incomplete Contracts: An Economic Theory of Default Rules.' *Yale Law Journal*, Vol. 99, 1989-1990, pp. 87-130.

Bailey, J. E., 'Facing the Truth: Seeing the Convention on Contracts for the International Sale of Goods as an Obstacle to a Uniform Law of International Sales', *Cornell International Law Journal*, Vol. 32, 1999, pp. 273-317.

Basedow, J., 'Lex Mercatoria and the Private International Law of Contracts in Economic Perspective', *Uniform Law Review*, Vol. 12, Issue 4, 2007, pp. 697-713.

Berger, K. P. *et al.*, 'The CENTRAL Enquiry on the Use of Transnational Law in International Contract Law and Arbitration – Background, Procedure and Selected Results', available at [https://www.trans-lex.org/3/_/background-procedure-and-selected-results/] https://www.trans-lex.org/3/_/background-procedure-and-selected-results/.

Bergman, L., *A Casebook on Choice of Law in Arbitration*, Landa, Stockholm, 2017.

Bergsten, E. E., 'Experimental Education through the Vis Moot', *Journal of Law & Commerce*, Vol. 34, Issue 1, 2015, pp. 1-15.

Bergsten, E. E., 'The Willem C. Vis International Commercial Arbitration Moot and the Teaching of International Commercial Arbitration,' *Arbitration International*, Vol. 22, Issue 2, 2006, pp. 309-314.

Bianca, C. M.; Bonell, M. J., *Commentary on the International Sales Law – The 1980 Vienna Sales Convention*, Giuffrè, Milan, 1987.

Blessing, M., 'Choice of Substantive Law in International Arbitration', *Journal of International Arbitration*, Vol. 14, Issue 2, 1997, pp. 39-66.

Born, G., *International Commercial Arbitration*, Kluwer Law International, Alphen aan den Rijn, 2014.

Brand, R. A., 'Arbitration or Litigation? Choice of Forum After the 2005 Hague Convention on Choice of Court Agreements', *University of Pittsburgh Legal Studies*, Research Paper No. 2009-14.

Brekoulakis, S., 'Systemic Bias and the Institution of International Arbitration: A New Approach to Arbitral Decision-Making', *Journal of International Dispute Settlement*, Vol. 4, Issue 3, 2013, pp. 553-585.

Bridge, M., 'Good Faith, the Common Law, and the CISG', *Uniform Law Review*, Vol. 22, Issue 1, 2017, pp. 98-115.

Bridge, M.; Fawcett, J. J.; Harris, J. M., *International Sale of Goods in the Conflict of Laws*, Oxford University Press, Oxford, 2005.

Butler, P., 'New Zealand', *in* L. A. DiMatteo (Ed.), *International Sales Law: A Global Challenge*, Cambridge University Press, New York, 2014.

Coase, R., 'The Nature of the Firm', *Economica*, Vol. 4, Issue 16, 1937, pp. 386-405.

Coase, R., 'The Problem of Social Cost', *Journal of Law and Economics*, Vol. 3, 1960, pp. 1-44.

Coase, R., *The Firm, the Market and the Law*, University of Chicago Press, Chicago, 1998.

Cooper, T. M., 'The Common and the Civil Law. A Scot's View', *Harvard Law Review*, Vol. 63, Issue 3, 1950, pp. 468-475.

Cooter, R.; Ulen, T., *Law and Economics*, Addison-Wesley, Boston, MA, 2007.

Cooter, R. D.; Feldman, M.; Feldman, Y., 'The Misperception of Norms: The Psychology of Bias and the Economics of Equilibrium', *Review of Law & Economics*, Vol. 4, Issue 3, 2008, pp. 889-911.

Cordero-Moss, G., 'Can an Arbitral Tribunal Disregard the Choice of Law Made by the Parties?', *Stockholm International Arbitration Review*, Vol. 1, 2005, pp. 1-21.

Cordero-Moss, G., *International Commercial Contracts: Applicable Sources and Enforceability*, Cambridge University Press, Cambridge, 2014.

Coyle, J. F., 'The Role of the CISG in US Contract Practice: An Empirical Study', *University of Pennsylvania Journal of International Law*, Vol. 38, Issue 1, 2016, pp. 195-240.

Cuniberti, G., 'International Market for Contracts: The Most Attractive Contract Laws', *Northwestern Journal of International Law & Business*, Vol. 34, Issue 3, 2013, pp. 455-517.

Cuniberti, G., 'Is the CISG Benefiting Anybody?', *Vanderbilt Journal of Transnational Law*, Vol. 39, 2006, pp. 1511-1550.

da Silva Velloso, C. M., 'Problemas e soluções na prestação da Justiça', *Revista dos Tribunais*, Vol. 664, 1991, pp. 215-235.

Davies, M.; Snyder, D. V., *International Transactions in Goods: Global Sales in Comparative Context*, Oxford University Press, New York, 2014.

de Churruca, J., *Introducción histórica al Derecho Romano*, Universidad de Deusto, Bilbao, 1994.

de Ly, F., 'De Facto Harmonization by Means of Party Autonomy and Model Contract Clauses (*Lex Mercatoria)*', *in* Morten M. Fagot (Ed.), *Unification and Harmonization of International Commercial Law – Interaction of Deharmonization*, Wolters Kluwer, Alphen aan den Rijn, 2012, pp. 151-160.

de Ly, F., 'The Relevance of the Vienna Convention for International Sales Contracts – Should We Stop Contracting it Out?', *Business Law International*, Issue 3, 2003, pp. 241-249.

del Pilar, P. Viscasillas, M., 'CISG Case Law in Spain', *in* C. B. Andersen & U. Schroeter (Eds.), *Sharing International Commercial Law across National Boundaries: Festschrift for Albert H. Krtizer on the Occasion of his Eightieth Birthday*, Wildy, Simmonds & Hill Publishing, London, 2008.

del Pilar, P. Viscasillas, M., 'Contract Conclusion under the CISG', *Journal of Law & Commerce*, Vol. 16, 1997, pp. 315-344.

Diedrich, F., 'Maintaining Uniformity in International Uniform Law Via Autonomous Interpretation: Software Contracts and the CISG', *Pace International Law Review*, Vol. 8, 1996, pp. 303-338.

Diedrich, F., 'The CISG and Computer Software Revisited', *Vindobona Journal of International Commercial Law and Arbitration, Supplement*, Vol. 6, 2002, pp. 55-75.

Dietz, T., *Institutionen und Globalisierung: eine empirische Untersuchung am Beispiel grenzüberschreitender Softwareentwicklungsverträge*, Mohr Siebeck, Heidelberg, 2010.

DiMatteo, L. A. *et al.*, 'The Interpretive Turn in International Sales Law: An Analysis of Fifteen Years of CISG Jurisprudence', *Northwestern Journal of International Law & Business*, Vol. 24, Issue 2, 2003, pp. 299-440.

DiMatteo, L. A.; Ostas, D., 'Comparative Efficiency in International Sales Law', *American University International Law Journal*, Vol. 26, Issue 2, 2011, pp. 371-439.

Dixit, A., 'Arbitration and Information', Working Paper, Princeton University, Princeton, NJ, USA, 2003.

Dodge, W. S., 'Teaching the CISG in Contracts', *Journal of Legal Education*, Vol. 50, 2000, pp. 72-94.

Drahozal, C. R., 'Private Ordering and International Commercial Arbitration', *Penn State Law Review*, Vol. 113, pp. 1031-1050.

Driver, J., 'Caesar's Wife: On the Moral Significance of Appearing Good', *The Journal of Philosophy*, Vol. 89, Issue 7, 1992, pp. 331-343.

Eisenberg, T.; Miller, G. P., 'The Flight to New York: An Empirical Study of Choice of Law and Choice of Forum Clauses in Publicly-Held Companies' Contracts', *Cardozo Law Review*, Vol. 30, 2009, pp. 1475-1512.

Fabre, R., 'Les clauses d'adaptation dans les contrats', *Revue Trimestrielle de Droit Civil*, Vol. 82, 1983, pp. 1-30.

Faria, J. E., 'A crise do poder judiciário no Brasil', *Justiça e Democracia*, No. 1, 1996, pp. 18-64.

Faria, J. E., 'O judiciário e seus dilemas', *Revista do Advogado, Associação dos Advogados de São Paulo*, No. 56, 1999. pp. 64-67.

Farnsworth, E. A., *Contracts*, 4th edn., Aspen, New York, 2004.

Fauvarque-Cosson, B., 'La confiance legitime et l'estoppel', *Electronic Journal of International Law*, Vol. 11, Issue 3, 2007, pp. 1-47.

Felemegas, J., "The United Nations Convention on Contracts for the International Sale of Goods: Article 7 and Uniform Interpretation", *CISG Database*, available at [https://www.cisg.law.pace.edu/cisg/biblio/felemegas.html]

Ferrante, E., 'Italy', *in* L. A. DiMatteo (Ed.), *International Sales Law: A Global Challenge*, Cambridge University Press, New York, 2014, pp. 399-413.

Ferrari, F., 'Interprétation uniforme de la Convention de Vienne de 1980 sur la vente internationale', *Revue Internationale de Droit Comparé*, Vol. 48, Issue 4, 1996, pp. 813-852.

Ferrari, F., 'La rilevanza degli usi nella Convenzione di Vienna sulla vendita internationzionale di beni mobilli', *Contratto e Impresa*, anno X, No.1, 1994, pp. 239-258.

Ferrari, F., 'Remarks on the UNCITRAL Digest's Comments on Article 6 CISG', *Journal of Law & Commerce*, Vol. 25, 2005, pp. 13-37.

Ferrari, F. (Ed.), *The CISG and Its Impact on National Legal Systems,* Sellier, Munich, 2008.

Ferrari, F., 'What Sources of Law for Contracts for the International Sale of Goods? Why One Has to Look Beyond the CISG', *International Review of Law and Economics*, Vol. 25, 2005, pp. 314-341.

Fitzgerald, P. L., 'The International Contracting Practices Survey Project: An Empirical Study of the Value and Utility of the United Nations Convention on the International Sale of Goods (CISG) and the UNIDROIT Principles of International Commercial Contracts to Practitioners, Jurists, and Legal Academics in the United States', *Journal of Law & Commerce*, Vol. 27, 2008, pp. 1-34.

Flechtner, H., 'Changing the Opt-Out Tradition in the United States', *University of Pittsburgh Legal Studies Research Paper Series* No. 2010-10.

Flood, J.; Sosa, F., 'Lawyers, Law Firms, and the Stabilization of Transnational Business', *Northwestern Journal of International Law & Business*, Vol. 28, Issue 3, 2007, pp. 489-526.

Fouchard, P.; Gaillard, E.; Goldman, B., *Traité de l'arbitrage commercial international,* Litec, Paris, 1996.

Fountoulakis, C., 'The Parties' Choice of "Neutral Law" in International Sales Contracts', *European Journal of Law Reform*, Vol. VII, Issue 3/4, 2005, pp. 303-329.

Fradera, V.; Meira Moser, L. G. (Eds.), *A Compra e Venda Internacional de Mercadorias: estudos sobre a Convenção de Viena de 1980*, Atlas, São Paulo, 2010.

Fraidin, M. I., 'Decision-Making in Dependency Court: Heuristics, Cognitive Biases, and Accountability', *Cleveland State Law Review*, Vol. 60, 2013, pp. 913-974.

Gabriel, H. D., 'The Inapplicability of the United Nations Convention on the International Sale of Goods as a Model for the Revision of Article Two of the Uniform Commercial Code', *Tulane Law Review*, Vol. 72, 1998, pp. 1995-2014.

Gaillard, E., 'Trente ans de lex mercatoria. Pour une application sélective de la méthode des principes généraux du droit', *Journal du Droit International*, No. I, 1995, pp. 5-30.

Galgano, F., *Lex mercatoria*, Il mulino, Bologna 2001.

Garoupa, N., 'A análise econômica do direito como instrumento de reforço da independência do Judiciário', *Revista de Direito Bancário e do Mercado de Capitais,* No. 37, 2007, pp. 81-87.

Garro, A. M., 'La formación del contrato en la convención de Viena sobre compraventas internacionales y en el proyecto de unificación', *Revista Jurídica de Buenos Aires*, Vol. III, 1987, pp. 12-58.

Gaviria-Gil, J. A., 'The Puzzle of the Lack of Colombian Case Law on the CISG', *International Law: Revista Colombiana de Derecho Internacional*, Vol. 13, No. 26, 2015, pp. 289-328.

Geis, G. S., 'Economic as Context for Contract Law. Framing Contract Law: An Economic Perspective by Victor Goldberg', *University of Chicago Law Review*, Vol. 75, Issue 1, 2008, pp. 569-600.

Gessner, V., 'Global Legal Interaction and Legal Cultures', *Ratio Juris*, Vol. 7, Issue 2, 1994, pp. 132-145.

Gessner, V.; Budak, A. C. (Eds.), *Emerging Legal Certainty: Empirical Studies on the Globalization of Law*, Ashgate Publishing Limited, Aldershot, 1998.

Gessner, V.; Schade, A., 'Conflicts of Culture in Cross-Border Legal Relations: The Conception of a Research Topic in the Sociology of Law', *Theory, Culture & Society*, Vol. 7, No. 2, Issue 6, 1990, pp. 253-277.

Gillette, C. P.; Scott, R. E., 'The Political Economy of International Sales Law', *International Review of Law and Economics,* Vol. 25, 2005, pp. 446-486.

Goff, L., 'The Future of the Common Law', *International and Comparative Law Quarterly,* Vol. 46, 1997, pp. 745-760.

Goldman, B., 'Frontières du droit et lex mercatoria', *Archives de philosophie du droit*, Vol. 9, 1964, pp. 177-192.

Goode, R., 'The Role of the Lex Loci *Arbitri* in International Commercial Arbitration', *Arbitration International,* Vol. 17, Issue 1, 2001, pp. 19-40.

Goode, R., *Commercial Law*, Butterworth, London, 2004.

Gordley, J., 'Mistake in Contract Formation', *The American Journal of Comparative Law*, Vol. 52, Issue 2, 2004, pp. 433-468.

Gordon, M. W., 'Some Thoughts on the Receptiveness of Contract Rules in the CISG and UNIDROIT Principles as Reflected in One State's (Florida) Experience of (1) Law School Faculty, (2) Members of the Bar with an International Practice, and (3) Judges', *American Journal of Comparative Law*, Vol. 46 (Suppl.), 1998, pp. 361-378.

Graffi, L., 'Remarks on Trade Usages and Business Practices in International Sales Law', *Journal of Law & Commerce*, Vol. 29, Issue 2, 2011, pp. 273-295.

Green, S.; Saidov, D., 'Software as Goods', *Journal of Business Law*, 2007, pp. 161-181.

Guthrie, C., 'Law, Information, and Choice: Capitalizing on Heuristic Habits of Thought', *in* G. Gigerenzer & C. Engel (Eds.), *Heuristics and the Law*, MIT Press, Cambridge MA, 2006, pp. 425-437.

Hackney, P., 'Is the United Nations Convention on the International Sale of Goods Achieving Uniformity?', *Louisiana Law Review*, Vol. 61, 2001, pp. 473-486.

Hall, K., 'Why Good Intentions are Often Not Enough: The Potential for Ethical Blindness in Legal Decision-Making (November 4, 2009)', *in* R. Mortensen, *et al.* (Eds.), *Alternative Perspectives on Lawyers and Legal Ethics: Reimagining the Profession*, Routledge, London, 2010, available at [http://ssrn.com/abstract=1500137].

Hermalin, B. E.; Katz, A. W.; Craswell, R., 'The Law and Economics of Contracts', *in* A. M. Polinsky & S. Shavell (Eds.), *Handbook of Law and Economics*, Elsevier, New York, 2007, pp. 3-138.

Heuzé, V., 'La formation du contrat selon la CVIM: quelques difficultés', *RDAI*, No. 3/4, 2001. pp. 277-291.

Heuzé, V., *La vente internationale de marchandises – Droit Uniforme*, GLN Joly éditions, Paris, 1992.

Hillman, R. A., *Cross-Reference and Editorial Analysis of Convention Article 7*, available at [https://www.cisg.law.pace.edu/cisg/text/hillman.html]

Hochstrasser, D., 'Choice of Law and "Foreign" Mandatory Rules in International Arbitration', *Journal of International Arbitration*, Vol. 11, Issue 1, 1994, pp. 57-86.

Honnold, J., 'The Sales Convention in Action – Uniform International Words: Uniform Application?', *Journal of Law & Commerce,* Vol. 8, 1988, pp. 207-212.

Honnold, J.; Flechtner, H., *Uniform Law for International Sales under the 1980 United Nations Convention,* 4th edn., Kluwer, Amsterdam, 2009.

Hwang SC, M., 'Commercial Courts and International Arbitration – Competitors or Partners?', *Arbitration International,* Vol. 31, Issue 2, 2015, pp. 193-212.

Janssen, A.; Spilker, M., 'The Relationship Between the CISG and International Arbitration: A Love with Obstacles?', *Contratto e impresa/Europa,* Vol. 1, 2015, pp. 44-74.

Jhangiani, S.; Amin, R., 'The Hague Convention on Choice of Court Agreements: A Rival to the New York Convention and a "Game-Changer" for International Disputes?', *Kluwer Arbitration Blog,* 23 September 2016.

Jolls, C.; Sunstein, C. R.; & Thaler, R., 'A Behavioral Approach to Law and Economics', *Stanford Law Review,* Vol. 50, Issue 5, 1998, pp. 1471-1550.

Kahneman, D., 'A Perspective on Judgment and Choice: Mapping Bounded Rationality', *American Psychologist,* Vol. 58, Issue 9, 2003, pp. 697-720.

Kahneman, D., *Thinking, F., & Slow,* Straus and Giroux, New York, NY, 2011.

Kahneman, D.; & Riis, J., 'Living, and Thinking About It: Two Perspectives on Life', *in* F. A. Huppert, N. Baylis & B. Keverne (Eds.), *The Science of Well-Being,* Oxford University Press, Oxford, 2005, pp. 285-304.

Katz, A. W., 'Contract Formation and Interpretation', *in* Peter Newman (Ed.), *The New Palgrave Dictionary of Economics and the Law,* Macmillan, London, 1998.

Katz, A. W., 'Contractual Incompleteness: A Transactional Perspective', *Case Western Reserve Law Review,* Vol. 56, Issue 1, 2005, pp. 169-186.

Katz, A. W., 'The Relative Costs of Incorporating Trade Usage into Domestic versus International Sales Contracts: Comments on Clayton Gillette, Institutional Design and

International Usages under the CISG', *Chicago Journal of International Law*, Vol. 5, Issue 1, 2004, pp. 181-190.

Katz, A. W., 'The Strategic Structure of Offer and Acceptance: Game Theory and the Law of Contract Formation', *Michigan Law Review*, Vol. 89, Issue 2, 1990, pp. 215-295.

Khan, P., *Les principes généraux du droit devant les arbitres du commerce international*, JDI, Paris, 1989, pp. 305-327.

Kiene, S., 'German Country Analysis: Part II', *in* L. A. DiMatteo (Ed.), *International Sales Law: A Global Challenge*, Cambridge University Press, New York, 2014, pp. 377-398.

Koehler, M., 'Survey Regarding the relevance of the United Nations Convention for the International Sale of Goods (CISG) in legal practice and the exclusion of its application', *CISG Database*, 2006, available at [http://cisgw3.law.pace.edu/cisg/biblio/koehler.html].

Koehler, M.; Yujun, G., 'The Acceptance of the Unified Sales Law (CISG) in Different Legal Systems: An International Comparison of Three Surveys on the Exclusion of the CISG's Application Conducted in the United States, Germany and China', *Pace International Law Review*, Vol. 20, 2008, pp. 45-52.

Komarov, A. S., 'Internationality, Uniformity and Observance of Good Faith as Criteria in Interpretation of CISG: Some Remarks on Article 7 (1)', *Journal of Law & Commerce*, Vol. 25, 2005-2006, pp. 75-85.

Korobkin, R. B., 'The Problems with Heuristics for Law', *UCLA School of Law, Law & Econ Research Paper No. 4-1*, 2004.

Korobkin, R., 'What Comes after Victory for Behavioral Law and Economics', *University of Illinois Law Review*, No. 5, 2011, pp. 1653-1674.

Korobkin, R.; Guthrie, C., 'Heuristics and Biases at the Bargaining Table', *Marquette Law Review*, Vol. 87, 2003, pp. 795-808.

Kotuby Jr., C. T. *et al.*, 'The Hague Choice of Court Convention Takes Effect, and With It Greater Certainty for International Transactions', Jones Day Publications, available at [www.jonesday.com/the-hague-choice-of-court-convention-takes-effect-and-with-it-greater-certainty-for-international-transactions-10-29-2015/], 2015.

Kritzer, A. H., 'The Convention on Contracts for the International Sale of Goods: Scope, Interpretation and Resources', *Cornell Review of the Convention on Contracts for the International Sale of Goods*, 1995, pp. 147-197.

Kronman, A., 'Paternalism and the Law of Contracts', *Yale Law Journal*, Vol. 92, Issue 5, 1983, pp. 763-798.

Lando, O., 'Culture and Contract Laws', *European Review of Contract Law*, Vol. 3, Issue 1, 2007, pp. 1-20.

Lando, O., 'Some Features of the Law of Contract in the Third Millennium', *Scandinavian Studies in Law*, Vol. 40, 2000, pp. 345-401.

Lando, O., 'The Law Applicable to the Merits of the Dispute', *in* P. Sarcevic (Ed.), *Essays on International Commercial Arbitration*, Boston, London, 1991.

Landolt, P., 'A Summary of the Swiss Case Law on the CISG from 2008 to 2013', available at [www.landoltandkoch.com/medias/landolt_jusletter_cisg.pdf].

Legrand, P., 'On the Unbearable Localness of the Law, Academic Fallacies and Unseasonable Observations', *European Review of Private Law*, Vol. 10, Issue 1, pp. 61-76.

Lew QC, J. D. M., 'Achieving the Dream: Autonomous Arbitration', *Arbitration International*, Vol. 22, Issue 2, 2006, pp. 179-204.

Lew QC, J. D. M., 'Novit Curia and Due Process', *Queen Mary School of Law Legal Studies Research Paper No. 72/2010*, 2011.

Lew QC, J. D. M., 'The Law Applicable to the Form and Substance of the Arbitration Clause', *in* Albert Jan van den Berg (Ed.), *Improving the Efficiency of Arbitration Agreements and Awards: 40 Years of Application of the New York Convention*, ICCA Congress Series, Volume 9, Kluwer Law International, Alphen aan den Rijn, 1999, pp. 114-145.

Lew QC, J. D. M.; Mistelis, L.; Kröll, S., *Comparative International Commercial Arbitration*, Kluwer, Alphen aan den Rijn, 2003.

Lookosfy, J. M., 'In dubio pro conventione? Some thoughts about opt-outs, computer programs and preemption under the 1980 Vienna Sales Convention CISG', *Duke Journal of Comparative and International Law,* Vol. 13, Special Issue, 2003, pp. 263-289.

Luhmann, N., *A Sociological Theory of Law*, translated by E. King and M. Albrow, Routledge and Kegan Paul, London, 2014.

Mackaay, E.; Rosseau, S., *Analyse Économique du Droit*, Dalloz, Paris, 2008.

Magnus, U., 'Harmonization and Unification of Law by Means of General Principles', *in* Morten M. Fagot (Ed.), *Unification and Harmonization of International Commercial Law – Interaction of Deharmonization*, Wolters Kluwer, Alphen aan den Rijn, 2012, pp. 161-174.

Mak, V., 'According to Custom…? The Role of "Trade Usage" in the Proposed Common European Sales Law (CESL)', *European Review of Contract Law*, Vol. 10, Issue 1, 2014, pp. 64-84.

Maule, J. A.; Hodgkinson, G. P., 'Heuristics, Biases and Strategic Decision Making', *The Psychologist*, Vol. 15, Issue 2, 2002, pp. 68-71.

Maureen, T. M., 'United Nations Convention on Contracts for the International Sale of Goods: Creating Uniformity of International Sales Law', *Fordham International Law Journal*, Vol. 12, 1989, pp. 727-750.

Mazeaud, D., 'La confiance légitime et l'estoppel', *Revue Internationale de Droit Comparé*, No. 2, 2006, pp. 362-392.

Mazzacano, P., 'Harmonizing Values, Not Laws: The CISG and the Benefits of a Neo-Realist Perspective', *Nordic Journal of Commercial Law*, Issue 1, 2008, pp. 1-36.

McConnaughay, P. J., 'Risks and Virtues of Lawlessness: A Second Look at International Commercial Arbitration', *Northwestern University Law Review*, Vol. 93, 1998, pp. 453-523.

McMahon, J. P., 'Drafting CISG Contracts and Documents and Compliance Tips for Traders – Guide for Managers and Counsel' (2004), available at [www.cisg.law.pace.-edu/cisg/contracts.html#a6].

Meira Moser, L. G., 'A cláusula compromissória, a conduta das partes e a força jurígena dos usos e costumes – comentário da Sentença Estrangeira Contestada nº 855', *Revista de Arbitragem e Mediação*, Vol. 35, Issue 9, 2012, pp. 317-340.

Meira Moser, L. G., 'A formação do contrato de compra e venda entre ausentes: a interlocução entre a Convenção de Viena (CISG) e o direito brasileiro', *in* V. Fradera & L. G. Meira Moser (Eds.), *A Compra e Venda Internacional de Mercadorias: estudos sobre a Convenção de Viena de 1980*, Atlas, São Paulo, 2010.

Meira Moser, L. G., 'Albert H. Kritzer, the 1980 UN Convention (CISG), and the Vis Moot: An Inseparable Relationship', *Pace International Law Review*, Vol. 24, 2012, pp. 258-265.

Meira Moser, L. G., 'Arbitragem em contratos empresariais: redução de custos e eficiência da transação', *Revista de Direito Empresarial (RDE)*, No. 13, 2010, pp. 33-55.

Meira Moser, L. G., 'Arbitration and Choice of Law in Cross-Border Transactions: A Potential Interplay?', *ASA Bulletin*, Vol. 34, Issue 1, 2016, pp. 95-111.

Meira Moser, L. G., 'CISG in Brazilian Courts: A Promising Start – Case Commentary on Inversiones Metalmecánicas I.C.A. v. Voges Metalurgia Ltda.', *Internationales Handelsrecht*, Vol. 16, Issue 4, 2016, pp. 133-136.

Meira Moser, L. G., 'Inside Contracting Parties' Minds: The Decision-making Processes in Cross-border Sales', *Journal of International Dispute Settlement*, Vol. 8, Issue 2, 2017, pp. 250-279.

Meira Moser, L. G., 'Parties' Preferences in International Sales Contracts: An Empirical Analysis of the Choice of Law', *Uniform Law Review*, Vol. 20, Issue 1, 2015, pp. 19-55.

Meira Moser, L. G.; Pignatta, F. (Eds.), *Comentários à Convenção de Viena sobre contratos internacionais de venda de mercadorias*, Atlas, São Paulo, 2015.

Mellers, B. A.; Schwartz, A.; Cooke, A. D. J., 'Judgment and Decision Making', *Annual Review of Psychology*, Vol. 49, 1998, pp. 447-477.

Menon, S., *Opening Lecture for the DIFC Courts Lecture Series 2015*, pp. 1-46.

Menon, S., 'Roadmaps for the Transnational Convergence of Commercial Law: Lessons Learnt from the CISG', *Colloquium*, 23 April 2015, pp. 1-40.

Meyer, J., 'UN-Kaufrecht in der deutschen Anwaltspraxis', *Rabels Zeitschrift für ausländisches und internationales Privatrecht*, Vol. 69, 2005, pp. 457-486.

Meyer, J., 'UN-Kaufrecht in der österreichischen Anwaltspraxis', *Österreichische Juristen-Zeitung*, Vol. 63, 2008, pp. 792-798.

Meyer, J., 'UN-Kaufrecht in der schweizerischen Anwaltspraxis', *Schweizerische Juristen-Zeitung/Revue suisse de jurisprudence*, Vol. 104, 2008, pp. 421-428.

Michaels, R., 'Economics of Law as Choice of Law', *Law and Contemporary Problems*, Vol. 71, Issue 3, 2008, pp. 73-105.

Miquel, J., *Derecho privado romano*, Marcial Pons Ediciones Jurídicas, Madrid, 1992.

Mistelis, L., 'CISG and Arbitration', *in* A. Janssen & O. Meyer (Eds.), *CISG Methodology*, Sellier European Law Publishers, Munich, 2009, pp. 375-395.

Morales-Olazábal, A. *et al.*, 'Global Sales Law: An Analysis of Recent CISG Precedents in US Courts 2004-2012', *Business Lawyer*, Vol. 67, Issue 4, 2012, pp. 1351-1381.

Moser, G., '2016 Queen Mary International Dispute Resolution Survey: Unveiling Technology, Media and Telecoms (TMT) Disputes', *Kluwer Arbitration Blog*, 15 December 2016.

Muñoz, E.; Meira Moser, L. G., '*Brazil's Adhesion to the CISG* – Consequences for Trade in China and Latin-America', *in* I. Schwenzer & L. Spagnolo (Eds.), *Globalization versus Regionalization – 4th Annual MAA Schlechtriem CISG Conference*, Eleven International Publishing, the Hague, 2013, pp. 79-96.

Murray Jr, J. E., 'The Neglect of CISG: A Workable Solution', *Journal of Law & Commerce*, Vol. 17, 1998, pp. 365-379.

Mustill, L., 'Arbitration: History and Background', *Journal of International Arbitration*, Vol. 6, Issue 2, 1989, pp. 43-56.

North, D. C., 'The New Institutional Economics: A Symposium', *Zeitschrift für die gesamte Staatswissenschaft/Journal of Institutional and Theoretical Economics*, Bd. 140, H. 1, 1984, pp. 7-17.

Oppetit, B., 'Autour du contrat international', *Droits*, Vol. 12, 1990, pp. 107-115.

Oppetit, B., 'L'adaptation des contrats internationaux aux changements de circonstances: la clause de hardship', *Journal du Droit International,* No. 4, 1974. pp. 794-814.

Oppetit, B., 'La notion de source du droit et le droit du commerce international', *Archives de philosophie du droit,* Vol. 27, 1982, pp. 43-53.

Oppetit, B., *Théorie de l'Arbitrage,* Press Universitaires de France, Paris, 1998.

Oviedo-Albán, J., 'La Convención sobre Compraventa Internacional de Mercaderías: antecedentes y desarrollos alternativos', *Foro de Derecho Mercantil,* Vol. 29, 2010, pp. 37-89.

Pamboukis, Ch., 'The Concept and Function of Usages in the United Nations Convention on the International Sale of Goods', *Journal of Law & Commerce,* Vol. 25, 2005-06, pp. 107-131.

Park, W. W., 'The Lex Loci Arbitri and International Commercial Arbitration', *International and Comparative Law Quarterly,* Vol. 32, Issue 1, 1983, pp. 21-52.

Park, W. W., 'The Predictability Paradox – Arbitrators and Applicable Law', *Dossier XI of the ICC Institute of World Business Law: The Application of Substantive Law by International Arbitrators,* 2014, pp. 60-70.

Pavić, V.; Djordjevic, M., 'The Scope and Sphere of Application of the CISG in the Balkans', *in* J. Stamm (Ed.), *Festscrift für Helmut Rüßmann,* Juris, Saarbrücken, 2013, pp. 887-916.

Perret, F., 'Resolving Conflicts between Contractual Clauses and Specific Rules of the Governing Law – Strict Application of the Law or Flexible Approach', *Dossier of the ICC Institute of World Business Law: The Application of Substantive Law by International Arbitrators,* 2014, pp. 109-111.

Philippopoulos, G., 'Awareness of the CISG Among American Attorneys', *UCC Law Journal,* Vol. 40, Issue 3, 2008, pp. 357-569.

Plamper, J., *The History of Emotions: An Introduction,* Oxford University Press, Oxford, 2015.

Posner, E. A., 'Economic Analysis of Contract Law after Three Decades: Success or Failure?', *University of Chicago Law & Economics, Olin Working Paper No. 14, 2002,* pp. 829-880.

Posner, R. A., 'Rational Choice, Behavioral Economics, and the Law', *Stanford Law Review*, Vol. 50, 1998, pp. 1551-1575.

Posner, R. A., 'The Law and Economics of Contract Interpretation', *University of Chicago Law & Economics, Olin Working Paper No. 229*, 2004.

Ratniece, L., 'An Economic Analysis of the Duty to Inspect Goods Pursuant to the CISG and CESL', *RGSL Research Papers No. 8*, 2012.

Rea, M.; Marotti, M. C., 'What Is All the Fuss? The Potential Impact of the Hague Convention on the Choice of Court Agreement on International Arbitration', *Kluwer Arbitration Blog*, 16 June 2017.

Reed, L., 'The 2013 Hong Kong International Arbitration Centre Kaplan Lecture - Arbitral Decision-Making: Art, Science or Sport?', *Journal of International Arbitration*, Vol. 30, Issue 2, 2013, pp. 85-99.

Regula, S.; & Kannowski, B., 'Nochmals: UN Kaufrecht oder BGB? Erwägungen zur Rechtswahl aufgrund einer vergleichenden Betrachtung', *Internationales Handelsrecht*, 2004/2, pp. 45-54.

Saidov, I., *The Law of Damages in International Sales – the CISG and Other International Instruments,* Hart Publishing, Oxford, 2008.

Samson, C., 'L'harmonisation du droit de la vente internationale de merchandises entre pays de droit civil et pays de common law', *Contemporary Law: Canadian Reports to the 1990 International Congress of Comparative Law*, 1990, pp. 100-125.

Sanders, P., 'New York Convention on the Recognition and Enforcement of Foreign Arbitral Awards', *Netherlands International Law Review,* Vol. 6, 1959, pp. 43-55.

Savare, M., 'Clauses in Conflict: Can an Arbitration Provision Eviscerate a Choice-of-Law Clause', *Seton Hall Law Review*, Vol. 35, 2004, pp. 597-611.

Schlechriem, P.; Witz, C., *Convention de Vienne sur les Contrats de Vente Internationale de Marchandises,* Dalloz, Paris, 2008.

Schlechtriem, P., *Uniform Sales Law, The UN-Convention on Contracts for the International Sale of Goods*, Vienna, Manzsche Verlags – und Universitatsbuchhandlung, 1986.

Schmidt-Ahrendts, N., 'CISG and Arbitration', *Belgrade Law Review,* No. 3, Year LIX (2011), pp. 211-223.

Schmidt-Kessel, M., 'Commentary on the UN Convention for the International Sale of Goods (CISG), Articles 8-9 (pp. 143-196) & 11 (p. 203-213)', *in* I. Schwenzer (Ed.), *Schlechtriem & Schwenzer, Commentary on the United Nations Convention on the International Sale of Goods (CISG),* 4th ed., Oxford University Press, Oxford, 2016.

Schroeter, U., 'Commentary on the UN Convention for the International Sale of Goods (CISG), Article 19', *in* I. Schwenzer (Ed.), *Schlechtriem & Schwenzer, Commentary on the United Nations Convention on the International Sale of Goods (CISG),* 4th ed., Oxford University Press, Oxford, 2016, pp. 350-372.

Schroeter, U., 'Empirical Evidence of Courts' and Counsels' Approach to the CISG (with Some Remarks on Professional Liability)', *in* L. A. DiMatteo (Ed.), *International Sales Law: A Global Challenge*, Cambridge University Press, New York, 2014, pp. 649-668.

Schroeter, U., 'Freedom of Contract: Comparing CISG and PECL Provisions', *Vindobona Journal of International Commercial Law and Arbitration*, Vol. 6, 2002, pp. 257-266.

Schroeter, U., 'The Cross-Border Freedom of Form Principle Under Reservation: The Role of Articles 12 and 96 CISG in Theory and Practice', *Journal of Law & Commerce,* Vol. 33, Issue 1, 2014, pp. 79-117.

Schultz, T., 'Arbitral Decision-Making: Legal Realism and Law & Economics', *Journal of International Dispute Settlement*, Vol. 6, Issue 2, 2015, pp. 231-151.

Schwartz, A.; Scott, R. E., 'Contract Theory and the Limits of Contract Law', *Yale Law Journal,* Vol. 113, 2003, pp. 540-596.

Schwenzer, I. (Ed.), *Schlechtriem & Schwenzer, Commentary on the United Nations Convention on the International Sale of Goods (CISG)*, 4th ed., Oxford University Press, Oxford, 2016.

Schwenzer, I., 'Commentary on the UN Convention for the International Sale of Goods (CISG), Articles 35-39', *in* I. Schwenzer (Ed.), *Schlechtriem & Schwenzer, Commentary on the United Nations Convention on the International Sale of Goods (CISG)*, 4th ed., Oxford University Press, Oxford, 2016, pp. 591-673.

Schwenzer, I., 'Conformity of the Goods – Physical Features on the Wane?', *in* I. Schwenzer & Spagnolo, L. (Eds.), *State of Play: The 3rd Annual MAA Schlechtriem CISG Conference*, Eleven International Publishing, The Hague, 2012, pp. 103-112.

Schwenzer, I., 'Divergent Interpretations: Reasons and Solutions', *in* L. A. DiMatteo (Ed.), *International Sales Law: A Global Challenge*, Cambridge University Press, New York, 2014, pp. 102-119.

Schwenzer, I., 'Who Needs a Uniform Contract Law, And Why?', *Villanova Law Review*, Vol. 58, Issue 4, 2013, pp. 723-732.

Schwenzer, I.; Hachem, P., 'Commentary on the UN Convention for the International Sale of Goods (CISG), Articles 1-6 (pp. 17-118), Article 7 (pp. 119-142) & Article 96 (pp. 1264-1266)', *in* I. Schwenzer (Ed.), *Schlechtriem & Schwenzer, Commentary on the United Nations Convention on the International Sale of Goods (CISG)*, 4th ed., Oxford University Press, Oxford, 2016.

Schwenzer, I.; Hachem, P., 'The CISG: Successes and Pitfalls', *American Journal of Comparative Law*, Vol. 57, 2009, pp. 457-478.

Schwenzer, I.; Kee, C., 'Global Sales Law – Theory and Practice', *in* I. Schwenzer & L. Spagnolo (Eds.), *Towards Uniformity: The 2nd Annual MAA Schlechtriem CISG Conference*, Eleven International Publishing, The Hague, 2011, pp. 155-164.

Schwenzer, I.; Kee, C., 'International Sales Law: The Actual Practice', *Pennsylvania State International Law Review*, Vol. 29, Issue 3, 2011, pp. 425-447.

Schwenzer, I.; Tebel, D., 'The Word is Not Enough – Arbitration, Choice of Forum and Choice of Law Clauses under the CISG', *ASA Bulletin*, Vol. 31, Issue 4, 2013, pp. 740-755.

Sefton-Green, R., 'Choice, Certainty and Diversity: Why More is Less', *European Review of Contract Law*, Vol. 7, Issue 2, 2011, pp. 134-150.

Selden, B. S., 'Lex Mercatoria in European and US Trade Practice: Time to Take a Closer Look', *Annual Survey of International & Comparative Law,* Vol. 2, Issue 1, 1995, pp. 111-129.

Shavell, S., 'Economic Analysis of Contract Law', *Harvard Law and Economics Discussion Paper No. 403,* 2003.

Shavell, S., 'On the Writing and the Interpretation of Contracts', *Journal of Law, Economics and Organizations - JLEO,* Vol. 2, Issue 2, 2006, pp. 289-314.

Sheaffer, C., 'The Failure of the United Nations Convention on Contracts for the International Sale of Goods and a Proposal for a New Uniform Global Code in International Sales Law', *Cardozo Journal of International and Comparative Law,* Vol. 15, 2007, pp. 461-495.

Sheehy, B., 'Good faith in the CISG: The Interpretation Problems of Article 7', *Review of the Convention on Contracts for the International Sale of Goods (CISG) ed. by Pace International Law* Review, 2007, pp. 153-196.

Silberman, L.; Ferrari, F., 'Getting to the Law Applicable to the Merits in International Arbitration and the Consequences of Getting It Wrong', *NYU Law and Economics Research Paper No. 10-40,* 2010, pp. 1-34.

Simon, H. A., 'A Behavioral Model of Rational Choice', *Quarterly Journal of Economics,* Vol. 69, 1955, pp. 99-118.

Slovic, P. *et al.,* 'The Affect Heuristic', *in* T. Gilovich, D. Griffin & Daniel Kahneman (Eds.), *Heuristics and Biases: The Psychology of Intuitive Judgment,* Cambridge University Press, Cambridge, 2002.

Smith, A., *The Wealth of Nations,* 5th edition, Methuen & Co., Ltd., London, 1904.

Sornarajah, M., 'Supremacy of the Renegotiation Clause in International Contracts', *Journal of International Arbitration,* Vol. 5, Issue 2, 1988, pp. 97-114.

Spagnolo, L., 'A Glimpse through the Kaleidoscope: Choices of Law and the CISG (Kaleidoscope Part I)', *Vindobona Journal of International Commercial Law and Arbitration,* Vol. 13, 2009, pp. 135-156.

Spagnolo, L., *CISG Exclusion and Legal Efficiency*, Wolters Kluwer, Alphen aan den Rijn, 2014.

Spagnolo, L., 'Green Eggs and Ham: the CISG, Path Dependence, and the Behavioural Economics of Lawyers' Choices of Law in International Sales Contracts', *Journal of Private International Law*, Vol. 6, 2009, pp. 417-464.

Spagnolo, L., 'Rats in Kaleidoscope: Rationality, Irrationality, and the Economics and Psychology of Opting in and out of the CISG', *Vindobona Journal of International Commercial Law and Arbitration*, Vol. 13, 2009, pp. 157-178.

Spagnolo, L., 'The Last Outpost: Automatic CISG Opt Outs, Misapplications and the Costs of Ignoring the Vienna Sales Convention for Australian Lawyers', *Melbourne Journal of International Law*, Vol. 10, 2009, pp. 141-216.

Stephan, P. B., 'The Futility of Unification and Harmonization in International Commercial Law', *Virginia Journal of International Law*, Vol. 29, 1999, pp. 743-797.

Swiss Institute of Comparative Law, *The 1980 Vienna Convention of the International Sale of Goods: Lausanne Colloquium of November 19-20, 1984: with trilingual text of the Convention*, Schulthess Polygraphischer Verlag, Zurich, 1985.

Taylor, D., 'Reflections on a Critical Aspect of CISG-Governed International Sale of Goods Transactions: The Impact of the Hague Convention on Choice of Court Agreements on Forum Selection', *International Trade and Business Law Review*, Vol. 15, 2012, pp. 42-59.

Thompson, D. A., 'Commentary, Buyer Beware: German Interpretation of the CISG Has Led to Results Unfavourable to Buyers', *Journal of Law & Commerce*, Vol. 19, 2000, pp. 245-263.

Tieder, J. B., 'Factors to Consider in the Choice of Procedural and Substantive Law in International Arbitration', *Journal of International Arbitration*, Vol. 20, Issue 4, 2003, pp. 393-407.

Tung, S., 'The Importance of Languages in International Arbitration and How They Impact Parties' Due Process Rights', *Contemporary Asia Arbitration Journal*, Vol. 10, Issue 1, 2017, pp. 113-132.

Truong, C. C. Q.; Fouchard, P., 'The Law Applicable to the Merits in International Distribution Contracts: An Analysis of ICC Arbitral Awards', *ICC International Court of Arbitration Bulletin*, Vol. 12, 2001, pp. 37-47.

Truong, C. C. Q.; Fouchard, P., *Les différends liés à la rupture des contrats internationaux de distribution dans les sentences arbitrales CCI*, Litec, Paris, 2002.

Tversky, A.; Fox, C. R., 'Weighing Risk and Uncertainty', *Psychological Review*, Vol. 102, Issue 2, 1995, pp. 269-283.

Tversky, A.; Kahneman, D., 'Judgment Under Uncertainty: Heuristics and Biases', *Science*, Vol. 185, 1974, pp. 1124-1131.

Tversky, A.; Kahneman, D., 'The Framing of Decisions and the Psychology of Choice', *Science*, Vol. 221, 1981, pp. 453-458.

Ullmann, H., 'Droit et Pratique des clauses de hardship dans le système juridique américain', *Revue de Droit et des Affaires Internationaux*, No. 7, 1988, pp. 889-904.

Villey, M., *Le Droit Romain*, Presses Universitaires de France, Paris, 1949.

Vogenauer, S., 'Regulatory Competition through Choice of Contract Law and Choice of Forum in Europe: Theory and Evidence', *European Review of Private Law*, Vol. 1, 2013, pp. 13-78.

Vogenauer, S.; Hodges, C. (Eds.), *Civil Justice Systems in Europe: Implications for Choice of Forum and Choice of Contract Law*, Hart Publishing, Oxford, 2017.

Voigt, S., 'Are International Merchants Stupid? Their Choice of Law Sheds Doubt on the Legal Origin Theory', *Journal of Empirical Legal Studies*, Vol. 5, Issue 1, 2008, pp. 1-20.

Widmer-Lüchinger, C., 'Switzerland', *in* L. A. DiMatteo (Ed.), *International Sales Law: A Global Challenge*, Cambridge University Press, New York, 2014, pp. 466-485.

Williamson, O. E., *Market and Hierarchies: Analysis and Antitrust Implications*, Free Press, New York, 1975.

Williamson, O. E., 'Transaction-Cost Economics: The Governance of Contractual Relations', *The Journal of Law and Economics*, Vol. 22, Issue 2, 1979, pp. 233-261.

Windship, P., 'Domesticating International Commercial Law: Revising UCC Article 2 in Light of the UN Sales Convention', *Loyola Law Review*, Vol. 37, 1991, pp. 43-68.

Witz, C., 'CVIM: interprétation et questions non couvertes', *RDAI*, No. 3/4, 2001, pp. 253-275.

Witz, C., 'L'interprétation de la CVIM: divergences dans l'interprétation de la Convention de Vienne.' *in* F. Ferrari (Ed.), *The 1980 Uniform Sales Law. Old Issues Revisited in the Light of Recent Experiences*, Sellier, European Law Publishers, Munich, 2003, pp. 279-333.

Zajonc, R. B., 'Feeling and Thinking: Preferences Need No Inferences', *American Psychologist*, Vol. 35, Issue 2, 1980, pp. 151-175.

Zeller, B., 'Intellectual Property Rights & the CISG Article 42', *Vindobona Journal of International Commercial Law and Arbitration*, Vol. 15, Issue 2, 2011, pp. 289-302.

Ziegel, J. S., 'The Future of the International Sales Convention from a Common Law Perspective', *New Zealand Business Law Quarterly*, Vol. 6, 2000, pp. 336-346.

Ziegel, J. S., 'The Scope of the Convention: Reaching out to Article One and Beyond', *Journal of Law & Commerce*, Vol. 25, 2005-2006, pp. 59-73.

INDEX

International Commerce and Arbitration (Series editor: Ingeborg Schwenzer)

Volume 1: Mariel Dimsey, The Resolution of International Investment Disputes: Challenges and Practical Solutions, ISBN 978-90-77596-52-4

Volume 2: Sarah E. Hilmer, Mediation in the People's Republic of China and Hong Kong (SAR), ISBN 978-90-77596-74-6

Volume 3: Christina Knahr, Christian Koller, Walter Rechberger and August Reinisch (eds.), Investment and Commercial Arbitration – Similarities and Divergences, ISBN 978-90-77596-81-4

Volume 4: Markus Jäger, Reimbursement for Attorney's Fees, ISBN 978-90-77596-98-2

Volume 5: Olivier Luc Mosimann, Anti-Suit Injunctions in International Commercial Arbitration, ISBN 978-90-77596-99-9

Volume 6: Edgardo Munoz, Modern Law of Contracts and Sales in Latin America, Spain and Portugal, ISBN 978-94-90947-03-3

Volume 7: Pascal Hachem, Agreed Sums Payable upon Breach of an Obligation, ISBN 978-94-90947-04-0

Volume 8: Ingeborg Schwenzer and Lisa Spagnolo (eds.), Towards Uniformity, ISBN 978-94-90947-10-1

Volume 9: Natia Lapiashvili, Modern Law of Contracts and Sales in Eastern Europe and Central Asia, ISBN 978-94-90947-20-0

Volume 10: Lara Pair, Consolidation in International Commercial Arbitration – The ICC and Swiss Rules, ISBN 978-94-90947-27-9

Volume 11: Ingeborg Schwenzer and Lisa Spagnolo (eds.), State of Play, ISBN 978-94-90947-46-0

Volume 12: Ingeborg Schwenzer and Lisa Spagnolo (eds.), Globalization versus Regionalization, ISBN 978-94-6236-020-4

Volume 13: Marie-Camille Pitton, Le rôle du jugement étranger dans l'interprétation du droit conventionnel uniforme, ISBN 978-94-90947-81-1

Volume 14: Andreas F. Müller, Protecting the Integrity of a Written Agreement, ISBN 978-94-6236-073-0

Volume 15: Ingeborg Schwenzer, Yeşim M. Atamer and Petra Butler (eds.), Current Issues in the CISG and Arbitration, ISBN 978-94-6236-097-6

Volume 16: Alain Hosang, Obstructionist Behavior in International Commercial Arbitration: Legal Analysis and Measures Available to the Arbitral Tribunal, ISBN 978-94-6236-100-3

Volume 17: Alissa Palumbo, Modern Law of Sales in the United States, ISBN 978-94-6236-439-4

Volume 18: Ingeborg Schwenzer and Lisa Spagnolo (eds.), Boundaries and Intersections, ISBN 978-94-6236-441-7

Volume 19: Ingeborg Schwenzer (ed.), 35 Years CISG and Beyond, ISBN 978-94-6236-624-4

Volume 20: Marçal Justen Filho, Cesar Pereira and Maria Augusta Rost (eds.), Brazil Infrastructure Law, ISBN 978-94-6236-640-4

Volume 21: Ingeborg Schwenzer, Cesar Pereira and Leandro Tripodi (eds.), CISG and Latin America: Regional and Global Perspectives, ISBN 978-94-6236-653-4

Volume 22: Ingeborg Schwenzer and Lisa Spagnolo (eds.), Growing the CISG, ISBN 978-94-6236-667-1

Volume 23: Ingeborg Schwenzer (ed.), The CISG Advisory Council Opinions, ISBN 978-94-6236-719-7

Volume 24: Ingeborg Schwenzer and Lisa Spagnolo (eds.), The Electronic CISG, ISBN 978-94-6236-751-7

Volume 25: Lina Thieme, Damages for breach of the obligation to arbitrate, ISBN 978-94-6236-791-3

Volume 26: Miquel dels Sants Mirambell Fargas, The Seller's Right to Cure under Article 48 CISG, ISBN 978-94-6236-830-9

Volume 27: Gustavo Moser, Rethinking Choice of Law in Cross-Border Sales, ISBN 978-94-6236-846-0

9 789462 368460

Printed by Libri Plureos GmbH in Hamburg,
Germany